. . . Religious . . . Violence . . . and . . . Abortion . . .

**University
Press
of
Florida**

. . . Gainesville . . . Tallahassee . . . Tampa . . . Boca Raton . . . Pensacola . . .

# Religious Violence and Abortion

## The Gideon Project

. . . Orlando . . . Miami . . . Jacksonville . . .

Dallas A. Blanchard and Terry J. Prewitt

Library of Congress Cataloging-in-Publication Data

Blanchard, Dallas A.
Religious violence and abortion: the Gideon Project / Dallas A.
Blanchard and Terry J. Prewitt.
p.   cm.
Includes bibliographical references and index.
ISBN 0-8130-1193-0 (cloth: alk. paper).—ISBN 0-8130-1194-9
(paper: alk. paper)
    1. Abortion—Religious aspects—Christianity.   2. Pro-life
movement—United States.   3. Bombings—Florida—Pensacola—Case
studies.   4. Terrorism—Religious aspects—Christianity.
5. Violence—Religious aspects—Christianity.   I. Prewitt, Terry J.
(Terry James), 1945–.   II. Title.
HQ767.25.B53   1993
363.4'6'0975999—dc20        92-39693

The University Press of Florida is the scholarly publishing
agency for the State University System of Florida,
comprised of Florida A & M University, Florida Atlantic
University, Florida International University, Florida State
University, University of Central Florida, University of
Florida, University of North Florida, University of South
Florida, University of West Florida.

University Press of Florida
15 Northwest 15th Street
Gainesville, Florida 32611

As life is action and passion,
it is required of a man that he should share
the passion and action of his time,
at peril of being judged not to have lived.

. . . Oliver Wendell Holmes, Jr.

# . . . Contents

**. . . Tables**

**. . . Figures**

# . . . Foreword

by

Lewis M. Killian

The bombing of three abortion clinics in Pensacola early on Christmas morning, 1984, called by the perpetrators "a birthday gift for Jesus," dramatized the lengths to which the anti-abortion movement would go to stop what they call "genocide." The two young men who planted the bombs and their female accomplices, characterized by their friends as "Christian young people," were tried in federal district court. They were convicted of interference with interstate commerce, making and exploding unregistered devices, and conspiracy. The prosecutor characterized the bombings as terrorism, as do the authors of this book. As a confrontation between the law and a social movement, the trial was of a kind with the trial of John Brown, the Scopes trial, and the trial of the Chicago Seven.

Let there be no mistake: the Gideon Project was not an irrational, deviant act committed by fanatics or psychopaths. It was part of the tactics of the anti-abortion movement even though not all the members would go to such an extreme and only these four activists were charged and prosecuted. The story of the project raises serious questions concerning the responsibility, moral or legal, of the ideologists of a social movement for the behavior of the followers whom they influence by their words.

This incident was one of thirty cases of arson and bombing of abortion clinics during 1984, and there had been twenty-five cases between 1977 and 1983. The following years, 1985–86, saw twenty-three more cases even after the nation's most highly placed anti-abortion advocate, Ronald Reagan, had finally condemned abortion clinic bombings as "violent, anarchistic activities."

It is fortunate for citizens concerned about the abortion controversy, be they voters, church members, politicians, or social scientists, that two diligent social scientists taught in the city of the Christmas Day bombings and were willing to follow the trial day by day throughout its course. This book is far more than just a case study of the events in Pensacola, however. The authors also queried by questionnaire, face-to-face interview, or telephone interview perpetrators or victims of abortion-related violence in other parts of the nation. The data are analyzed in the broader context of religious fundamentalism, the political aspects of the abortion issue, and the cultural milieu in which both pro-choice and anti-abortion movements, so-termed, have emerged.

Lay readers, perhaps uninterested in theories of social movements, will still be enlightened by the analysis of the relationship of religious fundamentalism to the anti-abortion movement with all its levels of activity. Conscientious religionists who are ambivalent and perplexed about the status of a fertilized ovum, the fate of a child during the many years of life after the nine months of gestation, and the right of a woman to control her own body will understand better why they are lumped with strong pro-choice advocates as "baby-killers" who, like Hitler, justify genocide. They will be fascinated by the account of the trial, which has all the excitement of a detective novel.

The current phase of the anti-abortion movement should be characterized, to be accurate, as a countermovement. Kristin Luker, in *Abortion and the Politics of Motherhood* (1984), has shown that a small group of Right to Life activists emerged in California as early as 1967 but experienced an almost unbroken string of failures until 1973. Then the success of the pro-choice movement represented by *Roe v. Wade* evoked a vigorous, burgeoning anti-abortion countermovement. Luker did not cover the intensification of movement activities that arose after the electoral victory of Ronald Reagan in 1980. The present volume takes up at this point and analyzes the process of radicalization during the 1980s.

Recognition of the characteristic heterogeneity of any social movement mandates analysis of the interaction among the participants, encompassing both the experience and behavior of the most radicalized activists and the influence on them of messages received from the more moderate members. The ongoing process includes also the consequences of the tactics of the extremists for the other members, particularly the leaders. Will they cast out the extremists as an embarrassment to the movement, or will they continue to embrace them even while denouncing their acts?

The interaction of the two young arsonists in Pensacola with preachers and church members who proclaimed that abortion is genocide ("Hitler would have loved it," read the billboards) and picketed abortion clinics daily is seen as the essential background out of which developed their decision to cease to be "nameless faces in the crowd of picketers" and to do something truly effective. Given the structural and ideological milieu they found in a fundamentalist religious network, it is easy to see how they could believe that God was speaking to them. It is part of the belief of the Assemblies of God denomination that God speaks both by signs and directly to believers.

As they stood before the bar, these "Christian bombers" received a wealth of support from "pro-lifers" from all over the nation. While most of them would not go as far as had the defendants, they still refused to regard the violent acts as any more than misdemeanors justified by the enormity of the real crime, the murder of unborn persons. Lawyers provided by the movement came from California, Kentucky, and Indiana to aid in their defense. They tried to make the immorality of abortion the issue in the trial. To the prosecution, the issue was whether one could get away with taking the law into one's own hands. The defense asked, "Which should the law protect—life or property?"

In the day-by-day account of the testimony and arguments in the courtroom, in the comments of supporters and the demonstrations they staged outside the courthouse, and in the events in the fundamentalist churches after the conviction, students of social movements will find an unusually comprehensive and graphic description of inter-action within a movement. The internal workings, the justifications for violent tactics, and the collective definition that made the four defendants martyrs, not criminals or traitors to the movement, are revealed with the detail of a blueprint.[1]

But a social movement is not an isolated group deriving its dynamics solely from within. It develops in a social and cultural milieu; it requires resources drawn from both internal and external sources; and it depends on validation of its values by some broader worldview, more widely shared in the society. Again, Luker did a masterful job of describing the worldview of anti-abortion activists, a profoundly religious one that is a reaction to what they deplore as the secularization of society. Blanchard and Prewitt, combining the insights of social movement theory and the sociology of religion, treat the anti-abortion movement and the Gideon Project as parts of a larger countermovement, politico-religious fundamentalism. The Equal Rights Amendment, homosexuality, pornography, capital punishment, prayer in schools, and textbooks promoting "secular humanism" are other issues that have been the targets of collective action in the broader movement. The religious Right in Pensacola, as in the rest of the nation, has been active in connection with all of these issues before abortion became its central concern. It is significant that the intensification of anti-abortion activity began about the time of the final defeat of the ERA, in which the Florida legislature played a critical part.

These authors make the case that it was another factor, not just the victory in the anti-ERA fight, that moved the anti-abortion movement into its radical, violent phase. They do not answer the question that some social movement theorists would raise: Was there a significant increase in resources available to the movement at the time of this and earlier escalations? Instead, they concentrate on the ideology of the movement and the change in the moral and political climate created by Ronald Reagan's election. The latter triggered what Doug McAdam (1982) has termed the process of cognitive liberation for the fundamentalist movement. While pointing out the weakness of the Moral Majority's claim to have been the crucial element in the Republican victory, Blanchard and Prewitt show that this triumph nevertheless provided Christians of the Right with their first significant sense of personal victory against the rising tide of secularization in America. This turn in their political fortunes provided an essential ingredient in the "sense of injustice" that Ralph Turner and Lewis Killian (1987) have suggested underlies any social movement—the belief that victory over unjust, evil conditions is *possible*. President Reagan's support for the anti-abortion ideology was unwavering even though as governor of California he signed the most liberal abortion law in the nation at that time. Public opinion polls showing that the majority of Americans disagree with the anti-abortion position did not discourage him or his successor, George Bush. Reagan's pronouncements created a permissive climate in which radicalization proceeded and extremism flourished. Of a total of 102 instances of arson and bombing of abortion clinics between 1977 and 1987, 12.7 percent occurred during Jimmy Carter's presidency and 40.2 percent during the first four years of the Reagan regime. Another 47.1 percent took place during the next three years, 1985–87. While Reagan condemned anti-abortion violence after the Pensacola bombings, it was easy for the bombers to believe that both God and their president were really on their side.

Some social movement theorists have sought to divorce the analysis of religious movements from the study of collective action in pursuit of political goals. The fundamentalist countermovement clearly constitutes a case of social insurgency fitting the political process model advanced by McAdam. Yet it seeks, like the fundamentalist Shiite movement in the Middle East and the protracted campaign of the Irish Republican Army, the realization of religious values through political action, through societal manipulation as well as through personal transformation. Quite properly Blanchard and Prewitt broaden their perspective to encompass fundamentalism and the radicalization of fundamentalist movements on the national and global levels.

As a contribution to theory of social movements, this work is far more than just a valuable case study. In describing the sort of utopia that the fundamentalist movement envisions, the authors remind us of the power of ideology in influencing the behavior of participants in social movements. In placing the anti-abortion movement and its most violent manifestations in the context of the larger movement, they give convincing evidence of the importance to the vitality of a social movement of a worldview and its validation by significant segments of the society.

*University of West Florida*

# . . . Acknowledgments

While Dallas Blanchard took primary responsibility for most of the first and subsequent drafts of this work, we both contributed significantly to the editing and framing of the approach.

We appreciate the editing efforts of Glenda Blanchard, Karen Haworth, Andy Lipscomb, and especially Barclay Blanchard. The University of West Florida Press Committee gave some very helpful suggestions. The substantive comments and suggestions of our colleague Ramon A. Oldenburg were particularly helpful. Of inestimable help were the comments and suggestions of a number of reviewers; several were anonymous to us, but Steven Markson, Faye Ginsburg, Judith Ochshorn, Harvey Cox, and Keith Roberts had especially helpful suggestions for improving the work. We are especially grateful to Lisa Compton, our superb copyeditor at the University Press of Florida, and to George Bedell and Walda Metcalf for their support of this project. Of course, none of them is responsible for the book's final form or the conclusions we make.

We are indebted to the *Pensacola News Journal*[1] executive editor, Kent Cockson, who released photos to us, and librarian, Sherry Collon, who was extremely helpful in locating essential materials. The *Buffalo News* granted us permission to reprint Toles's editorial cartoon. We are also grateful to the National Abortion Federation and the Bureau of Alcohol, Tobacco and Firearms for sharing their data on abortion-related violence with us.

This research was supported partially with funds from the University of West Florida's Department of Sociology and Anthropology; Alfred B. Chaet, associate vice president for Research and Sponsored Programs; and the University Research Committee. We also appreciate the support of the university's Computer Services, Russell Lee, director, and Karen Brotherton, word-processing supervisor.

The work would have been incomplete without the cooperation of those who let us interview them, especially Lindell Ballenger, Linda Taggart, Bo Bagenholm, William Permenter, John Burt, Sharon Glass, David Shofner, Vicky Conroy, Debra Jean Armond, Shirley Gallagher, Gloria Mattingly, David Mayo, and David Del Gallo.

David Paladino, Florida Education Association/United (American Federation of Teachers, AFL-CIO), gave us assistance which only he knows about, but which was invaluable to us.

Most of all, her husband is most grateful to Glenda Blanchard for her support, encouragement, patience with hearing more than she ever wanted to hear about abortion, violence, and religion, and then offering substantive comments and suggestions.

# Background

 . . . Part . . . One . . .

## ... 1
## Introduction
## The
## Abortion
## Stalemate

We had begun another collaborative project on the ethics of abortion when the Pensacola abortion clinic bombings occurred on Christmas Day, 1984. When James and Kathren Simmons, Matthew Goldsby, and Kaye Wiggins were arrested, we decided to shift our focus to the trial and the violence surrounding the abortion controversy in Pensacola. As we followed the trial, we realized the need to develop a comparative background on abortion-related violence, as well as additional local perspectives on pro-choice and anti-abortion activism. We began, then, asking questions about violence related to abortion across the nation.

Our interest in abortion, religion, and violence stems from several lines of prior work. Dallas Blanchard's primary training has been in the sociology of religion and social ethics; he is also a United Methodist minister. He was already engaged in long-term research on a group of southern Christian socialists, which was set aside during the course of this work. That group, the Fellowship of Southern Churchmen, was also a protest movement, primarily a forerunner of the civil rights movement. During the late 1940s, members of that group engaged in acts of civil disobedience related to racial segregation in the South.

Blanchard was involved to a limited degree with the civil rights movement in the 1960s and, at that time, became more aware of the religious justifications for political activism on several sides of most issues, especially in the South. This book offers a clear example of a kind of highly focused political action stemming from religious ideology. Wide religious diversity and intense social commitments pose a critical problem for modern American society, since mass communications and secular values increasingly conflict with "traditional" religious perspectives. Thus, for Blanchard, this book develops from a local situation themes pertinent to every community—the abortion controversy deserves detailed attention by social scientists attuned to the wider issues of religiously inspired or justified political activity.

Terry Prewitt's earlier work on religion has stressed the social context of religious beliefs and practices. In addition to work with Native American religions, mainly among the Oklahoma Delaware, he has pursued two other lines of anthropological research into religion. First, he has written on social and cultural interpretations of the Hebrew Bible, mainly the Book of Genesis as it relates to formative Judaism. In this context he developed interest in contemporary ethical and legal interpretations of the Hebrew scriptures by fundamentalist Christians. Second, he has investigated the recent history of political evangelism in the United States and associated missions in the Caribbean. Part of the concern of both these areas of research has been the theological treatment of capital punishment, abortion, and other social issues as viewed by culturally conservative American readers of Hebrew law and narrative. The Pensacola bombers based some of their actions on Old Testament readings and were associated with a strongly political evangelical religious community. These connections offered a basis for analysis of theology in action with clear relevance to current social changes in America.

## Theoretical Considerations and Approaches

While most sociology and a growing part of contemporary anthropology are devoted to a lawlike style of theory, this book is founded in pattern theories more typical of traditional ethnography and structural linguistics.[1] Such "concatenated" theories draw together diverse empirical generalizations in an effort to generate understanding of a large-scale situation. This interpretation of the Pensacola clinic bombings and their aftermath is presented in a context of other such violent acts perpetrated against abortion clinics. We offer this work in the spirit of qualitative sociology, ethnography of complex societies, contemporary social history, some forms of general systems theory, and other perspectives on understanding that bridge humanistic and scientific goals.

In many respects, this kind of work, linked broadly to the *Verstehen* theory of Max Weber and his followers, is less prominent in contemporary sociology than in anthropology. However, the line between sociology and anthropology is blurred because, in the broad discussion of "who" will define ethnography and "what" its theoretical grounding will be, sociologists have for the most part provided the essential formalizations accepted by both disciplines. Ethnography nonetheless remains an anthropological "method." To the extent we have engaged in relatively short-term and superficial contact with our subjects, our work is consistent with sociological conceptions of ethnography. We nonetheless share a long-term familiarity with the cultural premises underlying both sides of the abortion controversy, including the communities of charismatic and fundamentalist religions. Our writing, then, reflects the "authoritative"—if perhaps grandiose—style of the anthropological ethnographic tradition.[2]

Our holistic orientation calls into question our use of other generalizing efforts of sociologists, such as writings on the sociology of violence or religion. Where we have found works that ring true to our experience in this community we have cited them. We have also offered our own generalizations for some of the patterns we have observed, sometimes even using our intimate knowledge of "our case" to suggest directions for understanding the more limited facts of our "background cases." The Pensacola situation allows the reader to see how cultural positions on abortion become part of media presentations, courtroom proceedings, church activities, and public demonstrations. Our descriptions, though minimal, are aimed at showing the conflicting applications of cultural premises to which, taken individually, most Americans would subscribe.

It remains for us to outline some other works that immediately inform our analysis and writing. Limited as these studies may be, their importance in our thoughts about how to proceed and what to view cannot be overestimated. Yet we make no attempt to be comprehensive in any particular area of social theory. Our substantive goal of understanding the Christmas Day bombings in Pensacola and ostensibly unrelated, but similar, acts of violence must remain the focus of this book.

There have been studies of violence from a sociological perspective, probably the best example of which is Gamson's (1975). The only study of violence as it relates to religion, to our knowledge, is the one of the Jonestown phenomenon,[3] which was, however, primarily a case of self-inflicted violence. Our analysis bridges these types of studies to examine the links between religion and violence directed toward others.

While we approach this subject from primarily sociological and anthropological perspectives, we also examine psychological and sociopsychological explorations that might shed light on these events. Because we assume that no single perspective can explain the complexities of human behaviors, we examine studies of rapists, torturers, and terrorists, as well as theories concerning violent criminals in general and especially social movements, that might help us to understand the activation of abortion clinic bombers and arsonists.

Beyond abortion, there are many issues before the American people and government that garner religious activism and could also lead to violence: the evolution/creationism controversy, prayer in the schools, gay rights, sex education, and pornography, to name but a few. Thus, this study has implications for possible future arenas of violence.

While it was not our intention to develop new theories, this study does yield some new insights on (1) the number of levels of different types of organizations in the anti-abortion movement, which is generalizable to other social movements; (2) the development of changing constituencies at different levels of social movement activism; (3) the interactions among theology, social position, social isolation, and violence; (4) the place of governmental authority in encouraging or discouraging violence; (5) the complex relationships among psychological, social, and cultural factors in encouraging violence; (6) the depth of subcultural rifts in American society; (7) the characteristics of multireligious fundamentalism in the United States; (8) a broader, more detailed definition and description of the basic traits of fundamentalism than heretofore given; and (9) the important potential effects of subgroup encapsulation in this country.

## Methods

A variety of data form the basis of our study and the attendant conclusions, as described below.

*1. The Trial of the Pensacola Four.* Chapters 2 through 13 contain essentially what sociologists and anthropologists call "data." That is, they provide a primary case study that may be interpreted, in part, through the expanded information set forth in the rest of the book. Dallas Blanchard attended all the days of the trial and sentencing but one, while Terry Prewitt attended that day and three others. In addition, a colleague, William Barnes, attended all but two days and shared his notes with us.

Although our description of the trial of the Pensacola Four is long, it represents only a small part of the full proceedings, concentrating on the defense and the cross-examination of defense witnesses. We have selected those elements of testimony that seem to capture best the themes stressed by the prosecution and defense attorneys. These themes involve points of law—in the main, matters having little to do with abortion itself—and cultural statements about abortion that were ultimately introduced into the trial only in the context of the insanity plea. Our readers should understand that abortion and bombing are quite unrelated issues from the point of view of the court. On the other hand, within the community most people interpreted the trial through their value perspectives on abortion, women's rights, civil disobedience, or other orientations apart from the technical legal issues in the case.

We present the trial of the Pensacola Four and its context as a description keyed to issues we believe are central to the abortion controversy in general. In this respect, our view of the trial is but one interpretation. The level of detail is appropriate to allow comparison with the vast majority of other cases of violence in recent years, while giving a full sense of what happened in Pensacola. We have found in the Pensacola situation continual restatement of common stimuli, motives, methods, rationales, and processes as in virtually every other instance of abortion-related violence. More important, the types of persons involved—viewed in terms of age, sex, social class, personality, degree of social isolation, and religiosity—present a pattern worthy of close scrutiny by the American public. Our footnotes to the trial and its background cite the links between the Pensacola case and national events and processes. Those footnotes also point out key events and statements for our later analysis. We chose this descriptive format to retain the integrity of those local events.

We believe our descriptive compromise between total detail and a more superficial treatment of the trial and its cultural context is a necessary prerequisite to understanding the dynamics of a deep cultural schism. We might have accomplished this goal by detailing any of several other trials that have occurred in recent years, but the Pensacola trial presents the clearest juxtaposition of opposed viewpoints of any case we have seen and offers distinctive strategic advantages for analysis.

First, the youth and almost pure religious motivation of the bombers elicited extreme cultural and emotional reactions from all sectors of the community. The bombers gained an inordinate amount of sympathy and public support from some elements of the anti-abortion community, even though many of those explicitly denied advocacy of violence.

Second, the fact that three clinics were bombed at once on Christmas morning in an intended symbolic gesture brought the case to the highest levels of national awareness. The national media widely publicized the bombings, and many news organizations, such as the *Village Voice*, United Press, and the *Chicago Times*, sent reporters to the trial. In addition, a number of television consortiums set up satellite relays outside the courtroom. These media representations of Pensacola failed to capture the community as we know it and tended to stereotype the Pensacola Four and members of the anti-abortion movement as crackpots. We felt that a more balanced characterization of the community and local activists would enhance understanding of the place of the Pensacola events in the national movement.

Third, public statements by one of the defendants, as well as sworn testimony developed in the trial, linked the bombings to the national information network of radical elements in the anti-abortion movement, even though the bombers themselves had not actively participated in other anti-abortion efforts. Exhibited in the trial were publications read by the defendants from various national anti-abortion organizations, which the defense maintained had a pronounced impact on the defendants. National anti-abortion figures, such as Joseph Scheidler, also made appearances during the trial. Our treatment of the trial attempts to sort out local involvement and motivations from the more widely publicized national anti-abortion presence during the proceedings.

Fourth, because four defendants with slightly different levels of involvement were tried simultaneously on varying charges, the defense required careful and complex preparation. The three primary attorneys for the defense took essentially different stances and used different tactics during the trial, yielding examples of most of the kinds of defenses used in trials of other individuals charged with abortion-related violence across the country. This aspect of the trial gave voice to the abortion issue in all of its complexity.

The Pensacola bombings, the events surrounding them, and the subsequent trial provide an almost perfect example of what Max Weber called an "ideal type,"[4] an example of ideology carried to its extreme, which is rarely found in real life. The situation seems ready-made for generalization and was indeed the source of various conclusions in the press, among the general public, and in the pro-choice and anti-abortion movements. These somewhat "committed" responses, however, often lacked depth of examination or appreciation of the cultural variety underlying the issues. We believe the complexity of the case, together with its "ideal" form, makes it valuable for detailed analysis. Those who call themselves fundamentalists are a highly varied group, as are those who call themselves pro-lifers. The violent wings of these groups are probably unique in the degree to which they take ideology seriously and in their degree of commitment to the ideology.

*2. Questionnaires to Perpetrators of Abortion-related Violence.* We obtained current addresses for all but three individuals convicted of abortion-related violence and mailed them a questionnaire. The questionnaires sought information on social background (e.g., age, marital status, occupations of parents, religious affiliation as a child and at the time of the crime, education); knowledge of and acquaintance with other perpetrators and key figures in the anti-abortion movement; previous involvement in the movement, if any; and the rationale for the individual's acts. Five subjects responded to these questionnaires.

*3. Interviews of Perpetrators.* Dallas Blanchard was able to interview several subjects in prison or jail to obtain essentially the same information as above or to flesh out returned questionnaires with greater detail. Others agreed to being interviewed by telephone. While we were not allowed to tape the prison interviews (due to prison regulations), we did, with permission, tape the telephone interviews and furnished a copy of the tapes to those subjects. In addition, we mailed the interview subjects copies of our characterizations of them (presented in chapter 13) as a check on our accuracy. Those interviewed include Peter Burkin, Joseph Grace, Edward Markley, Michael Bray, and John Brockhoeft.

When we were unable to obtain sufficient data because of interview refusals or through examination of reports in both local and national newspapers, we interviewed reporters who covered the trials for additional information.

*4. Newspaper Accounts.* Whether a person agreed to an interview or not, we secured all newspaper articles about the violent act, the perpetrators, and their subsequent trials. We found the coverage usually to be broad and detailed. Our files of newspaper articles totaled more than three cubic feet of material. Only rarely did an interviewee correct essential data as reported in the press, and those corrections tended to be about minor points or facts.

*5. Interviews of Local Anti-Abortionists.* We interviewed a number of key persons in the Pensacola anti-abortion movement. Most notable were John Burt, David Shofner, Vicky Conroy, and Sharon Glass. Each interview lasted at least an hour and concerned the structure of the local movement, its ties to national organizations, and other data relevant to the movement.

6. *Data on Fundamentalism.* We used three essential sources of primary data on contemporary (as opposed to historical, which we also researched) fundamentalism: (1) interviews with several key leaders and knowledgeable local fundamentalists, especially charismatics (major interviewees were Vicky Conroy, Sharon Glass, Lindell Ballenger, John Burt, David Shofner, David Mayo, and David Del Gallo); (2) attendance at a number of worship services at several different Assemblies of God congregations; and (3) previous personal interactions with fundamentalists. For example, Dallas Blanchard had pastored both rural and urban United Methodist churches in Alabama, Tennessee, and Kentucky over a period of seventeen years, and noncharismatic fundamentalists were members of all those churches. Both of us had interacted with fundamentalists in Pensacola in university-sponsored debates and over public issues before the school board or the county commission.

7. *Interviews of Personnel at the Victim Clinics.* Dallas Blanchard called every abortion clinic in the nation that had been victimized by violence and was still in operation, and he interviewed a person there, usually the clinic manager. We also interviewed personally the Pensacola clinic operators William Permenter, Linda Taggart, and Bo Bagenholm. Information sought from each concerned the frequency and types of incidents (such as demonstrations and illegal acts) that had occurred both before and after the bombing/arson or other violent act. No consistent pattern was discovered to allow us to predict when a particular clinic might become the object of violence.

8. *Other Data.* Additional information was garnered from Planned Parenthood, the National Abortion Federation (NAF), the National Abortion Rights Action League (NARAL), and the National Organization for Women (NOW). The NAF, for example, provided us with an important list of the dates, places, and arrested or convicted perpetrators, where appropriate, of every incident of extreme abortion-related violence in the United States. The NAF also provided year-by-year data on violent incidents. The Bureau of Alcohol, Tobacco and Firearms gave us additional information about perpetrators and where they could be lo-

cated. In addition, because of their involvement in counterdemonstrations and escorting women during clinic picketing, we interviewed officers of the Escambia County chapter of NOW, Shirley Gallagher and Gloria Mattingly.

## A Note on Terminology

The terms *pro-life* and *pro-choice* are political statements by opposing sides in the abortion controversy, and each side resents and protests the name(s) chosen by the other side. Each is seeking to seize the "high-ground" of the ethical/moral debate while appealing to as wide a constituency as possible. Those calling themselves pro-lifers hold that pro-choicers are really pro-death, while pro-choicers maintain that the anti-abortionists are really anti-woman.

However, it is clear to us that "pro-life" is a misnomer for that movement. It might be more accurately termed "pro-fetal-life" or "anti-abortion." There are some segments of the movement that are closer to a broad "pro-life" stance, opposing not only abortion but also the death penalty, euthanasia, and nuclear and biological/chemical weapons. On the other hand, there are groups opposing the death penalty while approving abortion, as well as organizations opposing nuclear and biological/chemical weapons while also approving abortion.[5] There are also many individuals who personally oppose abortion but support the right to choose it. The anti-abortion movement at large tends to ignore those issues, and some constituent organizations and individuals actually support the death penalty and the arms race. Its seizure of the self-designation "pro-life" implies that its opponents are pro-death, while it ignores, discounts, or essentially casts aside considerations of the implications of an unwanted pregnancy on the potential mother's life.[6]

One might argue that the choice is not pure. That is, in the extreme position, the choice for the fetus may be against the life of the woman, as in an ectopic pregnancy or the pregnancy of a preteen-ager. This argument could be extended in some cases of euthanasia, nuclear warfare, and chemical/biological warfare to ask, *Whose* life is being given value over other lives? As the conservative theologian Dietrich Bonhoeffer (1966) stated, "Life conflicts with life."[7]

Thus, there are no purely neutral terms that both sides, or even the public at large, agree on. Therefore, we will follow the general social-science approach, using for each the term that is generally used in that field: *anti-abortion* and *pro-choice*.[8] These tend also to be the terms used in the wider community. Occasionally we will use different, but obvious, terms for each in the interest of variety.

### Abortion as a Symbol of Cultural Rift

Like the anti-abortion movement, the pro-choice movement is diverse and has inspired its own radical elements—individuals willing to use illegal action to promote their cause—though to a much more limited extent.[9] But pro-choice violence, besides being too infrequent to form a basis for generalizable conclusions, is beyond the scope of our immediate concern. Nonetheless, our treatment of the Pensacola confrontations by nonviolent activists on both sides gives an example of how deep the cultural rifts are in this community and, to an extent, on the national front.[10] We point out that should federal abortion standards change, our society might merely experience a shift in the sources of violence surrounding abortion. For example, the July 3, 1989, Supreme Court decision in *Webster v. Reproductive Health Services* ruled that states could forbid abortions in public hospitals or other publicly supported facilities, could prohibit public employees from performing or assisting in any abortion not necessary to save a woman's life, and could require medical tests to determine the viability of any fetus at least twenty weeks old. Furthermore, the court agreed to hear in its 1990 term three other cases that could require private clinics performing abortions in the first three months of pregnancy to meet hospital standards such as those in operating rooms and the informing of parents of females under eighteen years of age.

The effects of the current and potential restrictions on *Roe v. Wade* could eventually be similar to those of the repeal of prohibition.[11] The abortion battle is already effectively returned to the arena of the fifty states. Battles within states are expected to arise quickly over potential restrictions on the availability of abortions. It is possible that states will pass laws similar to the "local-option" regulations relating to alcohol sales.[12] Thus, where abortion is concerned, there may be "dry" states and "dry" counties. The result will inevitably be the activation of more pro-lifers and pro-choicers at the state and local levels. An additional result of that mobilization, we contend from this study, will be an increasing kindling of extremism and violence. Another predictable result of localization of the issue will be the reappearance of illegal abortionists in the "dry" states or counties.[13]

Therefore, among our goals in this work was to understand the dynamics of an extreme faction of a social movement. We conclude that at heart we have a cultural conflict between groups (anti-abortion and pro-choice) that, while using the same language, attach entirely different symbolic meanings to words and behavior and therefore actually speak different languages. Their failures to communicate are exacerbated by the fact that while they do use the same words, they operate out of contrasting and conflicting worldviews in which the words have dramatically different meanings.

Furthermore, the personal and social profiles of those who are most likely to be attracted to violence in the anti-abortion movement should provide clues to the social types who are likely to be attracted to violence in any social movement. As we indicate in this book, there are marked similarities to these persons and other violent American criminals, including rapists and "ordinary" terrorists.

We are left with several serious and demanding questions. How can we accommodate diverse and conflicting worldviews in a society as diverse as America is and much of the world is becoming? What shall be the bounds of our tolerance? Are our present constitutional safeguards sufficient to protect the interests of all people, majority and minority alike? Are there social questions where majority opinion should take more serious account of minority positions? Can we in some way convince groups that by their worldview are intolerant to become tolerant of others? Can we break the cycle through which powerful media and political groups form pronouncements of "popular interests" that misinterpret the diverse opinions underlying our values and cultural actions?

Our work forms one beginning toward answers to these questions. Although our own pro-choice commitments to the abortion issue are evident enough in our treatment of the material, we believe that those who disagree with us espouse many quite reasonable and important alternatives to solutions we might advocate. Truly democratic solutions to value conflicts will work in such a way as to minimize the potentials for violence precisely because they take into account the widest range of cultural viewpoints and move beyond value conflict toward effective compromises. A national rethinking of our abortion practices is needed if our society is to move beyond the present stalemate and its attendant potentials for open conflict.

# ...2
# A Birthday Gift for Jesus

And there rose up fire out of the rock . . .
Judges 6:21

It was shortly after midnight when Bo and Debhra Bagenholm wearily pulled into their driveway, finally home after the Christmas Eve party. As they walked toward the door, Bo debated with himself. "I need to change clothes and get my gear together," he thought, "and get over to the office." But then his mind swung to the negative side and he began a litany of all the reasons he shouldn't do it. "The night is already half over. I'm tired. I just spent the last two nights there. Nothing has happened for six months. And this fog is so heavy. Besides, it's Christmas."

Each weekend since the June 25 bombing of the Ladies Center, Bo Bagenholm, sensing that it had to happen again, dressed in his scrub suit, threw the folding lounge chair in the car, and, armed with his .38-caliber revolver, staked out his office through the night—in good weather in the dry retention pond behind the building, in bad weather in the dark lobby inside. This evening, rather than get out his chair and gun and dress again for the cool, damp night, he went to bed with his wife.

Psychiatric nurse Debra Jean Armond wiped her hand across her tired eyes as she felt her way through the dense fog in the hospital parking lot toward her car. The fog surrounded her like a misty wet shroud, dulling her senses of sight and hearing. "What a way to spend Christmas Eve!" she thought. Glancing at her watch in the pale lights, she corrected herself: "No, it's already Christmas Day, three hours into it."

After working the 2:45 to 11:15 shift last night at University Hospital, she went to midnight mass and then returned to the hospital to discuss a patient with the doctor. Now she was on her way home to her apartment to catch what sleep she could before she reported back for duty at 2:45 Christmas afternoon.

As she drove slowly up Ninth Avenue, deserted at this hour, she felt lost and disoriented in the fog. The sides of the street were invisible; it took great concentration and effort to determine exactly where she was. Familiar landmarks were no longer there. The usually bright neon signs were soft and indistinguishable glows in the darkness. All the homes were dark now; parents, having finally finished putting bicycles and swing sets together, had unplugged the blinking lights of their Christmas trees and gone to bed to grab a few hours' sleep before the children would shake them awake. There was no other car on the street, and she felt isolated and alone.

Suddenly, she felt something like an explosion right under her car—as if the wheels had been blown out beneath it. Her first thought was, "Someone is trying to kill me!" Stunned and thinking the car had been bombed, she stopped in the middle of the road, looked around at herself and the car, and hesitantly decided both were all right. Shaken and anxious, she warily continued home to a restless sleep.

Further down the same street, at the same moment that Debra Jean Armond was jolted, Matthew John Goldsby, clad as was his companion, Jimmy Simmons, in black shirt and pants with a dark green ski mask over his head, was standing on the roof of the office of Dr. Bo Bagenholm and lowering with a rope a forty-one-pound, six-by-twelve-inch pipe through the broken skylight. He was trying to move quickly because there was an identical package ticking away in the trunk of Simmons's car in the parking lot below, and the concussion he heard meant there were only ten minutes until these two remaining detonators exploded.

At 3:28 A.M., Station No. 6 fire fighters had just spent fifteen minutes settling back in from a call when a new alarm came to send three trucks to the Ladies Center, just down the street. When the fire fighters arrived, they found smoke pouring from the doors and windows, adding to the deep foggy haze, and debris scattered outside on the ground. It looked as if an explosion had hit the rear of the building; the back door had been blown ajar. After removing the electric meter, they entered to search the building to make sure no one was inside. With flashlights barely able to cut through the haze, they climbed through overturned cabinets and equipment, finding electrical wiring hanging loosely from all the plasterless walls and the distinctive odor of gunpowder suspended in the air.

Goldsby and Simmons hurried to the Executive Plaza Road office of Dr. William Permenter. They saved this site until last because they were unsure of the type of security system or whether there was one at all. They checked the two detonation systems. Like the other two, there was an energy-control timer, which was attached to a hobbyist's rocket engine for a detonator, plus a one-and-a-half-foot fuse and a two-minute detonator, in case an alarm should go off when they broke open a window to place it. At the office, no alarm sounded when they smashed the window, so they did not light the fuse.

Placing the ticking bomb on the floor just inside the window, they raced to the First Assembly of God and parked in the rear lot out of sight of passing cars. They huddled, listening, beside one of the false buttresses of the building. Roughly equidistant from all three sites, the church was an ideal, secluded spot for their short wait. On schedule, they heard the bomb at Bagenholm's office go off. Hearing nothing from the direction of Permenter's office, they drove out Ninth Avenue past the Ladies Center and saw only a police car parked across the street with the patrolman sitting inside it. Once past the area, they quickly drove back to Dr. Permenter's building. Turning into Executive Plaza, they saw no police officers or fire fighters, but red and blue flames soared a hundred feet into the night fog, creating a surrealistic canvas on the low sky.

At 3:40 A.M., Captain Richard Currow of the Pensacola Fire Department received a call to go to Dr. Bagenholm's office. He found a haze of smoke hanging in the street and around the building that smelled like gunpowder. There was no indication of fire. All doors and downstairs windows were secured, so the fire fighters got out their door-lock puller and tried to enter the building. But the doors had two well-constructed locks that resisted removal. Bagenholm arrived and opened the door with his keys. Looking up the stairs, Captain Currow saw flames in the building and returned to the truck for the hoses. As the fire fighters pulled out the hoses, flames were coming through the roof. They took the hoses in and upstairs; at the top of the stairs there was a hole in the floor as big as an automobile, but they were able to extinguish the fire quickly.

At 4:00 A.M., James Sanders, captain of the Brent Volunteer Fire Department and an off-duty county deputy sheriff, got a call to go to Permenter's office. The Brent department sent one fire truck, which was joined by six others from the Ferry Pass Volunteer Fire Department. When they arrived, the building was engulfed in flames and the roof had partially collapsed. The north wall was blown completely away, and brick and mortar debris were scattered as far as two hundred feet away. Securing the scene required sealing off a city-block-sized area around the totally destroyed building.

About the same time Deputy Sanders was first awakened, Goldsby and Simmons reached the house where Jimmy's wife, Kathren, and Matt's fiancée, Kaye Wiggins, were praying and reading in the Book of Judges the story about the slayer of those who offered infant sacrifices to Baal—the story of Gideon.

## ... 3
## The City
## of
## Five
## Flags

Pride goeth before destruction . . .
Proverbs 16:18

Pensacola in early 1985 represented a collection of people and cultural contradictions resulting from a rich history. Surrounding the urban core is a mosaic of neighborhoods called the Historic District, the Belmont-Devilliers District, North Hill, and East Hill, the expansion neighborhoods from the sixteenth century to the early twentieth century. In the central urban area, an abundance of parks and schools breaks the sea of houses among live oaks draped with Spanish moss and pecan and magnolia trees. Small and large, sometimes well finished and occasionally broken-down, new, old, and refurbished, surrounded by the ubiquitous azaleas and camellias, the houses shelter a plethora of human types: retired couples, widows, widowers, fishermen, ministers, unemployed laborers, young professionals, students, renters, owners, lawyers, and many, many more.

The November 1984 elections had demonstrated that the federal-court-mandated single-member city council districts can provide democracy in a small city, despite the periodic *Pensacola News-Journal* editorials favoring the old system of at-large elections. The new system provided one more irritant to devotees of tradition.

Some families of the black community are among the oldest families of Pensacola, forming a continuity with the Spanish period. There are prominent black and white families who are related only a few generations back, although the subject is rarely broached by anyone except by circumlocutions. Interracial couples are seen occasionally in the malls, still another obvious irritant to some. The military and university presences have radically influenced this aspect of official and public life in Pensacola—clearly the city is more national now than it is Southern. Even the more charismatic and Pentecostal churches are interracial, a reflection of national value changes on local religion. Indeed, the fundamentalist churches are generally far more interracial, as opposed to integrated, than the mainline denominations, which are far more liberal in their social views.

Yet, even if racial tensions do not divide Pensacola overtly, racial politics are the rule of the decade. The public school system is predominantly black in many parts of a city too small for busing. There are many private "Christian" schools, some exclusively white, and two unaccredited Bible colleges. But it is frequently difficult to distinguish black from white neighborhoods, and the newest expansions of the city attract many middle-class blacks. However, transitions may also be abrupt, and the I-110 spur entering the city is gracefully elevated over one of the most neglected and depressed black areas of the city.

Dotting the city are some of the best Chinese, Italian, and Greek restaurants in the South, evidence of large Taiwanese, Vietnamese, Korean, Italian, and Greek communities. Seafood abounds, from steam houses and oyster bars to fancy restaurants serving the best the Gulf of Mexico has to offer. Locals frequent fish houses to buy shrimp, snapper, mullet, flounder, and oysters fresh off the boats. From the new Three-Mile Bridge, commuters see lines of fishermen in every kind of weather on the old bridge, its channel span now removed. From April to October groups of shrimp boats, now often operated by Vietnamese refugee families, work different sections of the bay.

The larger rigs work offshore—the sleek snapper boats, run by three- or four-person crews, and shrimp boats, constructed with bulky steel hulls, sometimes working as far as the Mexican coastal waters. The port also enjoys a constant traffic of freighters, mostly grain haulers, and barges using the Intracoastal Waterway through the bay as a link between the rivers and the Atlantic. On the clearest days the flattop profile of the USS *Lexington*, the training carrier for fledgling navy pilots, stands silhouetted across the bay. The narrow ribbon of sand beyond the carrier marks the fragile island barrier between bay and Gulf. With binoculars one can see the inverted V of the fins of sharks circling and waiting to feed on trash cast from the *Lexington*. Larger and mirroring the shark fins are the numberless colorful sails of all sizes, trailered in for day sails or brought from the several bayous where they are permanently moored.

To the north and west, Pensacola's growth reaches beyond its official boundaries to include several smaller towns and unincorporated communities. Here live the older, more rural members of the population being swallowed by urban growth. Small frame houses line the old main routes that give access to modern look-alike subdivisions. From these neighborhoods traffic flows hesitantly into the city from the north along any of six closely related access routes. A mere ten by ten miles is sufficient to embrace all the variety of the city, which is yet the major outpost of Florida in the panhandle. Pensacola lies only fifteen miles east and thirty miles south of the Alabama state line. Its hospitals, businesses, and tourist facilities are the vital hub of the region, drawing people from hundreds of miles away.

Growth also draws people from across the nation. The city is cosmopolitan; natives are outnumbered by outsiders. Active and retired military families, refugees, and young professionals from elsewhere are a major component of the community, infusing it with new blood and new ideas. These diverse elements have given the city a look and feel a world apart from what one would expect in a Southern city.

Yet there remain elements of Southernness in the mix. Within and surrounding Pensacola are people who represent a very traditional Southern culture and espouse a fundamentalist faith. There is a business named the Born Again Glass Company, and one can hardly go a mile in several parts of town without seeing two-square-foot signs bearing biblical quotations such as "Ye must be born again" and "He that soweth to his flesh shall of the flesh reap corruption." Almost as frequently one will see bumper stickers reading, "When the Rapture Comes, This Car Will Be Driverless"; seen more rarely is the hostile response: "When the Rapture Comes, Leave Me Your Car." Spotted usually at least once a day by anyone driving two or three miles in the town are pickup trucks with four-by-eight-foot side panels or autos with two-foot-high boxes strapped to their tops with vivid depictions of the fires of hell and appropriate verses.

In north Escambia County and across the Escambia River in Santa Rosa County, the accepted standards of life contrast sharply with those of Pensacola. The northern end of Escambia is noted for its penchant for pork-barrel politics and feisty politicians who take care of their "neighbors." It is the home of numerous Pentecostal and independent churches, which push even the mainline denominations there into a more conservative stance. There is also a strong, prosperous Mennonite community, whose members can be distinguished by the women's black-scarf-covered hair buns and high-necked dresses.

Local folklore holds that Santa Rosa County has more churches per square mile than any other county in the United States. At the same time, several politically motivated murders, attacks, and bombings mar the otherwise tranquil atmosphere of rural northwest Florida. These grow out of the lingering family-feud mentality, the history of private law, the notion that one has a right to enforce personally the community value consensus, only one expression of which was lynch law. Traditional values are enthroned and extolled. Changes similar to those in Pensacola have only begun to affect the county regions and communities. Fewer residents of the outlying areas attend college; those who do tend to be the first in their families to do so. They are aligned with diverse Protestant sects, usually in small, intimate, family-centered congregations. Although occasional problems, such as incest or organized racism and sexism, come to the attention of the authorities, the vast majority of the rural people are simply good, God-fearing, and honest small-town Southern Americans.

At best, the people in the city and those living outside it are not in tune with each other. Even those in the city with a rural background continue to "go home" on weekends and maintain the rural traditional outlook and values. When the *Rocky Horror Picture Show* began its long run in a Pensacola theater in 1982, letters to the editor decried the satanic aspects of the film, and Monty Python's religious comedy, *The Life of Brian*, received a similar response.

Pensacola is a small city with many subcultures. It is cosmopolitan, to be sure, and proud of its progress and growth. For the most part, it is a happy place, filled with people who enjoy what it offers and accept each other. Yet the foundations of cultural conflict are well established. Change toward the "national culture" has occurred in the midst of a large traditional population that once dominated and controlled the life of the region. The traditionalists are now only a vocal minority, and many of them have not enjoyed the benefits of Pensacola's growth and prosperity. To them Pensacola frequently appears as a prideful place, working against nature, God, and the best qualities of humanity. What comes to their minds when they read Proverbs 16:18–19, which Kaye Wiggins quoted to Matt Goldsby in November 1984? "Pride goeth before destruction, and an haughty spirit before a fall. Better it is to be of an humble spirit with the lowly, than to divide the spoil with the proud."

# ... 4
# Onward,
# Christian
# Soldiers

Will ye plead for Baal? . . . If he be god, let
him plead for himself.
Judges 6:31

For the purposes of this study, it was not enough to review what kinds
of people Pensacolans[1] were; we felt we must also look at recent de-
cades in more depth, especially since 1973, the year of the Supreme
Court's *Roe v. Wade* decision. We decided to review the community
issues of the Equal Rights Amendment, homosexuality, pornography,
capital punishment, abortion, textbooks, and other issues. We wanted
to know who had been involved in these "causes" and if perhaps one
issue had connection to others. We especially wanted to know how
"religious" and "secular" groups had met each other in public debate.
So we found ourselves spending hours in the local newspaper morgue
refreshing ourselves on important events, issues, and persons.

Pensacola has not existed in a vacuum; state, regional, national, and
international events since World War II have had dramatic impacts on
all American communities. In those forty years television has become a
major information source. Americans have fought two Asian wars, in
Korea and Vietnam, the latter sometimes called the "Living Room
War" to describe the effect of television on the public's perceptions of
armed conflict.

Desegregation has brought great social change to Pensacola schools, jobs, and some neighborhoods. The 1954 *Brown v. Board of Education* Supreme Court decision was only the first of many white-racist Southern disillusionments with that once august body. And the failure to achieve integration has brought additional disillusionment to many blacks.

Yet Vietnam and desegregation do not provide the critical impetus for the modern issues of the abortion controversy in Pensacola. A different issue serves as a much better starting point for our inquiry. On March 22, 1972, the U.S. Congress sent the Equal Rights Amendment (ERA) to the states for ratification. Shortly thereafter in Florida, the state house of representatives passed the amendment by a 90–4 margin, but the Senate failed to act on it.

The ERA ultimately came to represent the impetus for many of the "moral" issues of the new religious Right in the United States. This conservative religious coalition is well represented in Pensacola, and the community has been at the center of several regional controversies linked to the national trends toward conservatism that characterize the late 1970s. But if the ERA was the beginning, abortion came as the swift second step, alerting the senses of the tradition-minded across the nation.

### The Turbulent Rise of the "New Right"

On January 22, 1973, the Supreme Court ruled that first-trimester abortions could not be limited by the states, effectively legalizing "abortion on demand" during early pregnancy. Yet in October of that same year, Dr. Kenneth C. Edelin of Boston was charged with manslaughter for letting an aborted fetus die. Mixed signals went out across the country, and many wondered exactly what the rules were.

In 1973 the Florida house rejected the ERA in a 64–54 vote, while it died in a senate committee with a 3–3 vote. In 1974 it was the senate's turn to defeat the ERA by 21–19, and the house's turn not to act on it.

Ratification of the ERA required endorsement by thirty-eight state legislatures within ten years of its passage by the U.S. Congress, and by early 1973 thirty states had ratified it. As the number crept upward toward the magical thirty-eight, supporters and opponents alike intensified their lobbying efforts. As a proposed new law, the ERA had the effect of mobilizing both support and opposition as did no other issue in northwest Florida or the rest of the nation. Existing and new organizations—local, state, and national—held rallies, enlisted members, solicited money, lobbied legislators, demonstrated, marched, and picketed for the next ten years. Cries of doom were raised at both the threat of passage and of defeat. It was an issue marked by rhetoric, hyperbole, and events created for the media. Proponents on both sides of the issue tended toward extremist language and behavior. Opponents charged that the ERA would bring unisex bathrooms; women in combat sharing foxholes, sleeping quarters, and bathrooms with male soldiers; and further breakdown of the family by allowing homosexuals to marry one another and to adopt children. Some charged that the ERA was a communist plot to destroy America, would force homemakers to get jobs, and would compel the Catholic church to have 50 percent of its priests be women.

Groups supporting ratification in the Pensacola area included the local chapters of the National Organization for Women, the League of Women Voters, the Federation of Business and Professional Women, the National Women's Political Caucus, the AFL-CIO, the YWCA, the American Association of University Women, and both political parties. In 1976, 110 national groups joined in the coalition ERAmerica. Several major liberal Protestant denominations took positions favoring the amendment.

Opposition came from such groups as Women's Right to Be Women, Women for Responsible Legislation, Gals With Guts (GiGi), Stop-ERA (Phyllis Schlafly), and the John Birch Society. Religious groups opposing the ERA included the Latter Day Saints and the conservative and fundamentalist bodies that hold to male dominance in the home and traditional family values. Locally, this included several Southern Baptist, Church of Christ, and Assemblies of God congregations. For many of these groups, the ERA was identified with secular humanism, sexual licentiousness, homosexuality, abortion, anti–capital punishment, and anti–national defense.

On July 4, 1974, thousands of gay-rights activists came to Pensacola for a "national convention." Gay bars along the waterfront and shoreline were filled; transvestite strip shows were common. The city police arrested twenty people in the bars in an attempt to keep a lid on the activities. Little was mentioned in the local press except in small, inside-page police reports. But the word got around town, and evangelical churches mobilized people to write their city council members. In the same year there were four failed attempts to set fire to two gay bars.

In April 1975, thirty-four states had ratified the ERA and the Florida house had endorsed the amendment by a 61–58 vote. Just before the senate was to vote on it, 1,500 to 3,000 supporters (depending on whose estimate one trusts) held a march on the state capitol, singing songs such as "Move on over or we'll move on over you." Speakers included Governor Reuben Askew, Betty Friedan, Marlo Thomas, and Alan Alda. A group of self-styled lesbian feminists carried a banner reading, "An army of lovers shall not fail." Other signs read, "We've shoveled it long enough" and "Vote for the ERA or get cut off." In the news there was a threatened national boycott of Florida citrus should the senate vote no. Despite a poll showing that 62 percent of west Floridans supported the ERA, both Pensacola senators voted against it to aid its defeat by a 21–17 margin.

By July 4, 1975, tensions had heightened around the expected and now annual gay-rights gathering in Pensacola. Prominent in the news were articles on the "Homosexual Bill of Rights" and on appeals from the American Civil Liberties Union against police harassment of gays and an editorial supporting the ACLU petition. After the July 4 assembly had passed with few if any incidents and the news had cooled, the *Pensacola News-Journal* published an editorial supporting the military's position on dishonorable discharge for gays in the service and another article sympathetic to the problems of homosexuals.

In August 1975, local interests were focused on other issues. A federal appeals court overturned the Florida law requiring that unwed mothers-to-be obtain parental consent and married women obtain spousal consent before having abortions. This decision effectively removed minor pregnant females from legal parental control and married pregnant women from control by their husbands. At about the same time, the number of gynecologists offering abortions—and even advertising their services—increased as a result of a Supreme Court decision allowing lawyers and doctors to publicize their services and prices. The number of legal abortions being performed increased dramatically. That which had once been available only through illegal operators or through legitimate physicians under various subterfuges now became an open event, advertised in the daily want ads and Yellow Pages.

Also in August 1975, the Escambia County Commission was confronted by religious groups about the sale of alcoholic beverages near churches and schools. The county was not about to ban hard liquor altogether; it was too essential to the tourist industry and county revenues. However, the commission did ban the sale of liquor in newly established stores and bars within 1,500 feet of churches and schools.

That same year a schoolteacher in Okaloosa County, some fifty miles east of Pensacola, filed a federal court suit to overturn a school board regulation requiring Bible reading and prayer in the classroom. Pensacola was drawn into the dispute since the federal court sessions were held in the city and since many Pensacolans spoke publicly on both sides of the issue. For six months the controversy held the headlines, was disputed in letters to the editor, and was the subject of several editorials against compulsory prayer in the schools. The issue was finally "resolved" when the local federal judge ruled that the school board requirement was unconstitutional.

However, the decision did not settle the issue in all minds. In December Governor George Wallace of Alabama, in support of Bible reading in the schools, addressed a prayer rally in Fort Walton Beach that was attended by 3,500, far fewer than the 13,000–20,000 participants expected by the sponsors. The same month a local state legislator announced his intention to introduce a bill to restore prayer and Bible reading in the public schools. His defiance resulted four months later in a bill permitting "silent meditation."

The prayer issue is not dead today, but in the mid-1970s other issues began to capture public attention. In early 1976, it was revealed in the press that a murdered, reputed homosexual from Atlanta had been in the Pensacola area and had temporary custody of two young males from the local youth ranch for troubled teenagers. The local Lambda Society, a gay rights group, attempted to question candidates for county offices, and the newspaper published three editorials on homosexuality.

According to a May 1976 *News-Journal* editorial, Pensacola had long had "a number of nightclubs featuring topless female dancers or female impersonators." The same editorial concluded: "There are certainly limits to the amount of 'porn' the community is willing to tolerate . . . but we believe the community's main concern at this point is that [pornography] . . . not intrude upon the lives of those who want no part of it."

The newspaper's estimate of community tolerance was belied the next month when the local state attorney, Curtis Golden, met with fifty-five people to form Pensacola Citizens for Decency, whose purpose, according to Golden, was to locate pornographic material for sale in the county and report it to his office, as well as determine what constitutes a violation of community standards. One county commissioner at the meeting stated that the new Fellowship of Christian Politicians would "disbar crooked lawyers who just defend these people [pornography publishers and distributors]." No one pointed out that this would be a fundamental violation of basic rights of defendants and no grounds for disbarring any attorney.

Three days later an editorial suggested the group might be over-zealous and advised it to limit its work to "making sure that offensive material is not displayed openly to the public, that it does not degrade the neighborhood, rather than trying to tell other adults what they may or may not read."

Less than a month later, the entire community was shocked when a local state legislator, Ed Fortune, accused a professor at Pensacola's University of West Florida of showing *Deep Throat* to a class attended by Fortune's daughter, who was also the wife of an assistant state attorney. It was later brought to light that viewing of the film for the "Mass Media and the Law" class was voluntary. Many faculty organized to support academic freedom, to the strong opposition of the Christian Businessmen's Committee.

Fortune then introduced a bill to require censorship committees on each of the nine state university campuses to review course materials. With his bill faltering, Fortune made another shocking disclosure in June, charging that the sex act was simulated in a theater class by UWF students performing a scene from *Equus*. His bill passed both houses, but Governor Reuben Askew vetoed it. Fortune responded by promising to introduce a bill to make showing of hard-core pornography on campus a reason for dismissal of faculty. With the legislature out of session for six months, the issue was allowed to fade.

Meanwhile, State Attorney Golden's office had contacted bookstores around town and advised them to remove specific materials or face prosecution. In June, the *Pensacola News-Journal* ran an article proudly headlining Pensacola as the "Cleanest City in the Southeast."

The year 1977 brought the Dade County referendum on homosexual rights. Several editorials in the Pensacola paper and numerous letters to the editor opposed the proposed homosexual rights law in Miami, a city quite distant from Pensacola, both socially and in mileage. Meanwhile, representatives of Parents of Gays continued offering the newspaper "Viewpoint" articles that sought to educate the public about gay-rights issues.

By this time thirty-five states had ratified the ERA and attention focused once again on the Florida legislature. Based on legislative polling, proponents were optimistic that the bill would finally pass both the legislature and the senate. A newspaper poll of Floridans showed that 56 percent of those polled and having an opinion favored the ERA. But the actual vote in the senate again defeated the ERA in Florida.

In 1972 the Supreme Court had effectively repealed all death penalty laws on the grounds that they gave both judges and juries too much leeway. In July 1976 the Court approved, by a 5–4 majority, new death penalty laws of three states, including Florida. In October of that year, Florida Citizens Against the Death Penalty was organized. During this period there was much publicity on the idea of televising executions. An April 1977 poll of the state revealed that only 14 percent of respondents favored the idea. Those most supportive were blacks and people without a high school education. Those who tended to say they would actually watch executions were the same two groups and political conservatives. At the same time, 74 percent favored the death penalty itself, but only 64 percent of north Floridans did.

Santa Rosa County, next-door to Escambia County but more rural, had long ago banned the sale of all alcoholic beverages except beer and wine. With the growth of Pensacola, portions of Santa Rosa had become bedroom communities of the city and somewhat dependent on the tourist trade, especially the new and growing community of Gulf

Breeze, just across the Three-Mile Bridge from Pensacola and separating the city from the other Escambia County community of Pensacola Beach. By 1977 pressure to legalize hard-liquor sales in the county had grown, and a petition for a referendum was presented to the county commission. A hot and angry four-month campaign ensued, with the wets mustering only 41 percent of the vote.

In September 1977 Florida followed federal Medicaid guidelines and decided not to fund elective abortions for those who could not pay.

In February 1978 a furor arose over the showing of *Oh! Calcutta!* at the Pensacola Municipal Auditorium. Under pressure initiated by Rev. Chuck Baldwin, an independent Baptist minister and chairman of the Moral Majority in west Florida, the city commission attempted to void the contract, but the federal court held that the cancellation was a violation of the First Amendment and the show went on, to the distress of many. Baldwin's primary concern was the display of male nudes in the play, and he pledged to expand protests into other areas, including topless dancing.

Anita Bryant, the former Florida orange juice ambassador, spoke and performed in March for a crowd of 2,200 at the University of West Florida under the sponsorship of local religious groups. The Metropolitan Church, a church of and for gays, held a candlelight vigil to protest her appearance and picketed the performance. In May the Metropolitan minister, Susan Kliebenstein, held a week-long fast and pray-in across from city hall in support of gay rights.

In 1978, to the less vociferous opposition of the usual groups, Florida rather quietly passed its own state constitution revision to ban sex discrimination.[2] However, the spring of 1979 saw the Florida senate again defeat the ERA by a 21–19 margin.

In May, John Spenkelink, held in Florida's Starke Prison with five denied Supreme Court appeals, became the second person executed in the nation since 1967. The Spenkelink case aroused much public discussion, debate, and publicity on the death penalty. In June the local Catholic bishop, René Gracida,[3] called for abolition of capital punishment, and Florida Citizens Against the Death Penalty held a statewide conference in September.

In August, Rev. Chuck Baldwin and Rev. Andy Bloom, another independent Baptist minister, presented a petition with 1,000 signatures requesting an Escambia County Commission committee to close all but essential retail outlets on Sundays. The committee rejected this, as Baldwin termed it, "moral and spiritual legislation."

A new issue arose in 1980 over the adoption of biology and psychology textbooks for the Escambia County school system. Evangelical and fundamentalist church groups, stridently led by Baldwin and Bloom, rallied to protest the teaching of biological evolution and "secular humanism" in the public schools. They even ran an ad in the newspaper asserting that homosexuality, extramarital sex, and thievery were being taught in the local schools. The broadness of their attack made it clear that the issue went well beyond the teaching of evolution in the schools. (Similarly, an organization in Maryland called the Coalition of Concerned Parents opposed teachers discussing, without parents' permission, such topics such as one-world government, interpersonal relationships, drug and alcohol abuse, and organic evolution. Clearly, evolution is but a surface issue among a complex of underlying issues.)

One Escambia County School Board meeting had to be rescheduled because the usual chambers would not hold the crowd. The meeting took place a couple weeks later in a high school gymnasium, where bleachers were loaded with partisans on either side—pro-evolutionists sat on the right, pro-creationists on the left, and the school board under the north basketball goal. Rooted on with applause and loud amens, conservative ministers and laypersons spoke heatedly and with passion into a microphone at mid-court against the committee book selections, to mutterings and groans of the "liberals." A few liberals, teachers, professors, and a minister or two spoke against teaching creationism in the schools, to the jeers and hoots of the opposition.

Finally the vote came: four for the committee recommendation to adopt the disputed books, one against. Mutters rose from the pro-creationists: "We'll be back. You're not through with us yet."

### A Victory for the Minority

Traditionally, the American people have elected to the presidency practical politicians, those who are willing to compromise principles for the possible, who are not bound to their ideologies come hell or high water. After rejecting perceived ideologues of first the Right and then the Left in Goldwater in 1968 and McGovern in 1972, Americans sent to the White House their first ideologue in the last half of the twentieth century in the person of Ronald Reagan.

The 1980 election was preceded with intense mobilization by the religious groups of the Right, along with conservative political organizations. These groups were not only successful in selling Ronald Reagan to a plethora of highly committed one-issue voters, but they also achieved local successes that changed the face of the Congress in 1980. Those most committed to "moral" issues were also most vulnerable to the negative media images of the Carter presidency, especially the tough-sounding Reagan rhetoric that found a kind of national shame in the Iranian crisis. Although Reagan scored a surprising victory, the popular vote was close, and on most single issues the "majority" view was not Reagan's view.

Polls and research conducted since 1980 demonstrate that there is little broad support for the Moral Majority and similar groups. Some analysts say that the religious Right had little effect on voters' behavior in 1980. Farmers, wage laborers, students, professionals, the elderly, some women, and even some minority voters formed the coalition that elected Reagan. Many of these people seem to have set aside, for the most part, their feelings about such "moral" issues as prayer in the schools, abortion, and other projects of the radical Right. More crucial in the Reagan election were the unemployment and inflation staggering the national economy, and the Iranian hostage situation. The voters were seeking leadership that, at the least, appeared to know where to go and what to do. However, the Moral Majority and its allies considered the election a mandate to bring American law—national, state, and local—into line. The Reagan victory provided Christians of the Right with their first significant sense of personal victory against the rising tide of secularization in America. This perception motivated them to even more enthusiastic mobilization on subsequent issues.[4]

The cheers of victory were still resounding in 1981 as the state and local NOW organizations began their final push for ratification of the ERA by the 1982 Florida legislature. In September the statewide kick-off rally took place in Pensacola, accompanied by the announcement of lobbying plans. December brought the national president of NOW to a Pensacola rally, a petition drive to change local legislators' positions, and a media blitz over radio urging supporters to call Senator W. D. Childers, who said his phones were completely tied up. Opponents of the ERA also responded to the ads, helping to tie up the lines. One opponent stated a widespread feeling: "I don't think the majority of people in Florida are for ERA. I don't care what the polls say."

In June 1982, on the same day that the Florida legislature approved the ERA by a 60–58 vote, the state senate again voted down ratification. Amid hunger strikes and sit-ins in which one Pensacola woman was arrested for trespassing, the old-time power politics of Florida's smaller legislative body played itself out, this time by a 22–16 margin. ERA opponents held victory rallies throughout the region, some attending a Washington celebration honoring Phyllis Schlafly and Dempsey Barron, the Panama City senator credited with single-handedly killing the ERA in Florida.

Other issues returned to the public consciousness. Executions had proceeded slowly in Florida, whose late-1981 total of 163 prisoners on death row led the nation in convicted capital murderers. The *Pensacola News-Journal* published almost annual editorials calling for speeding up the execution process. Gay activism continued to heighten into 1982, manifest in a widely publicized demonstration on the opening of the state legislature in Tallahassee. Activism was becoming a norm, but on the local level in Pensacola the most involved groups represented the religious Right and focused on the issues of nudity and abortion.

Trader Jon's is probably the most famous Gulf Coast bar east of New Orleans. It has a long history as a gathering place, especially for navy personnel drawn by the naval aviation memorabilia covering its walls and, until recently, topless dancers and strippers. When Prince Charles of England visited Pensacola Naval Air Station, it was virtually obligatory for him to tour Trader Jon's, and unfavorable international publicity followed. The success of Trader Jon's, with its photos, autographs, and mementos of the Blue Angels and famous navy pilots, inspired other local establishments to hire topless waitresses and go-go dancers. As the news spread through the city of how extensive such bars were, the same religious groups and persons began pressuring the county and city authorities again.

In March 1982 the U.S. Court of Appeals threw out Escambia County's antinudity law, declaring it too vague. Topless dancing continued and expanded amid the legal void. In July the county commission forbad nudity in any place selling alcohol. In September, again under pressure from church groups led by Chuck Baldwin and Andy Bloom, the county commission passed a regulation forcing the closing of bottle clubs at 2:30 A.M., only thirty minutes after the closing of bars. This effectively closed the bottle clubs, the real goal of the evangelicals.

Encouraged by these successes, the religious groups began pressuring the city commission to pass a similar city ordinance. In January 1983, 175 people from local churches attended a city council session, which led to a new law that same month against topless dancing in bars. Some places, like Trader Jon's, responded by separating with a doorway the selling of liquor and topless dancing. But the law itself, although it was appealed by some operators, gave the churches another public victory. The issue faded as all topless dancing eventually ceased pending the appeals.[5] Many establishments featured dancing without nudity, and one was converted to a discotheque.

The first abortion clinic bombings in the United States occurred on May 29, 1982, in St. Petersburg and Clearwater, Florida.[6] About a week later a clinic in Fairfax, Virginia, was blasted by six bombs, which threw the wife of the owner from the building, although she was not injured.

In 1983 Ronald Reagan became the first president to publish an article on abortion, "Abortion and the Conscience of the Nation." In that article he urged "the antiabortion forces not to lose heart" and went on to state passionately: "The abortionist who reassembles the arms and legs of a tiny baby to make sure all of its parts have been torn from its mother's body can hardly doubt whether it is a human being. The real question . . . is whether that tiny human life has a God-given right to be protected by the law—the same right we have."[7]

By March 1983, Pensacola had three abortion clinics and at least two physicians openly advertising their abortion services, while all but four or five of the more than twenty obstetricians-gynecologists provided early abortions on demand. John Burt, a member of the Brownsville Assembly of God congregation, passed a newsstand and noticed an article stating that in 1982 Pensacola had seven abortions for every ten live births, a deceptive statistic since most people give birth in their home communities, while those seeking abortions may come from a much wider territory. Angry at what he believed to be a high rate of outright murder of unborn babies, he initiated the first picketing of the city's abortion clinics on March 3, 1983, and fourteen demonstrators, members of the local Citizens Against Abortion, were arrested for trespassing outside the Ladies Center. Thus began the abortion confrontation in Pensacola.

The arrested picketers were placed on probation the following week and prohibited from "using bullhorns, megaphones, or . . . shouting or screaming at passersby." The next day Burt demanded that clinics allow them to picket in their parking lots "to speak to patients entering and leaving the building rather than relying on signs and posters to convey their message." The clinics refused.

On Mother's Day of the same year, hundreds marched downtown and held a rally in Seville Square. Mayor Vince Whibbs proclaimed it "Respect for Life Day" in Pensacola, thereby stamping the so-called pro-life movement with political legitimacy.

On May 26, 1983, a clinic in Norfolk, Virginia, was destroyed by arson. A clinic in Dover, Delaware, was destroyed by arson on January 13, 1984. Also in January, Ronald Reagan became the first president to inject the abortion issue in a State of the Union address. That month he also spoke against abortion to the March for Life leaders and to the National Religious Broadcasters.

The clinic destroyed by the May 1983 attack in Norfolk, Virginia, was rebuilt and then bombed on February 17, 1984. Eleven days later, arson caused $100,000 in damage to a College Park, Maryland, clinic. A clinic in Bellingham, Washington, was hit by a Molotov cocktail on March 4. The Everett, Washington, clinic was torched on March 4 and again on March 26; on April 19, it was set afire a third time.

In April 1984 about fifty picketers marched outside the Pensacola office of Dr. Bo Bagenholm, and John Burt demanded that Bagenholm give him the aborted fetuses for a "Christian burial." When asked if the demonstrations might spark a bombing in Pensacola, Burt replied, "I don't care."

Early that same spring Matt Goldsby and Jimmy Simmons saw the films *Assignment Life* and *Silent Scream* at their church, the First Assembly of God. The films show graphic photos of fetuses aborted at various

January 20, 1984. Judy Riley, vice president of Okaloosa County National Organization for Women, joins demonstration outside U.S. Representative Earl Hutto's office. (Courtesy of the *Pensacola News Journal*.)

August 13, 1984. Karen Burt of Brownsville Assembly of God, daughter of John Burt, leads a group of approximately 300 protesters in a chant to close down the Ladies Center. (Courtesy of the *Pensacola News Journal.* Photo by Gary McCracken.)

stages and a sonogram of an abortion. After this experience, supplemented by reading a newspaper-sized leaflet titled "The American Holocaust," Matt Goldsby and Jimmy Simmons began discussing the issue of abortion and what could be done about it. Matt was particularly impressed by "The American Holocaust," which had full-color pictures of aborted fetuses surrounding a letter from Ronald Reagan to a California pro-life group. Reagan was a hero to Goldsby, who took personally the president's words, ". . . we must strengthen our resolve to end this national tragedy." He was captured by Reagan's condemnation of silence and inaction and by his statement that "something must be done." Jimmy and Matt agreed that picketing seemed a waste of time, changing nothing.

On May 15 a caller, traced only to Pensacola, told the Miami head-

May 11, 1984. Group from area Baptist churches, led by the Rev. David Shofner, picketing the Ladies Center. (Courtesy of the *Pensacola News Journal*. Photo by Gary McCracken.)

quarters of the Pensacola Ladies Center, one of a statewide chain of clinics, that a bomb had been placed in the center. None was found.

### Reassessing the Road to Violence

It is not surprising that the fundamentalist, evangelical,[8] and other conservative Christian groups did not organize seriously or activate themselves strongly in support of the death penalty, for, after all, they had the law on their side in most states. Organization and mobilization come in opposition to the present state, rarely to support it. However, the conservatives individually expressed through frequent letters to the editor their support for the death penalty and their anger at the long delays of executions through legal appeals. Only token support was shown by counterpicketing outside the state prison during executions.

But beginning with open expression of homosexuality, one issue after another had arisen over a ten- to twelve-year period to offend the moral sensibilities of the conservative, fundamentalist, and charismatic Christians of Pensacola. Their widest and strongest mobilization began with opposition to the ERA. That coalition, wrapped around family-based values, carried over to the abortion issue, although the casts of central and leading characters tended to shift from issue to issue. The religious Right experienced a few successes, some of them only temporary: closing bottle clubs, withholding of homosexual rights, eliminating nudity in bars, defeating the ERA, and securing a crackdown on so-called massage parlors and open prostitution.

On the other hand, the conservatives had suffered significant defeats. *Playboy* continued to be sold in the 7-Eleven convenience stores. Several nightclubs still offered nude dancing by means of various subterfuges. Evolution was taught in some of the schools. Liquor sales continued unabated in the county. Homosexual bars, both male and lesbian, and bottle clubs continued to do business.

Meanwhile, the paths of protest, especially regarding abortion, escalated—from letters to the editor, to small appearances before governing bodies, to large and vocal appearances before the same bodies, to peaceful picketing, to picketer harassment of patients at the clinics. Patients entering clinics had their auto tags traced, and calls were placed to their parents or other relatives charging them with getting abortions. Some anti-abortionists followed patients home and shouted at them from the front yard. Doctors practicing abortions received threats against their lives; their homes were picketed; agents of the Bureau of Alcohol, Tobacco and Firearms trained physicians to search their cars for bombs. Bomb threats were called to doctors' offices and clinics, and the office and home telephones of doctors and staff were occasionally tapped by law enforcement agents in unsuccessful attempts to trace threatening callers. At some offices, hydrogen sulfide bombs were placed in the air intake vents, sickening staff members and patients recovering from anesthesia. Patients were harassed and intimidated in the waiting rooms by infiltrators disguised as patients and by the reinstated use of bullhorns by picketers outside.

Each defeat radicalized more of the minority, and the abortion issue became for some the focal point of all their discontent. A few placed their full attention on the issue, as nothing they did, no matter how offensive and daring, seemed to have any effect. The frustration built.

On June 25, 1984, a bomb exploded in the Ladies Center in the early hours of the morning.

# ... 5
# Marching
# as
# to
# War

And this shall be a sign unto you . . .
Luke 2:12

Because he feared . . . the men of the
city . . . he did it by night.
Judges 6:27

The June 25 explosion at the Ladies Center came at 3:23 A.M. Full
damage to the building and contents was ultimately estimated at
$250,000. Clues to the type of bomb used were scarce. Investigators
speculated to the press that a window had been broken open and that
about twelve sticks of dynamite with a lighted fuse were placed on a
chair in the office. Although investigators from the Bureau of Alcohol,
Tobacco and Firearms were called in, they kept a low profile, and little
was said of them in the press.

It was later determined that the bombers used large PVC pipe, the
type normally used for water lines, to make their dynamite. PVC is
easily shaped with a handsaw and is readily available, as are easy-to-
glue-on end caps, from any building supply store.

Several picket leaders were given lie-detector tests; others were interviewed. No suspects were found. Public reaction was mixed. Officers
of NOW condemned the bombers. John Burt, one of the picket leaders,
said, "I'm not grieving about it. I'm glad nobody was hurt, you understand. But I'm glad that the killing has stopped. After all, nobody shed
tears over the closing of Nazi Germany's death camps."

In a letter to the editor of the *Pensacola News-Journal,* one individual

June 25, 1984. The Ladies Center following the June 25, 1984, bombing. (Courtesy of the *Pensacola News Journal*.)

stated: "Thank God for someone who had the know-how to do this at the right time to not kill anyone. And the guts to do it."

David Shofner, Baptist minister and president of the Pro-Life Coalition, the organization sponsoring the picketing, echoed John Burt: "I'm sorry for that [the bombing]. But I am . . . glad one of them [abortion clinics] isn't operating."

Two days later, a minister's car that resembled Dr. William Permenter's auto and was parked in his clinic lot was set afire by an unknown person or persons.

Picketing resumed immediately and expanded to include new abortion sites. John Burt advocated increasing the level of activism to nonviolent sit-ins. On August 10 fifty pickets marched outside Bo Bagenholm's office and again demanded the remains of abortions for "Christian burial."[1]

The pickets, carrying placards depicting aborted fetuses and signs such as "Babies Killed Here," brought videotaping equipment in anticipation of trouble with the police. Asked if the demonstration might initiate another bombing, John Burt replied, "I don't care."

Marching as to War . . . 43

In a press interview Bo Bagenholm said the picketing had increased his practice: "I'm busier now than I ever was in the past." He later told us that his practice increased 30 percent in each of the first two years of picketing. Another sign that the picketing was not completely effective was that it provoked a number of letters to the newspaper from his obstetrical and gynecological patients supporting his practice.

On August 13 the Ladies Center reopened in a new location on Ninth Avenue and shortly thereafter began performing abortions again.

### The Silent Scheme

Prior to the June 25 bombing, Matt Goldsby and Jimmy Simmons decided that they would not march or demonstrate against abortion; they would respond to others' comments about abortion, but they would initiate no discussion themselves. During the early investigation of the June bombing, Matt and Jimmy waited for a knock at the door. But none came. They took their escape from detection as a sign from God, a divine stamp of approval on what they had done, and they began planning the next step. Parking nearby, they surveyed the clinic and doctor's offices for three to four hours at a time through the night over a week-long period to determine when there was the least traffic and when the buildings themselves were empty of people. Like Aaron and Caleb sniffing out the Promised Land, they cased the enemy, whose land they were determined to take. They drove into the parking lots during early morning hours to discover whether there were any detection sensors in them. Apparently, their visits failed to coincide with Bagenholm's stakeouts or failed to arouse his suspicions if they did enter the lot while he was there.

After confirming there was no security surveillance at night at any of the sites, they checked out the buildings themselves for the most vulnerable approach to them. The Ladies Center had a crawl space beneath it, making it the most easily attacked and most vulnerable building. On the other hand, Bo Bagenholm's building appeared to have alarms on the doors and windows; but they spotted a skylight on the roof and concluded that there was no sensor attached to it. "Pinky" Permenter's office was the most problematical. The building was brick construction, and internal security devices were not readily evident. Its roof offered no ready access.

Thus, Jimmy and Matt decided to attack the buildings in reverse order of difficulty and danger of detection. The Ladies Center would be first, followed by Bagenholm's office since the roof appeared to be accessible from a tree, and finally they would hit Permenter's office through a window.[2]

Meanwhile, their time was also taken with other concerns. Jimmy and Kathy were busy planning their September wedding. Matt and Kaye began dating again in August after a two-month break in their three-year romance, and they were planning a wedding of their own for March 1985. In preparation for his marriage Matt bought a house in a small black neighborhood in Cantonment, a nearby town. He also felt himself under siege from the Internal Revenue Service for unpaid taxes over several previous years of temporary work. The IRS threatened to take his house.

Matt also continued to pursue his ambition of becoming Mr. Olympia, the ultimate bodybuilder, by exercising at a local spa for at least an hour and a half each afternoon immediately after work. Bo Bagenholm, another but less dedicated aficionado of bodybuilding, frequented the same spa about three afternoons a week. As Bagenholm entered the exercise room, he would customarily wave or nod to the regulars there. Matt Goldsby returned Bagenholm's greetings with a grim, cold stare. After several such rebuffs, the physician ignored the strange young man, whose name he did not even know until he recognized the picture in the January 2 newspaper.

### The Voice of God

Those belonging to the Assemblies of God believe that God speaks directly to the believer—not necessarily through words, although that may take place through the gift of tongues. However, the gift of tongues involves "generalized" or nonspecific revelations understandable only to someone inspired with the gift of interpretation of the utterance. On the other hand, one may receive more specific directions from God, usually referred to as "a burden laid on my heart." Other specific revelations may come, such as what should constitute one's own life vocation, but both kinds of revelation are usually accepted only when accompanied by a confirmatory experience—for example, someone else might receive the same direction or revelation from God without being cognizant of the prior revelation, or some event might occur that appears to confirm the revelation, such as receiving a job offer. Sharon Glass of Pace Assembly of God provided an example: God revealed to her that she was to become a member of the staff of her church, and six months later her pastor testified that God had told him that she was to be on his staff, validating her earlier revelation.

It appears that the logic of this process was operating between Matt Goldsby and Jimmy Simmons. Both felt God was calling them to end abortion. Since two of them felt this compulsion, they concluded it must have been a specific direction from God.

Assemblies of God followers also believe that God speaks through signs. He gives confirmatory and disconfirmatory "signs" about personal behavior. For example, if one desires a job in a particular place or of a particular type, an offer of such a job constitutes a "sign from God." Later statements and testimony would suggest that for Matt and Jimmy not being arrested for the June 25 bombing constituted such a sign, confirming the righteousness of what they had done. So they decided to expand their efforts.

### The Scheme Continues

After their wedding in September, Jimmy shared with Kathy what he and Matt had done in June and their plans for the future. During the summer the two young men had ordered sixteen T-shirts emblazoned with "Protector of the Code," a phrase they intended as an indication of their concerns with the code of chivalry and knighthood, the "proper" relationships between men and women. In late fall they determined a name for their endeavors, the Gideon Project, since Gideon had laid low the altars of Baal, on which firstborn children were sacrificed. To purchase materials, they established a bank account into which they placed their tithes. In the presence of Kaye Wiggins, according to her later testimony, they were enigmatic about the meaning of the Gideon Project.

They began the execution of their plans. They asked Kathy and Kaye to purchase only two pounds of black powder (sold over the counter) from several different shops in the area; and they bought some black powder in the same places themselves until they had a total of twenty-four pounds. Matt took GE energy timers from a construction project of the company he worked for, Norton Del Gallo. Matt ordered three steel pipes, each twelve inches long and six inches in diameter, and six end caps for them from a building supply company. Norton Del Gallo dealt regularly with the supply outlet, and people there knew Matt by sight. Matt charged the order to the Norton Del Gallo company. He had to return three more times before he got the kind of pipe he wanted, one threaded at both ends; on each trip he conversed with the owner or his son about the order.

During all these preparations, Kathy was urging them onward, suggesting that they would all make a name for themselves with the Gideon Project.

On the Friday before Christmas, Norton Del Gallo had a cookout in the afternoon for its employees. While the other workers were cooking and eating, Matt asked Tony Del Gallo, a relative of the owner, to help him bore holes in the three pipes, each one-half inch in diameter. They then screwed on and welded the end caps. While they were doing this, Tony asked what the pipes were for, and Matt told him that he was making boat buoys for some members of the First Assembly of God congregation.

That same day, while Matt was perfecting the pipes, Kaye was purchasing black powder from a couple of shops while she and a friend were shopping for their upcoming weddings. Each planned to be maid of honor for the other. Kaye later maintained that she did not know the ultimate use of the powder until she delivered it to Matt's driveway at about 6:00 that afternoon. At that time he showed her the June 25 newspaper and told her what he wanted the powder for, she would later testify.

That afternoon, Matt had transported the pipes in the trunk of his car to his home, where he was joined by Jimmy and Kathy. Kaye joined them about 11:30 P.M. Matt met her at the door and told her they were building the bombs in the kitchen.

While Kaye and Kathy went to the other parts of the house and cleaned and vacuumed it, Matt and Jimmy tapped screws with a hole in their middle into the bored holes, attached end caps to the three pipes, and covered the bored holes with Vaseline to prevent their collecting black powder and setting off an explosion when the screws were placed in them. They connected the wiring of the energy-control timers to the detonators (hobbyist's rocket engines) and used a funnel to pour seven pounds of black powder into each bomb so that each had the optimal mixture of 60 percent powder and 40 percent air. Then they placed the bombs, with detonators disconnected, on the floor of the closet in Matt's spare bedroom.

While they were engaged in these tasks, the women remained outside the kitchen, and Kaye concentrated on cleaning the rest of the house. She later stated, "I didn't want to know anything about it," although it was obvious she did know what was happening. About 12:30 or 1:00 A.M., after the bombs had been completed, Kaye went home.

On the afternoon of December 23, after church and lunch together at a restaurant where they saw Jimmy and Kathy, Matt and Kaye went to Olde Sarge's Army-Navy Store, where Matt bought a pair of solid black SWAT pants—the type used by police officers—and a dark green ski mask. While there, Matt asked the price of black T-shirts. The next day he returned and purchased a second pair of pants, stating that a friend had liked the first pair so he had given the pants to him. (Evidently, Matt's high school literature classes had not exposed him to Thoreau's warning, "Beware of all enterprises that require new clothes.")

Matt spent Christmas Eve with Kaye and her mother and stepfather. Leaving about midnight, he returned to his house to meet with Jimmy. They dressed in black shirts and pants and carried dark green ski masks out to the car. Then they placed the bombs in the trunk of Jimmy's car, leaving the detonators outside the bombs. Before leaving on their mission, Matt went inside and called Kaye, telling her to go to Kathy's and read with her the story of Gideon in the Book of Judges.

Matt and Jimmy drove directly to the Ladies Center in the heavy fog, thankful for its protective cover. They parked in a nearby office parking lot, pulled on their ski masks, opened the car trunk, and set all three timers for forty-five minutes, to give them three simultaneous explosions. They thought that three blasts at once would confuse the fire and police departments and reduce their chances of getting caught while maximizing the damage.

Carefully, they inserted the first detonator and carried the heavy bomb to the building, where they removed a section of the latticework covering the crawl space. The combination of low flooring and the weight of the bomb required that both Matt and Jimmy handle the device. They crawled into the darkness beneath the building, gingerly towing the bomb with them. Matt was thankful for his weight-lifting training, which helped him handle the weighty package. The ski masks shielded them from occasional cobwebs as they made their way toward what they believed to be the central support point for the building, where they left the bomb.

Hurriedly returning to the car, they drove to Bagenholm's office and parked a few doors down the street. After connecting the second detonator, they carried that bomb to the rear of the office. Several times Matt tried unsuccessfully to reach the roof via the tree that grew close by. Then they noticed a TV antenna beside the building, and Matt shinnied up it as quickly as he could. Meanwhile, worried about the delay, Jimmy returned to the car and drove it to the office parking lot. He added ten minutes to each timer.

Using a nylon rope, Matt gingerly pulled the bomb and a blowtorch to the roof. He began trying to open the skylight with the blowtorch, but that took longer than expected and the glare of the torch made it more likely a passing motorist would notice him. Giving up on the torch, Matt began hacking at the skylight with a heavy knife he had brought. Finding that technique also too slow, he tried kicking at the already damaged skylight until there was enough of an opening to lower the bomb. Then he heard the explosion at the Ladies Center. Moving quickly, he dropped the rope after the bomb below. Then he and Jimmy gathered their other materials, left Bagenholm's building, and drove quickly to Permenter's office while the last timer ran in the trunk.

At Permenter's office they gave up worrying about detection; time was passing too quickly. So they armed the final device, went to the office window, smashed it, and, hearing no alarms, placed the bomb inside on the floor without lighting the attached fuse.

They drove back to the First Assembly of God and pulled behind the building. Located close to the three sites, they waited to hear the last two bombs detonate. Soon they heard the explosion at Bagenholm's through the fog. Not hearing another explosion, they worried about the bomb at Permenter's. Had it not gone off? They drove out Ninth Avenue past the Ladies Center, seeing only a police car parked across the street with the patrolman sitting, seemingly inattentively, inside it. Once away from the area, they drove quickly to Executive Plaza. Turning into the street, they found no police or fire fighters, but flames leaping into the sky were devouring the building.

The simultaneous blasts, though only two instead of the planned three, had the desired effect in the case of Dr. Permenter's office. Although several nearby residents had called to report the blast, the dispatcher, receiving the calls from sites not too distant from Bagenholm's office, assumed the Permenter building calls were repetitions of the Bagenholm office reports. About twenty minutes elapsed before it was clear that two separate explosions had occurred and the dispatcher summoned fire fighters to Permenter's office. As a result, the building was completely gutted by fire and secondary explosions.

Matt and Jimmy returned to Jimmy's house. Kaye met them in the driveway, and she and Matt hugged briefly while she cried in relief. She returned home, and they all went to get some sleep before the morning news broadcasts.

## ... 6
## The
## Visit
## of the
## Magi

And they said to one another, Who hath
done this thing? And when they inquired
and asked, they said, Gideon the son of
Joash hath done this thing.
Judges 6:29

It was later determined that total damage to the three clinics was more than $706,000 and possibly as much as $900,000. Only the Ladies Center was able to reopen in the same location. Dr. Permenter, who shortly before had considered and rejected total retirement from medical practice to concentrate on other interests, had already planned to phase out abortions and concentrate on his gynecological practice. The bombing moved up this decision for him by only three months.

Dr. Permenter suffered the greatest personal financial loss since he had just recently reduced the insurance on his building contents to $20,000. Lost in the total destruction of his building were several original Norman Rockwell paintings as well as all his medical equipment and patient files. Bo Bagenholm's building was the only one of the three that was fully insured.

Police and fire officials were overwhelmed by the number of sites to investigate and immediately contacted the federal Bureau of Alcohol, Tobacco and Firearms, which had a local office at the federal courthouse. The BATF agents joined Pensacola, Escambia County, and state police and fire officials in the investigations.

Immediately after the fires were extinguished, the sites were secured with bright yellow plastic crime-scene tape to keep the public out. Securing the Permenter site required quarantining the equivalent of a square block since debris was scattered as far as two hundred feet from the former building.

The local BATF agents were also overwhelmed by the amount of investigation required. Bob Hofer, agent in charge of the local office, notified Dan Conroy, the Miami-headquartered chief of the Florida BATF office, for assistance. On Christmas afternoon additional BATF agents began arriving, and by the following day some twenty agents from all over the Southeast had assembled in Pensacola. With other local and state agencies represented, a total of some thirty-five investigators worked on the case under the direction of BATF agent Jerry Robinson of the New Orleans office.

Many Pensacolans knew nothing of the bombings until they read the headlines as they sleepily retrieved their morning papers on December 26. A rare front-page editorial of the *Pensacola Journal* defined the bombings as "terrorism" and asked rhetorically what would be next, "A Catholic Church? A synagogue?" A general consensus assumed that pro-lifers were responsible, while the picketing spokespersons bristled at this and postulated that the perpetrator was a pro-choicer trying to discredit them or a vengeful male whose wife or daughter had undergone a traumatic abortion.

John Burt was quoted in the local paper as follows: "If there is an element of our society that does that [bombing], and no one is hurt, I'm glad the killing (of babies) has stopped." Burt also felt the bombings would help his movement. "I think you will see some larger demonstrations now," he said. David Shofner stated: "Bombings and fire will certainly stop it. Picketing doesn't. You might stop one or two girls every now and then or help them to change their minds [by picketing], but certainly there won't be any babies killed in these clinics for a while."

On Thursday, December 27, the federal officers offered a $10,000 reward for information leading to the arrest and conviction of the bomber. That same day the *Journal* received an anonymous letter claiming credit for the bombings. The author claimed to be a WAVE who had undergone an abortion of a six-month pregnancy and had suffered deep guilt afterward. The signature read, "A Woman Who

December 25, 1984. Bo
Bagenholm, outside his
clinic in the early morning
hours shortly after the
bombing on December 25,
1984. (Courtesy of the
*Pensacola News Journal.*
Photo by Gary McCracken.)

Knew What She Was Doing." Both Permenter and Bagenholm labeled
the letter a publicity ploy.

By Friday, news of the bombing investigation had descended to the
bottom half of the front page. The crime-scene investigation ended
without publicity that day. The newspaper reported a statement by the
president of a local association of obstetricians-gynecologists: "Most
OB-GYN doctors do abortions on existing patients, but they're not in
the business to do abortions." David Shofner told a reporter: "I can't
help but thank the Lord that they are not killing babies. But, my word,
we would never resort to this as a means to stop it."

On Thursday afternoon and Friday agents sifting through the debris
found at each of the sites pieces of twelve-inch pipe, end caps, parts of
toggle switches, pieces of timers and wiring, portions of batteries, and
other fragments of the bombs. Enough parts were located to reassem-
ble almost completely each of the three devices.

On Friday BATF agents began the search for a local source of the
pipe used in the bombs. They first went to Pipe and Equipment, Inc.,
and inquired of Ron Yeakle if the company sold six-inch pipe in lengths

January 5, 1985. Rev. David Shofner of West Pensacola Baptist Church leads
a group of approximately 20 anti-abortion protesters in front of Dr. Bo
Bagenholm's residence. Bagenholm's sprinkler system was operating all
during the protest. (Courtesy of the *Pensacola News Journal.* Photo by Gary
McCracken.)

as short as thirty-six inches and that were nippled, or threaded, at both ends. Yeakle responded that this was unusual, that most users of pipe that size weld caps to them rather than thread them, and that only a couple of places in Pensacola could thread pipe that large. He referred them to Pensacola Tool and Supply Company, among other sources.

At Pensacola Tool and Supply the agents discovered that three identical sections of pipe along with six end caps had been sold on December 14 to Matthew Goldsby for Norton Del Gallo. The owner's son, James Cowley, located for the agents the receipt for the pipe signed by Matthew Goldsby and charged to Norton Del Gallo in the amount of $293.27. The investigators also learned that the threading had been done by Runyan Machine and Boiler Works.

The agents purchased a similar six-by-twelve-inch section of pipe and took it to Runyan, where they had it threaded by David Griffin, who, as he finished the threading, warned the agents not to touch it since it was quite hot. One of the agents, eager to compare the new pipe and the pieces from the clinics, picked it up anyway and burned himself. While the agents were there, Griffin identified the evidential pieces as ones he had threaded.

On Saturday agents George Bradley and Lloyd Erwin placed Matt Goldsby under surveillance. They followed as he picked up Kaye Wiggins, although they did not yet know who she was, and as the two visited Tony Del Gallo's house, went to a formal-wear rental store, and shopped in a mall.

Early that afternoon agent Robert Rowe met with Matt Goldsby's supervisor, Frank Webb, at the Blount Building construction site. There Webb got for him a GE mark-time timer from the storeroom, one of about twenty-five timers the company had for use on the job. Rowe also learned that Goldsby had access to the locked storeroom.

By Sunday, newspaper coverage of the bombings was relegated to the bottom of the first page of section C (the Gulf Coast section) and was simply a recapitulation of previous news. However, shortly after the papers hit the streets and front porches of Pensacola, a BATF agent pulled into the driveway of Matt Goldsby's house in Cantonment. It was about 9:00 A.M., and as agent Gordon P. "Gus" Gary of the Jackson, Mississippi, office opened his car door, a large dog approached him, so he returned to his car. He finally had to call downtown over his car radio to get someone to telephone and awaken Matt Goldsby to control the dog so that he could get out of his car. In the meantime he was joined by a second agent, George Bradley.

Gary identified himself to the sleepy Goldsby, who was dressed only in cutoff jeans, as a Department of the Treasury agent and then asked, "You know why we're here, don't you?" Goldsby responded, "Sure, income tax," and invited them into the house.

Bradley showed his search warrant, and Gary stated they were there to ask some questions about some pipe and advised Goldsby of his rights. Gary asked, "Did you pick up some pipes from Pensacola Tool and Supply?"

"Yes."

"What did you do with them?"

"I put them in my car, took them to the Blount Building, and left them there."

The agents then asked him to go downtown with them for further questioning. Goldsby asked to change clothes first and then, having changed, asked to call his girlfriend. The agent standing in the room with him heard him tell Kaye Wiggins, "BATF agents are here and I'm going with them to take a polygraph. Everything is fine. I may be late for church."

As two of the several agents who had arrived by that time escorted Goldsby to the sheriff's office, the others divided up the searching territory. Bradley went through the three bedrooms, in one of which he found a funnel, a roll of black electrical tape, a cash register receipt from Olde Sarge's Army-Navy Store, and the filter from a vacuum cleaner. He also searched the trunk of Matt's car and discovered a one-half-inch tap for threading the inside of a pipe and an eleven-sixteenth-inch drill bit.

Back in the house, in Goldsby's own bedroom, he found pictures of Kaye Wiggins, six T-shirts with Greek-style lettering reading "Protectors of the Code," and two letters from Wiggins to Goldsby. One, written on shorthand-pad paper and undated, read:

Dearest Matt,
didn't want to go home so Kim and I came & straightened up a bit. I know your [sic] mad cause I moved your dresser out & put the old one in

But look how much better it looks  I love you much. Can't wait til I can stay here all the time  Kim says Hello, and she still loves you  Even though you don't love her! I'll see ya at Church! If ya get cold, your sleeping bag is in the hall closet!

> I love you Babydoll!
> Sweet dreams
> Kaye

The letter implied that Kaye Wiggins had a key to Goldsby's house or some method of entering the house at will.

The other letter, dated November 20, 1984, and typed, was addressed to "Matthew John Goldsby I." It contained a long quotation from Proverbs 16:18–26. One sentence, "There is a way that seemeth right unto a man but the end thereof are [*sic*] the way of death," was underlined in heavy green. Among other things, the letter said:

> . . . God has told you he's going to restore to you seven foul [*sic*] what satan has taken from you. . . . After you read this letter, I want you to go and Pray for the Giedion [*sic*] Project. Pray about the time, the date, and pray for the plans. I feel strongly about this as I know you will. Ill [*sic*] be praying for you also. . . . Well, as you can see, I have to [*sic*] quickly ran [*sic*] out of paper. . . . THIS TIME I HAVE FALLEN IN LOVE WITH THE BOSS. . . .

> WITH ALL MY LOVE,
> s/Kaye
> KAYE M. WIGGINS
> KAYE M. GOLDSBY

Agent Bradley also noticed as he walked through the house that a dark green ski mask lay on the living room coffee table, but it held no significance to him at the time.

The agent who worked with Bradley, Lloyd T. Erwin, found dark camouflage clothing and black pants in Goldsby's bedroom. Agent Frank B. Lee searched the inside of the automobile. Between the seats he found a list headed "The Gideon Project." Items on the list included red paint, three half-inch galvanized plugs, penlight, and switches. In the hall air-conditioning compartment inside the house, he located a paper bag behind the unit with four empty pint-sized black powder cans. In the kitchen he discovered a roll of duct tape, a spool of wire, a rocket engine label, and another label for one eleven-sixteenth-inch drill bit with a one-half-inch shank. Sweeping the floor, he recovered specks of black powder and bits of plastic wire coatings.

Going out to the garage, Lee found a receipt from a hardware store for two drill bits, three half-inch plugs, and other items on the list from the car. In the garbage he came across plastic shavings from electrical wire and a receipt from Lock & Gunsmith for two items totaling $17.33.

The agents did not find the drill used to bore the half-inch hole in the pipes, nor did they locate welding tools used in the construction of the bombs.

After the call from Matt, Kaye got to church well after the service had started. She met Kathy and several other people on the front steps and told them what had happened. One of the people there asked if the black powder cans were still at Matt's,[1] and Kaye answered, "I don't know." Skip Latham went inside the church where Jimmy was working the lighting system and asked Jimmy if the powder cans were still there. When he learned that they were in bags next to the garbage can, he returned and told the women, who decided to go to Matt's to recover the cans and get them out of the house.

By shortly after noon the search at Goldsby's was completed and all the agents had left except Erwin and Bradley, who discovered that another agent had left with their car keys. They called downtown and had someone return with them. As the agents who had brought back the keys left the house in one direction, Erwin and Bradley headed out the other way.

They were barely out of the driveway when a car passed in the opposite direction. Erwin recognized Kaye Wiggins staring straight ahead in the passenger seat; another female was driving. He quickly mentioned it to Bradley, and they both noticed that the car continued past Goldsby's house without slowing or stopping.

Bradley quickly turned his car around to follow. Around a curve they saw the car parked in the driveway of what appeared to be a house with no one at home, and the women were almost to the front door. They continued on to the circle exit, where they caught up with the agents who had brought their car keys and stopped them. Talking it over, they decided the women's behavior was suspicious, and they drove back in opposite directions—one car along the circle, the other to the second exit of the circle on the main road—to stop and question the women.

As the agents neared Welcome Circle again, they saw the women's car exiting, so they followed them until the other agents caught up with them. Then they pulled the car over and approached it.

Agent Bradley reached the car on the driver's side and asked the women if they knew Matt Goldsby. Each twice denied knowing him. Agent Erwin then said to Kaye Wiggins, "I've just been looking at your picture." About the same time, Bradley noticed an electric drill and extension cord atop folded clothing in the back seat of the car and asked the women to step out of the car and walk to the rear of it.

While two agents remained with the women at the rear of the car, the other two began searching it. In the back seat they found the drill and a dark ski mask. When Erwin opened the glove compartment, he found a Radio Shack bag and in it a rocket engine and three toggle switches, along with a series of igniters for rocket engines.

At this point the agents asked the women to go downtown with them and make a statement, which they agreed to do. With one of the agents beside her, Kathy Simmons drove her car to the sheriff's office, while Kaye Wiggins rode with one of the other agents.

Meanwhile, Matt Goldsby was being interrogated by agent Phillip Bruzzichesi. While denying any connection with the bombings, Goldsby admitted to two life ambitions: becoming both a millionaire and Mr. Olympia. They talked about his childhood, during which Goldsby said he had been raised by his mother and that "I was raised as I should be raised, with a rod." They discussed his feelings about abortion, and Goldsby said, "I am against abortion. That is the black and white of it. There is no gray area." Finally, Bruzzichesi, quoting the Douay Version of Job 15:6, said, "Your own lips condemn you," adding, "The day you tell the truth is the day you will be in the national limelight. You want to be a hero, right? You've got a lot of support in this thing. I think you did it out of conviction."

At this point Bruzzichesi brought in three other agents, including Gary and Morris Pelham, and told them, "I think he wants to tell you the truth about it. He's doing this out of conviction; he's not a criminal—he's a religious guy." Knowingly, Goldsby responded, "You're trying to present to me a glamorous aspect. I see you're an expert in psychology." Pausing for a moment as if thinking, he went on, "I did it. It was Matt Goldsby and God. No one else was involved." During the ensuing interrogation Goldsby stated, "I'd hate to see it come to the case when real estate meant more than human life." Turning to agents Pelham and Gary, he apologized for keeping them from their families during the Christmas season, adding, "But your kids are alive, although their Christmas presents may be late."

The discussion turned to the details of the bombings, the purchase of supplies, the construction, the prior planning, and the final placement of the bombs. Goldsby sketched the plan for the bombs and "autographed" it at Bruzzichesi's request. He also discussed scenes from the film *Silent Scream* and how strongly it had impressed him, as did the other movie, *Assignment Life*. Goldsby also mentioned his weight lifting and, proudly, his ability to squat 440 pounds. He also expressed pride in his high grades in high school and the fact that he had graduated.

In self-justification he proclaimed, "The legislative avenues have become deteriorated. There are more laws protecting people who do wrong things than people who do right. There are too many people trying to rip off the government, charging $800 for a hammer. Government is of the people, by the people, for the people. What I did was morally right." He went on to say that he felt he had to follow God's law, not man's, and as long as there were abortions he would feel the same way.

"I realize the seriousness of what I have done," he said at one point, "and, if I was going to get caught, I didn't want to give myself a bad name. I don't want it to be in vain." Bruzzichesi interpreted that as, "If it's worth doing, it's worth doing right." Goldsby then added proudly, "I stopped it, didn't I?" "You sure as hell did," Bruzzichesi responded. Throughout the interrogation Goldsby maintained that he had carried out the entire operation with no assistance.

When Kaye Wiggins and Kathren Simmons reached the sheriff's office with the agents, the Miranda rights were read to Kaye. She admitted seeing Matt Goldsby on Christmas Eve from about 6:00 until "late" that night but maintained she did not see him again until about

6:00 Christmas morning. She claimed to know nothing of the bombings or of Matt's participation in them.

At 8:30 on Monday morning, December 31, Matthew John Goldsby was arraigned before the federal magistrate, who set a hearing for seven days later for "probable cause" for holding him. A few details of his statement were revealed at that appearance to justify his being held without bond as a danger to the community.

About 9:00 A.M. agents Bradley and Lee went to Pensacola Glass Company, where Jimmy Simmons worked, but Simmons was not there. As they were discussing what to do, Simmons arrived. When they identified themselves, he said, "I've been expecting you. Let's go."

At the sheriff's office he admitted only to having seen the pipes in Goldsby's car trunk. He claimed he did not notice how many there were or whether there were end caps on them. When asked about the rocket engines and toggle switches in his car, he said that he was going to make bottle rockets and that the switches were for auxiliary lights for his Jeep, which was at his mother's home in Crestview.

After releasing Jimmy Simmons, the agents questioned his brother, Michael Simmons, a deputy sheriff. He maintained that he knew nothing of Jimmy's possible involvement in the bombings and was clearly surprised at the idea.

On New Year's Day Jimmy Simmons called the BATF office and told them he would be in to see them at 10:00. He appeared at the sheriff's office accompanied by his brother and gave a statement. He confessed to beginning the planning of the bombings in late October with Matt Goldsby; it was then they began to gather materials and to examine the security at the three sites. His statement indicates, among other things, that they chose pipe bombs to cause greater damage than the June bomb had done and that they decided to use timers to make the explosions simultaneous.

On the morning of January 2, at 11:00, James Thomas Simmons was arraigned before U.S. Magistrate Robert Crongeyer and held under the same conditions as Matt Goldsby. Following the hearing, Simmons's mother told reporters, "We're not fanatics."

Also at 11:00, agents James Watterson and William Riehl went to the home of Kaye Wiggins, arrested her, and read her rights to her

January 2, 1985. James Thomas Simmons, following his arrest, is led into the federal courthouse by ATF caseworker Robert Hofer. (Courtesy of the *Pensacola News Journal*. Photo by Jerry Kovach.)

again. On the way to the BATF office she admitted purchasing two pounds of black powder at each of two stores about ten days before Christmas at Goldsby's request. She said that she believed the powder was for a Christmas gift for Jimmy Simmons, who owned a black-powder gun. She told them that she found out what it was really for when she gave the cans to Matt Goldsby. She also admitted being present in Matt's house the night the bombs were constructed but added that she stayed out of the kitchen, where Matt and Jimmy were making them, and cleaned the bedroom.

At the BATF office, when the agents asked her what she knew about the Gideon Project, she began crying. Later in the questioning she said she had wanted to go along to help place the bombs but the men would not let her because it was too dangerous.

At the same time Kaye Wiggins was being arrested and interrogated, other agents were arresting and questioning Kathren Simmons. She told them that on Christmas Eve between 11:00 and midnight she and Jimmy had gone with her parents to view the Christmas lights displayed at St. Ann's Catholic Church and then she and Jimmy had gone home to bed and had stayed home all Christmas Day.

In a second interview that afternoon, Kathy Simmons broke and admitted knowing about the bombings, purchasing some of the powder, knowing what the "Gideon Project" meant, and being present while the bombs were made. She also admitted going to Goldsby's house on December 30 to try to remove the empty powder cans, and she admitted using the tithe bank account she and Jimmy maintained to make the powder purchases for the bombs. She said Jimmy had claimed they got the idea for the bombings "from the Lord, and He told him how to build it."[2] Asked about the "Protectors of the Code," she said, "That was chivalry; [it] was just a joke between the two of them; they carried on like little boys."

The next day Kaye Wiggins and Kathren Simmons were charged with conspiracy and three counts of aiding and abetting in the bombings. They were told to stay in town and were released in the custody of their mothers.

Following his arrest, Goldsby was originally represented by attorney Robert Kimmel, who was reportedly also prepared to represent Kaye Wiggins. However, by the time of the arrest of the women, David Del Gallo, Matt's employer and a fellow member of First Assembly, and others had apparently convinced the four defendants that one attorney should represent them all. The attorney representing the four, Paul Shimek, commented on that Wednesday afternoon (January 2) to reporters about their contention that God told the defendants to carry out the bombings: "If they pray and believe this is where they are being led in God's will, then it is possible to receive some revelation, [but it] could just as well have come from Satan." Thus Shimek set the theme he was to play through the trial and sentencing. Magistrate Robert Crongeyer gave in effect an anticipatory response to this at Simmons's hearing when he said while denying bond, "There is no guarantee God won't call him again."

Morning and evening newspapers gave judgments of the defendants from their co-workers, teachers, and ministers, all of whom were shocked by the arrests. They described each of the four as fine, person-

January 6, 1985. Kathy Simmons with Arthur Shimek, son of her attorney, Paul Shimek, entering the federal courthouse for her arraignment. (Courtesy of the *Pensacola News Journal*.)

able, upright, Christian young people—another theme to be played throughout the trial to sentencing.

Thursday, January 3, was the beginning of a media trip for Kaye Wiggins. In Shimek's office, carefully coiffed and stylishly made-up with eye shadow and lipstick, she faced national and local reporters and, for the first time, openly publicized the bombings as "a gift to Jesus on his birthday." She also expressed her conviction that both men were now sorry for what they had done and would never repeat the crime. She went on to voice her shock at her own arrest and her pride in Matt as her "knight in shining armor."

Shimek also participated in the press conference, denouncing abortion and intimating that abortion was the essential trial issue. The split in the local legal fraternity was publicly revealed when Robert Kimmel criticized Shimek for holding the press conference and thereby endangering the defense.

On the same day as Kaye Wiggins's press conference in Paul Shimek's office, President Ronald Reagan finally spoke out forcefully against abortion clinic bombings, just after a bomb blew up a clinic not far from the White House. He promised to throw the weight of federal law enforcement efforts behind solving these "violent, anarchistic activities" and bringing the perpetrators to justice.

The next day Wiggins flew to Atlanta for an interview on Cable News Network's "Crossfire" program, hosted by Tom Braden. Although she had cleared the trip with the U.S. probation officers, she had failed to get the permission of the magistrate. While most of the program centered on a lackluster debate over abortion between Nannette Falkenberg, executive director of the National Abortion Rights Action League, and Joseph Scheidler, executive director of the Pro-Life Action League, the opening few minutes centered on Kaye Wiggins. Dressed in a high-necked lavender lace dress with a black shawl over her shoulders and relatively heavy makeup, Wiggins struck an image that contrasted sharply with the way she later presented herself in court.

While she claimed all four defendants regretted what they had done, she contended that she was not responsible in any way for the bombings. She also contended that neither she nor Matt knew anyone who had ever had an abortion. On the other hand, she said, "Matt does not have any regrets of the publicity it is bringing to abortions."

Continuing under Tom Braden's questioning, she added, "I don't feel bombing a building is half as bad as killing a child. . . . It has been proven to me that life begins at conception. I don't know what the Supreme Court decision says about it. I just know what I feel about it." She set one theme for the upcoming trial when she blamed the victims by saying, "There wouldn't be a bombing if it were not for abortions." That logic was picked up later in the program by Joe Scheidler when he asked, "Why should anybody be so upset that they [the bombers] would blow up a building? There must be something terrible going on in there [for them to do this]."

For her part, Kathy Simmons resented the media attention centered on Kaye Wiggins, a relative latecomer to the conspiracy but the more photogenic and articulate of the two.

On Saturday, January 5, Matt Goldsby and Jimmy Simmons held a press conference, apparently arranged by Shimek and only for four out-of-town reporters, at the county jail where they were being held. At that conference Goldsby said, "The more we learned about it [abortion], the more it began to deal with us—the anger and frustration."[3]

The previous day a local television channel, WEAR-TV, conducted a call-in poll on the question, "Would your religious beliefs, under certain circumstances, lead you to violate civil law?" The response was 58 percent yes and 42 percent no. Disregarding the ambiguities of the question as it was worded and citing the results, Goldsby held they were evidence of support for what he and the other three defendants had done.

He went on to say, "Both of us are just your average young kids raised in the church. . . . We have a deep respect for God and the true moral ways. We're very patriotic and, you know, we just love to hunt and fish. . . . There's no conspiracy . . . This is Spanky and Alfalfa right here." Asked if they had discussed the plan with others, he responded, "We also knew the majority of religious leaders would not agree with what we did. . . . We saw children being killed and we reacted in the quickest manner."

On Monday, January 7, in the early morning hours, someone broke a window at the First Assembly of God and tried to set fire to the pseudo-Spanish-colonial steel-frame building, which resembles the federal courthouse in downtown Pensacola. Whoever started the fire made a major mistake by trying to set it in a room with no draperies, wooden items, or other easily ignited materials. The fire extinguished itself with only minor damage done; however, an ascription on the window read, "An eye for an eye."

On Thursday, January 10, the Canadian Broadcasting Network conducted an interview, which would be broadcast the following Sunday, with Kaye Wiggins and Kathren Simmons in Paul Shimek's office. Among other things, Kaye Wiggins said, "I don't see how you can say that what we did was so wrong when what they were doing inside the buildings was more wrong [than what we did]. Killing is more illegal than the blowing up of property: it's the taking of human life."

Two hours after the interview, judges Roger Vinson and Winston Arnow, along with Magistrate Robert Crongeyer, issued a gag order on all the principals in the case.

# The Trial

. . . Part . . . Two . . .

# ...7
# Between
# the
# Times

The Lord sent a prophet unto the
children of Israel.
Judges 6:8

The question of who would represent the defendants and how that
should be done became an ongoing issue. Paul Shimek was chosen by
Simmons and his wife as their attorney at the time of their arrest. Both
Goldsby and Wiggins initially chose Robert Kimmel, a thirty-two-year-
old criminal attorney in the Blount Building, where Goldsby's primary
job had been. On the Sunday of Goldsby's arrest, Paul Shimek, known
as a First Amendment and constitutional attorney, and Robert Em-
manuel also went to the county jail to represent him. The confusion
extended to the hearing before the U.S. magistrate on Monday, December 31, at which both Shimek and Kimmel told the magistrate's
secretary that they were representing Goldsby. Kimmel was present at
Wiggins's original interrogation, and she requested that he represent
her when she was arrested on January 2. On the same day, Goldsby
dismissed Kimmel as his attorney and hired Shimek. Following her
news conference on January 3 in Shimek's office, Wiggins followed
suit.

When Paul Shimek was first brought into the case, and later at the
January 7 hearing before Magistrate Crongeyer, he was cautioned by
the magistrate that by representing all four defendants he might pose a

January 7, 1985. James Simmons (right) with Matthew Goldsby (center) being led into federal courthouse for arraignment. (Courtesy of the *Pensacola News Journal.*)

conflict of interest and a danger to their individual rights to full representation. Shimek responded that he was "the only attorney in Pensacola who understands the scriptural and spiritual aspects of this case." The magistrate had all four defendants sign a three-page waiver of their right to independent counsel.

Shimek maintained that there was no conflict of interest and insisted that he would represent all the defendants or none. Shimek also made it clear early on that he would try to make abortion, rather than the bombing, the central issue in the case. He began this tactic at the hearing when he tried unsuccessfully to introduce into evidence the leaflet from Matt Goldsby's Bible, "101 Uses for a Dead (or Live) Baby" by Olga Fairfax, an anti-abortion activist.

Kaye Wiggins was the only defendant to testify at the hearing. Shimek used her testimony to attempt to get charges against her dropped, but during her testimony she testified to her involvement on and after December 21 and some of the involvement of the other three.

January 7, 1985. Anti-abortion demonstrators outside the federal courthouse during the arraignment of the Pensacola Four. Karen Burt (left) is followed by her father, John Burt (center). (Courtesy of the *Pensacola News Journal*.)

The magistrate refused to dismiss the charges against Wiggins and held the two males without bond.

During the pretrial period, especially before the gag order, Shimek became an interpreter of the "spiritual" aspects of the case to the public. For example, on the claim by Goldsby and Simmons that God had told them to do it, Shimek explained, "I doubt there was an audible voice" and defined it as "an overwhelming inner conviction, an inner peace. . . . If they pray and believe this is where they are being led in God's will, then it is possible to receive some revelation, [but it] could just as well have come from Satan."

Some members of Pensacola's legal community were critical of Shimek's defense tactics, particularly his use of press conferences. While the majority of local attorneys were publicly silent and would speak only within small groups of friends and close acquaintances,

Robert Kimmel expressed a not uncommon feeling when, on January 3, he asked, "How is a press conference going to help Matthew at the trial? They're helping the prosecutors prepare their case. My heart goes out to Matthew. I am sincere in my worries for this young man." He later added, "I think it's way too late to help the defendants [due to] the showmanship that Shimek has already pulled off." The *Pensacola News-Journal* voiced the questions more pointedly in a January 13 article that asked, "Is Paul Shimek a hero . . . [or] a publicity-seeking showman setting his clients up for disaster?"

Roughly five feet nine inches tall and looking about forty-five years of age, Paul Shimek had practiced law in Pensacola for fifteen years. He wore a waxed, black handlebar mustache through most of those years; but recently he had sported a neatly trimmed mustache that, noted in conjunction with his hair falling over his forehead, had led some of his detractors to compare his appearance with Hitler's. He began as a civil rights lawyer, frequently handling American Civil Liberties Union types of cases—defending, for example, businesses accused of selling pornography. His support of unpopular causes earned him the reputation of a "left-wing liberal" among the relatively conservative population of the local community. However, sometime in the 1970s, according to his own testimony, he "got religion" and refused to represent pornography cases any longer. His partner Stephen Sutherland stated, in answer to a question addressed to him by one of the authors in 1982, that Shimek quit representing pornography cases because "those folks don't pay their bills." By 1984 Shimek was defending abortion clinic picketers arrested for trespassing.

On January 5, Judges William Stafford and Roger Vinson held a closed-door meeting with Shimek in which they reminded him of "Rule 15" of the Northern District of Florida, which states: "It is the duty of the lawyer or law firm not to release or authorize release of information or opinion which a reasonable person would expect to be disseminated by means of public communication . . . if there is reasonable likelihood that such dissemination will interfere with a fair trial or otherwise prejudice the due administration of justice." Kaye Wiggins's father asserted, "I think somewhere in all of their minds they've got some idea that [as a result of all the publicity] God's going to shake the prison walls and let them all out."

A key person in the decision to hire Paul Shimek for the defense was David Del Gallo, Matt Goldsby's employer and a member of First Assembly of God, who had Jimmy and Kathy Simmons spend the night of Goldsby's arrest at his own house. Del Gallo also housed Goldsby after his conviction and temporary release and reemployed Goldsby, Wiggins, and Simmons before their sentencing. It should be noted that Del Gallo also knew Dr. Bo Bagenholm, having entertained him at his home once or twice to show Bagenholm his exercise room.

On February 27, a motion was filed with the court to add three attorneys to the defense. The press interpreted this to mean that T. Patrick Monaghan of Bardstown, Kentucky, would defend Matt Goldsby; Frank E. Booker, a member of the University of Notre Dame law faculty, would represent Jimmy Simmons; Booker's daughter, Mary Frances Hasson, of South Bend, Indiana, would defend Kathy Simmons; and Paul Shimek would continue as Wiggins's attorney.

But on March 6 Susan Novotny, assistant U.S. attorney, filed a motion with the court "to clarify legal representation of defendants" in which she stated that Booker claimed to her only two days previously that he represented only James Simmons, while the next day Shimek maintained to her that he represented all four of them and the other attorneys were only assisting him. Also, on March 5 she had participated, at Shimek's request, in a conference telephone call with him and Monaghan, during which Monaghan asserted he was representing only Goldsby and Shimek finally agreed that he would represent only Wiggins, after which Monaghan asked Shimek to hang up so he could speak privately with Novotny. However, while the three of them were talking, Charles Rice, also of Notre Dame, filed a motion with the court to represent both the Simmonses and Goldsby. Thus, less than a week before to the scheduled trial, mass confusion seemed to reign among the defense.

When the trial was postponed from March 11 to April 15, Hasson, who was expecting a baby in April, was replaced by Christine Kasun, a former prosecutor from San Francisco. All the new attorneys had previous experience in abortion-related cases or had been active in national or local anti-abortion movements.

In reaffirming the gag order on March 14 in his Supplemental Order to Ensure a Fair Trial, Roger Vinson stated that "regular press conferences and statements tantamount to confessions, but appealing to a higher law than man's law and condemning the abortion clinic 'murderers' in inflammatory language, could only be viewed by the Court with alarm."

The gag order prevented the public from learning much about the dynamics of the decisions to add attorneys to the defense, on why these particular ones were chosen, or whose voices were dominant in the decisions. However, the informal attorney network in Pensacola wondered whether the decisions were out of Shimek's hands—that is, whether the assistance was virtually forced on him by national anti-abortion forces. Perhaps one of the primary determinants lay in the need for outside funding for the defense effort, even though it is reported that some "significant" amount of fund-raising was accomplished within the First Assembly of God.

With Goldsby viewed as the pivotal defendant, his attorney, Monaghan, effectively became the central figure in the defense, followed by Booker, Kasun, and Shimek, in the order of each defendant's reported involvement in the crime, although local attention remained focused on Shimek up until the trial. Moreover, until the actual arrival in Pensacola of the outside legal contingent for the trial, Shimek carried the burden of maintaining public awareness. Under the gag order, one effect of the filing of legal appeals and briefs (which, of course, probably would have been filed with or without a gag order) was keeping up the level of publicity. From January to April there were several appeals of the gag order to both the district and the appeals courts. The primary arguments used in these appeals were that the gag order strangled the defendants' First Amendment (free speech) rights and that it hindered their efforts to raise defense funds. Shimek's continual raising of the issue of the need to appeal for defense funds gave an impression, intended or not, that this was a *pro bono* (without fee) case, one in which the lawyer donates his or her time, which it was not.

Shimek also asked for the dismissal of the grand jury indictments because the panel was not adequately representative of persons eighteen to thirty years of age in the federal district, composed of some ten north Florida counties. A third tactic was his motion to suppress the evidence taken from Kathren Simmons's car in the December 31 search. This, he maintained, was an illegal search and seizure. Then, in late February Shimek moved to add "innocent by reason of insanity" to the original innocent pleas of the defendants.

Between January and late March three motions were filed to release Goldsby and Simmons on their own recognizance. In the final attempt, Booker and Monaghan emphasized the religious issues and the youth of the defendants by affirming that the two detainees would swear on the Bible "in open court that they will keep all of the court's conditions just as if eternal life were subject to be lost for a violation thereof" if they were released. The written motion went on to state, "To the Christian, as these young men are, no more binding device can exist." It compared the defendants with John the Baptist; like him, they were subject to a loss of faith from imprisonment.

Except for the addition of insanity to the defense plea, all motions and appeals were denied. In denying the third request for the release of Goldsby and Simmons, Judge Vinson stated: "They might construe that as a sign. They might feel compelled to carry out a mission they felt called to in the first place."

In April the defense attorneys appealed to the Eleventh Circuit Court of Appeals the portion of the gag order forbidding public appeals for defense funds. In the appeal Shimek stated that he had been "expecting that the tens of thousands of members of the public who share the pro-life view, and despise abortion as the vilest evil in American law since human slavery, would rally with the small contributions they can afford to a defense fund. . . ." This appeal was also denied.

Simultaneous with the legal maneuverings were other events. The Pro-Life Coalition in particular seized upon the arrests and trial as a vehicle for presenting its message. During the arraignments, grand jury sessions, and subsequent hearings, the coalition picketed and held prayer vigils outside the federal courthouse in groups of five to twenty-five. They carried signs with pictures of aborted fetuses and garbage cans with blood-soaked dolls.

John Burt, David Shofner, and Sharon Glass became the focal spokespersons for the Pro-Life Coalition, especially John Burt, who tended to get the most media attention. Burt acknowledged that in his youthful association in the Ku Klux Klan he learned how to get media attention through the use of extreme and terse statements. He also stated, "The more we can bring the abortion issue to the forefront, the

January 16, 1985. Mary Dowdy (left background) and Violet Gratton picket the federal courthouse. (Courtesy of the *Pensacola News Journal*. Photo by Don Grassmann.)

better it will be [for the anti-abortionists]." Thus, the coalition's efforts duplicated and reinforced those of the defense: shifting attention from the bombings to abortion.

Burt was clearly willing to accept the "public" position among the anti-abortion forces. He maintained that he was in a more independent position than others, which freed him to speak more daringly: "I don't have boards to contend with. I have no qualms about breaking the law—picketing, trespassing."[1] While not accepting responsibility for inspiring the bombings, he did assert, "We're in a battle of good and evil. Just like the commander-in-chief of the armed forces can't be held

accountable for every person killed in battle, so I can't be held accountable."

Also keeping the incidents and defendants in the media was Dr.
Bagenholm's unsuccessful February petition to the Escambia County
Commission for permission to carry a concealed weapon because of
the telephone threats against him and his family. The most the commission was willing to do for the physician was to advise him to avoid
routines and be careful where he parked.

Meanwhile, protests continued at the Ladies Center on Saturdays
even though the clinic no longer performed abortions on that day. The
picketers were augmented by Pace Assembly of God's assistant pastor,
Steve Zepp, and his bullhorn. The use of the bullhorn was given legal
status since its purpose was ostensibly to issue directions to the picketers. Its actual use was more frequently to communicate with patients
entering and leaving the center and those inside it. Members of NOW
and clinic personnel complained that Zepp's communications crossed
the bounds of propriety. For example, they report him saying to one
entering patient, "Don't abort your baby! Who will defend us against
the Russians in twenty years?" However, when the police investigated
the reports, they found no improper use of the bullhorn. The interest
in the coming trial among anti-abortion supporters at times swelled
the numbers of picketers at the clinic and offices from a typical ten or
fifteen to as many as a hundred.

In mid-February John Burt announced to the press his intention to
enter Bagenholm's office, reopened at a new location, to confront
patients there. Burt admitted to two purposes: publicity and stopping
some of the abortions. He added that basically he wanted "to cause a
heck of a lot of confusion. I hope that it will turn away some people
when they see all this confusion." His plans were thwarted when the
press asked Bagenholm to react to Burt's announcement, thereby fore-
warning the doctor. Thus, when Burt and two members of Our Father's
House (his shelter for pregnant women and abused wives) entered
Bagenholm's office on Friday, February 14, they were met by sheriff's
deputies just inside the door, and Burt was charged not only with
trespassing but also with carrying a concealed tape recorder, a third-
degree felony in Florida.

The bombing trial was originally scheduled to begin on March 11. In

January 19, 1985. Yvonne Harrell (left), holding her son Jeremy, and Susan Skipworth stand side by side but on different sides of the picketing, outside the Ladies Center. (Courtesy of the *Pensacola News Journal*. Photo by Don Grassmann.)

January 27, 1985. Steve Zepp, assistant pastor of the Pace, Florida, Assembly of God, with his bullhorn outside the Ladies Center. (Courtesy of the *Pensacola News Journal*. Photo by Bruce Graner.)

January 27, 1985. Escambia County National Organization for Women counter-protest, Ladies Center. (Courtesy of the *Pensacola News Journal.*)

the last week of February, someone fired a rifle bullet through a window of Supreme Court Justice Harry A. Blackmun's apartment, which was blamed on an anti-abortionist, and in Pensacola it was announced that there would be a massive pro-life march terminating at the Ladies Center on the Saturday before the trial. When questioned, Sharon Glass, one of the march coordinators, said that the trial and march were not related and the timing was merely coincidental. The march, whose theme was "I Believe in Life," was initiated by Penny Lea,[2] a thirty-eight-year-old gospel-country singer from Minnesota, who had reached greater fame in the anti-abortion movement than she had ever found on the music circuit. She claimed God had begun moving her toward this march on January 7, although she did not announce it until after the trial date was set. She described the intended march: "This will be a solemn assembly of God's people with no talking, only intense prayer as we march. . . . We will surround the death chambers of the city, and as the trumpets sound [reminiscent of Gideon?], the people will shout 'Let my children go!'" She said God wanted seven

February 3, 1985. Protesters outside the Ladies Clinic. (Courtesy of the *Pensacola News Journal*. Photo by Bruce Graner.)

thousand people for the Pensacola march and she had mailed invitations to five thousand churches and individuals across the country.

On the Sunday before the scheduled march, Lea conducted a two-hour service at Pace Assembly of God for two thousand worshipers. In the church vestibule Lea's son sold T-shirts, record albums, and lapel

March 7, 1985. Kaye Wiggins, Kathy Simmons, and Paul Shimek (left to right) enter the federal courthouse. (Courtesy of the *Pensacola News Journal*.)

pins, while onstage Lea was espousing the "new" fundamentalist political activism: "We got our president reelected, didn't we? We're winning our country back." She went on to characterize nonpolitical Christianity as "lies of the devil."

On the Thursday before the trial was to begin, the local NOW chapter announced it would show a film commemorating women's rights following the scheduled weekend anti-abortion march. That same day Judge Vinson granted defense motions to explore an insanity defense on the condition that the defense request a delay of the trial to allow the prosecution time to prepare, which the defense complied with. The trial date was moved to April 15.

On the morning of the Saturday march, NOW called a press conference and announced a program to get stricter local laws on picketing. The march began at noon with a parade permit for eight hundred participants. The media reported that two thousand marchers actually participated. The one-and-one-quarter-mile, relatively silent march was led by Penny Lea, clad in a green surgical scrub suit, and John Burt, Sharon Glass, and half a dozen others, who were dressed in the

March 19, 1985. "I Believe in Life" march participants gather in the parking lot at Pensacola Junior College. (Courtesy of the *Pensacola News Journal.* Photo by Gary McCracken.)

blue scrub suits that Lea sells. They were followed by a group of ministers, fourteen bearers of American and Christian flags, and a white coffin holding a doll. On arrival at the Ladies Center, the marchers found numerous police officers, including a SWAT team. They quietly assembled before the building, eight trumpeters blared, and the crowd shouted "Let my children go!" seven times. Then they knelt and prayed, some in tongues.

Inside the Ladies Center, the staff, Bo Bagenholm, and NOW supporters had awaited the marchers by snacking on tuna and potato salads and sipping strawberry daiquiris or coffee. They wore their own symbols: double heart patches, representing compassion for women seeking abortions. Upstairs, two police officers videotaped the demonstrators as they gathered before the building.

The press interviewed several marchers and observers. One participant, Dr. Richard Ziemba, leader of Pensacola Right to Life, called for clemency for the accused bombers and announced another march for the Saturday before the new trial date. Later, at the rally in a nearby park to which less than 40 percent of the marchers had gone, sixteen speakers addressed the crowd. One of the headliners, Rev. David Dia-

March 19, 1985. Rev. Steve Zepp of the Pace Assembly of
God uses his bullhorn to make sure his message is heard
inside the Ladies Center during the "I Believe in Life"
march. (Courtesy of the *Pensacola News Journal*. Photo by
Bruce Graner.)

mond[3] of Louisiana, said, "I wouldn't mind seeing those heathen doctors' hands cut off and hung up on a string for the world to see."

Thirty minutes later, less than forty of the two thousand marchers
appeared at the West Pensacola Baptist Church, where they dedicated a
granite memorial to the fetuses aborted since 1973 and Lea prayed for
the alleged bombers.

In a live interview on local television at 10:00 that evening, John
Burt began unwrapping a small package on camera. Before he could
finish opening it, the cameras were cut off and the interview was

abruptly terminated. His package contained a five-month-old, saline-aborted fetus (which he later named Baby Charlie) preserved in a jar of formaldehyde. He told reporters he planned to use it as a "counseling tool" and added, "Maybe it will become a common tool with the pro-life people." A subsequent police investigation concluded that Burt had violated no Florida laws by exhibiting the fetus, and in a press conference the following week Burt displayed the fetus to reporters.

On the Saturday following the march, the *Pensacola Journal* published an editorial condemning the demonstrators' "abuses of common courtesy" by picketing doctors' homes and "making pejorative remarks to individuals entering or leaving . . . clinics." However, the editorial also opposed more restrictive picketing laws in the city, while calling for a "reasonable dialogue in this issue."

On Monday, March 19, David Shofner, head of the Pro-Life Coalition, called a press conference in the office of Paul Shimek, who was present along with a silent Kathren Simmons and Kaye Wiggins. Kathren Simmons appeared as she would throughout the pretrial period and trial, wearing neat, everyday clothing that did not draw particular attention to her. Kaye Wiggins, on the other hand, was carefully made-up and her hair was styled, matching her prior media appearances. Describing the accused four as heroes, Shofner announced a legal defense fund for them established by the coalition, and he solicited donations. "We're not endorsing the bombing of buildings. We're endorsing four young people who need a legal fund. . . . They'll go down in history as heroes, not criminals. In my mind they are heroes," he said. He added that $7,700 had been collected to start the fund. He went even further to identify the bombings with the anti-abortion efforts by saying, "[People want to contribute because] folks are waking up about this pro-life movement and they're getting involved."

Two days later, Judge Vinson warned Shimek, Wiggins, and Kathren Simmons that the Monday press conference was a violation of the gag order and that any additional violation would subject them to punishment for criminal contempt. At that press conference it was stated that Shimek would handle the defense fund. Howard Messing, vice chair of the Florida Bar Ethics Committee and speaking from his south Florida office, said this might be a violation of legal ethics: "I'd have someone else administer the fund. . . . A lawyer raising money . . . that might be something the bar might choose to look at." However, Shimek continued to handle the fund, and there never was any indication that the bar investigated his actions.

Late in March the National Association of [State] Attorneys General petitioned the Justice Department to investigate abortion clinic violence and "illegal harassment and intimidation of people who work in or visit abortion clinics." Two days later a group of fifteen anti-abortionists presented to the city council petitions with 2,568 names opposing any changes in picketing restrictions. The council received the petitions with little comment except to note that it had received no proposed changes.

Early in April, Goldsby filed with the court a statement of willingness to plead guilty to the charges against him if the charges against Wiggins were dropped. There was no response from the prosecution.

Throughout this interim period, Goldsby and Simmons were reportedly receiving thirty to fifty letters a day at the county jail in support of the bombings. The newspaper reported receiving numerous letters on the issue, and hardly a day passed without the morning or evening paper carrying one or more letters on abortion, most of them anti-abortion in sentiment and several openly supporting the bombings. The paper reported just prior to the trial that "the eyes of the nation seem trained on Pensacola."

The national focus on the city was emphasized the week before the trial when Jerry Falwell, on a fund-raising tour for his Virginia College, came to Pensacola and said he would seriously consider contributing to the defense fund, although he felt that violence such as this harmed the anti-abortion movement. While opposing the violence of bombing, he also said it may have assisted the anti-abortion movement by focusing attention on the issue.

The scheduled April 13 anti-abortion march was canceled, but the seminar portion was held that morning at the municipal auditorium. The sponsor, Pensacola Right to Life, had one thousand seats set up for the expected attendance, but only 125 people showed up, among them several young children brought by their parents to view the film *Silent Scream*.

The next morning no direct mention was made at First Assembly of God of the coming Monday trial. Matt and Jimmy, of course, were not there but were still in the county jail. Nor was Kaye or Kathy present. But their presences hovered in the atmosphere throughout the hour-and-a-half service.

David Del Gallo and his wife presented their fourth daughter for dedication, the Assemblies of God equivalent of infant baptism.[4] Pastor Lindell Ballenger commented several times about how beautiful were the three identically dressed older girls. Then he held up the infant to the congregation in one outstretched hand, turning in a half-circle for the audience to see her. Smiling broadly, he repeated several times in a reverential, building voice, "Isn't she beautiful?" Turning to the Del Gallos, he said, "You need a son! I wish you would go and have four more just like these." Then, facing the congregation again, he said, "That's the way we'll win the world for Christ, by having more children than the heathen do!"

At the end of the sermon the normal shuffling of feet and papers stilled rapidly as a woman began to speak in a tongue, her soft voice carrying well over the hushed house. She continued for about three minutes. The ensuing silence was broken by a male voice interpreting what the woman had said. The phrases he uttered had a biblical pattern to them, with expressions such as "My children . . . " The prescriptions were very general, dealing with the gentle life-style: "Be not haughty. Love one another."

The altar call followed, and many worshipers began moving to the front of the church to be met by others to pray with and for those who had come. Those at the altar stood or knelt in a semicircle. Others drifted to the exits, chatting softly with one another as the activities at the altar continued.

# ... 8
# The
# Prosecution

Then the men of the city said unto Joash,
Bring out thy son, that he may die:
because he hath cast down the altar of Baal.
Judges 6:30

### The First Day[1]

On Monday morning, April 15, there was an air of excitement outside the federal courthouse in downtown Pensacola. Two remote-
broadcasting television saucers pointed to the southwestern sky. Cameramen wandered the sidewalks, trying to determine the best spot for
filming the attorneys and defendants who would enter the building in
approximately thirty minutes. Others watched the first half-dozen
picketers gathered on the corner who were organizing themselves and
passing around signs in preparation for their final number of about
thirty, who paraded for only an hour.

Yellow police tape blocked off the south stairs of the courthouse, as
well as all other entrances and driveways, front, side, and rear. More
yellow tape, tied to police sawhorse barriers, edged the sidewalk at the
gutter and closed off the normal parking places in front of the building.
City police with walkie-talkies clipped to their shoulders stood singly
and in pairs at the corner and at the north end of the building, as well
as across the street at the edge of the boulevard median.

At the side of the building, beside a basement-level entrance used in

April 15, 1985. Protest in front of the federal courthouse as the trial of the Simmonses, Goldsby, and Wiggins begins. (Courtesy of the *Pensacola News Journal*.)

less publicized trials to bring in defendants and now roped off with yellow tape, someone had scrawled in red against the cream-colored paint, "THE TRUTH SHALL MAKE YOU FREE." Defendants Jimmy Simmons and Matt Goldsby would not read that, for they would enter and leave the building each day via the former mail loading docks at the rear.

Promptly at 8:30 the marshal unlocked the courtroom doors, and we spectators poured through before he could open them completely. Directed to the seats reserved for the press, I moved to a pewlike courtroom bench two rows behind the defense table and examined my surroundings.

The earlier newspaper reports on the small size of the courtroom were not exaggerated. Most of the space was taken by the arena for the combat to come: the judge's bench in the center, flanked on the left by a chair for his law clerk; another chair, lower and slightly in front and to the judge's left, for the court reporter, John Suda; a third chair, to the right, for the clerk of the court; and an "altar rail" stretching almost the entire width of the room. Against the wall on the right was the tiered jury box with two rows of seven fixed swivel chairs. On the far left and immediately against the rail, setting off the judge's territory, was the witness-box, also slightly raised. Between the witness stand and the jury box, directly in front of the judge and court clerk, stood a long, empty table to receive the offerings of evidence yet to be introduced by the prosecution and the defense.

Balancing out the pending field of legal conflict, immediately in front of the spectator area, were two tables, each about six feet wide and three feet deep, the one on the left for the defense and the other for the prosecution. The spectators were allotted four pewlike benches on each side of the center aisle, the front two on each side reserved for the families of the defendants and assistants for the prosecution and the defense. In an open space behind the spectators, a couple rows of wooden chairs had been placed to help accommodate the expected eighty to one hundred press representatives.

The scene was completed by a first for a federal court: the closed-circuit televising of the trial from a fixed camera in the left rear of the room to a nearby courtroom accommodating the overflow observers.

Two hours after our entrance the long-awaited trial appeared to be getting under way as defense and prosecution attorneys threaded in with cardboard boxes and briefcases filled with files. Patrick Monaghan and his assistants were weighed down by two folding easels six feet tall and bundles of two-by-three-foot enlarged magazine covers and commercial advertisements. Monaghan also plopped down on the defense table two large reels of 16-mm film. The easels were propped cruciform against the wall beside the defense table, where they would remain during the first two days of the trial.

Monaghan, the apparent leader of the defense, dressed in a dark blue suit and dark lavender tie, his trademarks throughout the trial, leaned his slim, six-foot frame over the table and began organizing his planned exhibits. He looked about forty years old, his dark hair turning early to salt-and-pepper. He had a jovial air about him, smiling broadly to the other attorneys, the defendants as they entered, and their families. When the two prosecuting attorneys arrived, he went over to their table and spoke sociably to them.

The official trial began with a knock on the door leading to the judge's chambers and the command from the U.S. marshal, W. L. "Mac" McLendon, "All rise! This court is now in session." By the time he had finished the ritual, the black-robed Roger Vinson had entered and was seating himself. Vinson was a relatively new judge, and the press had been speculating about how he would acquit himself in his first major jury trial. Slim and of medium height, Vinson occupied the chair with a natural ease, frequently leaning far back with his almost completely gray hair against the high-backed chair and at other times leaning forward to look out over his glasses.

The formal proceedings got under way with a series of defense motions that were either denied or referred to later evidentiary hearings. The defense table, large enough for two to sit at comfortably, was crowded with four lawyers; directly behind them the four defendants and two assistant attorneys sat in a semicircle.

Both female defendants wore plain white dresses. Kaye Wiggins looked very different to those who had seen her before; her now very subdued makeup gave her an appearance of innocent youth. Her reported loss of twenty pounds since her arrest probably added to the effect, making her appear more demure, with less of a "knowing look"—nothing like the poised, outgoing adult who had appeared on CNN and in local news conferences.

Kathy Simmons appeared somewhat bewildered, looking around occasionally and careful not to meet the eyes of anyone other than family and close friends. Jimmy Simmons, dressed in a soft blue shirt and light gray suit, his thinness making him look taller than his five feet ten or eleven inches, seemed to be in a world of his own, somewhat aloof from the activity around him or, perhaps, withdrawn into himself. Every now and then he seemed to remember to look at Kathy and smile, as he held her hand loosely.

Matt Goldsby was seated next to Kaye. In slightly different shades of blue shirt and gray pants, he slumped low on the bench. His suit and shirt fit his muscular frame rather tightly. While he spent most of the time looking at the floor beyond his feet, he seemed to have antennae sensing everything around him while he feigned indifference.

Susan Novotny, assistant U.S. attorney, and Thomas Dillard, U.S. attorney, sat at the prosecution table with an assistant behind them and several briefcases on the floor around them. Novotny, who had handled most of the preliminary hearings for the government, was strikingly attractive—a tall, corn-silk, sun-bleached blonde with a few brown and gray strands of hair. Her feminine suit and high-heeled shoes contrasted with the more austere style of the female defense attorneys. Her husband, mother, and father would sit two rows behind her throughout most of the trial.

The first day was taken up with jury selection[2] and defense motions for suppression of evidence. It was a disappointment to the media: no shocking revelations, no legal histrionics. Monday's low-key proceedings contrasted sharply with Tuesday's session, which began to set the tone and themes for the following week's events.

### The Second Day

When Kathy Simmons and Kaye Wiggins arrived at the front steps of the courthouse, a line of ten to fifteen press photographers and video camera operators were waiting for them. The women were still dressed plainly and wore little, if any, makeup. They did not acknowledge the photographers, who pursued them as they made their way up the steps.

When court convened on Tuesday morning, Judge Vinson called on the defense for its opening statements. While Shimek would later play upon the religious theme, Goldsby's lawyer, Patrick Monaghan, highlighted knighthood and chivalry, blending them with the religious motif. However, rather than appearing to lecture the jury, he seemed to be chatting with them. While his manner was forceful and emphatic, he maintained a conversational style, as when talking with friends about something one cares about deeply and sincerely.

"Matthew John Goldsby is not a terrorist. James Thomas Simmons is not a terrorist. Kathren Simmons and Kaye Wiggins are not terrorists. They are two young girls who are very much in love with their knights in shining armor," he opened. He then shifted to the insanity defense and the defendants' belief in the Bible by asserting that in carrying out the bombings Goldsby and Simmons were acting out the story of Gideon: "They saw themselves as protectors of human life. They saw themselves as destroying the altars of sacrifice."

During his oration, Monaghan moved to the blackboard at the wall opposite the jury and wrote "4109" on it without explaining the reference in any way. He began to lay the basis for the "cognitive-dissonance" theory of the defense by asserting that the accused suffered from conflicting signals on what was right about abortion.[3] One signal came, he said, from "the symbolic father of our country [Ronald Reagan], who bemoans abortion." An opposing signal came from the Supreme Court, which defines abortion as legitimate. From one side there are "the March of Dimes ads that say be kind to your unborn baby before it is born, and in the Yellow Pages it is fetal tissue to be terminated."

Kathy Simmons's attorney, Christine Kasun—of medium height and decorously clad in a conservatively cut dark suit, white blouse, and wide-heeled dark shoes, as if she were defining a formal style for the courtroom—declined to make an opening statement.

Paul Shimek rose and faced the jurors with an air of confidence and authority. He began by stating he had not planned to make an opening statement and went on to explain that the defendants believe in the "spirit world" and that to understand them one must have "knowledge of that spirit world." His voice picked up in strength and emotion as he asserted in a lecturing style that those who believe in that world "act in certain ways. They do good deeds. They have pure, unadulterated hearts, not divided, . . . like pure gold, unalloyed. They are pure, . . . peacemakers. That is a paradox. . . . They are preaching the gospel in their way." Shimek continued in a preachy cadence: "They obey God's law and not man's law. Take it or leave it. There are absolutes. And so it is that blessed are those who are persecuted for their [sic] namesake. That is how they think. . . . Remember there is a satanic world, too. Satan seeks to divide, destroy, devour, especially those doing God's work."

Frank Booker, the final defense attorney, with his glasses appearing about to slide down his nose and with his thinning reddish-brown hair, made a brief statement to the jury in which he sounded like a law professor addressing a class of would-be lawyers: "The law has been my life. . . . If you will just follow the law, [then] we will do right."

Susan Novotny was less emotional in her opening statement to the jury. Proceeding calmly, deliberately, and logically, with a quietly forceful and serious demeanor, she pointed out that the prosecution would establish that the defendants planned together a premeditated act. She claimed that they bought the materials over a period of months, that they purchased black powder in small amounts to avoid suspicion. She added that the males wore dark clothing during the placement of the bombs to avoid detection, which was also why they chose early Christmas morning as the time to carry out their plan. Kathy Simmons opened a bank account just for the bomb materials, she maintained, and Kaye Wiggins purchased some of the powder. Furthermore, all the defendants, when first confronted, denied any involvement.

Throughout the first day of jury selection the defendants had appeared rather lighthearted, smiling and whispering occasionally to one another. During Novotny's opening presentation, however, they grew noticeably more serious, even gloomy.

Following her initial statements, Novotny began presenting the prosecution's case. She first called Deputy James Sanders, Captain Richard Currow, nurse Debra Jean Armond, and Lieutenant John M. Wise to describe the initial effects of the blasts, the extent of damage, and the potential danger to human life, particularly the lives of the fire fighters called to the scene. The prosecution presentations were straightforward and factual. However, in cross-examination Monaghan brought the jurors' attention back to the topic of religion when he asked Currow, after having him redescribe the dangers of the fire and the large hole in the second floor of Bagenholm's office and the unusual situation of his being able to see the hole under those conditions, "Do you think somebody may have been praying for you that night?" Novotny's objection to the question was sustained.

Debra Jean Armond testified in a soft but firm voice about her fright when the Ladies Center bomb exploded near her. In his cross-examination Monaghan pushed her to admit to the fact that she was not hurt in any way.

Monaghan asked the fire fighter Wise if he considered life more important than property, if he would rather see any building destroyed than one person be hurt. Wise responded affirmatively. Monaghan then asked, "That building [the Ladies Center] is still conducting interstate commerce, isn't it?" Before Wise could respond, Monaghan said, "Thank you for valuing life over property." Again Novotny objected and was sustained.

The issues were becoming clear. For the prosecution to sustain its case as a federal offense, Novotny had to prove interference with interstate commerce,[4] and Monaghan had chosen the issue of life versus property on which to try this part of the case. In other words, he chose to take the prosecution's strength and make it a weakness by weighing the destruction of property against the saving of lives.

Novotny proceeded to call the medical secretary at Bagenholm's office, the owner of the Ladies Center building, the Miami home-office supervisor of the Ladies Center, and a nurse from Permenter's office to testify to the extent of damage at each site and the fact that each office was engaged in interstate commerce through the purchase of supplies and materials from outside Florida.

Once again, the most interesting part of the testimony was the cross-examination. For example, Monaghan asked Linda Jane Ferguson, Bagenholm's medical secretary, "Do you buy curettes?" Then he described the vacuum machine for abortions and asked, "Is that made in Florida?" While the prosecution had elicited testimony about office supplies and medicines purchased out of state, Monaghan was trying to bring into issue the abortion instruments themselves through the guise of "interstate commerce."

After Ferguson pled ignorance, he went on to ask, "Dr. Bagenholm delivers babies, doesn't he? When a pregnant woman comes [to see Dr. Bagenholm], is that baby a patient?" Following her affirmative answer, he asked, "On Fridays, when an individual comes for an abortion, the child is not recognized as a patient?" Ms. Ferguson responded that the patient is the woman.

Kasun followed Monaghan with, "On the days when abortions are not performed, is [sic] the woman and the baby treated as a patient?"[5] Ms. Ferguson reiterated, "We treat her [the woman] as the patient."

Following the direct testimony of Greg Ravenscroft, owner of the Ladies Center site, Monaghan asked him where the trash cans were located around the building. Shimek picked up the cross-examination with questions about the amount of rent Ravenscroft received prior to the bombing, eliciting the admission that the monthly rental was $2,200.[6] When Shimek asked how much he received now, Ravenscroft responded, "$1,800, since all the space is not now usable."

Questioning Ellen Goldenberg, Miami overseer of the Ladies Center and whose Jewish-sounding name he would later use in his summation to draw images of the Holocaust, Monaghan asked, "Do you sell tissue in interstate commerce?"[7]

Goldenberg responded with a terse no.

Monaghan persisted in a derisive tone, "Are the by-products and materials of this *business* disposed of in interstate commerce? Do you dispose of the contents of that jar in interstate commerce?"

"They are medically tested," she answered.

"Is it part of your business to sell any of that product?" he went on.

"No," she quickly said.

Kasun picked up with, "What are the items in those jars?"

"They are the contents of the uterus," Goldenberg answered.

Kasun asked, "Are the contents of the uterus an unborn child?"

Novotny interrupted with an objection that was sustained.

In the course of the direct examination of Linda H. Johnson, William Permenter's office nurse, Novotny asked her how many patients the medical office handled, to which Johnson responded, "Thousands." When asked what kinds of information had been contained in records destroyed by the bombing, Johnson answered, "Allergies, previous treatments, and such."

Novotny began adding the next layer of prosecution evidence by calling BATF agents who had investigated the bombing sites and questioning them about what evidence had been recovered at each of them. All sites had yielded twisted and blackened pieces of heavy pipe; bent and equally blackened, distorted, and weighty end caps; and bits of timer pieces, wiring, battery casings, and toggle switches.

From the half-dozen boxes on the floor near her, Novotny brought out piece after piece of steel pipe and other parts for identification by the agents until the table before the judge was covered and boxes littered the floor under and around the table. The sheer quantity of bomb parts recovered was overwhelming to the observers.

Monaghan continued emphasizing the abortion issue, rather than the bombing, by asking such questions as "Did you look in the trash containers?" and "Have you talked to high school young people about fetal alcohol syndrome?"[8] All three agents replied in the negative.

Then Novotny questioned James Cowley of Pensacola Tool and Supply Company about the sale of the pipe to Matt Goldsby. Cowley testified to the confusion over the order until it was finally sent to Runyan Machine for threading and also attested that it was charged to Norton Del Gallo Development Company. When Novotny showed one of the blackened pipe parts to Cowley for identification, Monaghan objected, but Judge Vinson allowed it. During the dispute Matt Goldsby leaned forward to view the piece of pipe and nodded as if verifying the identification of it.

Monaghan began his cross-examination of Cowley by asking, "If someone came to you to buy some pipe to blow up a railroad car carrying people to a death camp, would you sell it to him?" As Cowley hesitated, Monaghan went on to ask, "You liked Matt Goldsby didn't you? You saw him as an ordinary, nice fellow?" Following Cowley's agreement, he returned with, "What about a car taking young people to be killed? Some people make a distinction between the old and the young. . . . " Novotny's objection was sustained, and the question went unanswered.

Novotny then called Cowley's son to identify Goldsby as the one who purchased the three six-inch-diameter pipes in twelve-inch lengths. Looking around the courtroom, the younger Cowley focused on the defense table where Matt Goldsby was hidden from view by Kaye Wiggins. Goldsby leaned forward to help Cowley get a clear view of him. Monaghan tried again with his "railroad car" question, but it was not allowed as a hypothetical question.

David Griffin of Runyan Machine and Boiler Works was the next witness called by Novotny. He testified first that his threading of pipe was unique and identifiable. He told about the BATF agents bringing a new piece of the same kind of pipe for him to thread and about one of the agents burning himself on the hot pipe. Having established the interstate-commerce nature of the businesses in the three buildings through the testimony of Linda Jane Ferguson, Ellen Goldenberg, and others, and having connected Matt Goldsby to the purchase of the pipes for the bombs, Novotny continued to build the case by calling BATF agent Frank Lee, who testified to the materials he recovered from Matt Goldsby's car, house, and garage: the Gideon Project list of supplies, black powder cans, tape, wire, and other parts. He also described the stop and search of Kathren Simmons's car and the evidence recovered from the glove compartment.

In his cross-examination Monaghan began with inquiries about the rocket engines, asking if they were "finger-sized" or about the size of a firecracker and the "normal thing for kids to have."[9] A question or two by each of the other defense attorneys ended the second day of the trial.

### The Third Day

As Pensacola's weather entered a warming period with temperatures reaching into the eighties, the third day of the trial began. Outside, about ten protesters kneeling on a quilt on the courthouse steps continued their prayer vigil. In the courtroom, the opening testimony came from agent George Bradley in his first appearance before the jury.

Bradley told about the surveillance of Goldsby and Wiggins on December 29 and then about his part in the search of Goldsby's car trunk and house bedrooms the next day. His most startling testimony lay in his reading of Kaye's November letter to Matt, which mentioned praying for "the Gideon Project." When Bradley mentioned seeing the dark green ski mask on the living room coffee table, Kaye Wiggins's mother jumped up and rapidly left the courtroom as if in distress. Bradley concluded by describing the events leading to and terminating in the stop and search of Kathy Simmons's car.

In cross-examining Bradley, Monaghan asked about the "Protectors of the Code" T-shirts in the house and introduced a replica of them, laying it across some of the bomb parts on the evidence table in clear view of the jury.[10] Monaghan's placement of the T-shirt is difficult to interpret. On the one hand, he could have been asserting the chivalrous nature of their act in terms of "life interests," while not refuting that Goldsby and Simmons had placed the bombs. On the other hand, he could have simply been attempting to distract the jury from the evidence on the table. Both views of the tactic have some validity, especially considering Monaghan's demeanor toward witnesses to that point. Concluding, he thanked the agent for his testimony, and Novotny protested that Monaghan was attempting to "curry the favor" of witnesses. Judge Vinson instructed Monaghan to quit thanking witnesses.

Novotny's next witness was agent Gordon Gary, who testified to his initial waking of Goldsby on that Sunday morning and to overhearing Goldsby's telephone conversation with Kaye Wiggins. Monaghan asked him if he had anything to do with income tax. Gary replied, "I file mine annually," which brought laughter from the observers. While Monaghan delved into the details of the telephone conversation, Matt and Kaye sat holding hands, their knees jiggling nervously.

Agent Lloyd Erwin was called next. He affirmed that he had found the ski mask and dark, camouflage-type clothing at Goldsby's house, as well as the switches and rocket engines in Simmons's car. Monaghan asked if he found the mask "ominous" when he first saw it, to which Erwin replied, "No."

Monaghan then referred to the American Rangers taking the high precipice on Omaha Beach on D day and asked, "If you were going to do a brave deed, would you put this on your head [holding up some feminine hair ribbon] or this [lifting a dark green ski mask in the other hand]? If you were being brave and daring like a knight in shining armor, you might wear something like this [ski mask]?" The prosecution's objection prevented a response to the question.

The next testimony came from Patrick Milton of Old Sarge's Army-Navy Store, who testified that Goldsby and Wiggins came to the store and Matt had purchased some SWAT pants and a ski mask. Monaghan showed Milton a pair of garish green-plaid pants and asked if he could buy those at that store. Milton replied, "Not likely." Monaghan then inquired, "If you were going to do a great deed, save a maiden in distress, would you wear black pants or these other ones?" Milton responded, "The black ones." When Monaghan attempted to enter the plaid pants into evidence, Judge Vinson denied him with one of his occasional flashes of judicial humor, saying, "I don't want you to lose them by submitting them into evidence."

Next, Novotny began tying Kaye Wiggins more directly into the alleged conspiracy by calling James Rankin and Frances Martin, employees of two different gun shops. Each testified that Kaye Wiggins had purchased black powder from them. Rankin was asked if Wiggins looked different at the time of the purchase, and he replied, "Her hair was up. She looked like she had more makeup on. She looked older." Martin in particular recognized Wiggins easily because Kaye lived about a quarter mile from her home in Cantonment and had occasionally worked for Martin's mother.

Judge Vinson used the conclusion of Martin's testimony to call for a lunch recess. Since the jury was transported to more distant restaurants, the midday recesses left the trial spectators milling in the lobby for at least thirty minutes after their meal waiting for the trial to resume. During these moments and the regular ten- to fifteen-minute recesses of morning and afternoon, it became clear that the spectators formed two or three distinct groups. One was the family and close friends of the defendants. They congregated together in small clusters, usually of two or three persons, with individuals frequently moving from one cluster to another. A second group was the reporters, who also huddled together but often in slightly larger numbers of three to five and also singly moving from one coterie to another.

A third group was the out-of-town supporters of the defendants.[11] These individuals were largely unknown to the immediate family members since they came from as far away as Kentucky and Virginia, and they too remained largely together, their isolation reinforced by having to view the trial in the overflow room. It appeared that they either made friends quickly with one another or that they had already established networks among themselves before they arrived.

Most interesting was the relationships among these groups, especially between the family/supporters and the press. The immediate families and friends seemed to welcome contacts with reporters, especially the local ones who had interviewed them before or had reported about them. There was an openness, a lack of all pretense, even a strong friendliness and warmth as family members and supporters chatted willingly with the press. For example, the mother of one defendant thanked a reporter for her articles. As the mother moved on to another group, the reporter turned to me with amazement at the naïveté of the woman, for the reporter's direct quotations of her had held the mother up to much informal community ridicule. The majority of the family members and friends appeared to assume that everyone would naturally agree with them in their views on abortion, in their understanding of religiosity, and in their support of the defendants.

On the other hand, the outside supporters appeared to be more experienced with the press and more sophisticated in dealing with them. They were more careful to find out with whom they were talking and were more guarded, deliberate, and intentional with their responses to questions. Some were clearly experienced in giving a dramatic, succinct, quotable sentence or phrase, indicating a desire to use the press to the maximum.

For their part, members of the press tended to hold themselves aloof from both of the other groups, except for occasional informal and brief interviews. Among themselves, especially those from outside the local area, many were sarcastic about the defendants, their families and friends, and the defense attorneys. They seemed to find such overt fundamentalist religiosity a foreign world that they could not understand or appreciate, nor wished to understand or appreciate. Even though they and the fundamentalists spoke the same language, the two groups had great difficulty communicating with one another.

The first afternoon witness was Escambia County Sheriff's Deputy Phillip Bruzzichesi, who testified to Matt Goldsby's original interrogation in which Matt denied any knowledge of the bombings. When Monaghan began his cross-examination, Matt Goldsby's leg began jiggling rapidly, while Kaye Wiggins, who had one leg crossed over the other, was waving her foot almost as quickly. Monaghan elicited from Bruzzichesi Matt's greatest ambitions, to be Mr. Olympia and a millionaire, and Matt's eventual admission that he had done the bombing, that he alone with God had done it.

BATF agent Gus Gary then testified to Goldsby's confession of the purchase of materials, the construction of the bombs, and the placement of them on Christmas morning. In the cross-examination Monaghan tried to implicate the government in bombings and terrorism by asking Gary if he was acquainted with the Nicaraguan manuals,[12] of which Gary denied any knowledge. Turning to Goldsby's statement, "It was Matt Goldsby and God," Monaghan asked, "Did you file a report on God? Is God an unindicted coconspirator?" "No, sir," answered Gary.

Shimek then picked up the examination of Gary by asking abrasively, "Do you believe a nation can be cursed . . . with the curse of abortion?" Thomas Dillard's rapid and irritated objection was sustained.

The prosecution then moved to the evidence against Jimmy Simmons when Novotny called agent Bradley to the stand. Bradley told of the first interrogation of Simmons, in which he too denied any complicity in the bombings or knowledge of them. According to Bradley, Simmons said the toggle switches in his car were for his Jeep.

Agent Frank Lee followed Bradley to the stand and related Simmons's confession made on New Year's Day. Lee testified that Simmons had said he and Goldsby had begun the planning in late October and soon began gathering the materials and scouting the sites. Simmons had admitted that they chose these devices because they would do the greatest damage and could be set to go off at the same time. He had detailed the construction and drawn a diagram of the electrical circuitry. Lee concluded by asserting that Simmons showed no regret for the bombings.

Monaghan began cross-examination by picking up on the remorse theme and asking Lee, "He knew it was legally wrong but morally right?" Lee acknowledged that was correct.

Monaghan then moved to the bomb construction, eliciting from Lee the admission that there were no false wires on the bombs and that the toggle switches were on them as safety devices. Monaghan shifted to the "Protectors of the Code" T-shirts. Lee said Simmons had stated that they were not connected with the bombings but were intended to honor women. "He and Matt felt like they were the only ones left," Lee commented on the meaning of the shirts to Goldsby and Simmons.

About the planning of the bombings, Lee read from Simmons's confession: "About three years ago we began feeling a conviction about abortions. I don't want to sound like a religious fanatic. Everything just fell together, like supernatural knowledge came to us and built it." On that note, the third day of the trial ended.

**The Fourth Day**

Thursday morning opened without the jury present as Thomas Dillard sought to limit the testimony of an anticipated defense witness, William Brennan. Dillard maintained that Brennan, as a sociologist, was not competent to testify to the sanity of the defendants or to their having a "severe mental disease or defect." He maintained that the defense wanted Brennan's testimony as a subterfuge for raising the issue of abortion.

Monaghan argued before the judge that Brennan was an expert on the theory of cognitive dissonance and would testify to the conflicting messages society has sent the defendants. Judge Vinson reserved judgment on the issue until later.

The discussion shifted to the prosecution's plan to introduce into evidence a model of the bombs. Christine Kasun protested the introduction of the model because it was not the "real thing," the prosecution had not revealed how it planned to use the model in the trial, such use would prove nothing new, and she feared that the model would prejudice and unduly frighten the jurors. She also argued that the model would be cumulative; that is, it would help establish a point already proved by other evidence.

Novotny retorted that while there were two diagrams drawn by Goldsby and Simmons, those drawings did not help show the mechanics and destructive potential of the bombs. The model, she argued, was relevant for showing the steps necessary to make the bombs and their destructive potential. The defense, she said, had compared the bombs to a firecracker and a child's toy. The model would rebut that contention. She then outlined how the materials in the model were identical to direct evidence from Goldsby's home or to material producing fragments at the clinic and office sites. She went on to enumerate the different types of pieces introduced into evidence and the matching parts of the model.

Kasun asked, "How does the government plan to use it?"

"Your honor, we plan no in-court demonstration, if that is what the question is," retorted Novotny. "We will use it to indicate the function of the bomb and the mechanism of explosion."

After additional discussion, Judge Vinson allowed admission of the model. He carefully instructed the jury that the model was for illustrative purposes only, that it was not a working bomb or evidence actually collected from the clinic sites, and that the rocket engine was guaranteed not to go off.

Robert Rowe, a BATF agent from the New Orleans office, began the morning's testimony before the jury by recounting his trip to the construction site just a block from the courthouse where Matt Goldsby worked for Norton Del Gallo. There he obtained timers identical to those used with the bombs.

Rowe was followed by Lloyd Erwin, a forensic chemist on the investigation team, who described his reconstruction of each of the three bombs. Novotny then introduced a model of the bombs that Rowe had built from identical but mostly new materials. He had, however, used some of the leftover materials found at Goldsby's house, such as the duct tape. Compared with the smaller bits and pieces of the originals, the model, placed prominently on the corner of the evidence table nearest the jury, was ominous in its size, in the mechanics of its wiring and switches, and in its completeness, including the disarmed rocket engine hanging on the outside. As the agent described the details of it, Matt Goldsby leaned forward to examine it carefully, as if checking for its accuracy.

As Novotny strained at the weight of the model when placing it heavily on the corner of the evidence table, Judge Vinson asked if there was any black powder in it. Novotny reassured him that there was not.

Frank B. Lee took the witness stand next and described the interrogation of Kaye Wiggins. She had, he said, maintained that she had not seen Matt Goldsby between late Christmas Eve and 6:00 Christmas morning.

Agent James Watterson then picked up with the arrest of Wiggins on January 2. He told of the conversation they had in the car on the way to the formal interrogation and after she had been informed of her rights. She had admitted buying black powder from two separate stores before Christmas at Matt's request, he informed the court. Only after that, she had said, she learned that the powder was for bombs. She had also stated that while the bombs were being constructed she stayed outside the kitchen and cleaned the bedroom.

Shimek took charge of the cross-examination and asked Watterson how Wiggins had been dressed when he reached her house, to which Watterson replied, "I don't recall."

"Was there a dog there?" asked Shimek.

"I don't recall," responded Watterson.

Shimek persisted, "Did you ask if she had anything that belonged to Matt Goldsby?"

"I don't recall."

"Did you allow her a phone call?" asked Shimek.

"I don't recall."

"When did you ask her about the gunpowder?" asked Shimek.

Watterson answered, "Someone asked her a question and she responded. I'm not sure when."

Under redirect examination by Novotny, Watterson stated that he was certain that he had taken no items from Wiggins's home but he was not sure whether others had or not. He asserted again that he did not remember a dog being there. The questioning revealed that he had called for a female officer to come and be with Wiggins while she got dressed, but he did not remember who the officer was.

When court reconvened, the next witness, agent William Riehl, said he had asked Wiggins during the interrogation, "What do you know about the Gideon Project?" At that she "got emotional and started crying." Sitting next to Matt Goldsby at the defense table, Wiggins again had tears rising in her eyes. Riehl's testimony reiterated Watterson's; however, he added that Wiggins said she had wanted to go along to place the bombs but the "boys" wouldn't let her because it was too dangerous. She also told him that God had wanted them to do it, but that maybe he didn't because they got caught.

Under questioning by Shimek, Riehl said there were two other officers present all the time he was at Wiggins's house and that she had been dressed in a nightgown. Asked by Shimek if they had searched her house or clothing, Riehl responded negatively.

"Who asked if she had anything belonging to Matt Goldsby?" asked Shimek.

"I recall her saying only the ring on her finger," said Riehl.

Shimek pressed, "In the vehicle, on the way downtown, did anyone ask her any questions?"

"Agent Watterson conducted the interview," answered Riehl.

Kathren Simmons's first interrogation was detailed by George Bradley. He related that she had said she and her parents had gone to see the Christmas light display at St. Ann's Catholic Church on Christmas Eve and had returned home about midnight and gone to bed. She had added that she had not gone out at all Christmas Day.

Christine Kasun, Kathy Simmons's attorney, began the cross-examination, asking, "How many times did she say she was scared?"

"Several."

"Inhumane!" charged Kasun, implying that the questioners had taken advantage of a weak, frightened woman.

The redirect by Novotny revealed that when Simmons was asked her own feelings about abortion, she had responded, "It's not my place to judge. I wouldn't do it myself."

Agent Robert Bilbo then bore witness to Kathy Simmons's second interrogation on January 2. This time she had admitted having prior knowledge of the bombings and purchasing some of the materials, including black powder, with money from a bank account established for that purpose from their tithes. Jimmy had, she had said, taken her to show her each of the sites before the bombings. With that the prosecution rested its case.

Each defense attorney rose in turn and argued for the judge to issue a directed verdict of acquittal on all charges against his or her client. Shimek presented the strongest and longest argument, contending that all the government had proved against Kaye Wiggins was "a desire or a prayer" for the bombings. But, he argued, such are not crimes. Judge Vinson delayed ruling on Wiggins until the other lawyers had made their motions for their defendants.

Roger Vinson, in denying all motions for acquittal, admitted that "the evidence against Mrs. Simmons and Miss Wiggins is largely circumstantial." He added that the evidence against Wiggins in particular was possibly totally circumstantial but it was still sufficient for the jury to consider.

Following Vinson's half-smiling denial of his halfhearted acquittal request for Matthew Goldsby, Monaghan turned back to the defense table and shrugged. "No guts, no glory," he said.

# The
# Defense

This is nothing else save the sword of Gideon
the son of Joash, a son of Israel: for unto his
hand hath God delivered Midian.
Judges 7:14

The defense began its presentation by calling John Murdoch, an engineer, who described the bomb construction as "a very simple device . . . a device that I would expect a high school kid or someone with knowledge of handyman stuff to be able to construct."

Thomas Dillard, the district U.S. attorney, assumed the cross-examination. He carefully led Murdoch through a step-by-step explanation of how the bomb was built. With the final part in place, Dillard pointed out that the witness had not warned him to be sure the threads were clear of black powder or the whole thing could explode in his face when the final screw was placed.

The judge then recessed the trial for the day.

### The Fifth Day

The handful of demonstrators outside the courthouse continued kneeling and praying during the first hour of the fifth day of the trial. Some of them stretched their hands and arms skyward as their lips moved with indiscernible sounds.

Friday's court session began without the jury present as the opposing attorneys debated the range of questions that would be allowed of the defense character witnesses. Judge Vinson determined that questions about the defendants' "truth and veracity" would not be allowed but that questions relating to their "general reputation as a Christian" would be permitted.

The issue of William Brennan's testimony was raised anew, with Vinson expressing doubts of its appropriateness. Patrick Monaghan again tried to justify Brennan as an expert witness on cognitive dissonance. During the arguments Monaghan asserted that he planned to use material by Dr. Seuss, the movies *Dune* and *Beast Master*, and magazines such as *Time* and *Newsweek* as exemplars of society's conflicting signals about abortion.[1] Again, Judge Vinson reserved judgment on the issue until later and called for the jury to enter the court so that testimony could resume.

The defense called its first character witness, David Del Gallo, owner of the Norton Del Gallo company and employer of Matthew Goldsby. Questioned by Frank Booker, who looked professorial in his rather formally cut clothing, Del Gallo testified that he had known Matt Goldsby for ten to twelve years from church and from Matt's working for him at his house since Matt was about twelve. "He's the closest thing I've got to a son," Del Gallo asserted.

Dillard assumed the cross-examination for the prosecution by asking if there had been any change in Matt's behavior during November and December. He nodded in satisfaction as Del Gallo's negative response bolstered the prosecution's contention that Matt Goldsby was sane when he committed the bombings.

Booker then called Jimmy Simmons's brother, Michael, to the stand. Michael affirmed that Jimmy was a law-abiding person, "except he drives like a stumpman in the backwoods," and that Jimmy attended church every time the doors opened. He also pointed out that their father, a Pensacola police officer, died in May 1982. He further testified that he saw his brother in the parking lot at the county jail on December 30 in the presence of David Del Gallo and that Jimmy had then admitted committing the bombings. He said, "David Del Gallo suggested that Jimmy talk with an attorney. I went to get him some clothes, and Jimmy spent the night at David Del Gallo's," where several persons gathered that evening to discuss the situation. Those there included Jimmy and Kathy Simmons, David Del Gallo, Michael Simmons and his wife, George Raney (an assistant pastor of First Assembly of God), and Jimmy's brother-in-law.

Alfred Kirk, who attended the church Kaye Wiggins used to attend before she went to First Assembly, testified that she was "a nice, sweet, young girl." He said that her father and mother had divorced and her brother had drowned at a family outing when she was younger.

Under Dillard's questioning, Kirk admitted that he had not seen her "for about four years . . . when we started attending Pace Assembly," except for a twenty-minute conversation in the mall two months before.

Christine Kasun called Grace Madison, Kathren Simmons's senior English teacher, who asserted, "If I had a hundred students like Kathren, my job would be a lot easier. . . . She made A's and B's."

Kasun asked, "Did Kathy's values include chastity?"

"Yes."

"Obedience to her husband?"

"Yes."

Dillard continued with his efforts to undercut the insanity defense by asking, "Did Mrs. Simmons ever exhibit poor judgment?"

"No," said Madison.

"Was she ever an unstable person?" probed Dillard.

"Sometimes she had emotional problems. But she was never rebellious or angry. She was very mature for a high school student. . . . She showed obedience to her husband, parents, school officials, did what they expected her to do," Madison responded. Her testimony clearly suggested that Kathy's submission was consistent with Madison's own image of maturity.

On her redirect, Kasun emphasized Kathy's view of the role of loyalty and responsibility to her husband and the "biblical" role of a wife: "Obey your husband. The husband is head of the house."[2]

Booker next called David Mayo, a twenty-two-year-old paraplegic who lifted weights with Matt at least once a week. He pointed out that Matt had been the man of his mother's house as long as David had known him. Again, Dillard searched for changes in Goldsby's behavior during November and December, but Mayo affirmed Matt's maturity.

Monaghan's assistant, Christine Short, had spent much of the trial sitting on the first bench behind the defense table. Shorter than Kasun by six inches but dressed in a similarly severe style, she made her first official appearance before the jury when she examined Chester Richards, the husband of Jimmy Simmons's great-aunt and commander of the Royal Rangers (the Assemblies of God substitute for the Boy Scouts)[3] at First Assembly. He described Jimmy's participation in the Rangers as a youth. "Jimmy abided by the rules," he said. "He was not pushy, not a leader, but he would participate."

Under further questioning, Richards told of Jimmy's mother beginning to "court" about a year after her husband died. Jimmy was upset over this and "moved in with his sister," he said. Monaghan had Richards describe the conditions under which Jimmy lived at his sister's. Richards said that Jimmy had lived there for four or five months "in a camp trailer, no lights, no facilities, no water."

Dillard extracted from Richards the admission that he had had no close contact with Jimmy for two or three years. Dillard moved to the camp trailer situation, and Richards acknowledged that Jimmy had used the "facilities" at his sister's house.

Paul Shimek called John Pollock to testify to Kaye Wiggins's character. Pollock was the coach of the softball team at the company where Wiggins worked. When asked Wiggins's response when she was hit by hard grounders on the ball field, Pollock said, "She cried."

Shimek also called Glenda Switalski, who had gone shopping with Wiggins on December 21. They had been classmates in school, and Switalski testified that Wiggins "was always the good person in school. If she didn't want to do anything, she would say no."

Other witnesses were called, including Sunday School teachers, Jimmy's mother, fellow church members from years back, and the former pastor of First Assembly of God. Most of these, except Jimmy's mother, had been in no close contact with the defendants for four to nine years. In each instance Dillard or Novotny elicited affirmation of the stability of the defendants.

At about 4:30 there was a short break after the testimony of the last character witness. Jurors and audience moved about to ease stiffness and fatigue after sitting still for most of eight hours. But all grew still when Paul Shimek rose and said dramatically, "The defense calls Kaye Wiggins."

Kaye sat in the witness chair with her hands folded in her lap and her feet solidly planted, erect and leaning slightly forward toward the jury. Shimek handed her a piece of paper and asked her to identify it. She said it was a letter to her from Matt, written while he was in jail. At Shimek's request she read it:

Dear Kaye,
I'm sorry to put you through so much. I'll be able to do more for the cause from here. I told you I'm willing to give my life for the unborn.

I love you,
Matt

Then she testified to a second letter, which, she maintained, had been taken from her by the BATF agents when she was arrested and in which Matt had written that he was sorry to put her through this and that he "never thought it would go so far." Under Shimek's further questioning, she declared that the first time she knew anything about what was going on was when she delivered the black powder to Matt on December 21.

Paul Shimek then handed her the typed letter to Matt dated November 20 and asked her reasons for writing it. "He was in trouble, in need; he had problems with the IRS . . . severe financial difficulty," she said, with tears in her eyes.

Shimek then keyed in on the sentence referring to the Gideon Project and asked what it meant to her when she wrote it.

"I had heard the term between Matt and Jimmy," she said. "I thought it was a raft trip."

"Why were you concerned about the raft trip?" Shimek asked.

"In '83 [on a raft trip] Matt had been bitten by a spider," she responded.

Shimek continued, "'The time, the date, the plans'—what did that mean?"

"I resented their going. I felt left out, I guess," she said.

Speaking of her sympathies over Matt's financial problems, she commented, "He had bills. He was always being cheated, always had pressures on him. He never got to be a kid."

Returning to the day she delivered the powder to Matt, Shimek inquired of her reaction when Matt told her what it was for. "I was in it [by purchasing the powder]. I was scared. I didn't want to be any more involved. I didn't want to know," she said emotionally.

Moving to the Sunday she and Kathy had driven past Goldsby's house, he asked her why they had gone there. "I knew the black powder cans were still in the house. The last time I was there I saw them. I wanted to get them out," she stated.

Throughout this portion of her testimony Matt did not look at her but stared fixedly at the floor.

Then Shimek asked about movies she had seen with Matt: *Dune, Beast Master, Assignment Life*. He asked if she had read Dr. Seuss while baby-sitting and what magazines she read. Shimek's general literature questions were made more specific under Monaghan's questioning about specific titles and issues. Then he showed her the Reagan letter in "The American Holocaust" leaflet and quoted the sentence "Something must be done." Entering the original letter from the president into evidence, Monaghan balanced it delicately atop the model bomb before the jury. Asked about Matt's attitude toward the letter, Kaye Wiggins answered, "President Reagan is Matt's idol."

With the completion of the direct examination, since it was past 6:30 in the evening, Judge Vinson recessed for the day.

### The Sixth Day

Because the jurors were sequestered in a local hotel and wanted to complete the trial expeditiously, Judge Vinson continued the trial on Saturday. When the court reconvened, Kaye Wiggins was back on the stand for the prosecution's cross-examination. While Dillard had conducted almost all the previous cross-examinations, the trim, self-assured Susan Novotny rose to face Kaye Wiggins.

In a strong but matter-of-fact voice, sometimes in a quizzical or puzzled tone, she probed at Wiggins's relationship with Matt, drawing from her the fact that they had gone together for four years and had been engaged since August.

"You did a lot of things together?" Novotny asked.

"Yes," Wiggins responded tersely.

Novotny elicited from her that she had been with Kathy Simmons only two or three times before the arrests. "Jimmy and I were pretty close. It was me and Matt and Jimmy before Jimmy's marriage," stated Wiggins.

Novotny, appearing both bewildered and sympathetic, probed at inconsistencies between Wiggins's testimony and statements made at her several press conferences. In her testimony Wiggins had said she thought the gunpowder was for Matt to give to Jimmy for Christmas, while at several press conferences she had said it was for a gun of Matt's. Her response was that she did not recall saying that the powder was for Matt's gift to Jimmy.

Moving back to the afternoon Kaye gave Matt the powder, Novotny said, "He's showing you the newspaper [of the June bombing]. Why didn't you say, 'Give me those [cans] back'?"

"It wasn't my money. It was money Matt had given me from a check," she said.

Novotny pushed more accusingly. "You knew Matt's severe financial difficulties. . . . You had purchased close to thirty dollars of black powder. Did you ask, 'Why are we spending money on this?'"

"It wasn't Matt's money. . . . The check was from George Raney," Wiggins said.[4]

Susan Novotny paused, as if debating with herself about the direction she should take. Then, attacking again, Novotny asked, "Did you say to Matt in the car, 'Why do you treat me like this?'"

"He never meant to get me involved," Wiggins countered. "I was scared, shocked, hurt."

"After he showed you the newspaper, you didn't say, 'I want no part of this'?"

"No. He's my fiancé."

Novotny pressed, "You knew there were going to be additional bombings?"

"Yes, I did."

Turning to December 21, Novotny asked what happened when she arrived at Goldsby's. Wiggins responded, "Matt met me at the door and told me they were building bombs in the kitchen. I decided to stay out of the kitchen and cleaned house."

"Did you understand the bombs were completed when you left?"
"Yes."

Shifting to the clothing purchases at Old Sarge's, Novotny questioned, "Did you ask him [Goldsby] why he was buying a ski mask?"

"They were going to wear them the night that they went. I knew they would wear the mask and black pants and T-shirt."

"Did you make any objection?"

"I couldn't. I'm just his fiancée. I can't live his life for him, can't tell him what to do. I never tried to stop any of my friends."

Novotny moved to the raft trip by asking when it was to take place. "Before the wedding [Jimmy's and Kathy's]. Possibly in September or October," Wiggins answered.

"But in November you wrote about the Gideon Project?"

"Yes."

"Why pray for 'the time, date, locations and plans'?" Novotny asked.

"There were problems on the last trip. Where to put it into the water, bites . . ."

Novotny proceeded, " 'I feel strongly about this and I know you will too.' Why did you say that?"

"I had decided if he wanted to go, he could go."

" 'The ends thereof are death.' Does it relate at all to a rafting trip?"

"How I felt about the raft trip, working out, and everything," Wiggins explained.

"Is it coincidence that on the twentieth he's ordering pipe?"

"I guess so. Yes."

During this interchange, Kaye Wiggins appeared to be getting more and more nervous. Her foot was bouncing on the floor, her right knee rising and falling rapidly. She seemed to catch herself and began breathing deeply and slowly as if to steady herself.

Following a fifteen-minute recess, Shimek began the redirect examination; he had Wiggins recount her interpretation of the Gideon story, during which she identified the "false god" in the story as "Ball." Shimek corrected her pronunciation.[5]

Abruptly, he asked, "Are you still a virgin?"

"Yes," she responded firmly.

With the completion of Wiggins's testimony, the jury was excused and the defense shifted to the insanity defense by calling Dr. William Brennan, the sociologist from St. Louis University. Monaghan tried to establish Brennan's expertise to testify on the sanity of the defendants. Judge Vinson decided to postpone a decision on accepting Brennan's testimony until after the evidence of Nancy Mullan, the defense psychiatrist.

Mullan, a Freudian psychiatrist from Burbank, California, took the witness stand, bringing with her a copy of the third edition of the *Diagnostic and Statistical Manual of Mental Disorders*. Following the preliminaries establishing her credentials, she testified that Jimmy Simmons suffered "a borderline personality disorder." Asked for details, she thumbed through the manual and began reading the cluster of potential symptoms. She referred to Simmons's reaction to the film *Assignment Life* when, viewing a second-trimester saline abortion, he said, "It was like a piece of me being torn out." Mullan stated, "The death of his father was the beginning of the unraveling of James's life."

Regarding Matt Goldsby, she asserted that he had a "major affective disorder." She turned again to the manual and enumerated the symptoms of that disorder. Matt, she held, had an abortion mania, was hyperactive, had an inflated self-esteem and a sense of grandiosity, as manifested in his feeling he had a special relationship with political figures and God. "Jesus," she said, "is his imaginary friend."[6]

Asked by Monaghan about Kathy Simmons, Mullan asserted that she, like her husband, had a borderline personality disorder, although her symptoms differed. Kathy, she said, suffered from "emptiness, boredom, anger, temper, and unstable interpersonal relationships."

In the middle of describing Kathy she shifted to the relationship between Matt and Jimmy. "Before Kathy came along," she said, "Matt and Jimmy were a couple. A manic person [Matt] is fun to be around. He is most cheerful, outgoing, affable. But he must be in control." Referring to Matt's not having a father, she asserted, "He turned himself into everybody's father, into his mother's father at about eight years old. The Reagan letter would definitely have inspired him."[7] She went on to state that *Assignment Life* "was a catalyst for Jimmy Simmons," who first brought up the idea of the bombings. During this discussion of himself, Matt stared at the floor about six feet in front of him and occasionally smiled to himself.

Returning to Kathy Simmons, Mullan declared that she was "rigidly, primitively defensive, and neurotic, brittle like a dry stick." Asked directly by Monaghan if Kathy was psychotic, Mullan maintained that she was "on the border between neurotic and psychotic." Kathy, her head low, eyes searching her lap, but with no place to hide, was clearly distressed at this public airing about her personality and personal life.

Mullan proceeded to describe the Simmonses' marriage: "Kathy thought it was going to be a new beginning, that marriage would make her life. . . . She found a profound disappointment with her marriage; it didn't fit her dreams at all."

During the questioning, Mullan would occasionally coach Monaghan and on at least one occasion suggested to Judge Vinson what he really wanted to ask her. This tendency arose especially as Monaghan led her through *Time, Newsweek,* and *Life* magazine covers depicting fetuses, laying the groundwork to introduce cognitive dissonance.[8] "These are nice kids," she said, with a "focal area [abortion] of psychosis."

Kaye Wiggins, she said, exhibited a "neurotic depression" and the warning signs of a suicidal adolescent. When asked to cite the warning signals of suicide, she responded that suicidal individuals "don't want to go to a psychiatrist." Wiggins, she said, suffered from "dysthymic disorder," characterized by relatively frequent depressed moods.

Because Mullan maintained that *Assignment Life* was the precipitating factor in James Simmons's actions, Monaghan argued for the showing of the film and Mullan's analysis of its effects on James. After heated objections and arguments from Dillard, Vinson allowed the film to be shown but called for a brief recess to allow for rearranging the courtroom for the screening.

After the recess, spectators scrambled for seats with good views of the projection screen. The thirty-minute movie is an obviously staged "documentary"; that is, it purports to follow an objective female newspaper reporter dispassionately researching an article on abortion, but it quickly shifts to showing the "horrors" of abortion, including a woman moaning during an abortion procedure and pictures of dead fetuses at various stages of development, emphasizing photos of late-term abortions.

Mullan's analysis of the film's effects on Jimmy Simmons essentially repeated what she had said earlier. However, she summarized effectively by saying, "*Assignment Life* was the precipitating factor in James's psychosis. It depicts the bloody murder that abortion is."

When Dillard rose to question Mullan, he began by recounting the following sequence of events in Jimmy Simmons's life: seeing the film in June 1983, the abatement of his persistent thoughts on abortion after six to eight weeks, the loss of his job in September, his enlistment in the Marine Corps in the fall of that year, and then his failure to complete basic training before being discharged and sent home just after Christmas. Under Dillard's questioning, Mullan got increasingly nervous, seldom completing a sentence and frequently ending or breaking a statement with the interjection "OK?" Once she asked, after a long, rambling response, "Did I miss the question?" Another time she coached Judge Vinson on what the jury had or had not heard. When Dillard's questions went beyond her broad terms, such as "dysthymic disorder," and sought greater specificity of symptoms, she thumbed rapidly through the manual searching for the symptoms that defined the disorder. It appeared that spectators were witnessing the public collapse of a personality in a matter of minutes.

Dillard moved from James Simmons to Goldsby. "His mother was Jewish and converted. You say Matt has a confusion of himself with Jesus Christ. He says, 'I am Jewish,' but he has an identification with Jesus Christ?" he asked incredulously.

"That's the beauty of the American Psychiatric Association criteria," she answered. "They are based on observation, history, or . . . ." At that point she lost her way and trailed off.

Dillard probed for details about Kaye Wiggins's "death wish," which Mullan illustrated by saying that on a very hot summer day Kaye might sit at a traffic light, while all her friends were at the beach, wishing "that her life might come to an end."

"Sounds like me yesterday," countered Dillard.

When Dillard had retired, Shimek arose for redirect examination centering on Kaye Wiggins. He had Mullan recount the tragic events of Wiggins's life: the drowning of her brother in 1976, her father having an affair with his secretary and then divorcing her mother to marry the other woman. According to Mullan, Kaye summed it with, "I lost my mother, my father, my brother." She offered as further evidence of Kaye's disturbance the fact that Kaye had been out of high school almost a year and still held no steady job.

Kasun keyed in on Kathy Simmons's reaction to the psychiatric examination, her hating it "because it depicts her as abnormal." Mullan affirmed that and said that Kathy was the most rigidly defensive of the four. She said that Kathy "needs anchors, security, needs things in black and white."

While the redirect was not completed, the hour was late and Vinson recessed the trial until Monday.

## The Seventh Day

On Monday morning the area outside the courthouse was reserved by local anti-abortionists for demonstrators from area Southern Baptist churches. David Shofner had contacted about twenty pastors over the weekend and asked them to get their congregations to the courthouse. He also announced this to his own congregation on Sunday morning, urging their attendance. He stated that he had requested that non-Baptists not demonstrate that day and that the other denominational representatives had agreed. When I[9] heard him make that announcement at his church on Sunday, I immediately thought, "He's letting them know that John Burt won't be there." Not everyone needed to carry a picket sign or walk in the picket line, he added. It would be acceptable just to stand in the median across from the courthouse in silent protest and to witness or to pray, however the individual might feel led.

As I approached the building early Monday morning, there were four or five ministers carrying signs and seven or eight standing on the corner in a huddle with reporters. I did not see a single layperson among them.

John Burt arrived, despite his supposed pledge not to, and began circulating a statement from the West Virginia–headquartered Defenders of the Defenders of Life.[10] Addressed to Roger Vinson and Susan Novotny, comparing them to Herod and accusing them of having "your devilfather, Hitler," the letter demanded that the courts cease persecuting those opposed to abortion while defending and protecting "murderers." It went on to state that "the defenders of life deserve commendation and medals, not condemnation and prison sentences."

Meanwhile, the trial reconvened inside the courthouse. Kasun resumed the questioning of Mullan, probing for more details about Kathy Simmons's problems, particularly in her adjustment to marriage and sexual intercourse, which resulted in her being nauseated throughout her honeymoon. Mullan seized on Kathy's statement that "I don't have a house to myself; I live in other people's houses" as symbolic of her lack of identity.

Kasun went through Kathy's symptoms enumerated earlier by Mullan and had the psychiatrist illustrate each. Then she asked Mullan about Kathy's religious experience, and Mullan maintained it was an example of "splitting," separating the past from the present, repressing the past.[11] Since she had "met the Lord," Mullan said, Kathy felt that "now life is full of happiness, joy, good memories." Mullan interpreted this as an "obvious misperception of reality."

Mullan reinforced the cognitive-dissonance theory of the defense by asserting that all the defendants received two different signals about the same thing. "Abortion is the issue with the crack in it," she concluded.

Dillard interrupted with an objection to the witness's passing a note to the defense attorney. Mullan, like a child in elementary school, said, "Mr. Monaghan, if you hadn't pulled that out, no one never would have known," a remark that made the spectators laugh and Monaghan blush. Judge Vinson instructed Mullan to refrain from coaching the defense and making extraneous comments.

Thomas Dillard began the recross. "Is it unusual for an eighteen-year-old to get married, to try to find out who she is, to have an identity crisis at that age? Normal people don't?"

"Everybody has some basis . . ." Mullan trailed off. "What she doesn't know is how she feels all the time or what she thinks."

"When she told you about not having a house of her own, was she referring to after her arrest?"[12]

"Yes."

Asked about Kathy's chronic boredom, Mullan said her religious experience was a big break in her life. But her religiosity was excessive, displaying signs of anxiety. Illustrating, Mullan said, "When I am anxious I say 'OK' a lot."

"Is that a personality disorder?" Dillard asked pointedly. His obvious reference to Mullan's excessive use of "OK" amused the spectators.

Dillard shifted to Mullan's own psychiatric experience and elicited from her that she had testified for Monaghan in a case just last December and that she was personally opposed to abortion. He also extracted from her the admission that she had not talked with any of the defendants' family members until after she received a copy of the reports of the prosecution psychiatrists, who had interviewed the families routinely. Defensively, she said, "If I can establish the criterion [sic] from the patient himself, there is no need to talk with family and friends."

"Is abortion the only thing that would create cognitive dissonance?" Dillard probed.

"Yes."

"Isn't it healthy to have a level of cognitive dissonance? Won't a low level of cognitive dissonance create boredom?"

"No."[13]

Later Dillard focused on the term "borderline personality disorder," trying to determine whether this fits the legal definition of "a severe mental defect." Mullan hedged, not admitting that it was "a severe defect" but maintaining that it was more than neurotic.

When Dillard asked her if Jimmy Simmons suffered from an affective disorder, Mullan responded hesitantly, "It's tough doing four defendants," and she had to check her notes before she could correct him with "a borderline personality disorder."

As Dillard probed and questioned the specifics of Mullan's diagnoses, she grew more restive, reflecting her nervousness in comments such as, "I can't focus. What was your question?" "What were you asking me about?" "Do you know when I mentioned that?" "The question is not registering." She was particularly flustered when, during her discussion of Goldsby's fantasies, Dillard asked, "Might that not be your fantasy instead of his?"

Later Dillard asked, "Are there characteristics all personality disorders share?" In response, Mullan picked up her manual and started looking through it. Interrupting her search, Dillard directed her attention to page 12 of her manual and the statement that the book should not be used to determine legal responsibility or insanity, but that the mental-status examination (which, apparently, Mullan had not administered) should be used to do so.

The redirect examination tried to recoup and reaffirmed her diagnosis that all four suffered from a severe mental disease or defect.

Mullan was excused, as was the jury, and arguments began over the admissibility of Brennan's testimony. While Monaghan argued for the necessity of this evidence and Dillard contended it was a subterfuge for bringing abortion into the case, Kaye Wiggins was trying to get Goldsby's attention by patting his hand. When he did not respond, she started scratching his hand with her nail, then escalated to pinching it and finally pulled strongly on his thumb. Goldsby just stared at the table before him. She gave up and returned to pumping her foot rapidly. As the arguments shot back and forth, Kathy Simmons's mother passed snapshots of her daughter's wedding to the other family members on the same bench. Finally, the judge concluded that he would give the defense latitude and admit Brennan's testimony.

With Brennan sworn, Monaghan introduced the pamphlet "The American Holocaust," directed Brennan's attention to the Reagan letter in it, and elicited from him that the pamphlet concerned "16,000 aborted bodies in metal containers outside Los Angeles in 1982." Monaghan went on to introduce the song "I've Never Been to Me" and the book *Horton Hears a Who*, by Dr. Seuss, which contains the statement "A person is a person no matter how small."

Asked to define cognitive dissonance, Brennan testified that it means getting conflicting signals, ideas, and values from society; that is, receiving one message that something is good and another that it is bad. Monaghan then covered the conflicting signals received by Goldsby from the movies *Dune* and *Beast Master* and from a *Life* magazine article on treating the fetus as a patient. Brennan went on to point out the impact of television, which barrages the public with diverse attitudes and moves society to seek instant solutions to problems.

During cross-examination Dillard asked Brennan, "How many people experience this phenomenon?" The witness responded, "Most of us to some degree at some time." Dillard drew from him other areas of dissonance today, such as attitudes about cigarette smoking. He then asked Brennan if the defendants had read other books, listened to other songs, and seen other movies dealing with other issues, to which Brennan responded that he did not know.

Then Dillard struck at Brennan's credibility with, "Are you the author of a book titled *Abortion: The Final Holocaust*?"

"Yes."

"You mentioned you are lecturing at Vanderbilt. Is that to be on 'Holocaust Parallels' [to promote your book]?"

"Yes."

"This crowd looks like a good vehicle for that, doesn't it?"

"Not really."

Following Brennan's dismissal, Shimek called James Darnell, a minister and teacher at Liberty Bible College, an independent charismatic congregation in Pensacola, to testify on what the Bible teaches about the beginnings of human life. Darnell began a litany of verses that implied to him that the origin of human life is conception. After he had cited two or three verses, Dillard objected that the witness was virtually going through the entire Bible.

Monaghan argued that "the works of Shakespeare, the Bible, and poetry belong to all attorneys. In the final arguments I'm going to read the Bible cover to cover."

"That doesn't surprise me at all," retorted Dillard.

Shimek's last question to the minister was, "Do you think God would tell someone to blow up an abortion clinic?" Dillard jumped up to object and was sustained by the judge. Turning toward his chair, Shimek growled, "The government doesn't want to hear the answer."

Dillard rose again and said testily, "Your Honor, at least three times Mr. Shimek has made side comments after an objection and it's been sustained." He went on to request the court to remind Shimek of proper courtroom behavior.

Vinson addressed Shimek as if instructing a law student in a moot court: "You are an experienced attorney and these comments are inappropriate." Paul Shimek apologized deferentially to the court.

In his cross-examination Dillard asked Darnell, "Is God real to you?"

"Yes."

"Does God talk to you?"

"Yes."

"Are there certain signs from God in everyday life?"

"Occasionally."

"You wouldn't characterize that as a mental disorder, would you?"

"No."

On redirect Shimek asked Darnell to tell him what kind of signs he had experienced.

Darnell mentioned that when he was in college he had "a strong urging in the spirit to be a preacher" and that he had wanted to major in an art [religion?] and minor in a science, but the college had never allowed that until one week before he sought approval for it. He said, "That was a sign that God was working on my behalf." Shimek then asked, "Do you think God would tell someone to blow up an abortion clinic?" Dillard objected strenuously and was sustained. When Shimek muttered on his way back to his chair, Dillard again protested this unprofessional behavior. Shimek quickly apologized to the court.

Next Shimek tried to call Dr. Reed Bell, a local anti-abortion physician, to testify to the medical evidence for the beginning of life. As Dillard objected to this witness, Kasun, trying to get abortion back into the testimony, interjected, "What was going into interstate commerce?" Testily, Dillard argued, "They stand here with a straight face and tell us abortion is not the issue. I don't see how they can do it." Judge Vinson determined that Bell's testimony would be irrelevant to the issues at hand.

The defense rested its case and the jury was dismissed. The defense attorneys then moved for dismissal of all charges against their respective defendants. The motions were denied.

Even though it was nearly 5:30, Judge Vinson ordered that the testimony continue, and the prosecution began calling its rebuttal witnesses on the sanity issue. Dr. Daniel Dansak, a psychiatrist at the University of South Alabama Medical School in Mobile, was sworn in first.

Under Dillard's questioning, Dansak explained the result of his examination of James and Kathy Simmons. He spoke first of Kathy's family history: a mother who was the primary, strict disciplinarian; a father who was passive to avoid conflict. He testified that Kathy's purchase of the powder had not affected her sleep patterns, appetite, or marital relations. He stated that her mental-status examination showed that she was normal, fully oriented, and that her emotional responses were appropriate at all times. He detailed the various tests he administered and described Kathy's performance. He concluded that her judgment was "intact" and that she suffered from no severe mental defect, "not then or at any time."

Dansak testified that Jimmy Simmons considered himself to be like his mother; both of them enjoy the outdoors and caring for injured animals. Jimmy had said that his father's death was sad "but [was] God's will." There was no evidence that Jimmy was functionally unable to work after he lost his job in 1983 for reasons beyond his control. Also, his Marine Corps discharge was a disappointment but had left no profound effect on him. Regarding the abortion issue, Dansak said that the effects of viewing *Assignment Life* had not been long lasting and did not impair Jimmy's functioning. He added that Jimmy had no confusion of his identity with a fetus. In sum, he stated that James Simmons had no severe mental disease or defect.

Dillard then went through the major points of Mullan's testimony about Jimmy and Kathy. Dansak denied Mullan's conclusions, including the presence of a borderline personality disorder in either defendant. In any case, he stated, a borderline personality disorder is not a severe disturbance. Asked about cognitive dissonance, he dismissed it as something everyone experiences. He went on to say that this phenomenon has nothing to do with conflicting signals from society but that it refers to the dissonance between a person's behavior and that individual's beliefs about how he or she should behave.

At 6:40 P.M. Judge Vinson recessed for the day.


**The Eighth Day**

When court convened at 8:30 the following morning, Frank Booker began the cross-examination of Dr. Dansak by reviewing with him his credentials, during which it was pointed out that Dansak was "board certified," in contrast to Nancy Mullan. Booker failed to shake Dansak's calm and assurance about his conclusions regarding James Simmons.

Kasun turned to his report on Kathren Simmons. Reviewing Kathy's relations with her parents, Kasun asked, "Did this have any significance with Kathy at all?" "I am amazed," said Dansak, "she is so mature, given the facts of her childhood," at which Kathy smiled broadly. As to her participation in the bombings, he asserted she had said she did it for her husband's sake, not for the sake of abortion. Other questions from Kasun elicited only reaffirmations of Dansak's previous testimony.

Paul Shimek then asked Dansak how much he was being paid for his testimony. Dansak reported, "A hundred dollars an hour, three hundred fifty dollars a day for testimony, a maximum of two thousand dollars."

Shimek asked the circumstances of the family interviews, revealing that Dansak and the other psychiatrist, Dr. Manuel Cepeda, had interviewed them all at one time in one room.

"How many times have you testified in court?" Shimek asked.

"About four hundred, but I was paid only ten times," Dansak replied.

Dillard's opening on redirect was terse. "You owe me four dollars for lunch," he said to Dansak. Shimek jumped up to object: "He's currying favor. That's despicable!" Judge Vinson, smiling slightly, said, "It's not despicable, but don't do it again."

"Are you being paid for a particular diagnosis?" Dillard continued.

"No. I am being reimbursed only for what I lose from my usual practice."

"Is it standard to write a report, submit it, and then interview the family?" Dillard asked, pointing indirectly at Mullan's failure to interview family members until after she had read the prosecution's psychiatric evaluations.

"No."

As Dansak left the stand, Kathy Simmons's mother smiled and nodded to Kathy.

Dillard then called Manuel Cepeda, also on the faculty at the University of South Alabama Medical School. Cepeda had examined Kaye Wiggins and Matthew Goldsby. He also interviewed members of their families for two and a half hours and said those interviews confirmed his diagnoses.

In his examination of Kaye, Cepeda said, the defendant stated she did not have strong feelings about abortion for others, but for her it was unacceptable. She had also stated that she was upset at the plans for the bombings, that they made her anxious and disturbed her. Her brother, she had said, had been the lead singer in their family gospel-singing group. After he drowned, she tried to take over his role, but it didn't work. Her father's affair, divorce, and remarriage had happened two years before, and she had been angry at him about it.

Cepeda reported on the mental-status examination, which showed no evidence of psychosis, thought disorders, delusional thinking, or dysthymic disorder. He added that Kaye was depressed at the time of the interview, but that was a normal response to the situation she was in and it should "abate when the stressor is removed." Otherwise, her judgment was normal. On probing from Dillard, Cepeda discussed dysthymic disorders and stressed that even in mild cases both the individual and those about him or her would recognize it, especially the family members.

Dillard then asked about the basis of his evaluation of Matthew Goldsby. Cepeda pointed to his six and one-half hours spent with Goldsby, his review of Matt's statements to law enforcement agents, and his interviews with Matt's family.

Cepeda then recounted Matt's family history. The father was an alcoholic who physically abused Matt's mother and sister. When Matt was three, his parents divorced. The father apparently had no redeeming qualities, according to Cepeda. His mother had difficulty holding jobs because, the psychiatrist said, "she talks when she shouldn't." He mentioned that she was once the housekeeper for two priests, and on one occasion, when someone came to see a priest who was out, she witnessed to her own religious beliefs and lost her job. She followed the same pattern with other jobs. Matt's older sister, Terry, was a motorcyclist and construction worker who had left the church after high school. His brother, six years older than Matt, was an atheist and avid chess player.

On the subject of abortion, Matt had told the psychiatrist he knew no one who had had an abortion, but that in church it was always equal to murder. He was offended by it, but it wasn't a major thing for him until he and Jimmy began talking about it and decided they should do something about it. They rejected picketing because they "would be only nameless faces in the crowd."

Cepeda maintained he found no evidence of grandiosity or of Matt's confusing himself with God or Jesus Christ, and the mental-status examination revealed no abnormalities. He found that Matt had an IQ of 120, which placed him in the top 10 percent. According to Cepeda, Matt showed no evidence of severe mental disease or defect then or at any point in the past.

Dillard then reviewed with him Mullan's diagnosis, and Cepeda asserted there were no data to confirm it. He concluded that Mullan "made a conclusion to support her diagnosis without a data base to fit it." If the diagnosis had been accurate, Cepeda said, the change in Matt's attitudes and behavior would have been noted by others.

Monaghan began his cross-examination by asking, "From your interviews, you conclude Matt Goldsby is not a religious zealot or fanatic?"

"I agree; he is not a religious fanatic."

Monaghan asked the doctor if Matt Goldsby was antisocial. Cepeda responded, "No."

"Matt Goldsby stated that he would never do this again but also stated that God's law is above man's law. Do you believe that God's law is above man's law?" asked Monaghan.

"No, sir, I do not," responded Cepeda, indicating that they must be used together.

"Then Jesus is not an imaginary friend of Matt Goldsby?"

"No."

"Not a delusional belief . . . a figment of imagination to Matt Goldsby?"

"No."

"Can he see him?"

"No."

"Is Jesus just a religious idea to Matt Goldsby?"

"No."

"But Jesus talks to the heart?"

"Yes."

Monaghan moved to how God speaks by asking, "Do you believe God speaks to the individual through the heart?"

"People report that to me all the time."

Monaghan pressed, "Do you believe that is true?"

"I have no theological background to answer the question."

"Could it be true?" Monaghan persisted.

"I am here as a physician. We have to agree on terms. I deal with observable data. When we get to nonobservable data, I can't put a microphone beside a heart. When someone says 'God speaks to me through my heart,' as a physician, I believe that they believe."

"Is it possible God did speak?"

"I believe that they believe it."

"Do you believe God can?"

"Not based on my psychiatric expertise."

"Personally, do you believe?"

"Yes, I do believe God speaks to the heart if someone is willing and capable of receiving him."

At this Judge Vinson interrupted Monaghan to move the testimony along and said, "I believe that he has answered that as well as he can."[14]

Shifting back to the interviews and confessions, Monaghan asked if Matthew Goldsby had expected to get caught.

"He said," paraphrased Cepeda, "that he wouldn't have gotten caught if he had stuck with plastic and hadn't changed to iron."

Turning to Goldsby's lack of remorse, Monaghan asked, "He didn't feel sorry for what he had done?"

"He had heard that one woman had changed her mind as a result of the bombings, and that gave him a sense of accomplishment."

"Then it was a one-time achievement?" asked Monaghan.

"The problem," mused Cepeda, "is that once one gets a sense of accomplishment, one tends to go back to what was successful."

"But," pointed out Monaghan, "he said he would never do it again."

"Yes, but that's what you usually hear," countered the psychiatrist. "I believe he believed it at the time he said it."

Shimek then picked up on the religious theme with the question "Are you spirit-filled?"

"No, I'm a Baptist."[15]

"What is a charismatic?" Shimek asked.

"I used Matthew Goldsby's definition, taking the Bible literally. I do not use the word 'charismatic.'"[16]

Shimek probed Cepeda's personal beliefs on demons, Satan, communication and miscommunication with God. Cepeda parried these questions by stating that his personal beliefs were irrelevant to his evaluation of Goldsby.

Asked how much he was being paid, Cepeda said, "One hundred dollars an hour, seven hundred dollars a day."

"Did you ask Kaye Wiggins her theory of the case?" questioned Shimek.

"I threw my hands up and said, 'What are they going to use for a defense? I can't find anything wrong.' She grinned and said she didn't think anything was wrong," responded Cepeda in his final comment. As he left the stand, he and Wiggins smiled at one another.

To rebut the prosecution's psychiatrists, Shimek called Tanya Simmons, Jimmy's sister-in-law, to testify about how much time Cepeda and Dansak spent speaking with individual family members in the group interview. "Very little," she said. Then Dillard asked her if the families met with Dr. Mullan before or after meeting with Cepeda and Dansak. "After," she stated.

Thus concluded the presentation of the evidence. All that remained were the summations from each side, the judge's instructions to the jury, and the jury's deliberations.

# ... 10
# Closing Arguments and Verdict

This is my beloved Son, in whom I am well
pleased.
Matthew 3:17

When court reconvened after the lunch recess on the eighth day, Judge
Roger Vinson addressed the jury: "Ladies and gentlemen of the jury,
you have heard all the evidence. We will now hear the attorneys'
closing arguments and summations. Please remember that what the
attorneys say is not evidence but will help you in summarizing and
interpreting the evidence."

Susan Novotny rose and walked into no-man's-land, the large floor
space between judge and attorneys, witness stand and jury. "It has
been a long trial," she began softly and slowly. "You have all the
evidence, have heard all the sworn testimony. You will have all the
evidence Judge Vinson admitted in the jury room. Our goal is to review the evidence.

"It is by the criminal justice system, by enforcement of the laws, that
our country exists. Please recall the grand jury indictment: First, conspiracy to create firearms or explosive devices to damage or destroy a
building engaged in interstate commerce. Second, building three firearms or explosive devices. And third, utilizing those devices to mali-
ciously destroy three separate buildings."

She then outlined what the judge would instruct them on: the definitions of conspiracy, malice, and insanity. "Regarding the insanity defense," she said, "if you have any doubt about Dr. Mullan and her diagnosis, the defense fails."

She continued: "You heard two and a half days of testimony. How the bombs were built, what steps they [the defendants] took, their purchases. Why Christmas Day was chosen, their use of a blowtorch, their fear of being caught, the opening of savings and checking accounts by Kathren Simmons and James Simmons, their surveillance of three buildings so the bombs would be effective and the perpetrators would not be caught.

"James Simmons and Matthew Goldsby heard one explosion and went back to watch another. Christmas afternoon they went back to Permenter's office. They went back to Bagenholm's and the Ladies Center.

"Life went back to normal. It was normal before that. Matthew Goldsby went to work, did his duties. Richey Richards, a co-worker, testified that on December twenty-first Matthew Goldsby did not seem unusual, he was normal. James Simmons maintained his job. David Del Gallo testified that Matt was normal. It is curious that nothing was wrong," she said, pausing with a finger at the edge of her mouth and a questioning look. "The psychiatrists said that if they had a severe mental defect, it would have been immediately noticeable to anyone.

"After the bombing, life was normal until the investigators pieced it together and learned that Matthew Goldsby had bought the pipe. When they searched his house and questioned him, he denied any knowledge. At that point there arose evidence of a conspiracy. Kathren Simmons had bought black powder, had opened a savings account. When she said, 'Maybe the agents will search the house [Matt's] and find the cans,' she was thinking rationally. What was their testimony? 'We went there to destroy the evidence,' in Kathy's own words. And Kaye Wiggins's speaking to her intent to return to that house is clear evidence of her interest in the conspiracy. All denied any knowledge of the bombings. On December thirtieth, they exhibited no irrational behavior.

"Let's look at Kaye Wiggins's defense. It is a double defense: 'I was involved, but I was unable to appreciate the wrongfulness of the act,' or 'I was not involved at all.' Let's review the calendar of events. The pipe was ordered the end of November. In mid-November Kathren and James used the savings and checking accounts. There is a lot of testimony that it was called the Gideon Project. But Kaye Wiggins says the Gideon Project was a rafting trip. Notice no other rafting trip was named. Her testimony is contradictory: she was in favor or not in favor of the trip. Then on November twentieth she writes Matt Goldsby, 'Pray for the time, the date, the plans. . . . I feel strongly about this.' This is about a rafting trip and spider bites? Kaye Wiggins found out and entered into the conspiracy on or before November twentieth. She purchased black powder. She certainly knew about it on December thirtieth when she returned to the house to destroy the evidence to further the conspiracy. Recall the letter to her from Matthew Goldsby: 'I'm sorry to put you through so much. I can do more for the cause from here.'

"Regarding her insanity defense: She played softball. She was a pleasant, nice girl. No one noticed anything wrong but Dr. Mullan, who saw a dysthymic disorder. Kaye Wiggins is no different from any other eighteen- or nineteen-year-old girl. She made a bad judgment, but it was not due to any mental disease. Dr. Mullan's diagnosis of Kaye Wiggins clouds her evaluation of the others. If Mullan can say Kaye Wiggins has a mental disease, then we must challenge her on the others."

She turned the jurors' attention to Matthew Goldsby as she paced slowly a few feet in front of them and looked from one juror to the other, making sure she made eye contact with each frequently. "He took numerous steps. He put together the bombs, the timing, the manner in which it would be done. Dr. Mullan says he has manic bipolar disease. But Dr. Cepeda said that came from Dr. Mullan's own speculations; there is no evidence of a mental disorder.

"Matthew Goldsby told us in his own statement that he is goal-oriented; he wanted to stop abortion in Pensacola and had accomplished it. That is a rational statement. And motive is different from 'intent'; motive is no excuse."

She cited again Goldsby's statement: "I weighed my priorities. I knew it was risky. . . . Picketing, political action—that's not my bag."

She charged that Kathren Simmons, James Simmons, and Matthew Goldsby had all said, "I know you think I was wrong. I guess you would call me a criminal."

"There is no evidence of any of Dr. Mullan's symptoms. And James Simmons shows no evidence of Dr. Mullan's diagnosis," Novotny stated, looking thoughtful. "He was aware of what he was doing, that he might get caught, and took steps not to get caught.

"And Kathren Simmons, she saved money, bought powder, knew it was for a bomb, and tried to destroy evidence. That is irrational? It's strange that Dr. Mullan calls loyalty to her husband a mental disease.

"The pastor of Liberty Church, the doctors, they also have religious beliefs. To suggest that a close relationship with God excuses these acts or is the presence of a severe mental disease or defect . . . is truly amazing.

"The evidence is clear: the buildings were damaged, firearms were made, and each participated in it," she concluded.

Paul Shimek rose from the defense table and strode purposefully to stand before the jury. "You have more power today than ever in your life," he began in his strong, preacherlike, authoritative tones. "The whole country is looking at you, to see if the curse on the government is going to be lifted. This country is in trouble and you can do something about it.

"To indict Kaye Wiggins is a naughty, naughty thing. This is not a search for truth. If the truth were apparent there would be no trial for Kaye Wiggins. The great crime would be for you to think you must find the truth. The Soviet Union puts a thousand away to get the guilty. We let a thousand go free to make sure one innocent doesn't go to jail."

At the word *jail*, Dillard jumped quickly and objected. Judge Vinson said only, "Overruled."

"Beyond a reasonable doubt," Shimek continued. "That means 'more than a probability.' If you violate that rule . . . no matter what your own views are, you have to acquit her even if she is guilty, which she is not. There is no way to correct a mistake by you against Kaye Wiggins. A judge's ruling you can appeal, but not your mistake. The jurors' decision is final.

"You have the power to draw inferences, plot suppositions. You can let them build and speculate Kaye Wiggins right into jail. Don't convict her unless you can erase all reasonable doubt. Reasonable doubt is the key to this whole case.

"Even if you acquit her, she will be punished. She will always be known as the gal who got off or whose lawyer got her off.

"If you look at the evidence, regardless of your personal sentiment, you must acquit her. Let's look at the reasons for doubts:

"Conspiracy. That's absurd. She mentioned the Gideon Project in the November twentieth letter. You heard the testimony. She believed it was a rafting trip. She was worried because of the spider bite before.

"The government has cast a big net. Surely there is reasonable doubt. She's a virgin. She denies him, like Peter denied Jesus, three times."[1]

Turning to the other evidence, he said, "When she bought the black powder, she openly took Glenda Switalski with her. If you were knowingly doing this, would you bring along a friend?

"That night, Matt startles her, shows her the clipping. She wouldn't listen to him. Then at the jail, they [Matt and Jimmy] just blurted out the truth. And they said, 'Kaye didn't have anything to do with it.' Kaye didn't want to hear about it. She wasn't thinking in terms of hiding something; she was stunned.

"Unfortunately, virgins who are betrothed as Joseph was to Mary are committed in all ways except for the benefits of marriage. She can't betray him. She will deny him but not betray. Obedience is a virtue.

"December twenty-first, they're making bombs. Asked to help, she refuses, staying away from the kitchen.

"She can't be convicted for loving, for knowing something is going to happen in a couple of hours and not telling.

"The agents come to awaken her. They read her letters, search her closets, even go in her bedroom. In the letter Matt mentions 'the cause.' He has never explained to her and he is explaining why he did what he did. Why? She never knew. It's Cain and Abel. Blood is being spilled. Miami money is spilling Pensacola blood.

"The Kingdom is out there, in a lot of power. If you believe there's a God, there's a Satan. He loves to destroy. He sits in the pew and preaches from the pulpit. He's a liar and a deceiver. There was a miscommunication. God talks to Adam and Eve in the Garden of Eden and tells them, 'If you do what I tell you, that's good. Do not, that's bad.' If Jesus hadn't come, we'd still be there. Matt knows Him. Kaye knows Him.

"The government is overzealous. They catch innocent people. Kathy wants to drive out. They see a burglary. They had no idea the BATF had ransacked the place. Pensacola is all astir. And the media are inundating us. She was the only one who didn't make a statement.

"The government can tear up a letter. That's your government. I'm not proud of a section of the government that says you can kill babies, either. There's a higher law. The psychiatrist had the gall to say God's law is the same as man's. Look at the history of Israel, Gideon and Baal. God's law prevails or man dies. It's a tragedy that many of us reject scripture. There is life and there is death, blessing and cursing. Abortion leads for a lot of women to depression and anxiety. They are sterile afterward.

"Jesus will return in power and glory. They," he said as he pointed toward the defendants, "will rule and reign with Him. They will reign with Him forever."

Then he began going through the Beatitudes: "Blessed are those who mourn . . . the poor in spirit . . . the meek . . ." He mentioned also the publican and the Pharisee; Elijah and the army of the heavenly host; Sodom and Gomorrah; Noah and the flood; and the defendants, "unadulterated hearts," "tried to save their marriages," "persecution—that's what they are doing to Kaye Wiggins, hounding her like chasing a rabbit."

"Kaye Wiggins has done nothing. There is a reasonable doubt, Kaye Wiggins is not guilty. Both of the women, they are not guilty," he finished.

Sitting down again, Shimek slumped slightly in his chair with his chin resting on his touching fingertips and his eyes closed as if he were praying, a position he was to maintain throughout most of the other concluding statements.

During the fifteen-minute recess following Shimek's summation, Kathren Simmons's mother ran to another woman in the lobby and said breathlessly, "The world has finally heard!"

Following the recess Christine Kasun, clad in her severe, businesslike dark suit, approached the jurors slowly, and spoke softly. "Do you remember where you were last Christmas? I was with my family, my parents and my children. When the news came of this case, never in my wildest dreams did I think I would be standing here. I came in this case at the last minute. I got a call. The other attorney was too close to her due date. My first response was that I couldn't do it. I have children, just had a baby. Besides, I have never defended a criminal case. But then I remembered what my mother said to me when the news of Matthew Goldsby's arrest came on TV. There was a picture of him being hustled in handcuffs into a police car. And she said, 'That's such a shame. He probably thought he was doing the right thing, and now he's going to be made an example.' So I packed up and brought my baby with me.

"Kathy Simmons is accused of seven felony crimes, the same as the men. During this case, I have been interested in the truth. I have wanted the evidence to come in. I wanted you to see what was going on.

"We have many points of agreement," she continued. "First, Kathy was not really interested in abortion. She had no passionate feelings on the subject.

"Second, both Mullan and Dansak acknowledged Kathy's statement 'When Jimmy told me about the first one, I was shocked, angry.' Then she put it out of her mind.

"Third, the important things to her are her religion and her marriage. Her religion and her problems at home led her to get married. She sought to escape.

"Fourth, both Drs. Mullan and Dansak and Kathy agree that she pushed the bombs out of her mind.

"Fifth, she bought four cans of black powder. One would hope she wouldn't have done this, that she would have had the gumption to say no, but she didn't. She's a fragile person. I'm not going to argue that she's insane. I don't believe it. You don't believe it. It just was not in her power to stand up to Jimmy. Kathy didn't have it in her power to oppose Jimmy.

"Sixth, she embraced religion in an almost fanatical fervor. It was her way of dealing with the world. She took Saint Paul literally: 'Wives submit yourselves to your husbands.' She believed it, acted on it. She is not Jimmy's peer. She's three years younger. She was an outsider to Jimmy and Matt's love. The judge will instruct you on insanity. It is a state of mind. Sanity involves 'intent as charged.' I am not asking you to find her innocent, but that she did not have the ability to *intend*.

"Seventh, not until December twenty-first did Kathy know the attempt was to be on Christmas. That indicates how much a part of this club she really was. She was not a member of that club. Kathy and Kaye stayed out of the kitchen. They had nothing to do with building bombs. The agent believed her.

"Eighth, on December twenty-fifth Kathy and Kaye prayed and cried. They prayed that no one would get hurt. They were gallant, foolhardy young men. They couldn't stop it. They did not think what they did was wrong, because the Lord told them to do it.

"When agents Bradley and Bruzzichesi told her 'If you tell the truth, it will go better for you,' Kathy believed them. Bradley testified she was not scared. But in the transcript she tells him eight times she was scared. He wants you to think she is a cold, calculating liar. She denied involvement because she was scared. That's important.

"When Gideon decided to destroy the altars of Baal, the place of infant sacrifice, covered with infant blood, he did it by night. Gideon was scared. But he was doing the right thing. She did not tell the truth for two days because she was scared. But being scared is not the same as being a criminal.

"When she thought Michael Simmons might lose his job, she confessed. And she told every thought, not just what she did.

"Her crimes were thought crimes. 'I wanted to go with them that night.' That is not a crime. They are using it to dirty her up.

"She said Jimmy had driven her by the scenes. That is not a crime.

"Kathren Simmons supposedly opened up a savings account for buying materials for the bombs. She did not say it was specially for building the bombs. She said she put their tithes for the church in it. Agent Bilbo put that interpretation on it.

"Finally, when she found out Matt was going down for a polygraph, she went to the house to get rid of the black powder cans. She didn't even get out of the car. She never did it. Bilbo lied to her when he told her 'It will go better for you' [if she talked], and she should not have. Things did not get better.

"All she did was love her husband and not tell a lie. Jimmy loved her, too. He didn't realize he had involved her, too. That's Jimmy's one regret, that he involved Kathy, because he knew she really wasn't involved. It's a travesty of justice that she's indicted on the same level. A tragedy of love.

"This case has national importance, and the government has overcharged this case.

"She had her nineteenth birthday yesterday. Her life lies shattered at her feet. Her private life has been dragged before the entire nation. Her husband has been in jail. Her belief in her Savior has been ridiculed in this court. She is unemployed. She has no place of her own to stay in."

Kasun then moved back to the Gideon story, where the people come after him. "'Where's Gideon,' they asked. Joash defended his son: 'Do you want the altars of Baal back?' Do you want the abortion clinics back? Do you? If Baal wants them back, let him speak for himself. Where are the abortionists? Let them come forward. Where are the abortionists that have been wronged? They're too ashamed, too busy, hiding behind the law. The abortionists are responsible for this, that Kathy's life has been ruined.[2] Only a few years ago, if you called the police you put a stop to it. But by a Supreme Court decision, the laws were struck down. So now these kids are accused of a crime.

"Forty years ago, if they had sabotaged concentration camps, they would be heroes. In World War II my father commanded a rifle company that liberated Lansburg, where Hitler wrote *Mein Kampf*. My father saw pile upon pile, thousands of emaciated bodies. Why did they do it? Because our Supreme Court in its omnipotence says we can do it as long as we are nice about it.

"My father made the townspeople come and bury the bodies. They came with handkerchiefs over their noses. The pictures of the agents going through the clinic rubble show them with hankies.

"A moratorium doesn't happen in the case of abortion. The abortionists say, 'You go ahead and picket, and we're not going to stop.'

"What do you do if someday you meet one of these babies and he asks, 'What did you do to help me?' Will you say, 'I wrote a letter'? I saw *Assignment Life* Sunday and I wept. I caressed my children and I thought of those gloved hands in the movie. If you felt bad when you saw it, how do you think Matt and Jimmy must have felt? Stand in their shoes. If that film was a closed circuit of what was happening in the very next room, what would you have wanted to do about it?

"By the standards of this world, maybe Jimmy and Matt *are* crazy. They believe what few young people do. They do things few young people do. Kathy's teacher spoke of her coming early to help. Matt and Jimmy helped people fix flat tires, were friends of a handicapped man, took care of sick animals. They helped the helpless. They take marriage seriously. They sincerely thought they would risk everything to save some babies. They did that, too. They had no legal alternatives.

"When they bombed the abortion clinics, Matt and Jimmy did not hurt one hair on the head of one person. Dr. Cepeda testified that they took elaborate precautions. What was lost? The abortionists lost dollars. But they were compensated by insurance. They were back in business in a few days. We need fear no repetition of it from them [Simmons and Goldsby]. Is it necessary to compensate them [the abortionists] further with these four lives, this god Moloch, with his insatiable appetite? He is selfish, bloodthirsty, greedy.

"Her crime? Loving her husband. There is a child's prayer: 'God bless all the little babies in the world.' Will God hear? My little girl, in California, prays every night for you, the jury. Kathy is guilty only of loving her husband and believing in him. All of us wept for that baby [in *Assignment Life*] dead on the table. He will not have died in vain if you acquit Kathy."[3]

Frank Booker, the Notre Dame law professor, was next. Assuming his studied, slightly stooped stance, he spoke to the jury in his fatherly manner: "In the American criminal justice structure it is our fortune to defend the rights of the defenseless. You are the tower of strength on which we rely. The unborn child is stripped of his rights, has no policeman to help him. Where is the national response team to help the helpless?

"In my opening statement I said, 'Follow the law!' I say it again. It is the defense of necessity. It is right to act of necessity to save life.[4] For a defense of necessity there must be no legal alternatives available. What alternatives did they have? No policeman, no magistrate would assist them. The state legislature *had* laws to protect the unborn that were struck down. Our Congress cannot pass a law to protect them. No legal alternatives. This goes on daily. It was interrupted briefly in your city. It is a production-line job. It takes two minutes.

"Therefore, there was no crime at all under the law. Unless there is a crime, there is no need of a specific defense, to probe the mind, the psyche, the intent.

"You are the tower. If that falls, then . . . You are the first place where the whole crime can be impartially examined. All before is but an accusation and not evidence of guilt. For there to be a crime there must be an act and a guilty mind. The mind and hand must concur for there to be guilt. Look at the evidence for the guilty hand and the guilty mind.

"I learned from my grandma. She had chickens, and when a 'flyer' would get out of the pen, she would cut off one wing. Then it would fly in a circle. Over here," he pointed to the evidence table, "is a junkyard of physical evidence. But where is the mental evidence, the other wing? The government case won't fly.

"Let me review for you: Jimmy Simmons is a young man, twenty-one, idealistic, of good character, a profoundly fundamental Christian. The government could have countered the character witnesses, but it didn't. The government's case was interstate commerce, pens, papers, paper clips. But we showed you the real commerce: the commerce of death.

"Even the prosecution's psychiatrists were saying this, that they helped people in need. Yet they appeared to have blown up three abortion clinics. They heard the story of Gideon: 'Let Baal plead for Baal.' The government chose to wrap this business in the flag. Only you can decide if this business is interstate commerce.

"We must have criminal intent, a guilty mind. I thought of that heavy cruiser, the *Pensacola*, an eight-inch [-gun] cruiser at Midway, the turning point of World War II. The *Pensacola* beat off a torpedo attack, and then it came to the *Yorktown* and towed it to try to save it. What was in the mind of those sailors and officers? Were they thinking of murder and havoc or of saving our fellow sailors? If the heart and mind are filled with saving life, they cannot be filled with criminal intent. Christ said, 'Love the Lord thy God with all thy heart and all thy soul and all thy mind.' If that be true, where could criminal intent lie?

"This case is about right and wrong. Unless Jimmy Simmons knew right from wrong, he believed it was right. Dr. Dansak testified that Jimmy continued to read the Bible and was never able to develop such a feeling [that it was wrong]. Did he have a severe disease or defect of mind? Dr. Mullan testified that he had a borderline personality disorder. He had a confusion with the unborn child. 'Borderline' doesn't mean marginal, but between neurotic and psychotic. The difference between those who build castles in the air and those who live in them. Jimmy slipped across that border.

"It is a question of right and wrong. The earliest test we have is the tree of knowledge in the Garden of Eden. But the serpent was more subtle. Moral responsibility, and now legal responsibility, rests on the appreciation of the wrongfulness of one's act. To a profoundly religious person, Jimmy slipped back to that lost paradise, knowing not right from wrong. And legally there is no crime if there is no sense of wrong. We have two windows to that—one is psychiatry and the other is religion. When James saw himself as the murdered unborn, to the psychiatrist it was identity confusion. But to the deeply religious it was 'Inasmuch as you do it to the least of these, you do it unto me.'

"Follow the law. If he was directed by God, there was no criminal intent. If he was not, he is a severely ill young man and didn't appreciate the wrongfulness of his act.

"Only six officers were created by the Constitution: president, vice president, congressman, senator, judge, juror. No man can dictate to you the implement of justice you will forge. Aristotle said injustice is to treat things different as the same. The sword of mercy has no cutting edge, but a blunted point. Tell them, 'Go and sin no more.' Follow the law. Find James Simmons not guilty because there was no crime."

It was 5:30 in the afternoon when Patrick Monaghan rose before a tired courtroom audience to deliver the final defense summation. He began: "Matthew Goldsby is not a terrorist. James Simmons is not a terrorist. You were almost put to sleep by the evidence of their character.

"This is a case about intent. The government presented its case like it was unfolding a mystery. What is intent? You are walking down the street. You look through a picture window and see a man about to smash a lamp into the head of a woman. What do you do? Go down to the police station? Go write your congressman? Or, run into the building, kick down the door, push the man down and stomp his hand? If you do that, you have just committed trespass, breaking and entering, and assault and battery. Let's change it: it is a community playhouse and Burton and Taylor were practicing a violent scene. But you didn't know that. You did not have intent.

"The burden of proof is on the government to prove intent. If the government is right, Matthew Goldsby is not guilty. Any man who does what God tells him to do does not have criminal intent. The prosecution must prove that God *didn't* tell him to do it. Matthew Goldsby either did what God told him to do or something is wrong up here," he said, pointing to his head. "That's the only explanation."

"The government psychiatrist says he had no delusions. Then God speaks in his heart. Matthew Goldsby and James Simmons put out a test and God was pleased with what they had done. Perhaps God is speaking to America. I put on the stand Dr. Brennan to testify about cognitive dissonance. And I found the 'necessity' defense, which holds it is not a crime to save someone from imminent harm. That defense is in your power. You are an American jury such as has not been for years. You can follow the law."

Sweeping his hand toward the defendants, Monaghan proceeded dramatically. "That is innocence sitting over there. Those kids are the best that we've got. We've got Tom Sawyer and Huck Finn in this court. Tom Sawyer took a caning for Becky Thomas. He lied. He wouldn't have wanted modern wimps taking girls into abortion chambers.

"Take Huck Finn. His father was an alcoholic. He got on a raft with Jim, a runaway slave. That would be interstate commerce back then. The whole theme of the book is the problem of Huck's wrestling over turning in Jim, to do what is legal or to do what is right. There is a conflict in his mind, and he's just a boy, but like an all-American boy, he came up right. When he saw Jim, he didn't see a piece of property.[5]

"And James Simmons and Matthew Goldsby, when they saw an unborn child, did not see a piece of tissue. It's American innocence that's on trial here.

"Take a fatherless boy twenty-one years old. . . . How old were those boys on Omaha Beach getting off those Higgins boats? They were following God and their commander in chief." Turning to the evidence table, he picked up the Reagan letter and read it again to the jury. "When an American boy saw this letter, he saw it surrounded by bodies. It took all his hesitation, erased all doubt.

"We laughed until that film was shown. When I played with the ribbon, trying to make it into something ominous, we all laughed. When I compared plaid pants to black pants, it was funny, because nobody got hurt. We could laugh about their putting Vaseline on the plug. And nobody has gotten hurt yet. The only people endangered with this," he said, gesturing toward the bomb close at hand, "were these boys, these loving, foolish boys. They were the only ones ever threatened by it."

Pausing slightly, he continued, "The worshipers of Baal, the abortionists, want a victim. And you can give them a victim and make them happy. But this trial, this ordeal, this trial of ordeal has punished these kids, has driven home to them the law. Now, it's enough.

"The U.S. attorney is extremely competent. He has an authoritative voice, as you can see from the way he has of asking a question and turning it. I am glad to have him; it is comforting that we have such a one in authority against cocaine dealers and pornographers. But this a terrifying army against Tom Sawyer and Huck Finn.

"You are the keepers of what it is to be an American. We bring you these children and say, 'Look at them.' Someone has said, 'We need an example.' But we don't need an example. Every now and then the government tries. When Jesus was on trial, the government won its case and Jerusalem fell. Socrates was tried and Athens fell. If Tom Sawyer and Huck Finn are convicted, America will be the loser. We cannot take those losses impending on us now.

"Two weeks ago Amy Carter was arrested for protesting at the South African embassy. Before that, she called her father, and he told her to do it with his blessing. Is there any U.S. attorney bringing charges on Amy Carter? This case is a statement about life itself.

"There is a young man. He sees an empty train pull up and people loaded on it. It goes over the hill. The trains come again, and again. Then he goes and sees. They're being killed. The kid makes a device exactly like this one, takes it to a railroad car, and blows it up. In Nazi

Germany what would have happened to him? What would America have done? We won't know until you return with your verdict.

"In the 1840s there was a Kentucky case. A man named Bailey Smith had married a black woman and they had four sons. He wanted to get them across the Ohio River, but he died before he could. Some long-lost relatives came from Pennsylvania and wanted all his property sold. Neely Smith found a lawyer who argued that the presumption of the law is that you're white. Twelve jurors looked at Neely Smith and the greed of those Northerners and decided that Neely Smith was white. I want you to be a jury like that, because that's Tom Sawyer and Huck Finn.

"Make an example? Why do we always have to make an example? But examples never work at all that way. Old John Brown was genuinely crazy. He was tried and convicted. They took him to the scaffold on a stretcher and hung him. Both Lee and Lincoln agreed that an example was needed. Three years later we had Shiloh and Antietam. The example didn't do any good.

"In that chair," he said, pointing at the seat left vacant by the ill and excused juror, "is the thirteenth juror, God himself. I urge you, in your deliberations, consult with God. He has been in this case as an unindicted coconspirator. He has been all around this case. Every law is founded on God's law.

"It is the duty and the burden of the government to prove God didn't talk to him [Goldsby]. The government has proven it [hearing voices] is not delusional."

Referring to the "necessity" provision, Monaghan went on to state, "There must be no legal alternative available. We are talking about harm to that life. Dr. Permenter lost his building, but now he might be on the path to save his soul. Somewhere one kid is alive because of this. That kid's father is there," he said, pointing to Goldsby.

"Nobody was killed. But when the buildings were open, people were being killed." Explaining "necessity" further, he said, "There must be a direct causal relationship between the act and the avoidance of harm. There may be out there some woman bearing a child who will cure cancer.

"It is up to the government to prove 'beyond a reasonable doubt.' Look at the power of the government. They brought one agent after another. Is that fair? Against four kids. Is that fair? They were ably trained witnesses, too. It is fair, because the counterbalance of that power is 'beyond all reasonable doubt.'

"This act was not malicious, not willful, not an act for gain. There is a lot of conflict in the testimony. It reminds me of a Kentucky farmer who was asked how much his cow was worth by a man with a suit on. He said he couldn't say because he couldn't tell if the man was an insurance adjuster or a tax assessor.

"These kids are idealistic, passionate, like Don Quixote. They've been impacted by a great controversy out there. It was a lawyer from Kentucky who said America can't exist half slave and half free. I say we cannot exist half killing, half saving. The first day I wrote a number on the blackboard there, 4109. That's the number of lives killed on the day of the president's letter. Since I wrote that, 36,981 have been killed. You can tell the Supreme Court of the United States they can do their own abortions.

"Get their preacher. Hang the author of the movie. Hang the judge." Hastily he added, "Not this judge."

Pausing briefly to let the courtroom laughter subside, he continued: "Hang the lawyers, the doctors, the abortionists. But don't let's get self-righteous and get these kids. They're American innocence. You're the elders of the city. You will decide.

"If I could bring back just one of my buddies [by doing it]," he said, referring to the Korean War, "I'd take out a few more buildings. The fireman testified, 'Life before property.' The Sons of Liberty threw tea in the harbor. Here we have the Sons of Pensacola. You can't take them outside the walls of the city and stone them. You can't destroy innocence.

"One thing is clear. The Protectors of the Code love you. They would die for you. If you find them guilty, they're still going to die for you. There is something afoot in this case that's beyond us.

"What's the story of Egypt? Pharaoh's heart was hardened. I pray this is America and not Egypt. Don't let your heart be hardened. Abraham heard God's voice, 'Take Isaac.' Then up there on the mountain, with his knife raised over his son, there came a voice, 'Abraham, Abraham, withhold your hand from the boy.' Abraham heard it. I want you to hear and listen, because we wait your verdict.

146 . . . The Trial

"We don't need a victim, an example, a martyr. We've got Huck Finn and Tom Sawyer. What they need is a tobacco stick across their backs.

"When I went to law school on the GI Bill and after our first exams, a friend, a marine, and I went after the exam to have a drink and some pizza. He left the table and didn't come back. I found him in the bathroom, crying at the sink, and he told me a story. The Americans came to one village. And the Communists came. There was a sudden battle. The chaplain was pinned down helping people. But wherever he went, there was a corridor of peace. But then an officer on the other side took careful aim and shot him and then pushed his body so it rolled back to the American side. Hate filled the whole thing.

"We can't destroy innocence, Tom Sawyer and Huck Finn. It is not a question of religion, politics, or morals. It's not motive but intent.

"I've tried the best I could. The law is clear in this case. Follow the law and give us America. For Matt Goldsby, we love you and we thank you."

Ginny Graybiel, *Pensacola Journal* reporter, captured the defense summations in the next morning's paper: "Who was behind the blowing up of the abortion facilities? According to defense attorneys, it was either God, Satan or the doctors who performed the abortions."

It was 6:15 as Thomas Dillard, looking somewhat like Christopher Reeve in build and manner except for his mustache and his slim six-foot-one-inch frame, rose and strode purposefully to stand about a yard before the jury for his closing response: "Those are four very good attorneys. They told you just what you wanted to hear. They're telling you each in their own way. We have heard five minutes on the issues and two hours and fifty-five minutes on other matters.

"I agree. The evidence is clear. These are fine young people, from good families, and religion is the focal point of their life. From the beginning of this trial the defense has referred to them as 'kids.'" A note of anger crept into his voice as he determinedly asserted, "They are not kids, and I'm sick of hearing them called that. By every standard they are adults, and they committed an adult act.

"But they did an act that everyone in their religious group said was all right, was justified. But that could also define the Palestinians at night blowing up Jews. Or the Protestants in Northern Ireland blowing up Catholics. Or the Catholics blowing up Protestants. They're all religious people and they're convinced they're right. Last week a sixteen-year-old Palestinian blew up himself and some Jews. Was that Palestinian Huck Finn? Huck Finn didn't put this together," he thrust his arm, firm and outstretched, toward the bomb, his finger almost touching it. "That's no firecracker. It's an awesome weapon.

"You've been told, 'Close your eyes. Tom Sawyer and Huck Finn did this. Let them go.' But the law is a very thin fabric. We are a nation of laws, not of men. The law is the only thing that keeps us out of the jungle. We don't decide which laws to obey. That's what we fought for, what our forefathers died for.

"What's next? God speaks to me. I didn't appreciate Dr. Mullan telling me I have delusions. All of a sudden they act like the insanity defense was never entered. Of course, there is no insanity here. The defense made a cold, calculated decision. Ask yourself if the law says I have to prove God didn't talk to them." At this point, Dillard read the portion of the law dealing with insanity and then said, "This is no defense to the crime. We can't have it. Today it's the God you and I believe in. What will it be tomorrow? What can we say to the next defendant, a Muslim, who blows up this federal building and says, 'Allah doesn't believe in federal law'?

"That's what the issue is. Not terrorists. Not abortionists. Not religion. At the beginning they said abortion and religion were not the issue. That lasted five minutes. How did abortion get on trial? Through the insanity defense, which has been abandoned. It is not fair to them," he gestured toward the defendants, "to say they're insane to get in the abortion issue. But it didn't work.

"We," he said, referring to the prosecution, "have been called the curse of the earth, Pontius Pilate, Satan, like we started this whole thing. But we didn't do it. That's what happens when you put religion in. We're not the forces of Satan. Satan isn't on trial. God isn't. Religion shouldn't be in the case. But that is what happens when we use religion as an excuse.

"It's Tom Sawyer and Huck Finn," he said sarcastically. "'We just blew up three buildings. We'll pick a time when nobody's there. But y'all don't mind, do you? I don't have to obey the law because a jury in

Pensacola, Florida, on the twenty-second of April, 1985, said it was okay.' That's what's going to happen. Huck Finn and Tom Sawyer.

"If we proved beyond a reasonable doubt and then you turn them loose, then you have set it in motion. We don't need a fourth branch of government, a terrorist branch, that obeys the laws it wants to and disobeys what it wants to. If we do, then we're headed back to the jungle. There are many people who believe in many gods. What's next?"

Slowly and deliberately, he concluded, "The issue is whether Matthew Goldsby and James Simmons, with the help of Kaye Wiggins and Kathren Simmons, constructed these bombs, placed them in the buildings, and then blew them to smithereens."

It was 6:30 and twilight was falling outside as Judge Roger Vinson addressed the jury: "There are two judges here, me and the jury. I am the judge as to the law. You are the judge as to the facts."

As he continued with clarifications of the laws and the indictments, Kaye Wiggins's mother bent over, her lips moving as in prayer. Kaye herself, Kathren Simmons, and James Simmons looked steadily and soberly at the judge. Matthew Goldsby continued looking at the spot on the floor that he had examined through much of the trial. As Judge Vinson concluded his forty-five-minute instructions to the jury and excused them to their deliberations, Kaye Wiggins burst into quiet tears.

Before sending the jury out to deliberate, the judge revealed for the first time the name of the remaining alternate juror and excused her from the deliberations. At 7:15, for the first time in the trial, Judge Vinson did not leave the courtroom before the jurors but stood for their exit with the attorneys, defendants, and spectators, in respect for the jury's task.

The spectators had barely reached the lobby to stretch and visit the bathrooms when word came that the court was returning into session. When Judge Vinson entered the court, he announced that the jury had voted to retire for the night and to begin deliberations the next morning. Those in the courtroom who had anticipated with trepidation a late-night vigil were relieved.

At 8:00 the next morning the court was back in session, and the jury retired to open deliberations. At 8:32 the marshal handed to the judge a note from the jury that stated that count one in the indictment was unclear to them. After a brief conference with all the attorneys, Judge Vinson returned a note of clarification to the jury at 8:38.

The spectators, except for several of the defendants' family members and close friends, had exited the courtroom to pace the lobby or find a cup of coffee. Left scattered through the lobby of the remodeled old post office were the circular writing tables, which stood almost chest high for addressing letters and packages, the slots formerly housing inkwells now used as receptacles for used Styrofoam coffee cups. People tended to gather around these tables or around the windows, peering out at the larger group of demonstrators gathered for the trial's climax.

Outside it was raining, an occasionally hard, driving rain with strong gusts of wind. Pensacola was under a tornado watch, and the low, heavy black clouds scudding overhead indicated that the weather forecaster might be right.

Kaye Wiggins stood at one of the far windows, alone, seemingly distracted. Throughout the trial the press had seemed almost deferential to her and Kathy Simmons inside the courthouse—not surprising, since the gag order was still in effect. In the lobby the two could wander at will without anyone approaching them, but the moment they or their attorneys stepped outside the building, they found TV cameras surrounding them, sometimes less than a foot from their faces.

While I[6] talked with a local reporter, Mrs. Ruby Menard, Kathy Simmons's mother, walked up to us and chatted about how she dealt with the tension. "I just put my burden on the Lord," she said. "When I go to bed, I sleep all night. After all, I can't do a thing about this."

Susan Novotny's parents stood off by themselves near one of the windows. At one of the round writing desks a group of five or six reporters gathered with their heads bent over a yellow legal pad on which one of them was writing.

I talked a little with an anti-abortion worker from Kentucky. I had seen him throughout the trial, but we had not talked before. He said, "If you ask the whole pro-life movement, 'What's wrong with blowing up an abortion clinic?' the answers of most of them would be, 'Nothing.'"

Outside there were nine or ten TV cameramen trying to keep their equipment covered from the rain. I counted five different network and television station trucks.

Several of us were talking about where to get some lunch and wondering if we would be told when the jury broke to eat, when at 12:11 a marshal announced that court was reconvening. Thinking it was the announcement of the lunch break, most spectators filed in languidly. But then I overheard a marshal saying that the jury was bringing a verdict, and an air of excitement, anticipation, and, among the defendants and their families, apprehension swept through the room.

As the judge and then the jury filed in, Paul Shimek stood with his eyes closed. The marshal took the papers with the verdicts, one sheet for each defendant, and handed them to the judge, who silently read them one by one and then passed them to the clerk. Judge Vinson then directed the clerk to read the verdicts.

She began with Matthew John Goldsby and, count by count, announced he was guilty on all seven counts. The process was repeated for James Thomas Simmons, also found guilty on all counts. The clerk then read the sheet for Kathren Simmons: "Count one, conspiracy, guilty." On the other counts she was found not guilty. "Kaye Michelle Wiggins. Count one, conspiracy, guilty." Like Kathren, Kaye was found innocent on the other six counts.

At the word *guilty* Kaye Wiggins and her sister burst into tears, but the other defendants remained stoic, looking straight ahead at the clerk.

At the conclusion of the reading of the verdicts, Judge Vinson accepted the decisions of the jury and announced that he was releasing the defendants pending sentencing on May 30. Meanwhile, he said, there would be a presentencing investigation of each defendant. He justified releasing Goldsby and Simmons on their own recognizance since he was convinced by the evidence presented at the trial that they were no longer a threat to the community.

# ... 11
# Gifts
# of
# the
# Spirit

Now concerning spiritual gifts, brethren, I
would not have you ignorant.
1 Corinthians 12:1

The choir of First Assembly of God had just finished singing. The congregation was settling down in preparation for a sermon on the mission of the church. Brother Lindell Ballenger took the microphone and was about to speak when a voice rang through the sanctuary in a crisp flow of polysyllabic utterance. Pure utterance, a gift of tongues, from God through the lips of Rhoda Goldsby, Matt's mother. Several hands were raised as the words flowed. Then, as silence fell on the room, a man's voice offered interpretation: "My children, I am going to show you a new way . . . . " And then came a second interpretation, continuing the point of the first, in a woman's voice guided by the Holy Spirit.[1]

Before the last echoes of the words had fallen on the room, a dozen voices were raised saying "Thank you, Jesus!" and Brother Ballenger began offering a prayer for the blessings of the manifest Spirit. The choir and orchestra then moved from their places to join the rest of the congregation. Matt Goldsby was with the others in the orchestra for the first time since his arrest. He put his trumpet away and took a place at the rear of the church with Kaye Wiggins and the Simmonses. The sermon followed as a continuation of the blessing, concentrating on maintenance of the proper attitude toward the Holy Spirit and the need for revival within this and all congregations. There were no special messages about right and wrong, no words about bombing or abortion.

Even a casual observer would have asked the critical question, What has all of this to do with God-directed bombings, Christmas presents for Jesus, or reactions to the presence of Matt Goldsby? Simple answers are impossible. Among the answers we must explore, there are none that are totally satisfying and some that are potentially terrifying. At the outset we must establish to what extent and in what ways the religious and cultural experiences of Matt Goldsby and Jimmy Simmons contributed to their resolve against abortion and their actions against the clinics. Throughout, we must attempt to understand the premises of the Pentecostal religion and the full-gospel conception of nature, or we will gravely misinterpret what happened in Pensacola and what could happen in other places. In the end we must face the cultural reality of differences within Christianity, the inability of secular law to deal with the religious issue, and the full implications of diversity in an increasingly secular world.

## Pentecostal Congregations in Pensacola

Pensacola shares its religious profile with the national one. As in many other communities, the city's Christian fellowships include a range of "full-gospel," Holiness, and Pentecostal congregations. Many are small, but three Assemblies of God congregations are among the largest and most active ministries in the community.[2] Across the country, Pentecostal churches vary widely in their styles of worship and their relative importance in communities. What it means to "receive the Holy Spirit" is a subject for debate, sometimes even within particular congregations. In recent years Pentecostal practices such as prophecy and speaking in tongues have been carried into congregations otherwise unassociated with the original Holiness viewpoint, usually under the term "charismatic" fellowship. Yet another trend is manifest across the nation. Large Pentecostal congregations, working through evangelistic conversions, are increasingly successful in attracting members from more "orthodox" Christian denominations. First Assembly of

God of Pensacola is a successful evangelical, full-gospel, urban congregation of this kind.

The Pentecostal community and charismatic movement are loosely tied to a broader movement in modern religion known as fundamentalism. Fundamentalists usually argue for a literal reading of the Bible, although such reading often is better characterized as "free interpretation." Thus, most of the national television ministries can be called fundamentalist, since they spring from strong personalities who are relatively independent of any external pastoral or denominational authority and offer highly individual treatments of scripture.

Many Americans equate fundamentalism with religious conservatism. However, the terms *liberal* and *conservative* are impossible to apply with clarity to fundamentalist Christians, except as political labels. It is more useful to recognize elements of orthodoxy versus independence in the relations of congregations to the Christian body. Assemblies of God and other churches are founded on the principle of congregational and pastoral independence and so represent a departure from the standards of orthodoxy that characterize larger denominations.

There are many senses in which the modern churches offer challenges to the fundamental elements of belief that were extant among Holiness churches earlier in this century. Proscriptions against wearing jewelry, going to movies, or using makeup and rules affirming the dominance of the father in the family are changing as the pressures of external cultural values affect the religious community. Women at worship in Pace and First Assemblies of God will be found wearing slacks, high heels, elaborate hairstyles, and the latest makeup styles. Fundamentalists will be found shopping for groceries after church on Sundays. Despite their stress on the "traditional" family, these Christians are also adapting to the realities of the current divorce rate. For example, many local fundamentalist churches sponsor special groups or classes for single parents and other divorced persons. In one sermon Lindell Ballenger affirmed the ideal that the mother stay at home full-time to rear the children, but in the next breath he added, "when it is possible." In spite of these changes, the original cultural traditionalism of congregations forms a base of resistance to "secular humanism" and a springboard for a much broader and current program of social action.

The new appeal of the gospel grows as modern cultural changes influence central and immediately observable areas of life. Perceived rising rates of crime and divorce, more open expressions of sensualism, and sexual and child abuse tolerated by—perhaps inspired by—the liberal ambience of the American political and social intellect are taken as proofs of moral decay. More and more Americans have begun to adopt religious solutions for social problems they cannot understand and feel powerless to combat.[3]

Abortion is not the only social cause taken up by "full-gospel" congregations. It is not even a central cause. The cultural traditions that lie at the core of the Holiness orientation are manifest in many other areas of life with much greater force. The Assemblies of God congregations in the Pensacola area are not especially traditional with regard to the tenets of Holiness orientation. But these congregations are deeply committed to the search for a spiritually marked righteous life and the struggle to resist being drawn into an increasing decline of a sense of community.

Like most other fundamentalist churches, Pensacola First Assembly of God and its sister congregations in Pace and Brownsville are independent fellowships. "Full-gospel" ministry, emphasizing belief and action consistent with the gifts of the Holy Spirit, places these congregations in the minority among the largest associations of Christian fellowship. Southern Baptists, although also existing in independent congregations and forming by far the most powerful denomination in Pensacola, do not usually involve themselves in Spirit-guided healing, speaking in tongues, interpretation of tongues, or discernment of demonic spirits.[4] Congregational and pastoral restraints in these churches limit the actions of those who believe in spiritual gifts. Thus, even though many churches link themselves to fundamentalism, some fundamentalists find reason to deny a place for spiritual gifts in the modern world.

The Assemblies of God congregations in the Pensacola area share strong elements of "political evangelism" with a handful of "orthodox" churches, including especially four or five of the Southern Baptist churches. Political evangelism involves the association of contemporary conservative political ideas with religious or biblical justifications, most often through the spiritual gift of prophecy. In this sense alone is the Assemblies of God a conservative fellowship. Yet political evangelism is tied directly to spiritual gifts and so is a part of the total context of Matt Goldsby's religious upbringing, Jimmy Simmons's scriptural understandings, and the supportive moral interpretations of Kaye Wiggins and Kathren Simmons.

## Baptism in the Holy Spirit

David Mayo, a member of First Assembly, smiled genially across the table at our question, "Was the message from the lips of Rhoda Goldsby two Sundays ago an unusual occurrence?" He responded clearly. From the point of view of spiritual manifestations at First Assembly of God, it was not. From the point of view of Spirit-filled action by Rhoda Goldsby, it was not. But the interpretation by two people was not typical, though there seemed to be nothing special in its intent compared to other messages from God heard in the church. In fact, the Wednesday after the trial, when Matt and Jimmy had first returned to church, was the exceptional time in that church—a time when the congregation received their own back with love, not condoning their actions, but also not rejecting them in a time of spiritual need. Perhaps few congregations would have suffered the adversity of this brotherhood or known how to celebrate their release after conviction.

David reflected on the trial and the shock at church over the involvement of Matt Goldsby, his longtime friend, with the clinic bombings. Matt had not associated with the anti-abortion workers from the church. Neither he nor Jimmy Simmons had been outspoken about abortion. Matt, Kaye, Jimmy, and Kathren were not strongly active in the young adult group, although they had been relatively consistent in their association with the church. None of the four, to his knowledge, had been involved in Spirit-directed actions.

David continued speaking about the spiritual gifts discussed by Paul in 1 Corinthians and noted the conclusion of the Gospel of Mark. There are nine gifts of the Spirit: wisdom, knowledge, faith, healing, miraculous powers, prophecy, discernment of the spirits, speech in tongues, and interpretation of tongues—three gifts of revelation, three gifts regarding powers, and three vocal gifts. As the Apostle Paul explains: "There are varieties of gifts, but the same Spirit. There are varieties of service, but the same Lord. There are many forms of work, but all of them, in all men, are the work of the same God" (1 Corinthians 12:4–6).

The nine gifts outlined by Paul lie at the core of full-gospel understanding. Of course, God's work is not seen as totally confined to extraordinary action. David stated it simply: "It's faith. That's exactly what it is. And First Assembly's concept of the born-again experience is no different from that of any Baptist church that you know, or probably any Methodist church. Their doctrines are pretty much the same on being born again. It's receiving the Lord Jesus as your Savior, and accepting him as Lord of your life, and confessing him as Savior."

David pointed out that understanding of the Pentecostal perspective should be founded in scriptural reading, not simply opinion. Prayer and scriptural study must guide or limit the human interpretations of daily life. Indeed, for many people of faith, righteous action involves a scripturally based search for God's direction and help in recognizing "signs" of the proper way in all things. David explained: "The difference in churches is the baptism of the Holy Spirit. . . . The difference in First and many other churches is that First teaches from the Bible that there is the subsequent experience after salvation, and that is being filled with the Spirit. Of course, He [the Spirit] was involved in being born again, but when you become filled with the Spirit, it is like a total possession kind of thing. Not only does He have your heart, but He wants to direct and control your life."

The actions of Matt Goldsby and Jimmy Simmons must have been grounded in these core tenets of religious orientation. But how does one know God's intent clearly? How does one discern divine impetus from the instigation of demonic forces? Those who possess the gifts of discernment, wisdom, knowledge, or prophetic utterance state that prayer and careful study of scripture are necessary in order to transform God's will to understanding and action. It is one thing to know what is good and what is evil, but quite another to have the wisdom to understand the proper course of action to achieve good. Spiritual maturity comes through a process of Christian fellowship, scriptural study, and submission to all the signs of God's intent.

To be "born again" or "born in the Spirit" is to recognize a personal relationship with God, but it is not a guarantee of Spirit-filled action. The congregation of First Assembly of God, like other congregations, is composed of many "seekers of truth" at different levels of spiritual maturity. Baptism in the Spirit is a customary experience. Public manifestations of spiritual gifts are accepted by those who are directed by God and by those who are seeking truth, but not all manifestations are received as equally valid. When God uses a person to bless the congregation, the blessing is received with love. But not all believers are used to bless the church through public displays or utterance. In the words of Paul: "Now you are Christ's body, and each of you a limb or organ of it. Within our community God has appointed, in the first place apostles, in the second place prophets, thirdly teachers; then miracle-workers, then those who have gifts of healing, or ability to help others or power to guide them, or the gift of ecstatic utterance of various kinds. Are all apostles? all prophets? all teachers? Do all work miracles? have all gifts of healing? Do all speak in tongues of ecstasy? Can all interpret them? The higher gifts are those you should aim at" (1 Corinthians 12:27–31).

### A Splinter of the Truth

We waited in the outer office at First Assembly of God, glancing through recent issues of *Charisma* magazine. Pastor Lindell Ballenger returned from an earlier appointment and we settled into his office. Ballenger listened thoughtfully to our questions. At a critical juncture, we approached the issue of Spirit-directed violence. How could one deal with the claim that God inspired the bombings?

"The bombings could not have been inspired by God because the overwhelming weight of the scripture is against violence," Ballenger began. He did not believe Matt and Jimmy could have been used by God in such a way. He did not believe that God directed them in their action. "I believe they had a splinter of the truth, but they didn't have the whole thing," he said.

Pastor Ballenger realized that four members of his congregation had been caught up in an issue that is volatile and capable of creating frustration even in those experienced with political struggle and confrontation. Yet these young people—Matt, Kaye, Jimmy, and Kathren—were baptized in the controversy they created. Ballenger cited the unfortunate truth that the four had neither availed themselves of the resources of the church in seeking God's direction nor associated themselves with the many aspects of legal church action against abortion. It would be unfair and inaccurate, he said, to state that religion had nothing to do with their motivations or that others in the church were totally unaware of the feelings of the four about abortion. Nonetheless, it is fair to observe that fellowship in the church was not capable of detecting the seriousness of Matt and Jimmy's intentions. Thus, some in the church may have unwittingly provided support for the idea of the bombings, while others undoubtedly ignored opportunities to dissuade the bombers from their plans.[5] Nobody took Matt or Jimmy seriously. The full congregation took its opportunity to make a difference after the fact.

Of the religious defense in the trial, Ballenger said, "They have some strong convictions about abortion . . . and they did want to use this as a forum to deal with that issue." Yet there was no doubt in his mind that the trial was more than fair. The defense had been successful in having the abortion issue admitted as argument in the trial, and "motive" would likely weigh heavily in the final disposition of the defendants, no matter how unrelated to the determination of innocence or guilt. He also pointed out, "How could they find the kids not guilty of bombing buildings? They said they did it. The evidence was clear."

Ballenger also noted that the trial had caused Matt and Jimmy to evaluate what it means to be a Christian and the meaning of Christian action: "I'm not saying I disagreed with the judge keeping them in jail for a while, because, believe me, it made a difference. . . . My opinion is that if our judicial system is to rehabilitate people and put them back in society, then that would be the thing to do, to get out from the trouble to start with. These kids are rehabilitated. I don't even question; they would never ever do this again."

Ballenger was perhaps in the best position to know the defendants at this point. He understood their plight and frustration. He understood their error. And he understood their confusion within an entangling web of media pressures, legal manipulations, and a poorly informed public willing to make the situation worse. He reflected on his own involvement with Matt and Jimmy since the arrests:

> I sat there one on one, and nobody around and no reason for them to be any different . . . and I've got angry at them, and I've yelled at them, and I hit the table with my fist to get their attention, because they got so much mail. You could not believe some of the things that came to them in that jail . . . thirty to fifty letters a day sometimes, from all over this country, saying, "You guys are heroes; you're martyrs" and "God sent you to do this" and "Don't worry about spending the rest of your life in jail; you've saved one baby." . . . And these are things we've had to contend with where the kids are concerned out there sitting in that jail cell.

Contrary to belief among some people outside the church, abortion was not a central concern of Lindell Ballenger's ministry during his year of adjustment to Pensacola. Ballenger and other leaders of the church were taken by surprise at the bombings, at the involvement of Matt and Jimmy, and even at the religious justifications that surfaced immediately and ultimately became a central part of the defense. He recognized the sincerity of many of those who espouse radical approaches to the abortion dilemma, but he rejected any form of violence as the means to confront the issue: "I think the bombings hampered the issue. . . . I started dealing with Right to Life and the abortion issue ten years ago in Oklahoma, because I began to realize this is going to be a major problem. . . . And we began to make effective change in government leaders who had the power to do something about it. Then I came to Pensacola and found this radical movement here, and they were saying, 'Well, you don't care about abortion or you would be out on the picket lines.'"

Ballenger also reflected on what a proper punishment for Goldsby and Simmons would be. He struggled toward a balance of the issues of law, perhaps at that time paralleling the thoughts of Judge Vinson, who had yet to impose the sentence. He knew firsthand some of the threats and agitation that, although in check for the moment, could be unleashed against anyone in the community as a consequence of the sentence. Reflecting on the total situation, he offered some options:

In my opinion, if the judge did what I think would be the best thing for the kids, he would put them out on probation and make them make restitution. Make them pay. . . . How long would it take them? A long time. How long before they forget it? Never. . . . I know the kids, and I'm telling you, it's probably the worst thing you could do to them, as far as really making examples of them. But on the other hand, if they just walk out without any jail sentence, the boys . . . I just somewhere in the back of my mind feel that it's going to say to all these idiots across the country, "Well, God has vindicated these kids and so we have a right if we don't like something, blow it up! If we don't like somebody, shoot them down, because God will get us off the hook!"

### Spirit and Anger

Sharon Glass talked to us in one of the prayer rooms at Pace Assembly of God. We broached the topic of God's direction in the bombings and trial, in the actions of the Pro-Life Coalition in Pensacola, and in the Penny Lea Crusade, for which she serves as Florida director. Glass had been an observer at the trial, drawn by her longtime involvement in the abortion issue. She reflected quietly on currents of interpretation among some people of charismatic mind: "I think everybody had an initial reaction to it that God couldn't have told them that, but then after the trial there were some people who are saying 'Well, I don't know, now, because of God's name being lifted up.'"

The scene outside the federal courthouse had offered a curious juxtaposition of images. After the first morning prayer vigil outside the building, the press photographers had passively observed the return visits of seven or eight people who knelt on the steps with their hands and voices raised in petition. We recalled how on one occasion a young reporter standing only a few feet away on the steps above glared with incredulity and blurted out, "These people don't care about abortions; all they want is publicity!"

The Gideon Project was not the brainchild of anyone active in the anti-abortion movement. But the trial was of tremendous importance to local activists who had worked for months writing, speaking, and picketing against abortion in Pensacola. These activists followed the trial closely. Many were present on several days of the deliberations, taking advantage of the closed-circuit television extension of the court-room. The most visible local activist, John Burt, was more aloof, except for his engagements at the courthouse steps. National anti-abortion workers also observed the trial. They were drawn by the media cover-age of such pretrial statements as those of Kaye Wiggins broadcast by the Canadian Broadcasting Corporation and PBS:

> I know that God is against abortion. . . . He's using Kathy and myself to let people know. He's using Jimmy and Matt sitting in prison over there because they tried to save a child's life. Matt and Jimmy did feel that it was of God; and nobody else has took three of them out in one city. But I just feel, in my heart, that God is using these three, because He sees in Matt's heart, they were done with pure motive; they were, you know, from unselfish motive. They were doing it for Him, and He sees that. He doesn't condone it, but He forgives them, and He's going to take this and use it to the glory of God.

But if the inspiration for the bombings was not of God, then only discernment of the evil forces would have stopped Matt and Jimmy from carrying out their plan. Discernment is not only one of the "higher" gifts, but even those people who possess discernment are extremely conservative in its use. Sharon Glass discussed discernment in the context of the occult and the contrast of powers derived from Jesus versus powers based in evil: "With a medium psychic you are being used by a demonic spirit. See, Jesus can be at all places at all times, but the devil can't. So he has to send his demon forces. So most of the time the devil doesn't even take the time to mess with anybody. It's always a demonic force, a demonic spirit."

A few years earlier Sharon Glass had been involved in the occult. When she speaks of discernment of the Spirit, she speaks as one with direct experience in life and also in the evil spiritual forces that she sees constantly confronting Christians.[6] Her activities in the church include counseling and action surrounding possession and other emotional difficulties caused by the evil forces. She speaks with authority on the confrontation of the devil and the power of Jesus over evil. She is not afraid to confront today the evil that a few years earlier had dominated her life: "You have to learn to reject that which the devil is trying to send into you, or the forces are trying to send into you. And . . . there's a very thin line there. That's why I say, yes, the devil, he can manifest himself in the ways of God. Now, he can't do more than God, but he can be a very great deceiver. And this is what happens to people in a Christian life; they think they are hearing from God. And that's why I'm extremely cautious. I don't speak anything unless I know I'm hearing the voice of God, because that can destroy someone."

Was this what happened with the Gideon Project? Did Matt and Jimmy lack the discernment to know that their plan was inspired by the devil? Were Matt, Kaye, Jimmy, and Kathren more destroyed by the bombings than the clinic buildings? Or does a "Pentecostal" perspective hold only the answer that the Gideon Project comes from either God or the devil? The scriptural parallel of the Gideon story provides one answer to these questions, especially when considered in light of the damaging evidence collected from Matt Goldsby's home and the behaviors of Matt, Kaye, Jimmy, and Kathren. They believed they would not be discovered. They believed they were being protected.

But when faced with arrest, they also took that as a message from God. As Jimmy Simmons said to Lindell Ballenger the first time they talked in the jail, "Pastor, it was the will of God that we got caught." Ballenger recognized the frustration surrounding the abortion issue for many Christians and the possibility that poor human judgment may bring about actions conceived in frustration and anger. But he also stated:

I think one of the main virtues of being a Christian is the love that we should have in our hearts for human beings. If they got love for the babies that are being aborted, they need to extend that same Christian love to those doctors. I think the doctors that are committing abortions in this town think all Christians are full of hate and bitterness and anger and malice and wrath. . . . But who wants that kind of attitude? I wouldn't want to be like somebody out there, calling me names, and making obscene phone calls to me, and all this kind of stuff. To me, that's not what Christians are. So I get on the stump from that standpoint. I say it's all right to take an issue, but let's do it in love. Jesus' forces speak the truth in love! And we can be very truthful to people and still not be angry. Anger is a good emotion if it's kept under control. Anger out of control is destruction.

# . . . 12
# Sentencing

TEKEL: Thou art weighed in the balances,
and art found wanting.
Daniel 5:27

The morning of May 30 was the beginning of a fine, sunny day in Pensacola. An hour before the scheduled sentencing, a news conference was held by the four defendants in Paul Shimek's office. When asked by a reporter if he would recommend that anyone else bomb an abortion facility, Jimmy Simmons replied, "No, not unless God tells them to."

Outside the courthouse, shortly before 8:30, about twenty picketers carrying the usual posters and placards were slowly circling near the curb. John Burt walked leisurely among them, bearing Baby Charlie in his outstretched right hand. Charlie's usual residence, a four-quart jar of formaldehyde, sat atop a newspaper dispenser at the curb near the steps leading to the second-floor lobby. At the foot of the steps stood Joseph Scheidler, director of the Chicago-based Pro-Life Action League, with five or six reporters gathered around him.

The courthouse looked unfamiliar without the yellow security tape surrounding it. Inside, filing one final time through the metal detector, spectators were unexpectedly directed upstairs to a new courtroom. A large crowd was gathered in the lobby, waiting for the courtroom doors to be unlocked. Perhaps it was because the lobby area was smaller that

May 30, 1985. John Burt holds a pickled fetus as demonstrators march in front of the courthouse at the sentencing of the Pensacola Four. (Courtesy of the *Pensacola News Journal.* Photo by Richard Hammond.)

there appeared to be more people than had attended the trial. There were fewer familiar press representatives and out-of-town supporters of the defendants, which suggested that the vast majority of attendees were family and friends of the defendants. Glancing around, I[1] saw individuals I had not seen at the trial, some of whom could not attend because they were subpoenaed witnesses. David Del Gallo and his wife, for example, were chatting with a small group of people. Lindell Ballenger was wandering from one small cluster to another, spending a few minutes with each like a minister with his before-church crowd. The four defendants moved nervously between groups, seeming to work hard at appearing relaxed and unworried.

When the doors opened, the spectators moved quickly to find good seats. This courtroom was much larger than the room where the trial had been held, probably two to three times as large. Still the crowd began filling it, so the marshal directed the press to use the jury box to accommodate everyone in the room. Sitting adjacent to the prosecution's table, I had a clear view of the defendants, paired on the first bench on the opposite side of the center aisle. Nearest me, on the aisle, was Kaye Wiggins in a red and white striped dress. She appeared jauntier, less demure and sober, than she had seemed during most of the trial. Her makeup had returned, and she wore stylish white stockings. She clutched a small pocket New Testament of the type that legend holds to have deflected enemy bullets during World War II. She leaned against Matt Goldsby's shoulder and pointed out to him several passages in the Bible. The coatless Goldsby wore a dark brown shirt and a light tan tie and pants. Next to him sat James Simmons in a light blue shirt and dark blue tie. Beyond him and clasping his hand, Kathren Simmons was clad in a ruffled, light blue dress. Although she had normally worn glasses during the trial, she appeared this time without them, which made her look less reserved and withdrawn.

All the attorneys looked the same as they had more than a month prior except Patrick Monaghan, who was now wearing a red tie and bright red suspenders, which, he later told reporters, he hoped would recall visions of William Jennings Bryan and the Scopes trial. Missing today was Thomas Dillard. Susan Novotny and someone I did not recognize—a short, slim male—sat at the prosecution table.

The single, loud rap came at the door near the judge's bench, followed by the ritual command "All rise . . . ," and Roger Vinson entered the room. After everyone was seated again, he asked if any of the defense attorneys had any comments before he pronounced sentence.

Paul Shimek approached the lectern and requested that errors in the presentencing report on Kaye Wiggins be corrected. After the third or fourth citation of a minor correction, Judge Vinson stopped Shimek and told him these were all inconsequential alterations with little or no bearing on the sentencing issue at hand.

Shimek conceded and shifted to the statement in the report that said Jimmy Simmons had said that Kaye knew about the planned bombings around September 1. He pointed out that Wiggins had denied this. He went on to stress that the defendants "are trusting, teaching, humble," and he requested probation for both women.

Christine Kasun followed Shimek to the lectern and contended softly but earnestly, "Kathy's involvement was peripheral and motivated by the love of her husband and the love of God." Mitigating factors in Kathy's case, Kasun asserted, were her age and the facts that she had no prior record, she did not initiate the bombings, and, again, her involvement was peripheral. Furthermore, Kasun maintained, "Since she has shown remorse and is unlikely to repeat the act, she should be placed on probation. May God guard Your Honor in your judgment."

Frank Booker, next at the lectern, asked for the formal dismissal of counts two and three of the original indictment, which dealt with the June 25 bombing and had been dismissed "with prejudice" at the opening of the trial and thus could be reinstituted for a second trial. He argued that the defendants, now convicted, should not have those counts hanging over them, that the case should end here, this day. "Sometimes," he continued, "I think I should have stayed home and planted my corn crop on time." After a pause, he returned to the issue at hand. "The range of the court's discretion is so broad, up to sixty-five years. That is your burden. There are many questions I am sure you have considered: how the defendants would react to leniency; how leniency may encourage others."

Referring to the defendants as "youngsters," Booker recommended they all be given suspended sentences and placed on probation for five years. In support he cited that 26 percent of those guilty of the same crime had received probation. "Prison," he said, "is for the most vicious and antisocial persons. I am afraid for my client; he would be a natural target inside those places. I fear these boys may be eaten alive. He is in the critical years of his marriage. Does my client sincerely repent?" As if unmindful of the news conference two hours earlier, he answered his own question: "He has said, 'Do not as we have done.'"

Using military illustrations, as he had done during the trial, he cited the dilemma of Admiral "Bull" Halsey during the battle of the Philippine Sea when his carrier planes attacked the Japanese fleet at the outer edge of their range: "The American planes were returning to the carriers, it was growing dark, and the planes were running out of gas. Moreover, the American fleet was within range of the Japanese planes." Halsey's dilemma, Booker indicated, was whether to place first priority on the safety of the fleet or on the return of the planes. "But," he concluded, "Halsey endangered the fleet by heading into the wind and turning on the landing lights. I plead with Your Honor to steer against the wind and turn on the lights."

In his friendly, almost folksy manner, Monaghan rose and softly asked, "Is there any particular area in which I can assist the court?"

"No," Roger Vinson replied with a smile. "I am thoroughly familiar with it all, I believe."

Undaunted, speaking more forcefully and less deferentially, Monaghan began his statement. "There is the possibility of tragedy here. These are crystal-clean boys, and that is in conflict with their act. It would be a tragic raft trip for them to go into the system. I would rather they have forty years under Your Honor than four under the bureaucracy [of the prison system]." He then requested that, if they must be incarcerated, the defendants be placed in a level-two, as opposed to a level-three, facility.[2] He went on to request that Judge Vinson designate a particular prison and specific level of prison to maximize their chances of being placed in a less dangerous prison.

"They are not terrorists," he contended. "They did not aim themselves at people, at persons. These boys have been caught and incarcerated. At the trial they were first described by the prosecution as lying, conniving conspirators. Then the defense presented them as Christians first and later as insane. Then the prosecution argued that they were not insane but Christians. And, finally, we said, 'You're right.'

"Don't," he pleaded, "cut them loose on that raft in these waters. We ask the court to determine that no serious bodily injury was intended [which the Bureau of Prisons would have to take into consideration in assigning them to a facility] and designate a level-one or -two facility and a split sentence.

"You," he concluded, "are the patriarch, the father figure. The boys are with you."

Judge Vinson then asked the defendants if there was anything they wished to say. Only Matthew Goldsby rose and addressed the court. Slumped and propped on one stiff leg, both hands on the lectern, he said, "Dr. Cepeda said I would be capable of repeating [the crime] if I were not severely punished. He does not . . . the government knows neither my mind or my heart. I assure the court I would not again do this."

Susan Novotny stood before her table and began her arguments. "It has been the strategy of the defense since the opening of the trial to refer to the defendants as 'boys,' 'kids,' 'Huck Finn,' and 'Tom Sawyer.'

They are not kids. They are all adults by any and every definition. They did an adult act, and they deserve an adult sentence.

"They say, now, 'Never again.' But when they were first arrested, they were proud of what they had done.

"There are other issues—nightclub ordinances, books, movies. Do we want someone taking the law into their own hands on those, too?

"It is almost trite to say it, but we are a land of laws. There are ways to indicate that laws are incorrect: civil disobedience. They chose a different way."

She then enumerated the conditions of civil disobedience: first, no innocent person is damaged; second, they (the law violators) need the law themselves, they seek out the law.

Throughout these opening comments Kaye Wiggins, grim and tight-lipped, glared at Novotny. Unaware, Novotny continued: "In civil disobedience the purity of their statement is in what happens after the law is violated. The defendants were going to take the law into their own hands, contrary to their legal, social, and Christian beliefs. They planned, executed, and reacted to avoid detection and first denied responsibility.

"In addition, there was just under one million dollars in damage. They say they attempted not to injure. But what would have happened to some innocent passerby? What about the danger faced by the firemen?

"There should be a sentence commensurate with the offense. Send a message to the community. The nation is watching this trial. Indeed, the world is watching."

Stating that he had to say one more thing, Paul Shimek commented, "We are in spiritual warfare, a war between God and Satan. If we are not careful, the forces of darkness will prevail. Our country is in trouble. Our people perish for a lack of knowledge."

When Shimek finished, Judge Vinson asked the defendants to stand immediately before him. They assembled, hands clasped in front of them. Behind each of them, his or her attorney stood, and to the right of all of them stood the two prosecuting attorneys.

Roger Vinson spoke, "I have received letters from all over the United States. It is an important case, but every sentence is important.

"Kaye Wiggins, you have been found guilty of conspiracy. I sentence you to five years and a two-thousand dollar fine to be paid at a minimum of fifty dollars a month." He then mentioned the legal provisions for sentencing defendants to make restitution but added that he did not feel that would be viable in Wiggins's case. He concluded her sentence by stating, "Jail sentence to be suspended and you are to be placed on probation for the term."

Turning to Kathren Simmons, he cited the same sentence for her as for Wiggins.

He then said, "James Simmons, you have been found guilty. . . . On counts four, five, six, seven, eight, and nine, I sentence you to ten years, to be served concurrently." As he said this, Kathren Simmons and Kaye Wiggins began crying softly. "On count one, I sentence you to five years. The sentence is to be suspended, and you will be placed on probation for that period following your release. You will make restitution in the amount of $353,073.66, to be paid at a minimum of one hundred dollars per month beginning sixty days from your release."

Anticlimactically, he issued the identical sentence to Matthew Goldsby. But he continued, "I think it is important that they be in a facility as close as possible to Pensacola. The one at Tallahassee [a level two] has no space. The next nearest level-two facility is in Texas. Therefore, I am recommending a level one, and specifically Eglin Air Force Base. I am also going to recommend that they be given parole consideration under the youthful-offender guidelines. As there is, I feel, some danger of flight, I will set bond at fifty thousand dollars, which can be made on three personal sureties. You may surrender to the U.S. marshal here or at the Eglin Air Force Base facility at noon, June 17. I will also recommend that you be considered for release at the minimum of the guideline period or earlier."

Grins spread over the faces of the defendants' supporters throughout the courtroom. As the defense attorneys turned back from the bench following the judge's exit, they were smiling elatedly.

Downstairs on the sidewalk, John Burt and Joseph Scheidler were huddled with groups of reporters, while Baby Charlie rested again in his jar atop the newspaper rack and their followers were talking animatedly among themselves. Sharon Glass commented, "It [the verdict] was God's doing. It proves that He answers prayers."

About thirty minutes later, after posting bond on the signatures of David and Shere Del Gallo and Lindell Ballenger and making arrangements with the Bureau of Prisons personnel inside, the four defendants exited the courthouse together. As they stepped out the brass doors at the top of the steps, grinning broadly, spontaneous applause broke out among their supporters and some reached out to touch them or pat their backs.

# The National Context of Violence

 . . . Part . . . Three . . .

# . . . 13
# The
# National
# Roll
# Call

Whom shall I send, and who will go for us?
Isaiah 6:8

The story had ended for many. Several of the guilty had been caught, tried, and sentenced. They would now have the rest of their lives to feel the effects of what they had done, to reflect on the value of it. Their families would try to pick up the pieces of their lives, try to resume a semblance of normality out of the public eye. The reporters moved on to their next event, to the new issue in a new place.

But we, the sociologist and anthropologist, were left with many unanswered questions. Although the sentences given the defendants were found acceptable in most social groups in the community, we wondered how comparable they were to those levied elsewhere in similar cases. We understood much of the background of these defendants, including their place in the larger circle of anti-abortion activism, but we wondered about commonalities between this case and others. Were patterns of Christian conviction involved to the same degree in other cases? Were other bombers and arsonists inspired by common political and activist literature? Was the Pensacola case exceptional, and is this the reason national anti-abortion activists had worked to exploit the trial as an event? As students of human behavior, we were moved to seek patterns in the mosaic, to discover the rhythmic pulse of order in the seemingly disorderly.

Our questions extended beyond the bombings and the bombers to the community and the nation. The Pensacola Four represented to us a sign of a conflict of ideas and values for which simple resolutions seemed elusive. What real effect might the sentences have toward reducing abortion-related violence in our community or elsewhere? Were the prosecutors' arguments for stiff sentences valid, and were they really satisfied? Even if the sentences had been stronger, would that deter other bombings? Was the reception of the bombers in their community motivated by personal concern for them as individuals, or was the trial seen as a kind of vindication of their motives, if not their acts? Are we to believe that activists motivated by Christian love could feel fully repentant under the judgment of secular law? Would the trial itself end the abortion controversy in Pensacola, or would the notoriety and apparently exceptional features of the case merely make Pensacola a target for other activists? Can we say that the judgment of the trial resolved anything, or, in the end, were the contending factions simply allowed to continue speaking past one another? The different cultures and ideologies that met in this case reflect a certain madness, born in ethnocentrism and personal interests. But even in madness social scientists seek the order, the pattern, the structure behind the events. We had to assume that the bombings, the burnings, and the invasions of abortion clinics and doctors' offices were not random events, but that a pattern and a structure lay within and beneath them.

Some question whether the order social scientists find is in the real world or a fabrication of mind, an order to which the chaos of reality unwillingly and reluctantly bends its head. To be sure, as social scientists we formally view the social world through different constructs than those of commonsense visions of society—visions that dominate the everyday assessments of lawyers, media representatives, politicians, the unobtrusive public, activists, and university professors. But we also know that formal constructs, far from forcing events and meanings into a hostile framework, enable us to see patterns and contradictions clearly. Social scientists seek truth in processes very different from those of the legal proceedings we have just described. Because they are not founded in the "commonsense" view, the interpretations of social scientists transform the ordinary world into a subject matter in which no particular moral or legal vision is given preeminent weight. In such a context we may not always find "good" or "bad" neatly sorted by community or belief.

Whatever the vehicle through which structure is represented, the "real" world is quite a different thing from any construction of it. Our task is to understand the different views of social order in Pensacola, in its national context of cultural plurality, and represent some of the potentials of the whole. Thus, our vision of "order" implies a heterogeneity that, once found and understood, may offer comfort to us, or may as easily open crucial questions deserving of attention by the different cultural groups that make up America.

In seeking the structure of behavior, sociologists have frequently invoked the stage as a useful model. The rationale is that human behavior in real life resembles that of the actors in a drama. But actors are not usually completely their own people, not free to construct their own lines as they go. They have the constraints of a script, within which they have limited freedoms of expression and interpretation.

For the sociologist, our culture provides "scripts."[1] They tell us how we should behave and act in everyday life situations. One aspect of culture is values, or attitudes and beliefs about how things *should* be— for example, how a man should behave in contrast to how a woman should behave. And the stage on which we act out our culture's scripts is our own society.

Therefore, to understand the bombings, to discover the structure, if any, behind them, we look first at the major incidents themselves and ask if there is a specific part of the stage on which the actors have played their roles and, if so, why. Second, we examine the known "actors," those who have committed violent acts, to discover if there are commonalities among them. Finally, we examine the current condition of Western culture, the conflicting scripts set before people today.

## The Nature of Violence

What about the other places across the country where abortion-related violence has occurred? Is the Pensacola experience unique? Or are there similarities from which we make generalizations about the Pensacola violence and that of other communities?

The problem starts with the question, What is violence? There is a continuum of behavior that may be called "violence." We may begin to define it as the use of force against property or persons. But property, like violence, may be broadly defined. For example, theft of an object is an act of violence. And so also is the damaging of a person's reputation, since one's reputation or "good name" is a legally recognized item of valuable property. Thus, when twenty-one anti-abortionists broke into a Wilmington, Delaware, clinic, invaded its operating rooms, stole pieces of the suction machines, and damaged other equipment, they committed an act of violence. Similarly, when protesters have taken license plate numbers, located the homes and workplaces of patients, and then called family and employers to accuse the patients of being baby-killers, that is an act of violence.

The number and extent of acts of such violence, broadly defined, is beyond the scope of our ability to research. However, some insight into the national patterns of abortion-related violence may be revealed by examining the most extreme cases, those in which the perpetrators are more readily available for examination. Thus, we will limit our discussion of abortion-related violence to the known cases of arson, bombing, "drastic" destruction of property, and intent to physically harm other persons, in which the perpetrators have sought to evade detection and punishment, which takes them outside the realm of civil disobedience.

As Novotny explained in the trial, true civil disobedience requires a fundamental respect for the law and, by implication, the existing social system. Thus, those engaged in civil disobedience may violate a law, but they wait for arrest, even seek arrest and trial, to make public and dramatize their judgment that a law is unjust. In addition, they typically try not to injure persons or property. In fact, one primary tactic of civil protesters may be to become the *objects* of violence to dramatize their cause.

Another distinction between anti-abortion protesters and the civil rights movement activists is that the latter were predominantly the personal victims of unjust laws. Of course, the anti-abortionists maintain that abortion victims are defenseless fetuses who cannot defend themselves. Moreover, protesters in the civil rights movement were seeking *access* to and *expansion* of choices, while the anti-abortionists are seeking to *limit* choices of others.

Classical civil disobedience also involves violating the specific law that is considered unjust. In the case of abortion, however, one of the dilemmas of the anti-abortion movement is that there is no way to violate a law giving persons freedom of choice.

On the other hand, one anti-abortion spokesman, Nat Hentoff, a columnist for the *Washington Post* and the *Village Voice*, compares the anti-abortion movement with the abolitionist movement, rather than with the civil rights movement. The abolitionists and the anti-abortionists, he maintains, are seeking to change the U.S. Constitution. He equates the fetus with a slave, since, he argues, *Roe v. Wade* and *Doe v. Bolton* effectively make the fetus a property of the potential mother. He goes further to equate the violent wing of the anti-abortion movement with John Brown in the abolitionist movement (Hentoff 1989).

In our examination of what types of persons commit abortion-related violence, we will limit ourselves to the cases in which the offenders have been arrested, tried, and convicted.

### The Frequency of Abortion-Related Violence

As shown in table 1, during the years 1977–80, while Jimmy Carter was president, 12.8 percent of the major abortion-related violent incidents occurred, while 75 percent of the incidents since 1976 took place during Ronald Reagan's second term in office, the years 1984–87.

One reason for this dramatic increase may lie in the demise of the ERA as an issue and a shift in the religious Right's attention to abortion. Abortion was a ready-made attention getter, for the "targets"— doctors' offices and clinics—are visible and public. However, the change in presidencies initially made little difference in the rates of violence. Major differences between Carter and Reagan on abortion, women's rights, birth-control education, sex education, and other family and sex-role issues became immediately apparent as the Reagan administration established itself. The dramatic increase in violent acts

toward abortion facilities during Reagan's second term cannot be ignored or discounted, but the association of Reagan policies with the
violence is both indirect and subtle.[2]

From 1977 through 1983 there were "only" 24 cases of arsons and
bombings. However, in 1984 the number suddenly jumped to 30 cases.
After 1984, cases dropped gradually each year through 1987 but remained at well above the pre-1984 average of 3.4 per year. From 1977
through 1983, then, the average number of incidents was 3.4 per year,
while the next four years produced an average of 19.5 cases per year—
a 570 percent increase. How can we explain this rapid and lasting
explosion of violent incidents?

We maintain that a key factor was the ideological interpretation of
the reelection of Ronald Reagan in the fall of 1984. The Moral Majority
had taken credit for Reagan's victory in 1980 and thus was encouraged
by Reagan's outspoken support for Moral Majority positions, including
its anti-abortion stance. But despite the administration's support for
such proposals as a Fetal Life Amendment and a School Prayer

**Table 1. Frequency of Abortion-related Arsons
and Bombings, 1977–87**[3]

| Year | No. | % |
| --- | --- | --- |
| 1977 | 5 | 4.9 |
| 1978 | 7 | 6.9 |
| 1979 | 1 | 1.0 |
| 1980 | 0 | 0.0 |
| 1981 | 2 | 2.0 |
| 1982 | 7 | 6.9 |
| 1983 | 2 | 2.0 |
| 1984 | 30 | 29.4 |
| 1985 | 22 | 21.6 |
| 1986 | 14 | 13.7 |
| 1987 | 12 | 11.8 |
| Total | 102 | 100.2 |

Source: National Abortion Federation. The percentages add
up to more than 100 due to rounding.

Amendment, no significant change had occurred in abortion availability or other areas of the radical Right's agenda.[4]

Many people have categorically rejected the notion that Reagan's public "presence" on the abortion issue can be related to the instances of violence at any time. Our point is not to cast Reagan as leading a "call to violence" but to cite the effects of Reagan's failure to issue a call *against* violence in the context of the ideological struggle that intensified after the 1984 election. Reagan's reelection was interpreted by Jerry Falwell and others of the religious Right as a renewed mandate for their positions, despite research which demonstrates that the majority of Americans do not support their positions and did not vote on that basis. We maintain that this interpretation of the election, coupled with the administration's vocal support, led some extremists to violence because of the material failure of their causes. On the abortion front, frustration over the ineffectiveness of picketing, coupled with Reagan's widely publicized statement that "something must be done," apparently placed many abortion activists in a situation wherein the pace of change did not match their perception of the national will. Moreover, extreme elements of the radical Right could find in Reagan's public statements justifications for violent actions. This clearly was a strong motivating force for Matt Goldsby and Jimmy Simmons.

Sociologists call such results reactions of "relative deprivation."[5] When a group with rising expectations perceives a "tolerable gap" between their goals and real conditions, they usually continue to operate "within the system" toward changes they deem necessary. When rising expectations are met with a reduced perception that goals are being realized, then an "intolerable gap" between goals and perceived success exists, producing a sense of political deprivation. Under these conditions, more radical efforts toward the enactment of social goals tend to emerge. From this viewpoint, the relatively low numbers of bombings and arsons from 1979 through 1981 may be associated with the religious Right's expectations that the Reagan administration would quickly enact an end to open abortion. When this did not happen, the violence returned to the levels of the earlier Carter years. In this context, the flurry of liberal postelection studies contradicting the claims of the Moral Majority after each of Reagan's elections may

**Figure 1. Violence against Abortion Providers, 1977–91**

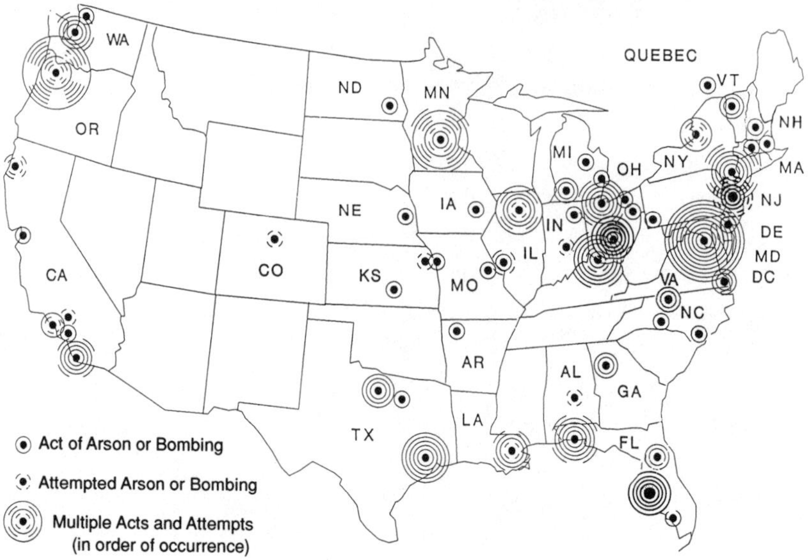

Source: National Abortion Federation.

be seen as partially contributory to the increase in violent acts in 1982 and the dramatic increase in bombings and arsons in 1984. Reagan's role was the unwitting encouragement of aspirations of the religious Right, creating frustration inasmuch as the agenda was not delivered.

In addition to a change in the numbers of arsons and bombings, a change also occurred in where the violence was taking place (see fig. 1 and table 2). From 1977 through 1981, all but one case of extreme violence took place in "inland" (noncoastal) states. From 1982 to 1985, coastal states were the sites of most bombings, including all 30 of the 1984 incidents. From 1985 to 1987, there was a gradual decline in the frequency of bombings in coastal states, accompanying the gradual reduction in bombings and arsons already discussed.

How can we explain these kinds of changes? Some research has shown that the states on the East and West coasts are more liberal in their attitudes toward abortion.[6] The same could be said of Gulf of Mexico coastal areas in comparison to their nearby inland areas. When we look at the cities where the major incidents took place, we also discover that many of those in the coastal states—Houston; Washing-

## Table 2. Coastal/Noncoastal Distribution of Serious Violence, 1977–87

| Year | No. | % Noncoastal | % Coastal |
|---|---|---|---|
| 1977 | 5 | 100.0 | 0.0 |
| 1978 | 7 | 100.0 | 0.0 |
| 1979 | 1 | 0.0 | 100.0 |
| 1980 | 0 | 0.0 | 0.0 |
| 1981 | 2 | 100.0 | 0.0 |
| 1982 | 7 | 25.0 | 75.0 |
| 1983 | 2 | 0.0 | 100.0 |
| 1984 | 30 | 0.0 | 100.0 |
| 1985 | 22 | 36.4 | 63.6 |
| 1986 | 14 | 64.3 | 35.7 |
| 1987 | 12 | 90.9 | 9.1 |
| Total | 102 | 42.2 | 57.8 |

Source: National Abortion Federation.

ton, D.C.; Baton Rouge; Everett and Bellingham (Washington)—are slightly inland from the coast.[7]

The coastal zone not only includes many larger urban centers but also is home to the majority of the U.S. population.[8] For this reason, the coastal areas tend to be seats of more "liberal" or cosmopolitan people. These areas tend to have many immigrant and ethnic enclaves and the majority of the nation's military bases, adding to their cosmopolitan nature. Perhaps the greater liberalism as well as greater urbanization in the coastal states[9] calls forth a more desperate reaction from its opponents, especially from those who live by a more traditional worldview, who are deeply offended by behavior that denies the validity of their orientation to kin and tradition.[10]

Four aspects of the data in table 2 fit well with our hypothesis of relative deprivation, again linking changes in pattern to the events of the 1980 and 1984 elections and Ronald Reagan's public statements on the abortion issue. First, at the beginning and end of the period observed, inland bombings and arsons are at comparable levels, between 5 and 10 incidents per year. Second, the relatively lower frequency of inland bombings from 1979 to 1983 reflects two distinct periods. The period from 1979 to 1981 was, as already noted, Reagan's period of campaigning and his first year in office, the honeymoon, a time of high expectations among the religious Right. The differentiation of coastal and noncoastal bombings during these years is uninformative because of the low numbers involved. Third, however, we note that the resumption and intensification of bombings from 1982 through 1984 was concentrated on the coasts, with the heaviest concentration in the New York–Washington, D.C., area, precisely in areas that would draw the strongest national media attention. It was at the end of this period that the Pensacola bombings occurred, followed by Reagan's first public statement against abortion-related violence in January 1985. Fourth, then, we consider the gradual reduction of coastal bombings in subsequent years to be a consequence of Reagan's transformation in public posture. Coastal bombings and arsons are significant because of the media exposure they generate. Violent acts in major cities, especially in the Washington, D. C., area, evoke strong public responses precisely because they are inconsistent with the dominant ethos of those communities. Violence against "immoral" activity in rural communities is more easily written off by the national media as reflecting local norms and thus creates far less pressure on government to hear religious demands on the abortion issue.

Another explanation of the locational trends in table 2 for the period beginning in 1985 lies in the reaffirmation of less violent methods by prominent anti-abortion activists. This change in tactics is exemplified by the growth of Operation Rescue, a national effort organized in 1988 to fully enact the ninety-nine principles set down by Joseph Scheidler (1985).[11] While questions still exist about the extent to which Operation Rescue strategy represents civil disobedience, the leaders of the national anti-abortion movement have clearly attempted to distanced themselves from bombings and arsons, calling them the acts of a few isolated zealots. To this may be added the fact that national coverage of their trials and convictions in 1985 left little doubt that bombers and arsonists would not be dealt with lightly. The media coverage also seriously damaged the credibility of the anti-abortion movement during that period, since the entire movement tended to be linked with the violence. Operation Rescue concentrated its efforts in large urban areas, providing a relief valve for expressing anti-abortion sentiments in ways that fell far short of bombing or arson. Thus, the pressure on clinics remains strong but has taken a form more palatable to the public and more useful to those in the Reagan-Bush administrations sympathetic with anti-abortion goals. The bombings and arsons, of course, make actions such as those taken by Operation Rescue appear less radical than they might have appeared without the violence.[12]

Few perpetrators of violence against abortion clinics were brought to justice before 1982. Since that time, bombers have been tried and convicted in Florida, Virginia, Washington, Delaware, Maryland, Washington, D.C., Louisiana, Illinois, New York, California, Minnesota, and Ohio. Five states account for thirty unsolved bombings and arsons between 1982 and 1987: California, Minnesota, Ohio, Oregon, and Texas. It is likely that a few individuals are responsible for multiple acts in each of these states, especially given the concentrations of incidents in certain cities (San Diego, Minneapolis–St. Paul, Toledo, Portland, and Houston).

The incidents in which the perpetrator was arrested, tried, and convicted illuminate questions about the backgrounds and motivations of individual bombers and arsonists.[13] Our information, collected in many instances directly from the perpetrators themselves, also suggests some underlying commonalities. As we turn to a review of others involved in violent actions against abortion clinics, we note that Matt Goldsby and Jimmy Simmons are the youngest central characters on the national roll call to be convicted of such actions. But the first person ever arrested was also twenty-one years old.

### Hempstead, New York: Peter Burkin

On February 15, 1979, twenty-one-year-old Peter Burkin became the first person arrested and tried for abortion clinic arson when he carried a container of gasoline and a torch into a clinic in Hempstead, New York—the first abortion facility opened in the United States following the 1973 *Roe v. Wade* Supreme Court decision. Charged with five counts of attempted murder and two arson counts, as well as reckless endangerment, he was eventually acquitted of attempted murder and one arson charge and found not guilty by reason of insanity on charges of setting a fire and reckless endangerment. A testifying psychiatrist asserted that Burkin had "developed somewhat of a messianic complex."[14] Both defense and prosecuting psychiatrists agreed that he was schizophrenic, although other psychiatrists held that he was not insane.

In a statement to us, Burkin maintained that he was attempting to "take hostages or, as I preferred to see it, make a 'citizen's arrest.'" As he put it, he was trying for "a great, massive publicity stunt" to publicize his theory that personality is lodged in the embryo. He had tried to get pro-lifers to take up the theory, but "to them, its [sic] irreligious, too complicated, and irrelevant—they think they got the 'proof' already."

Burkin describes himself as a "fake" terrorist; that is, he did not have a real weapon (only fifty cents' worth of gasoline) and he did not have the intention to use it. But he felt he had to convince the authorities and clinic personnel that it was real and that he could use it in order to achieve his aims.

Burkin's own account of the incident is interesting in itself:

I entered the clinic at about 5:00 P.M., lit the torch in the foyer, had to strip some of the paper from it so that it was not a large flame (though it was still bigger than I expected), and burst into the waiting room. In a near panic myself, I yelled, "Everyone out or this place is going up!" No one moved, instead they merely stared at me. I yelled again in a clearer and louder voice (I had a phobia about not being taken seriously), "Everyone out or this place is going up—I got gas!" while pointing to the door leading to the corridor which led to the rear exit. I stayed by the foyer door leading to the front exit, ready to turn and run if I had to, and waited until the last girl was through the corridor door before I started in that direction. I figured on entering an office off the corridor, surprising the people inside, closing the door, and forcing them to the other end of the room where I'd keep them at bay during the siege. Instead, just as I got through the corridor door, a husband of a nurse came out of an office and started towards me. I immediately stopped, raised the can and torch in the air to give him a good look, and yelled, "Get back, I got gas!" He was about ten feet away, perhaps more, and started back, upon which I started to take a step forward. Suddenly he lunged forward. Constricted in large part by the corridor door (which opened in the foyer and which I was more or less holding my leg against) my first instinct, rather than throwing the torch (for my arm was still held high and the only direction I could've thrown the torch was right at the husband of the nurse) I started back-peddling [*sic*], and almost immediately found myself falling backwards, my left foot trapped between the door and door frame as the door was slammed shut on me. Gasoline was spilled as I fell, a huge flame shot out from the can about a foot in front of my face, and I found myself flat on my back, seemingly engulfed in flames. I got up, turned, ran out of the building, and dived into the snow, rolling over several times in order to extinguish the flames.

About half an hour later a cop found me hiding in an alley only a few blocks away from the clinic. Of course, no one, aside from myself, was injured, though the clinic did burn down—which to my mind is no great loss.


Burkin says that as a teenager he became more and more religious and interested in the issues of world hunger and abortion. On hearing a philosopher on the "Dick Cavett Show" say that abortion was acceptable since fetuses do not have minds, it struck him that, since the embryo has the coding or instructions for forming mind, it was essentially the same thing as mind itself. Believing that the pro-lifers were botching the job of convincing the public of the humanness of the fetus, he set about his dramatic deed.

Burkin once said, speaking of himself, that he "is said to be schizophrenic, but I don't really think he is." He later said that he meant this comment humorously. He was and is unmarried, a self-described loner. He was reared as a Lutheran by parents who had themselves been reared as Russian Orthodox, but he was not particularly active in a church as an adult—even though he describes himself as very religious.

When asked how he perceived Ronald Reagan's attitude toward the bombings and arsons, he responded, "No doubt he understands the motives of the people responsible and regards the actions as a natural response to the brutality which takes place in such clinics every day."

## Minneapolis, Minnesota: David Corum

On October 28, 1981, David J. Corum, twenty-six years old, walked into the Meadowbrook Women's Clinic in Minneapolis. In his hand was an attaché case with a wire leading from it to his wrist. He told the receptionist that he had a firebomb in the case and would set it off if the clinic did not close for the day. Corum handed her a note repeating his demand and then sat down. The receptionist called the police, who came and talked with Corum. About two hours later, after examining the building and the attaché case and finding no bomb anywhere, they took him into custody.

Apparently Corum was expecting his former girlfriend to come to the clinic for an abortion that day and was trying to stop her. He was placed in a first-offender diversion program for a year, and his case was dismissed a year later.

## Granite City, Illinois: Anderson and the Moores

In January 1983, forty-two-year-old Don Benny Anderson and two brothers—Wayne A. Moore, eighteen, and Matthew M. Moore, twenty—abducted Dr. Hector Zevallos of Granite City, Illinois, and his wife at gunpoint and held them for more than a week in an abandoned ammunition bunker. The kidnappers demanded that President Reagan issue a strong statement against abortion or they would kill the couple.

Anderson was a Mormon elder and a real estate investor from Pearland, Texas. A turning point in his life occurred in 1980 when he was convicted of real estate fraud for conning a twenty-nine-year-old widow out of her $40,000 home for $460. Fleeing the state and effectively abandoning his family, he told his wife, "I'm not going to live by their unjust laws."

Anderson's wife described him as "a very spiritual man . . . He is a very kind and generous person who has a deep-rooted love for his children. He's devoted to the principles of family life." However, some of those who knew him described him as "a difficult fellow to like."

Anderson is reported not to have been active in the abortion issue until he received orders from God and the archangel Michael.

In Pearland, Anderson had come into contact with the Moore

brothers, also from a devout Mormon family. The young men were perceived as "soft-spoken, gentle and unassuming . . . from a very religious family." Their father said, "They were good boys. They never were a problem." One of Matthew's church teachers said the boy was "a superstar, one of the most impressive young men I have ever worked with." Matthew's attorney, William Lucco, asserted, "But for this course of conduct, I think they [Matthew and Wayne] could aptly be described as all-American kids."

Handcuffed and blindfolded, the Zevalloses were continually threatened with death and Mrs. Zevallos spent the first two or three days in continual tears. Calling themselves the "Army of God," the abductors claimed God had called them to fight abortion "to the death." Zevallos later said that Matthew Moore told him "they would continue to do any kind of violence until they accomplish their objective."

The Zevalloses were released after eight days of captivity, but two weeks later the kidnappers sent a letter to the Secret Service in which they said, "We all agreed that the will of God would be carried out if they were executed. The last two days was the most trying for all. We decided that they both were to be executed, and we were planning for the procedure." However, they claimed one of their many revelations from God finally told them not to kill the pair.

The trio also stole more than $300 from the couple, and the Moore brothers later confessed to at least two other robberies of clinics for $300 and $4,000 to finance their activities. They also admitted to arson of clinics in Clearwater and St. Petersburg, Florida, in 1982 and to the 1981 bombing of a clinic in Fairfax, Virginia, where a woman was thrown to the ground by the blast and four unexploded bombs were also found.

A letter received by a Tampa television station the night of the fires in Clearwater and St. Petersburg claimed that the "Army of God" had been protected by a band of angels while setting the fires.

On the third day of the kidnapping, the culprits had taped a forty-four page "Epistle" to a filling station restroom wall and anonymously called its location to the FBI. The document said, in part, "I, God, command you to disregard the instructions of law given by the trial judge [regarding abortions]." It also called for all those who desire to follow God to "kill the baby killers."

At the sentencing following the trial, Anderson told the judge that his conviction was "persecuting those sent by God to defend life and the U.S. Constitution." He went on, "I would like to thank God for being an instrument in His hands for doing this work I am engaged in."

Anderson received a thirty-year sentence. He got an additional concurrent thirty years for setting fire to the two clinics in Florida. In the Virginia case he also received a concurrent sentence, but eight years of it must be served after his current incarceration. Wayne Moore was sentenced under the Youth Corrections Act to an indeterminate term that can be no more than four years. His brother received an eight-year sentence.

While Anderson was awaiting transfer to a federal prison, Mearl Justus, the sheriff of St. Clair County, Illinois, charged that Anderson plotted with at least one other jail inmate to have the wife of a jail official kidnapped and held until Anderson was released and had escaped. According to the sheriff, Anderson promised the inmate as much as $15,000 to get him out.

### Norfolk, Virginia: Joseph Grace

In the early morning hours of May 26, 1983, Joseph Grace, a self-employed house painter and Vietnam veteran, set fire to a clinic in Norfolk, Virginia. Grace was convinced that the Russians were going to attack the United States with atomic weapons on May 28 and was on his way to the countryside to avoid the nuclear holocaust he expected for Norfolk. He said the clinic fire was to be a symbolic gesture as he left town.

After leaving the clinic, Grace wound through the nearby subdivision. Because it was early in the morning and he was afraid the police might stop most traffic because of the fire, Grace pulled his van to the side of a street to wait for traffic to pick up so he could get lost among the other vehicles while leaving the general area.

Without realizing it, Grace pulled over just a few blocks from the clinic on a main street that ran beside the arson site. A patrolman leaving the fire investigation saw the suspicious van, checked it out, awakened Grace, noticed the odor of kerosene on Grace and in the van, and arrested him.

His lawyer, Berry Willis, claimed that Grace had embraced pessimistic and extremist views on a variety of political issues. Willis went on to say that Grace was "looking for attention" and would have found it on another issue, if not this one. For example, Grace even went to Moscow at one time to support the Pentecostalists who had sought sanctuary in the U.S. embassy there. He reported to us that he had tried to marry one of the Pentecostalist women in the embassy, but she refused.

At the trial, a psychiatrist testified that Grace had grandiose ideas and was a fanatic. In addition, the psychiatrist claimed, he had paranoid feelings.

Grace was sentenced to a twenty-year term. He requested assignment to a nonurban prison to be as far as possible from the Soviet attack he was still predicting.

### Birmingham and Huntsville, Alabama: Edward Markley

Dressed in a jogging suit and accompanied by a still-unidentified man, forty-four-year-old Reverend Edward Markley, pastor of Our Lady of the Shoals Catholic Church in Tuscumbia, Alabama, entered a Birmingham clinic on Mother's Day weekend in May 1984 shortly after a lone woman opened it at 7:25 A.M. While his companion refused to let the woman use the telephone, Father Markley wielded a sledgehammer against the surgical equipment. The damage he inflicted on three suction machines ran somewhere between $7,500 and $8,500.

When the woman asked if they were going to hurt her, the unidentified man said, "Not unless you try to stop us." When she tried to walk out of the room, he stepped in front of the door and would not let her exit. Shortly, however, he did let her go outside, where she sought help from persons in a car in the parking lot who were early for the clinic opening.

Completing their work in less than ten minutes, the men drove off. Markley, a Benedictine monk and also the Birmingham diocesan "Coordinator for Pro-life Activities," was not identified until the clinic attendant recognized his newspaper picture following his arrest for an incident in Huntsville, Alabama, in June 1984.

On Father's Day weekend Markley entered the Huntsville clinic, shoved two female employees (according to court testimony; Markley maintains the employees grabbed him while trying to stop him), and spread red paint inside the building and on some of the people there. The two employees of the Women's Community Health Center testified that they were injured in the attack. One of the employees, counselor Kathryn Wood, testified that her medical expenses came to more than $13,000 from a broken neck vertebra and back injuries she suffered when Markley shoved her.[15]

Markley's Tuscumbia church reportedly raised 70 percent of his defense funds. A reporter interviewing Markley's secretary noted a color photograph of Ronald Reagan taped to a filing cabinet beside the priest's desk. The secretary claimed the church phone had been ringing constantly with calls from Markley's supporters.

Convicted in the Huntsville incident of first-degree criminal mischief and three charges of third-degree assault and harassment, Markley testified in his own defense that he "was there to eliminate the suction machines . . . to damage them so they couldn't be used that day." Contending that he was "following the law of God," Markley said the clinic employees should not have been there and that his first contact with one of the staff "came when she jumped on me . . . and bit my nose."

The city attorney, Charles Rodenhauser, then asked, "Did you think the people at the clinic would allow you to do this?"

Markley replied, "I thought I would be able to get in and do it before I would be apprehended."

"They were out of line," Rodenhauser inquired, "trying to stop you?"

"Yes," said Markley.

Markley was sentenced to a year and a day on the mischief conviction and thirty days on each of the assault convictions. His prison sentences were suspended, and the judge ordered him placed on five years' unsupervised probation. In addition, he was ordered to pay $2,402.65 in restitution to the employees for loss of wages.

Immediately following his conviction, Markley told a group of about thirty supporters, "We got our word out . . . and we're going to do better." Markley was quoted as saying of the restitution, "I won't pay. . . . Believing what I believe . . . to pay them restitution to fix their carpet to get them back going good, that's a joke. . . . If somebody was after you with a gun and you broke it, do you think you should pay for it?" However, his attorney said the restitution would be paid for the priest by someone else.

Following Markley's arrest for the Birmingham incident, his bishop, Joseph Vath, issued a statement citing Markley as a good priest and pastor. Vath went on to condemn violence but added, "If one is convinced that abortion is the taking of human life according to God's revealed Word, he is not acting unjustly according to God's law in defending the innocent unborn ones." Markley maintains that the bishop and his superiors may have preferred that he not be as "activist" as he was, but that they understood his motives and supported him.

The clinic director, Virginia Volker, complained about the anti-abortionists' trying to force their religious beliefs on others. Scott Houser, organizer of the demonstrations at the clinic, responded, "One's religious beliefs are merely his opinion. These are not my views; these are God's views that are objectively revealed to us in scripture."

Charged with first-degree criminal mischief and second-degree burglary in the Birmingham case, Markley told reporters just prior to this second trial that he should be acquitted because he was guided by a higher authority.

After a short trial, the jurors took one hour to return a guilty verdict on both counts. At the later sentencing hearing, the prosecutor argued that a prison term would do the priest good. Markley told the judge that his conviction was a mistake, that he was justified in doing what he had.

The judge sentenced Markley to two consecutive five-year terms, to be served on probation. Judge J. Richmond Pearson also ordered that during demonstrations Markley should remain at least five hundred yards from any clinic that performs abortions anywhere in the United States. Under Alabama law, if Markley were convicted of a third felony, he would receive a mandatory fifteen-year minimum sentence. The judge also ordered him to pay damages of approximately $2,300.

Sentenced in July, Markley was appointed by the bishop in August as director of retreats and abbey guestmaster at St. Bernard Abbey in Cullman, Alabama. However, he remained in his diocesan post in charge of pro-life activities.

In January 1986, when Markley helped organize several demonstrations and again picketed a number of clinics, his probation was revoked and he was sentenced to spend five years in prison, with no opportunity for probation, pardon, or time off for good behavior.

When we interviewed him in prison, Markley, who holds a master's degree in sociology, said, referring to our study, "I really had not felt [that] the appropriate response for someone to the crisis of the legalization of abortion is to make a sociological study of the background of people who were activists in it or who were involved in what might be so-called violence in it." He went on to say that he had never accepted the idea of "value-free science" (science that is completely open-minded and objective).

On May 1, 1988, Edward Markley was given the "Protector Award" by Joseph Scheidler's organization, the Pro-Life Action League. In announcing the award, the league's publication, *Action News*, stated: "In giving Father Markley the Protector Award, we neither condone nor condemn the specific instance of his attack against an abortion machine. We honor him because of his strong convictions about the sanctity of life in the womb and his willingness to sacrifice personal comfort for Jesus' sake. As a man of strong faith, Father can serve as a model to all true Right-to-Life activists."[16]

### Everett and Bellingham, Washington: Curtis Beseda

Curtis Beseda was convicted of arson on November 11, 1984, and sentenced to thirty years in prison for three times setting fire to a clinic in Everett, Washington, and once to a clinic in Bellingham. Born and reared in a nearby small town, Beseda had been a regular picketer at the Feminist Women's Health Center in Everett. Other picketers claimed that Beseda had helped calm them when they had gotten upset during their demonstrations. His attorney, Thomas Hillier, described him as a "loner."

In his defense, Beseda claimed that abortion was "the greater of two evils [as opposed to arson]" and that he had done what he had out of Christian love.[17]

## Washington, D.C., Area: Bray, Spinks, and Shields

In January 1985 Michael Donald Bray, Thomas Eugene Spinks, and Kenneth William Shields, all in their thirties, were charged with eight bombings in Virginia, Maryland, and Washington, D.C. Damages to the various targets and nearby buildings, including inhabited apartments, exceeded $1 million. Bray is a former Naval Academy midshipman and a sometime house painter, once an American Lutheran lay minister and later copastor of the independent Reformation Lutheran Church in Bowie, Maryland. He was also a member of the Pro-Life Non Violent Action League, although he and his companions had planned at least three additional bombings. Bray's brother, Daniel, is cochairman of the Defenders of the Defenders of Life[18] organization, which published the open letter to Judge Roger Vinson and the prosecutors of the Pensacola Four.

Spinks and Shields were arrested a day or two before Bray, who was interviewed by a reporter just after their arrests because of his activism in the local Pro-Life Non Violent Action League. Bray maintained that he knew Spinks, but not well, and that he had never heard of Shields.

Spinks ran a chimney-sweeping and roofing company in Bowie, while Shields was a comptroller for a corporation. Both were also active church members. Spinks, formerly a member of an Assemblies of God congregation, had attended Bray's church twice. Spinks's neighbors described him as a "fervent, born-again Christian" who often asked other residents if they had accepted Jesus as their savior. Otherwise, the Spinks family, including the children, did not socialize in the neighborhood. Shields had once belonged to the same Assemblies of God church as Spinks in another, nearby community.

The president of the Bowie-Crofton Right to Life chapter described the three as "hard-working family men, Christian-oriented." In Spinks's house BATF agents found hundreds of pounds of explosives, heavy pistols, rifles, shotguns, and a copy of *The Anarchist's Cookbook*, a manual on bomb construction, along with several ready-to-use bombs. In a storage warehouse rented by Spinks under the alias of Lou Burns, agents found an additional two hundred to three hundred pounds of chemicals, twenty compressed air cylinders, timers, fuses, and other bomb-making materials. During their trial, the men were characterized as "fervently religious opponents of abortion."

While Bray maintained up until his trial that he was against violence, Spinks and Shields pled guilty to the bombing conspiracy. Spinks testified against Bray, placed Bray at two of the bombings, and said Bray helped plan the other eight. Bray was sentenced to serve ten years in prison and to pay $43,782 in restitution.[19]

Following Bray's trial, Shields pleaded guilty to conspiracy in the bombings. At the court hearing, prosecutors revealed that Shields, who had a chemistry background, helped secure the materials and assemble the bombs, while Bray helped select and scout out the targeted clinics and Spinks carried out most of the actual bombings.

In our interview with him, Bray stated that he sees abortion as only one issue among a complex of political issues. He describes himself as a Christian reconstructionist.[20]

### Gaithersburg, Maryland: Arnold Ross

The same month that Bray, Spinks, and Shields were arrested, Dr. Alan J. Ross of Gaithersburg, Maryland, was charged with assaulting an anti-abortion activist with a hypodermic syringe outside Ross's office. Convicted of assault and battery and carrying a dangerous weapon with intent to injure, Ross was sentenced to one hundred hours of community service at a free medical clinic and twelve months' probation. Dr. Ross's clinic site in Bethesda, Maryland, had been the site of repeated sit-ins and picketer arrests. It was also marked by the frequent filing of charges and countercharges with the police against both picketers and NOW escorts of patients.

In an interview Ross maintained that he was "framed" and had no contact with any of the protesters, despite their regularly taking over his office and harassing his patients.[21]

### New York City: Dennis Malvasi

On the appeal of John Cardinal O'Connor of New York, Dennis John Malvasi, thirty-seven, turned himself in to the BATF office there in February 1987. Malvasi had been sought in connection with two 1986 bombings at the Eastern Women's Clinic and the Planned Parenthood Margaret Sanger Center. At the Eastern Women's Clinic, two passersby were hurt by flying glass.

The Planned Parenthood bomb consisted of fifteen sticks of dynamite, but it failed to explode. However, the blasting-cap detonator alone caused $30,000 in damage. Malvasi had reportedly posed as a person looking for office space and had gone with a rental agent to the seventh floor of the building, where Malvasi pulled a gun and handcuffed the agent to a radiator. Special Agent Robert J. Creighton of the BATF said that if the bomb had exploded the rental agent would have been killed.

Malvasi was also connected to a bombing in Queens, New York, in November 1985 and to the bombing of the Manhattan Women's Medical Center in December.

A former Marine who had fought in Vietnam, Malvasi had worked as a pyrotechnics expert during the Statue of Liberty celebration and had also been an entertainer on cruise ships. His other jobs had included emergency medical technician and ambulance driver. He used at least five aliases while avoiding arrest and had prior convictions in New York City for drug possession, assault, and weapons possession. He spent two years in jail on firearms charges from Florida.

Apparently a very religious Catholic, Malvasi said at his sentencing that he did not want to get into trouble with the Almighty and added, "I could never do it again, not because it would be wrong with God, but because the cardinal told me not to do it again." Pleading guilty, he was sentenced to seven years in prison and five years' probation for only the Queens and Eastern Women's Center bombings.

Before his court appearance and guilty plea, Malvasi informed BATF agents of the location of his explosive supplies, consisting of seventy-eight dynamite sticks, black powder, electric detonating plastic caps, and another, undefined explosive in a mini-storage locker.

His brother-in-law, Frank Wright, a thirty-eight-year-old plumber, and Carl Cenera, thirty-one, pleaded guilty to providing Malvasi with forty-five sticks of dynamite, although BATF agents thought the two did not know what Malvasi was going to do with them. In addition, Donald Pryor, Jr., forty-five, pleaded guilty to purchasing dynamite sticks for Malvasi from Cenera, who altered the serial numbers on the sticks. Cenera was sentenced to three years in prison; Wright, to two years; and Pryor died prior to sentencing.

### Indianapolis, Indiana: Wayne Kefauver

Wayne Kefauver, forty-six-year-old head of the Pro-Life Action League of Indiana, approached a police informant in October 1986 to arrange for the firebombing of the Clinic for Women, in Indianapolis. His meetings with the informant took place over a four-month period. Reputed to be "in real estate" in a small way for an occupation, and married with at least two children (who were present in his van during one of the meetings with the informant), Kefauver pleaded guilty to solicitation to commit a crime of violence and later had his sentence reduced to ninety days, the time he had already served, and a fine of $1,500.

Kefauver was highly active in the area in anti-abortion protests. He had been arrested and sentenced to jail a number of times for trespassing and resisting arrest. In fact, he began the solicitation to bomb the clinic while in jail by approaching another inmate, who informed authorities.

### Baton Rouge, Louisiana: Newchurch, Cheshire, Jarreau, and Braud

During 1985 two Baton Rouge clinics were set on fire, the Delta Women's Clinic on October 11 and the River City Women's Clinic four days earlier. Later evidence indicated there were similar plans for the Acadian Women's Clinic, but that plot was not carried out.

Arrested and charged with those offenses were John David "J. D." Newchurch, Charles Albert Cheshire, Jr., Darrick Jarreau, and Brent Paul Braud, all from the Baton Rouge area. Jarreau and Braud pleaded guilty shortly after their arrests and agreed to testify for the prosecution.

Newchurch, twenty-six, had planned to plead innocent by reason of insanity but changed his mind and pleaded guilty. He was sentenced to four years in federal prison and more than $250,000 in restitution. At his sentencing, U.S. District Judge Frank Polozola observed, "I don't think he can get the treatment he needs and the punishment he deserves with a lesser sentence."

Polozola stated that he felt Cheshire was the most culpable of the defendants. Cheshire, also twenty-six, was sentenced to five years and almost $270,000 in restitution, while Jarreau and Braud, both twenty-three, were sentenced to two years each.

The four had created their plot following a youth meeting at The Word Fellowship, pastored by Rev. David Diamond, a vocal opponent of abortion who denied any complicity in the violence.[22] Braud and Jarreau's attorneys argued that their religious convictions had been exploited. Apparently the judge agreed, noting that their deeds were the consequence of "a certain belief through the church they attended." Newchurch's attorney, Jim Boren, stated that if he had presented the case, he would have raised the issue of David Diamond's sway over the perpetrators. Boren said, "Dave Diamond is a hell of a preacher. His name would have come up and the influence he had on them would have been discussed." Boren went on to claim that "Newchurch suffered from a schizotypical [sic] disorder and that the cumulative effect of anti-abortion rallies, lectures and picketing helped drive him to the point of arson."[23]

According to his attorney, Newchurch had set fire to the Delta Clinic, walked to a telephone, called a friend from the church, and asked for a ride home. "When he got home," Boren said, "Newchurch came out with a pail of warm water and washed the feet of his friend, saying God had instructed him to do so."[24]

According to the testimony of Jesse J. Jones, Jr., special agent of the BAFT, the four defendants met in a restaurant after a church youth meeting and planned the arsons. Braud and Jarreau, he said, were to set fire to the River City clinic, while Newchurch was to burn the Delta clinic. Jarreau and Braud succeeded in destroying the River City clinic, but Newchurch set off a security alarm at the Delta site and ran, leaving a five-gallon can of gasoline hidden in weeds behind the clinic. Four days later Newchurch came back and used that can to set fire to the clinic.

Later, Braud and Jarreau were caught in flagrante delicto, setting fire to the Acadian Women's Clinic in March 1986.

Cheshire and Newchurch admitted that they wanted to use the arsons to "increase public awareness of the abortion issue."[25] Cheshire added that he wanted to offer in evidence "articles, books, tapes and films depicting the 'pain and suffering' of abortion,"[26] but the judge would not allow it.

During his hearing, Newchurch testified that for a living he made canvas bags that he sold at a flea market. He said he was a jack-of-all-trades "who used to be a mechanic and [was] self-employed since leaving the Navy."[27]

### Toledo, Ohio: Marjorie Reed

Marjorie T. Reed, a forty-six-year-old housewife and anti-abortion activist from Toledo, Ohio, was indicted in October 1987 for arson at Toledo Medical Services in June of that year. She was also charged with two counts of making telephoned bomb threats to the Center for Choice, also in Toledo, and aiding and abetting an unidentified person in the commission of arson.

When police approached her car to arrest her, she reportedly drove into an unmarked police car as she tried to escape.

The fire was set outside the Toledo Medical Services building near a fifty-five-gallon drum of xylene, a cleaning solvent also used as an octane increaser in aviation fuel. Toledo had suffered four previous abortion-related arsons, while Cincinnati had experienced a series of similar fires on or near the dates of several of the Toledo arsons.

Marjorie Reed had previously told reporters that she becomes transformed during her protests from a soft-spoken person to a crusader. "It's just like the Holy Spirit takes me over. God calls me to be his instrument. If I must go to jail, as Peter and Paul and some of the disciples, then so be it," she said. She had previously been sentenced to more than thirty-three months in jail for abortion-related incidents.

Reed's husband is an insurance agent. A Baptist, she reportedly usually picketed with a small group calling themselves Mary Grove Catholics United for Life. Speaking of her first picketing experience about five years previously, she said she thought, "I can't believe I'm going to a place where they are killing people. I just wanted to go in there and rip them apart."

While her pastor described her as "a rather caring person, never temperamental," one of her arresting officers said, "Her actions have been growing more and more violent. . . . She is engaged in a holy war, and it's going to reach a crescendo where someone will find themselves seriously injured."

## San Diego, California: Owens, Svelmoe, Kreipal, and Sullenger

In May 1987 a number of Right to Life supporters gathered in Atlanta for training in stopping abortions. One of the main speakers at that gathering was Joseph Scheidler, who announced plans to shut down all New York City clinics on Mother's Day 1988. During that conference, attendees were lectured on how to avoid the mistakes previous bombers had made that had led to arrests and convictions. Also attending were two women from San Diego, Jo Ann Kreipal and Cheryl Sullenger, members of the Bible Missionary Fellowship there. A police investigator later said, "When those two women walked out of there, they were loaded for bear. It was clear to them that something had to be done." Indeed, by the end of that month a conspiracy began to unfold within the Bible Missionary congregation to bomb abortion clinics in the San Diego area.

Sometime in late May 1987, Cathy Saie, a woman connected to the Bible Missionary Fellowship in Santee,[28] a suburb of San Diego, contacted law enforcement personnel about a plot to bomb several abortion clinics. As a result of her information, they staked out the Alvarado Medical Center and began tailing several members of the church.

Based on Saie's information, San Diego police detectives staked out the clinic for five nights, to no avail. On the evening of July 27, 1987, one detective was back again. When nothing eventful had occurred by late evening, he went home. However, worrying about the situation, he had trouble going to sleep and went back to the site.

Between 3:00 and 3:30 A.M. a pickup truck with a camper shell and its lights off drove up to the sight. The detective saw someone get out of the truck and later get back in and drive off. A few minutes later officers called to assist stopped the truck near the interstate highway. The driver was Eric Everett Svelmoe, twenty-nine years old, wearing a black woman's wig and black makeup on his face. Inside the truck police found a .357-caliber Magnum revolver and two quick-loading clips of ammunition.

Examination of the Alvarado clinic site revealed a pipe bomb taped to a two-gallon can of gasoline under the center's stairwell. The five-minute candle fuse had been lit, but it had sputtered out before igniting the bomb.

Svelmoe, an airplane mechanic, was charged with possessing, receiving, and constructing an unregistered explosive device and carrying a firearm during the commission of a felony—the latter charge was later dropped.

Just a month before, Mayor Maureen O'Connor of San Diego had participated in the thirteenth annual Lesbian/Gay Pride Day parade. She was the first lead officer of a major American city to walk in support of gay rights, primarily because of the AIDS problem. During the march a plane towed a sign reading "Homos deserve AIDS says Owens' church"; Dorman Owens was the pastor of the Bible Missionary Fellowship in Santee.[29] Others, wearing masks of gauze, bore placards reading "O'Connor has queer friends" and "People get AIDS from contaminated fruits."

Following Svelmoe's arrest, police searched his trailer and the home of Randall and Cheryl Sullenger,[30] who, along with Svelmoe, were connected with Owens's church. Questioned about the trio and the searches, Owens said he had known the Sullengers for only three months and described them as "good people." He portrayed Svelmoe as a "very sincere, dedicated person, committed to the Christian cause." In a later interview, he described Svelmoe as "a kind, dedicated Christian and patriotic American." He added that he found it difficult to believe that Svelmoe was involved in such an episode. He said that people should not believe that his church would support such behavior. "It's unfair to identify my church for something that may have been done by one member," he said.

It was revealed that Svelmoe had previously been convicted of disobeying a court order restricting picketing at San Diego's Birth Control Institute in 1984.[31] Also, Svelmoe had his pilot's license suspended for sixty days for flying a plane with an antigay banner reading "Repent fag" without a permit during the 1985 Gay Pride Day parade.

Svelmoe, who was married with two children at the time of his arrest, became a father for the third time while in jail. His co-workers described him as a nice, quiet, young man. A neighbor said, "He never talked to anyone and stayed to himself." Another neighbor said he was known as "the minister," adding, "Each Halloween he'd hand out prayer pamphlets instead of candy to the trick-or-treaters who dropped by." In 1983 Svelmoe and his wife were disciplined by the church when it was learned that their first child was conceived prior to their wedding in that year.

At the hearing for bail for Svelmoe, a police affidavit said Svelmoe "admitted to manufacturing the device at his mobile home . . . on a Sunday afternoon, July 26, using his own tools." In response to the defense attorney's contention that Svelmoe had no prior arrest record and was not a violent person, the prosecutor introduced photos of Owens's group picketing a clinic and a Gay Pride parade. In the Gay Pride parade protest Svelmoe held a placard reading "God says stone queers."

Despite the presence and support of Pastor Owens, Associate Minister Ken Felder of the same church, and Svelmoe's parents (retired missionaries to the Philippines), Magistrate Irma Gonzalez refused bail to Svelmoe, saying she felt he was still a danger to the community.

In November 1987, a federal grand jury charged Dorman Owens and six supporters with planning the Svelmoe bombing. The indictment also charged Owens with attempting to tamper with a witness (Svelmoe).

It was later revealed that Svelmoe, after four months in jail, grew disillusioned with Owens. Evidently, Svelmoe expected Owens to see that his wife and three children were taken care of during his incarceration. However, Owens had turned a deaf ear to their needs and had suggested that Mrs. Svelmoe go on welfare. Angered, Svelmoe agreed to testify for the state, asked Owens to come see him in prison, and, in several hours of conversation over a two-day period, had worn a "wire" to record Owens's conversations with him.

In those conversations Owens urged Svelmoe not to implicate anyone else in the church. Owens also said they were at war with the courts and "we're fighting the world." In a prayer with Svelmoe, he implored, "Stop the liberals before they totally destroy us and deliver us to our enemies." Owens also told Svelmoe that people were leaving his church, "and when that happens, finances are depleted. You can't run something on a shoestring." Owens went on to say, "The only way you're going to get anything accomplished is if you go to jail. It's the only way to bring it to the public's attention. Nothing's ever been accomplished without suffering."

The assistant U.S. district attorney, Larry Burns, charged that Owens was present at two or three meetings at his church and in his home when the bomb plan was formulated. Also arrested were the associate minister Kenneth Neal Felder (age thirty-nine); Jo Ann Kreipal (thirty-seven); Randall Ray Sullenger (thirty-five) and his wife, Cheryl (thirty-two); and Christopher Harmon (twenty-four) and his wife, Robin (twenty-two).[32]

The indictments charged Kreipal with introducing Svelmoe to other members of the conspiracy in May 1987. Randall Sullenger and Christopher Harmon were charged with discussing plans to bomb clinics with Svelmoe in June. Felder, it was charged, met with Svelmoe and Owens at the latter's home to talk about destroying the Alvarado clinic. Christopher Harmon was charged with giving Svelmoe literature about building a bomb, and Cheryl Sullenger gave Svelmoe gunpowder in a gift-wrapped box, a black wig to wear in the attempt, a gasoline can, firecrackers, and chemicals. In addition, the Sullengers bought firecrackers in Mexico to use in the device, Christopher Harmon purchased some chemicals for it, and Randall Sullenger provided the pipe for the bomb.

In the aftermath of the indictments it was revealed that Owens and his followers had demonstrated and picketed against abortion, homosexuals, humanists, adult entertainment, liberal politicians, draft resisters, and the Mormon church. Cheryl Sullenger was the head of Project Jericho, a Right to Life group inspired by Joseph Scheidler that had protested abortions and the disconnection of life-support systems for terminally ill patients.

The targeted clinic had been the object of weekly picketing, delivery of unordered pizzas, appearance of uncalled-for plumbers, vandalism, bomb threats, and threats to the manager's life.

Paul Owens, Dorman Owens's son and a minister himself, maintained that the arrests were a plot of "homosexuals, abortionists, and feminists who are very strong political groups that put pressure on the powers that be" in reprisal for his father's opposition to them.

At the hearing for bail for Owens, U.S. District Judge Earl B. Gilliam agreed with the prosecution that Owens should not be released. "With Owens' kind of logic, Gilliam said, 'He could participate in a bombing of this courthouse and the police station.'"[33]

Something of the mood and perspective of the group was revealed in an interview by Richard A. Serrano and Ralph Frammolino of the *Los Angeles Times* staff with Jo Ann Kreipal. They asserted that on the picket line she would say to patients things such as, "They're going to pull your uterus outside of your body and rip your baby out." She also condemned homosexuality and pornography, as well as abortion. During the interview, they said, she maintained that "AIDS wouldn't be a problem if America would abide by the Law of Moses, which orders society to execute the homosexual."[34] That, she said, "would be an 'act of love' for both the homosexual and society."

Svelmoe pleaded guilty to the attempted bombing and agreed to testify for the prosecution in the subsequent trial. His sentence was delayed pending the trial of the other seven, each of whom originally pleaded not guilty. However, on March 1, 1988, the other seven pleaded guilty to the charges against them. In June 1988 Dorman Owens's guilty plea (to charges of witness tampering and willfully concealing knowledge of the bombing) resulted in a prison sentence of twenty-one months and an additional five years on probation. He was forbidden to participate in any anti-abortion protests or to preach on the subject during his probation.

### Pensacola, Florida, and Columbus, Ohio: John Brockhoeft

In the early morning hours of May 7, 1988, BATF agents and local police arrested John Brockhoeft just outside Pensacola and charged him with planning to bomb the Pensacola Ladies Center. A resident of Hebron, Kentucky, and a postal service mail handler, the thirty-seven-year-old Brockhoeft was arrested after his wife, Bobbie Jo, told her father, Vernon Lovelace, what her husband was planning, and Lovelace informed law enforcement personnel, according to the subsequent court testimony.

It was testified that Brockhoeft drove to the Milton, Florida, location of Our Father's House and met there with John Burt, who accompanied Brockhoeft to a parking lot across the street from the Ladies

Center late in the evening, May 6.[35] They returned to Our Father's House, and then Brockhoeft drove alone toward Pensacola. Perhaps he noticed he was being followed, for he appeared to drive around Santa Rosa County randomly. Finally, about 3:00 A.M. the officers stopped him, searched his car, and arrested him. In his car they found steel pipe, explosives, and detonators. During the trial, Assistant U.S. Attorney Steve Preisser said there were so many volatile chemicals in the car that Brockhoeft could have killed himself had his car hit a bump on his trip to Pensacola.

At the trial Brockhoeft wanted to present a "necessity" defense—that is, he would claim that blowing up the clinic was necessary to prevent the larger crime of abortion. Judge Roger Vinson, however, ruled that because abortion is a legal activity, the necessity defense could not be used. Brockhoeft was convicted of possession of an unregistered explosive device, interstate transportation with intent to damage the Ladies Center, and attempting to damage a building involved in interstate commerce. He received a five-year sentence.

Brockhoeft had been a vocal picketer at clinics in Cincinnati and Columbus, Ohio. According to newspaper reports, his wife, pregnant with their fifth child, described his picketing activities as "terroristic" and added that she and her children lived in fear of him. In our interview, Brockhoeft denied such assertions, maintaining that he had a close and loving relationship with his children, while his wife was very supportive of his anti-abortion work.

Brockhoeft was reared as a Methodist in Erlanger, Kentucky, but now regards himself as a member of no denomination and as simply a Christian. He accepts the description of himself as a fundamentalist. He had one year of college at Northern Kentucky University.

In addition to picketing in Cincinnati and Columbus, he had joined the picketing in Pensacola on November 28, 1987. He had also traveled twice to events sponsored by Joseph Scheidler's group in Chicago, one of those times at Scheidler's invitation.[36] There he had met John Burt and Edward Markley, but he saw them only in a group-type activity. He had also participated in three of the Washington, D.C., Marches for Life, held each January on the anniversary of the *Roe v. Wade* decision. Arrested four times during his Ohio picketing, he was found guilty only once but was assessed no fine or jail sentence.

When we asked him why he chose to target a clinic in Pensacola rather than some clinic closer to his home, he said, "If the mission had been successful, it could have sent a message [to the Ladies Center]: if you are going to brutalize a Christian woman like Joan Andrews for such a token violation of the law in the face of such desperation as these little babies' being slain, then you can expect things like this to happen." He also mentioned the ten-year sentences of Goldsby and Simmons as justification. They and Andrews, he said, were suffering because of the Ladies Center.[37]

Brockhoeft was well versed in how to create sophisticated and powerful bombs. He explained he was self-taught in those skills and had conducted "numerous" remote tests of explosive devices. When arrested near Pensacola, he had materials for two types of bombs in his car, one of which could be made of astrolite, which he calls the most powerful nonnuclear explosive known. For encasing the explosive he had a two-inch pipe, one foot long.

In May 1990 Brockhoeft was indicted in federal court on five counts of arson and one of attempted arson at the Margaret Sanger Clinic in Columbus, Ohio, in 1985. After serving twenty-six months for the Pensacola conviction, he was sentenced to seven years' imprisonment for the Columbus arson.

### Syracuse, New York: Shari DiNicola

Shari DiNicola pleaded guilty to attempting to set fire to the offices of Planned Parenthood of Syracuse on three different occasions in 1990. She stated that she was angry at the ban against blockading clinics, which had been upheld by the Supreme Court. While not a member of Operation Rescue, she had attended one of its meetings and was, according to her attorney, motivated by materials she got there.

Her attorney also said that DiNicola, who was twenty-four years old at the time of her offenses, apparently had some mental problems as a result of a brain injury at birth, which affected "her ability to control her impulses."[38] She was sentenced to five years' probation and was, according to her mother, receiving daily therapy. The Planned Parenthood of Syracuse director, Jeff Gilbert, believed the young woman had been misused by anti-abortionists, according to DiNicola's attorney.[39]

### Greensboro, North Carolina: Robert H. Farley, Jr.

Two Greensboro clinics suffered arson damage in the early morning hours of March 17, 1991. The city's first Operation Rescue demonstrations had taken place the previous month. Robert H. Farley, Jr., aged thirty, was later arrested and charged with both arsons. The federal court magistrate ordered a psychiatric examination of Farley since Farley reportedly had a history of several years of schizophrenia and hospitalizations, had even damaged his own eye at one time, and had attempted suicide twice. His attorney reported that Farley would plead "not guilty by reason of insanity."[40]

### Commonalities among Bombers and Arsonists

Excluding the ambiguous-appearing cases of Ross and Corum, what are the common denominators among these Lutherans, Baptists, Mormons, Catholics, members of the Assemblies of God, and a one-time Methodist?

All are religiously ardent. All are dualists, viewing the world in clear-cut black and white. All their attorneys pled for their release on bail, and during the trials for their being found innocent, and at their sentencing for probation, on the grounds of their religiosity, their commitment to life, their being strong family men. Character witnesses invariably described them as good, hard-working, normal people. For example, Bray's copastor, Michael Colvin, described Bray as "the very antithesis of a kook or nut"—a description not unlike the character descriptions of all the others.

Except for Markley (the priest), Malvasi, Kefauver, Owens, and Reed, they all were under forty years of age when they committed these acts, and they were all lower middle class or, more frequently, working class or blue-collar workers.[41] Markley and Malvasi are the only Catholics. In addition, all of them are white and males, except for Marjorie Reed, Kaye Wiggins and Kathy Simmons (who were at the "edge" of that conspiracy), and Cheryl Sullenger and Jo Ann Kreipal.[42] Most appear to have been marginal to mainstream forms of political expression, including civil disobedience, but may also be considered politically naive in that they believed their actions would influence changes in the law.

Why is the group predominantly male? First, males are normally socialized in our society to an active orientation, to shaping things, while females are more frequently socialized toward conformity, fitting into the expectations of significant others.[43] Second, males are more frequently trained in the technical and mechanical skills involved in building bombs and setting fires, as well as in evading detection for wrongdoing. Third, probably the majority of the females in the activist wing of the anti-abortion movement are also actively mothering children, a deterrent to risking imprisonment.[44] In the fundamentalist community the fathering role is not viewed as a full-time occupation, while mothering is. Thus, males feel free not to be available to their spouses and children much more than females do.

Many of those convicted have occupations and family situations that isolate them from the normal tempering effects of work life in America. That is, most of them are employed by churches or are self-employed.[45] They have structures to take care of their families when they are caught and imprisoned, or they have no dependents at all. Thus prison sentences are not a major threat to them.[46] Most of them live on the fringe of urban areas and were reared in a more rural or small-town setting. Others are first-generation urban dwellers.

In sum, these appear to be people caught between old life-styles and the new urbanized, cosmopolitan world. Ammerman's (1991) characterization of Baptist fundamentalists as "in-betweeners" in their educational achievement can possibly be extended to include other aspects of marginality in our subjects' lives: occupations, family situations, friendships, and other aspects of integration into modern urban life.

We turn now to the implications of the common factors among these persons and explore various theories and research that may shed light on our subjects' uses of violence.

### Social Isolation

One very important characteristic is that all the convicted perpetrators appear to be isolated "loners" with a restricted number of significant relationships. Several of them have virtually no close personal relationships, especially no close female friends or romantic relationships. Others do have strong, even intense, personal ties that still typify the social isolate in that those relationships are limited or encapsulated within a network of a solitary worldview.[47] In particular, the majority are members of small Protestant sectlike churches rather than the larger "mainline" denominations. Such churches demand, and often receive, high degrees of commitment from their members. The Catholic church, on the other hand, has long been able to keep many "extremists," those with high degrees of commitment, somewhat under control by giving them legitimate avenues for expressing their commitment, such as monastic orders and the priesthood, which keeps their commitment channeled and thus somewhat in check.

### Rape and the Control of Women

The bombers and arsonists fit the social profile of other violent criminals in age, sex, social relationships, and occupational status. In particular, we are struck by their similarities to the "average" rapist, differing significantly only in their religiosity.[48] Perhaps the feminists are correct in their charge that these abortion-related acts express a basic sexual violence against women, rather than against buildings, and a desire to control women—a factor common to rapists. Thus, such behavior could be cited as a religious substitute for rape or, at the least, a male desire to control women.

We note that male domination of women is a cultural theme that permeates our society but is given more acceptable expressions in most people's lives. Women's subordination to men in marriage is generally recognized in the culture, manifest in the differential socialization of girls and boys, traditional ideas about women and work, male responsibilities in divorce, double standards of sexual fidelity, patterns of acceptability in pornographic representations of women and men, and the slow institutional response to the plight of women victimized by violent actions such as wife abuse and rape. Different social groups express the theme of dominance through different patterns of action, but no group is untouched by some of the more extreme dominance-asserting behaviors. In fundamentalist groups male dominance usually translates into the obedience of the wife and austere socialization practices. It may extend to a justification of pregnancy in the absence of birth-control use as "God's will," a sentiment more readily expressed by men than women.[49] Indeed, the problems of wife abuse and incest appear more frequently among rural conservative religious groups than in the general population.[50] Overall, the idea that radical action against abortion is an expression of an ideology of male dominance fits well with many Protestant fundamentalist worldviews.[51]

We are also struck by the parallels between legal defenses and justifications for these violent acts and the justifications offered typically by rapists: (1) It is the victims' fault. Scully and Marollo (1984) mention the common rapist allegations that "nice girls don't get raped" and "women are seductresses." This is comparable to the bombers' and arsonists' claims that if the clinics were not performing abortions, the justifiable violence would not have occurred. (2) The offense is not really serious enough to merit such severe punishment. Some rapists claim they committed only a minor wrongdoing, according to Scully and Marollo. (3) Psychiatrists testifying on behalf of those convicted of abortion-related violence have claimed the perpetrators' actions are a result of a personality disorder—feelings of inadequacy, antisocial personalities, passive-aggressive personalities, and borderline disturbances. Psychiatric testimony for rapists has typically cited the same syndromes.

Furthermore, the self-images of the two types of offenders are comparable. A majority of the Scully and Marollo sample of rapists projected themselves as "really a nice guy." The bombers also project the upstanding, moral-citizen image.

## Terrorism

Feminists have also charged that clinic bombings and arsons are acts of terrorism,[52] a definition denied by the Reagan administration in its refusal to assign such violence to the FBI for investigation.[53] The administration claimed there must be a central coordinating group behind such acts for them to be "terrorism." Since in the trial of the

Pensacola Four, as well as in several other similar trials, the issue of terrorism was also raised by both the prosecution and the defense, it is an issue worth consideration here.

The FBI definition of terrorism specifies it as "the unlawful use of force or violence against persons or property to intimidate or coerce a government, the civilian population, or any segment thereof, in furtherance of political or social objectives." However, as Stephen Segaller (1987, 223) points out, "A briefing paper adds: 'For an incident to be labelled terrorist by the FBI, one of two things must have occurred. First of all, the incident itself must fit the definition of terrorism, and secondly, either a terrorist group or individual must have claimed credit for the incident, or investigation by the FBI developed the fact that a terrorist or terrorist group was involved in the commission of the act.'" As Segaller observes, this gives the government room to maneuver for political reasons, for if just the twenty-five clinic bombings and arsons in 1984 were included in the U.S. terrorist statistics, the total would increase by 200 percent.[54] Thus, the FBI has not recognized these as terrorist acts because no person or group publicly claims responsibility for them.[55]

Ted Robert Gurr includes abortion facility bombings (but not arsons) among vigilante acts of terrorism of right-wing extremists in defense of the status quo.[56] He maintains that the decline in such incidents after 1986 results from prosecutions of offenders and calls by anti-abortion leaders such as John C. Willke for a halt to violence because of its negative impact on the public.

Franco Ferracuti of the University of Rome has made an extensive study of the terrorist's profile. He maintains that terrorists are "Utopians, with a total detachment from reality."[57] Carlos Marighella, another student of terrorism, adds that "from a moral point of view, the urban guerilla has an undeniable superiority. This moral superiority is what sustains the urban guerilla."[58]

John L. P. Thompson of Columbia University holds that "the stimulus to terrorism is political expectations. . . . It's possible that once you've activated these aspirations, you provoke, by some process that we don't entirely understand, a kind of polarization that becomes impossible to regulate.[59] In the same vein, Jerold M. Post of George

Washington University notes: "This all-or-nothing, black-and-white view of the world is very characteristic [of terrorists]. There's no gray zone for terrorists. Moreover, carrying out a kind of fantasy war against society and the Establishment is the most important part of a terrorist's life, and it is thus very difficult to deter him from it. You cannot hold a club over somebody's head and say, 'Stop doing the most important thing you've ever done.' It's like asking him to commit suicide."[60]

## Torture

Studies of torturers show a similar profile. Specialists in this area maintain that conditions leading toward becoming a torturer include (1) an impassioned ideology assigning evil to another group, (2) absolute obedience to some authority, and (3) a sense of support from some group.[61] Robert Jay Lifton, a psychiatrist at City University of New York, maintains that torturers use a "mental maneuver" of "doubling," forming a separate self who does acts their "ordinary" self would not condone. In effect, they form two personalities that do not overlap or intersect.[62] This personality condition, say the experts, is not a form of schizophrenia or serious psychosis. Rather, it is a compartmentalization of statuses, roles, and contexts. We argue that this may be a natural outgrowth of dualist thinking (see chapter 14).

An additional element, according to Ervin Straub of the Massachusetts Institute of Technology, is being able to divide the world into "us" and "them." He also finds that torturers feel that the victims are responsible for their own predicament, deserving what they get.[63] Another element he identifies is the torturer's sense that he enjoys the approval and support of those around him.

## Conclusion

Experts on international terrorism recognize abortion clinic violence as terrorism. The international journal *Terrorism* regularly includes statistics on American abortion-related violence in its reportage, as do the publications of the International Association of Chiefs of Police. Furthermore, all the clinic personnel across the country whom we inter-

viewed defined such acts as terrorism. In addition, the convicted violators we interviewed have admitted, and in some cases voluntarily
stated, that they were engaged in acts of terror.

The victims of these acts perceive them as terror. The perpetrators see
their acts as terrorizing. The scholarly community recognizes them as
terrorism. However, former Attorney General Edwin Meese and the
FBI were unwilling to recognize them as such.

In summary, the following parallels can be discerned in the profiles
of rapists, terrorists, and torturers and those of abortion clinic at-
tackers: Rapists are usually male and under thirty-five, have few social
relationships, and blame their victims; terrorists are utopians and ab-
solutists who see themselves as crusaders for the one true morality;
torturers, similarly, espouse ideological purity, authoritarianism, and
intolerance of others' beliefs, and they often depend heavily on a support group. All of these characteristics are shared by the perpetrators of
violence against abortion clinics.

Clearly, the perpetrators of violence against abortion clinics stand as
marginal participants in the prominent themes of American culture.
While many manifest superficial engagement in local and national
society, the attitudes that have driven their behavior are focused in
ways that are not immediately apparent to the people around them.
The values they accept concerning civil liberties, public responsibility,
obedience to divinely appointed authority, and gender roles are all
conveniently ordered to render their minority view moral, superior to
any other position, and, from their perspective, necessary for the entire
society. This produces, for outsiders, the contradictory juxtaposition of
violence as moral judgment. Like other violent criminals, these agents
of morality are indifferent to the real consequences of their actions on
other people's lives. Unlike other violent criminals, they are not as
clearly motivated by personal gain or pleasure since their efforts are
directed toward a "cause."[64] Whether the analogies to other violent
criminals, rapists, terrorists, and torturers are valid or not, those conducting violence against abortion facilities clearly share with all of
them (and each of them with each other) a strong egocentrism, an
objectification of their victims and a determination to control them and
others, and an ability to dissociate themselves from not only the conse-

quences of their acts to others, but also the consequences to themselves.

The critical point is that these violent crusaders are marginal even to the movement they purport to represent. The ambivalence of this relationship is signaled by the fact that the bombers' and arsonists' actions, while somewhat supported, cannot be fully embraced by the public representatives of the anti-abortion movement, if only out of interest in public relations.

# ... 14
# Sacred Universes in a Secular Society

All scripture is given by inspiration of God.
2 Timothy 3:16

Our study of those tried and convicted of abortion-related violence across the country reveals that there are commonalities among them. All are not Protestant fundamentalists, but we include rigid Catholics and Mormons under a wider umbrella of fundamentalists. All are not Pentecostalists or charismatics. But all are dualists, seeing the world sharply divided into the flesh and the spirit, body and soul, evil and good, wrong and right.

To understand fundamentalism and dualism, one must understand the world in which they exist, the secular world of modern society. So we will first examine secularization, and then we will turn to fundamentalistic dualism as a reaction against the secular society.

## The Development of Secularization

Secularization has been a central topic in the sociology of religion in recent years.[1] In particular dispute are the nature of secularization, its origins, and its effects. Is secularization destructive to societies, harmful to individuals, or beneficial to either or both? Our discussion will not enter directly into these debates but will follow one of the dominant approaches to secularization to interpret some aspects of the abortion controversy.

The modern debate began with a small but seminal volume by the economist D. L. Munby (1963), *The Idea of a Secular Society and Its Significance for Christians*, in which he described the secular society as one in which there is (1) a rational approach to problem solving; (2) institutionalized structures, such as courts, for the resolution of conflicts, as opposed to more informal structures such as the kinship group or the moral values of the society; (3) no official images of morality or definitions of the ideal persons; and (4) expectations that each individual find his or her own meaning system, such as religion.

This is contrasted with a "sacred" society,[2] common to traditional cultures of the kind typically studied by anthropologists and within which there is common agreement on what is important, on what is valuable. Such societies commonly have only one social organization, the family or kinship system, through which all economic, political, educational, and religious functions are conducted. Thus all men in the society do the same kinds of things, make a living the same ways, believe essentially the same things. The women likewise behave and think alike. Even in complex societies of traditional form the access of individuals to diverse roles is limited by rigid values that maintain the complementation of class and gender norms. Therefore, reactions to problems tend to be virtually automatic and based on tradition and custom. In this kind of system religion often functions as the primary component of self-identifying ideology. Thus there is no conscious distinction or difference in doing "religious" things as opposed to other things.

Religion, then, infuses everyday life and underlies all existence. When a person is planting a crop or hunting an animal, that person is also doing something religious. Furthermore, the "way things have always been" is freighted with divine will and beyond the control of humans. A person's task is to imitate the divinely established patterns.

In such a society, time tends to move in a circle, with each revolution taking one year to complete. People are attuned to the cycles of the seasons, the phases of the moon, and the rhythms of life. There is little, if any, sense of history except as the past becomes part of the fixed tradition. A human being's primary function is to maintain that tradition, which means resisting change, doing what one's ancestors did in the way they did it. Thus time is but one year long, and what is remembered are those repeating events, the cycles of life, rather than unique events.

Paralleling this distinctive view of time is a unique view of space in sacred societies. Meaningful space is the territory that the group inhabits. That area is also inhabited by the group's gods, who endow activities with ultimate meaning. Once a person leaves that sacred territory, he or she is in chaos, meaninglessness, for the new territory is the habitat of a different group with different gods and different meanings. The gods, then, are territorial, limited to the specific region. As Mircea Eliade points out, such a society has no concept of the secular, or the nonreligious, but distinguishes simply between the sacred and chaos.

With the birth of civilizations about six thousand years ago, a dramatic shift took place. Common to all civilizations is the invention and use of calendars. This indicates that civilizations replace the cyclical view of time with a linear one. That is, time is seen as nonrepeatable, having a beginning and going somewhere. History is invented. Unique events become important, and people begin keeping histories. With unique, special events seen as important, change also becomes valued. New ways of doing old things are not just sought, but they are welcomed. Tradition is remembered, but it loses its sacred quality. The secular society has emerged.

In a secular society the image of space is also transformed: sacred space becomes universalized. The gods themselves are viewed as being universal, unlimited in their spatial potency. In *The Secular City*, Harvey Cox (1965) argues that such views of time and space came into Western civilization through the Hebrew prophets.[3] While the priests of the temple upheld the traditional view that Jerusalem was inviolable by peoples such as the Assyrians because the temple was the house of Yahweh and the Assyrians had left their gods back home, the prophets maintained that Yahweh was universal and using even the Assyrians. Therefore, when the Babylonians conquered the Hebrews and carried many of them back as hostages, much to the priests' chagrin and horror, the followers of the priests in Babylon asked, "How shall we sing the Lord's song in a strange land?" (Psalm 137:4). The rhetorical question implies its answer: "We can't, for God is back in Jerusalem and without power here." The captives' only response could be to convert to Babylonian culture and religion.

The followers of the prophets, however, reacted to the captivity by inventing the synagogue because for them Yahweh was the God of the universe. "Whither shall I go from thy spirit? or whither shall I flee from thy presence?" they asked (Psalm 139:7). They denied that the heavens, the deepest sea, or darkness could separate them from the presence of God. For the prophets, then, all space is sacred space; there is no chaos. But when there is no distinction in spaces and all are equally sacred, the potential is, according to Cox, that all may be equally secular.

Another aspect of civilization is the development of distinct and separate organizations beyond the family. Religion is probably the first new organization to develop, with the temples atop their steep ziggurats, mountains raised in the flat plains, at the heart of the new cities. Priests were likely the first full-time specialists, the first persons not to farm like others. Soon the beginnings of government were formed, with the maintenance of full-time armies to protect from nomadic marauders the surpluses stored in the temple. About the same time skilled artisans became specialists working for the temple, trading their labor for portions of the offerings presented to the priest. Schools, even colleges, developed rapidly to train young people for specialized professions.

This process, which sociologists call "differentiation," is a continuing one. Interwoven with it is the increasing specialization of labor. It is estimated, for example, that civilization first developed with a base of less than 5 percent surplus food production that could be traded to specialists. In the United States today, less than 3 percent of the work force grows the food for all of us; we have more than reversed the ratio of the basis of specialization. The U.S. Bureau of the Census estimates that there are more than 30,000 different occupations in the country today, and every decade 10,000 disappear while a similar number of new forms of work appear.

In *The Division of Labor in Society*,[4] Émile Durkheim argues that this specialization of labor leads to the development of different values and beliefs by different segments of society. No longer performing the same tasks in the same ways, people begin thinking differently, and this process leads to a breakdown of a society's commonly held values and beliefs. This breakdown makes it difficult for people to communicate across occupational and, especially, class lines because the lawyer and the plumber speak different languages. In effect, they live in different worlds and their words, while from the same language, have different meanings.

As the differentiation develops, so there develop distinct areas of concern for the various organizations of society. Thus, "religious" concerns are distinguished from "political" and "economic" issues, and what is appropriate for one realm is not appropriate for the other. In the United States specialization and differentiation in organizations have expanded dramatically. In politics alone there are governments at the national, state, county, and municipal levels; this structure is complicated by intergovernmental and regional agencies responsible for coordinating activities of different levels.

The development of differing values also entails the collapse of commonly agreed-upon patterns of life, the "disenchantment," "demystification," and desacralization of the divinely decreed definitions of what it means to be male, female, husband, father, mother, and child, to be a family. In effect, people remove those patterns from the divine heavens and take them into their own hands to shape and redefine. Rare it is today, for example, to believe that "marriages are made in heaven." Just one result of this is the rise of differing and conflicting models of life-style and behavior.

The worldview of Western civilization, while not uniform or accepted by all segments of society, has been formed primarily by various dominant cultural images through time.[5] For example, during the late medieval period, the dominant image was that of the clock, that mechanical invention of replaceable parts.[6] In practical terms, the universe was viewed through that model into the eighteenth century and it still forms many of our images. The solar system as we imagined it first came from this. The ideas of the balance of power, checks and balances in government, deism in philosophy, the Newtonian universe of gravitation came from this meta-image. And it gave us the images of atoms, corpuscles and waves which persist into the 20th century.[7] The clock metaphor speaks to us through Adam Smith's economic theory,

Jeremy Bentham's utilitarian ethics, Joseph Haydn's symphonies, faculty psychology, and Alexander Pope's *Essay on Man*.

The mechanical model was followed by the Romantic rebellion and its organic model that compares organizations with the body, in which parts are not replaceable but the structure is greater than the sum of its parts. People and societies are pictured as having an inner nature working to realize itself. Both are born, mature, decline, and die. The organic model gave rise to Romantic literature, typified by the work of Wordsworth. It gave us Oswald Spengler's analysis of cultures and societies, Georg Hegel's dialectics, Karl Marx's failed vision of communism, the theory of biological and social evolution, process theology, and artistic realism.

The worldview of the modern age is increasingly informed by modern physics and the second law of thermodynamics, which states that the universe is winding down toward chaos. This view sees human life as temporarily running against the grain of the universe by increasing and expanding its organization, even spreading it via satellites beyond the solar system. Another aspect of the modern worldview arises from the laws of probability, by which we understand that nothing is certain, that we must live with ambiguity and contingency. Finally, Einstein's theory of relativity established the interchangeability between energy and mass and the instability of time. These scientific developments have led to a unitary view of human life—the assumption, usually unvoiced and unself-consciously held, that humans are one substance, not to be divided into body and soul, physical and spiritual. Whether we acknowledge it or not, we increasingly live as if that were so. Our commercials voice it for us: "You only go around once in life. Go for all the gusto you can!"

We Westerners view reality holistically. Rather than breaking things into their component parts, as in the mechanical model, we maintain that what is important is the way in which the parts relate to one another, the way they are organized, the system they form. Each part can be understood only in light of its relation to the other parts. This view is reflected in gestalt psychology in its assumption that the individual can be understood only in the context of total psychological, social, and biological relationships.

Such understandings have given rise to the assumption that ambiguity and contingency are constants in human life, that there is no ideal society we can build to answer all human problems, but that today's answers become tomorrow's problems. This acceptance of inherent ambiguity underlies situational ethics, which maintains that there are no moral absolutes appropriate to all situations in all times and that what is ethical is not found in right and wrong or good and evil, as previous ages have tried to define ethics. Rather, what is moral is that which is responsible in the given situation, which always comes to us freighted with ambiguity, in shades of gray instead of clear-cut black and white. Every human decision, then, involves guilt because no decision is pure.

The mechanical worldview, which envisions a flat earth at the center of the universe and suspended between heaven and hell, has been superseded by the modern view of a one-story universe in which humans exist on a small planet at the edge of a galaxy that is itself at the edge of the universe. Thus the human species is no longer at the center of all things.

The religion of the "respectable" churches is essentially secularized religion; that is, the established, mainstream denominations (such as Methodist, Presbyterian, Episcopalian, and middle-class Baptist) have accepted and support the separation of religion and law, the privatization of morality.[8] For many members the church is one more voluntary association among many. Their primary identity lies not in their religious belief systems but in their social status. In addition, they find themselves under cross-pressures from these many social and voluntary associations, which temper and moderate their values, beliefs, and behavior. They are forced to be tolerant due to the potential negative sanctions for extreme or "fanatical" behavior.

There are, of course, some in these mainstream denominations who take their religion seriously. But when they do, they tend to apply it to social issues such as racism, sexism, and other traditionally institutionalized social problems. Thus they are calling into question the taken-for-granted social order, which places them in direct conflict with the fundamentalist orientation to tradition. They also value education and science and are vocal advocates for a critical approach to scriptures (or, at least, a nonliteral approach), another anathema to the fundamentalists.

Using their understanding of the Bible and theology, they too have sought to establish a theocracy, albeit a more tolerant one, one that is more consistent with the traditional American values of success, equality, and justice. While predominantly middle class themselves and having a stake in the economic status quo, the mainstream denominational groups have tended to be more critical of the economic system and have supported racial and sexual equality, as well as programs to ameliorate the effects of poverty and other social ills.

On the other hand, they have raised the ire of the fundamentalists with their middle-class tolerance of the popular sins and their lack of enforced "orthodoxy." At least some of the hostility between fundamentalists and mainstream groups probably lies in inherent class resentments on both sides.[9]

### Fundamentalist Responses to Secularization[10]

From its development until World War II, fundamentalism tended to be composed predominantly of persons who had less than a high school education, who came from rural and small-town areas in the South and from urban industrial communities in the North, who held lower white-collar and blue-collar occupations, and who had relatively low incomes. They tended to feel that their income was average or worse than average.[11] However, since that time both evangelicalism and fundamentalism have made dramatic inroads into the middle and upper-middle classes,[12] so that Chalfant, Baeckley, and Palmer (1981, 246) assert, "They are confined neither to the southern nor midwestern 'Bible Belts'; instead they seem to be a part of a nationwide Bible Belt that has neither geographical nor social class boundaries."[13]

Protestant fundamentalism arose in the 1880s, originally as a response to the use by Protestant scholars of the relatively new linguistic techniques of text and form criticism in their study of the Bible. Those scholars determined that the Pentateuch was a compilation of at least five separate documents written from differing religious perspectives.[14] Similar techniques applied to the New Testament questioned the traditionally assigned authorship of many of its books. The mainline denominations of the time (Episcopalian, Congregational, Methodist, Unitarian, and some Presbyterian), valuing education for their clergy, began to teach these new insights in their seminaries. With the acceptance of these approaches came a general receptivity toward other new and expanding scientific findings, such as evolution.

By 1900, urbanization and industrialization of the United States were well under way, along with their attendant social dislocations. One response to this was the Social Gospel movement, which strove to enact humanitarian laws regulating such things as child labor, unions, old-age benefits, and guaranteed living wages.[15] Accompanying the Social Gospel and acceptance of new scientific discoveries was an optimism about the perfectibility of human nature and society, which was epitomized by a banner welcoming national Methodist youth to a West Coast conference: "Courage God; We're Coming!"

Fundamentalism solidified its positions in opposition to these trends and as a response to social change and to the loss of the religious consensus caused by the influx of European Jewish and Catholic immigrants to America. While fundamentalism was a growing movement prior to 1900, a major milestone was reached with the publication in 1910 of the first volume of a twelve-volume series titled *The Fundamentals*.[16] Prior to the 1920s and 1930s, fundamentalism was primarily a Northern movement. Its growth in the South came mostly after 1950.

There are divisions within Protestant fundamentalism, but there is a general common basis of belief. Customary beliefs include a personal experience of salvation; verbal inspiration and literal interpretation of scriptures as worded in the King James Version of the Bible; the divinity of Jesus; the literal, physical resurrection of Jesus; special creation of the world in six days, as opposed to the theory of evolution; the virgin birth of Jesus; and the substitutionary atonement (Jesus' death on the cross as a substitution for the punishment of each of the "saved"). The heart of Protestant fundamentalism is the literal interpretation of the Bible.[17] And while there may be shades of difference among various fundamentalists on several of the above doctrines, the second foundation of it is the substitutionary atonement.

Another aspect of fundamentalism has been a strong tendency toward separatism, separation from the secular world as much as possible and separation from "apostates" (liberals and other non-fundamentalist denominations). Fundamentalists have also supported "traditional" family values through opposition to abortion, divorce, the Equal Rights

Amendment, and civil rights for homosexuals.[18] While their separatism has been expressed prior to the 1970s in extreme hostilities toward Roman Catholicism, fundamentalists and Catholics share a large set of family values, which has led to their pragmatic cooperation in the anti-abortion movement.[19] Another tie between some Protestant fundamentalists and some Catholics lies in the Charismatic Renewal movement. This movement, which coalesced in the 1920s (Harrell 1975), emphasized glossolalia (speaking in tongues) and faith healing. Adherents were denied admission to the World's Christian Fundamental Association in 1928 because of these emphases. By the 1960s charismaticism began spreading to some of the mainline denominations and some Catholic churches. While Presbyterians, United Methodists, Disciples of Christ, Episcopalians, and Lutherans sometimes reluctantly accepted this new charismaticism, Southern Baptists and Churches of Christ have tended to adamantly oppose it, especially the speaking-in-tongues aspect of it. But the Catholic charismatics have tended to be quite conservative both theologically and socially (Fichter 1951, 53), giving them ideological ties in common with the charismatic fundamentalists and fostering cooperation between the two in interdenominational charismatic conferences, a prelude to cooperation in the anti-abortion movement.

We maintain that there is also a Catholic "fundamentalism," which may or may not be charismatic and which centers on church dogma rather than Biblical literalism, the a priori dogma of Protestant fundamentalism. Catholic fundamentalists accept virtually unquestioningly the teachings of the church.[20] They share with Protestant fundamentalists the assumption that dogma precedes and supersedes analytical reason, while in liberal Catholic and Protestant thought and in the nation's law, reason supersedes dogma. Similar to Catholic fundamentalism is that of the Mormons, which also takes church dogma at face value.[21]

We contend that there are at least six basic commonalities among what we call Protestant, Catholic, and Mormon fundamentalisms: (1) an attitude of certitude—that one may know the final truth—which includes antagonism to ambiguity; (2) an external source for that certitude—the Bible or church dogma; (3) a belief system that at root is dualistic; (4) an ethic based on the "traditional" family; (5) a justi-

fication for violence;[22] and (6) a rejection of modernism (secularization).[23] We are not alone in this position.[24]

Along with those doctrines and characteristics a group of attitudes and
beliefs that are less biblically based is found among most fundamentalists—
Catholic, Protestant, and Mormon. These include individualism (which
supports a naive capitalism); pietism; a chauvinistic Americanism
(among some fundamentalists) that sees the United States as the new
Israel and Americans as God's new Chosen People; anti-intellectualism;
antiscience; anti–Social Gospel; and anticommunism. (Some liberal
Christians may share some of these views.) Underlying this complex of
beliefs, which includes an opposition to evolution, is an espousal of
social Darwinism,[25] the "survival-of-the-fittest" ethos that presumes
that American society is truly civilized, the pinnacle of social progress.
This continuity with nineteenth-century American neocolonialism
dominates contemporary political views of the religious Right. It is also
inherent in the fundamentalists' individualism and opposition to social
welfare programs.[26]

Particular personality characteristics also correlate with the fundamentalist syndrome: authoritarianism;[27] self-righteousness; prejudice
against minorities; moral absolutism (i.e., a refusal to compromise on
perceived moral issues); and antianalytical, anticritical thinking. Many
fundamentalists refuse to accept ambiguity as a given in moral decision
making and tend to arrive at simplistic solutions to complex problems.[28] For example, many hold that the solution to changes in the
contemporary family can be answered by fathers' reasserting their pri-
macy in the family, by their forcing their children and wives to blind
obedience.[29] Or, they say, premarital sex can be prevented by training
children toward abstinence. One popular fundamentalist spokesper-
son, Tim LaHaye (1980), asserts that the solution to sexual urges,
especially of teenagers, lies in censoring their reading materials,[30] and
strict discipline of children by parents will virtually engender self-
discipline in them automatically.[31] The implication is that enforced
other-directedness by parents produces inner-directed children, while
the evidence indicates that such children are more likely to exchange
parental authoritarianism for that of another parental figure. To develop inner direction under such circumstances requires, as a first step,

rebellion against and rejection of parental authority—the opposite of parental intent.[32]

One aspect of fundamentalism, particularly the Protestant variety, is its insistence on the subservient role of women.[33] The wife is expected to be subject to the direction of her husband, children to the direction of their father. While Luker (1984) found that anti-abortionists in California supported this position and pro-choicers favored equal status for women, recent research has shown that reasons for involvement in the anti-abortion movement vary by denomination. That is, some Catholics tend to be involved in the movement more from a "right-to-life" position, while Protestants and other Catholics are more concerned with sexual morality.[34] The broader "right-to-life" position is consistent with the official Catholic position against the death penalty and nuclear arms, while Protestant fundamentalists generally support the death penalty and a strong military.[35] Thus Protestant fundamentalists, and some Catholic activists, are more concerned with premarital sexual behavior than they are with the life of the fetus.[36] This is not to say that each group disagrees with the positions of the other, but rather that the groups differ in their *primary* concern.

However, Protestants and Catholics (especially traditional, ethnic Catholics) are both concerned with the proper role of women.[37] Wives should obey their husbands, and unmarried females should refrain from sexual intercourse. For the Protestants in particular, abortion is an indication of sexual licentiousness.[38] Therefore, the total abolition of abortion would be a strong deterrent to such behavior, helping to reestablish traditional morality for females.[39]

At the same time, the current sexual morality casts the virgin female as deviant. The male virgin, however, has long been regarded as deviant. The fundamentalist ethic has accepted this traditional double standard by its relative silence on male virginity.

Another aspect of this gender-role ethic lies in the home-related roles of males and females. Women are expected to remain home, bear children, and care for them, while serving the needs of their husbands.[40] Again, this ethic is also related to social class and the social role expectations of the lower and working classes, including the attitude that women should "stay in their place."

Luker's (1984) research reveals that anti-abortion women are motivated by a concern for maintaining their ability to rely on men (husbands) to support their social roles as mothers,[41] while pro-choice women primarily want to maintain their independent status. The men involved in anti-abortion violence are clearly acting out of a desire to maintain that dependent status of women and the dominant roles of men. Some of those violent males reveal an inability to establish "normal" relationships with women,[42] which indicates that their violence may arise from a basic insecurity about performance of normal male roles in relationships with females. This does not mean that these men have no relationships with women. Indeed, it is in the context of relationships with women where dominance-related tendencies (including the forms of violence noted throughout the preceding chapter) become more manifest. It is likely that insecurity-driven behaviors are characteristic of violent males generally, but we do not have the psychiatric data available to assure this inference even for the population in question. However, the ideologies to which abortion facility bombers and arsonists subscribe and their only partial integration into modal patterns of American family life support the conclusion that these males, whether linked to women or not, see women as "naturally" subordinated to men.

In his study of activists from Toronto, Canada, Cuneo (1989, 85ff.) finds three dominant types: civil rights activists, who tend to be non-religious and are embarrassed by the religious activists; family-heritage activists, who are spokespersons for the "traditional" family and the status of women in it; and Catholic revivalists, who are equivalent to Catholic fundamentalists, seeking to revitalize the Catholic church in Canada.[43] Cuneo also finds an activist fringe composed of religious seekers; sexual therapeutics, "plagued by guilt and fear of female sexual power" (p. 115); and punitive puritans, who want to punish women for sexual transgressions. The "fringe" activists Cuneo found in Canada are closest to our population of bombers and arsonists, especially the sexual therapeutics and punitive puritans. Perhaps the bombers and arsonists are a unique group in the anti-abortion movement, operating essentially out of motivations that set them apart from the less violent activists in general.

Fundamentalists reject the assertion that religion is a private concern, something for each individual to determine for himself or herself. For them, there is only one right way, and they have it. Thus, the only way the nation can be "right" is for it to institute their definition of right in the public law. Government is an agency of God. Just as science should bow before creationism, so must law institute "Christian" morals and all "sin" should be legally outlawed.[44] All upright behavior should be legally supported. This is a crucial understanding, for the state, by definition, holds a monopoly on the use of violence. Thus, underlying fundamentalism is a willingness (in some cases, perhaps, the desire, if not compulsion) to enforce its moral definitions. There is not a great distance between the willingness to use public law and legal violence and a willingness to use private law and illegal violence. A strong bent toward violence is inherent in dualism itself, especially in its encouragement of physical punishment of children and its overt emphasis on obedience. However, this is not to claim that all or most fundamentalists are prone to or support such violence. We maintain only that the thought pattern encourages violence in suggestible adherents or in those already prone to violence.[45]

The bent toward violence is encouraged by the fundamentalist tendency to see conspiracies lurking behind what is perceived as moral decay. During the 1950s, fundamentalists found the conspiracy in the guise of communism. Today, for example, Tim LaHaye, while praising the reign of the church over all aspects of life in the medieval period (which others have termed the "Dark Ages"), sees virtually all modern deviance in America as the result of an overt conspiracy of secular humanists.[46] His answer to this state of affairs is to forcefully drive the secular humanists out of all positions of authority in government and education. Of course, most of the people he labels secular humanists would probably deny their guilt.

Fundamentalists hold a thoroughly egocentric belief system: they have no curiosity about other beliefs or images of the world, as if they already know the options and there is only one correct view.[47] They have no questions to ask, only a story to tell and an eagerness to tell it. The beliefs of others are irrelevant because those beliefs have nothing to offer and can only be wrong.

As secularized persons in modern society, most of us operate with multiple universes of discourse. When consulting with a physician, we accept the medical model of explanations. As students in a classroom, we research and draw conclusions running against our common, everyday assumptions because we move into a critical-thinking mode of discourse. When meeting with an attorney, we accept legal explanations for success or failure in the courtroom. But for a thoroughgoing fundamentalist there is only one universe of discourse, the theological one. If a person loses his or her job, it is because God wants that person to work some other place; it has nothing to do with the individual's job performance. Divine will becomes a virtually universal explanation for daily events. Other explanations are, again, irrelevant.

However, divisions do exist among fundamentalists. Some are millenarians (and there are also premillenarians and postmillenarians)[48] who emphasize the imminent return of Jesus, while others virtually ignore this doctrine. Still others are willing to cooperate with non-fundamentalists, such as the National Council of Churches or other denominations, while others refuse to cooperate with even other fundamentalists. Some emphasize speaking in tongues, while others deny biblical validity to it. Some are extremely exclusive, denying validity to every other group, while others are more accepting of the salvability of members of other denominations. Some even express a concern for political and social reform in tune with the agenda of the Social Gospel, supporting racial equality and feminism, as well as a more humane economic system. While virtually universally militant, fundamentalism is not monolithic. Fundamentalists do, however, tend to cooperate on agreed-upon issues.

At the heart of fundamentalism in its Protestant, Catholic, and Mormon expressions is a dualistic view of the world—a modern version of Manichaeanism,[49] a heresy roundly condemned by the early church. It divides reality into soul and body, spirit and flesh, good and evil, heaven and earth, God and Satan, male and female. Dualism sees the world and its individuals caught in a cosmic war between good and evil, spirit and body, faith and reason. These dualisms originate in the merger of Greek and Christian thought in early Christianity and were exacerbated by Thomist theology. The "real" worlds in this pattern of thought are the ideal worlds of good, God, ideas, and spirituality, rather than the observable physical world.

Fundamentalism also tends to personalize these forces. Thus there is a directly perceivable personal God with whom one talks and who talks back, not necessarily in words but in "burdens laid on the heart" or in feelings that overwhelm the individual's rational being. Also, there is a real Devil—albeit a finite one who can be in only one place at one time—and he has assistants, demons, who mimic God and try to trap the believer.

How does one know whether a "burden on the heart" is from God or from Satan? It requires verification or validation by another's having the same revelation independently. That is, feeling such a burden, the person tends to hide it in his or her heart (as did Mary with the angel's declaration to her), to ponder it and wait. Then if someone else raises a similar feeling or revelation, it is validated, legitimated as an authentic revelation from God. Sharon Glass of First Assembly of God spoke of one of her experiences, saying that she was convinced God had told her she would get a particular job with her church. She kept her conviction to herself, and six months later the pastor testified that God had told him who was going to be on his church staff and she was to be among them. This authenticated for her the original revelation.

Fundamentalist dualism extends to its view of the "natural" world. As Kristin Luker (1984) points out, fundamentalists picture the world as divided into two arenas—public life and private life—with the proper place of women being in the home, the private sphere, while men have dominion over the public realm.

Dualism also sees the world in stark black and white. This is particularly true of morality. A specific behavior is either right or wrong, good or evil; there are no shades of gray and few, if any, difficult moral decisions. Moral dilemmas are resolved by the good that is felt to be the highest, and all other results of following that greatest good, in spite of even tragic consequences, are borne as the will of God.

The moral concern is with what people do, how they behave. In its extreme, fundamentalism assumes that the end justifies the means. For example, Joseph Scheidler told us on the day of sentencing of the Pensacola Four:

We had a goal of closing twelve clinics across the country by July. We have now closed eighteen. We have an Adopt an Abortionist program, where a woman who has had an abortion goes to the doctor who did it and tries to talk with him about it, writes him letters, meets with his wife, gets to know him as a person. If he doesn't respond, then we harass him. We go to his home, if he is having a party with his friends, and picket with signs. We follow him to the airport, when he is leaving town, with signs like "Dr. So-and-So is an abortionist." Then we have a welcoming group for him when he lands wherever he's going and then again when he returns.

In the name of a higher good, fundamentalists believe, it is acceptable to harass, embarrass, intimidate, and discomfit.

Scheidler's ethic of violence is also revealed in a citation from an undated National Organization for Women memo: "In Kansas on August 5, 1983, Scheidler told his 'pro-life' soldiers to picket clinics, claiming that the medical complication rate for women having abortions increases by 4 to 5 percent on days when there are pickets outside the clinics. He later raised the figure to 8 percent. 'I'm saying that we're being effective in disturbing the doctor, the counselors, the women going in,' he said in April 1984 on a Washington, D.C., television program" (cited in Diamond 1989, 95). Testifying before the House civil and constitutional rights subcommittee in 1985, "Scheidler told the congressmen that he believes the antiabortion movement is above the law, because it answers to a higher law."[50]

Dualism also fosters a highly individualized religion. If God is so intensely personal that he speaks directly to the individual, then different individuals may receive different, but not contradictory, "burdens" from him. Thus, a fundamentalist group may legitimize widely divergent activities among its members—some demonstrating against abortions, others concentrating on soul-winning, and still others dwelling on more church-oriented activities. Therefore, the building of a movement to accomplish something may require a dynamic and charismatic (sociologically speaking) person to convince others to take up the same burden.

Whatever happens is interpretable consistent with the thought structure. Thus Matt Goldsby and Jimmy Simmons rationalized that not being caught after the June 25 bombing meant God supported their efforts. On the other hand, being caught after the Christmas bombings meant God wanted to use the trial to publicize the horror of abortions. Their capture, at least to them, did not mean that they were wrong about God's view of abortions or that he was disapproving the bombing itself. The prison sentence, being as light as it was, meant that prayer works. Many fundamentalist Christians in Pensacola did not ask, "Why any sentence at all? Why not a verdict of complete innocence?" This is comparable to the concept of "mana" in tribal societies, which is also a post hoc explanation for whatever happens, good or ill. Thus, whatever happens confirms the worldview. Nothing can possibly disconfirm it.[51]

All events are interpreted in the light of fundamentalist theology. Thus Kathren Simmons's mother responded to Paul Shimek's summation, which concentrated on spiritual warfare, God and Satan, with "They finally heard the Word!" She did not ask, "How valid is this as a defense?" or "How effective is this as a defense?" It appears that the legal and public purposes of the trial were irrelevant to her. Hence, there was a double agenda in the trial: that of the prosecution and the judge and that of the supporters of the defense, while the defense counsel themselves were trying to satisfy both agendas.

Pensacola fundamentalists were not concerned about abortion until the 1973 Supreme Court decision. They were not concerned about prostitution until prostitutes paraded the streets. They were unconcerned about topless bars until one was next door to one of their churches. We can safely predict that abortion would disappear as an issue as long as it was illegal. Indeed, this has been the case in the past. According to a knowledgeable informant, the Enzor Brothers Hospital, about forty miles northeast of Pensacola in Crestview, performed abortions virtually on demand in the 1930s and 1940s, as did a doctor in Century (only thirty miles to the north), who also sold black-market babies, but there was no public outcry. Thus, the fundamentalists' major concern, as shown by their public actions, is public morality—or legalized and positively sanctioned immorality as they define it. As long as the law does not legitimate what they see as immorality, the issue fades from primary attention and concern. Out of sight, out of mind.[52]

In his classic work *The Mind of the South*, W. J. Cash (1941) pointed out this essential schizophrenia of traditional Southern culture, its penchant for the public display and disattention to private behavior.[53] Discretion is not only the better part of valor; it is also the better part of morality. The popular and ribald tales of young Southern swains going to revivals to seduce the newly converted young women had a firm foundation in fact.[54]

Dualism is most attractive to the economically dispossessed—lower-middle-class, working-class, and lower-class persons whose work is rote, who have little or no control over their work or impact on the other significant social organizations, particularly politics. Dualistic religion may give them a sense of control, or at least a sense of knowledge and insight about what is *really* going on in the world. The ideology of male dominance has an inherent contradiction in it: the male is to be head of the house and is to be the provider; yet his ability to provide is frequently precarious. He may be a carpenter and work only when the company has a job and when the weather is good, making his income undependable, erratic, and contingent on forces outside his control. Thus, in his home he is or may be a relative failure, for life is a constant economic struggle. Even worse, he may depend on his wife's working outside the home to help raise the family's income and social status, as well as give the family a predictable income base, which tends to give her a larger voice in decision making. This, by the way, is true cognitive dissonance, a disjuncture between behavior and values. The dualistic ideology provides reinforcement and reaffirmation of tradition in the face of this dissonance. Furthermore, the fundamentalist church gives the lower- and working-class male the one place where he can exhibit dominance and control.[55]

In sum, fundamentalists largely adhere to the mechanical model of the universe,[56] which is also dualistic; thus they see a basic dialectical difference between energy and substance, body and spirit, mind and matter, faith and reason. Yet theirs is a thoroughly modern expression of the medieval thought pattern. It mimics science and uses the testimony of "experts" in its opposition to science. It differs fundamentally from science, however, in the belief that science must be subject to specific values. The values come first, and scientific findings that fundamentalists perceive as contradicting those values must be wrong.[57] The only scientific findings that are acceptable are those that can be shown to support their positions. Fundamentalism uses the scientific technology of communications to oppose modernism.[58]

More basic, fundamentalism also uses the thought patterns of modernism—especially systematizing—in building its own models, such as the various timetables for the coming millennium.[59] Without modernization, fundamentalism would not exist.[60]

## Fundamentalism and Radicalization of the Anti-Abortionists

Radicalization is an interactive process; that is, a person or group is radicalized only over against and in interaction with another person or group, and the reaction of each to the other is necessary to sustain the cumulative process.[61] Frustration at not achieving goals is one of the processes at work leading to the heightening of activity by one side, which leads in turn to a heightened reactivity by the opposition—an escalating process, unless something or someone breaks the cycle with a nonescalating (or de-escalating) response. A concomitant process involves the successive stimuli to action on the part of subgroups within each of the opposed interacting movements. Thus, on the individual level, the more one has invested in the group (in time, sacrifice, ego, or whatever), the more reluctant one becomes to drop the group. Indeed, there is a tendency to escalate the investment, even (or especially) in the face of the frustration of goals, to throw even more good money after bad.[62] From a group perspective, different actors may find appealing or unappealing the particular level of engagement at any stage of confrontation. The abortion struggle in the United States has sustained itself through a continual replacement with progressively more radical actors as the general goals of the anti-abortion movement have remained thwarted. However, more moderate groups such as the National Right to Life Committee persist, though probably somewhat weakened, and try to distance themselves from the incivilities and violence of the more radical succeeding headliners.

So, too, the anti-abortion activists in Pensacola increased their level and type of activities as they faced disappointment in realizing their goals. They began with simple picketing at the Ladies Center, which was then located at the rear of one of Pensacola's largest shopping malls. There they also tried to confront women entering the clinic by facing them as they exited their cars in the parking lot. When the clinic used a court injunction to force the picketers out of the parking lot and off the private property of the mall, the picketers were left with only the main artery roadside for their demonstrations, and this was located out of sight of the clinic itself.

Their response was to expand their picketing to the more visible and accessible locations of the offices of Dr. Bagenholm and Dr. Permenter, each in a building directly facing a public street. But again, injunctions kept them out of parking lots and prevented them from accosting patients. This inspired them to use a bullhorn to reach the women who might be seeking an abortion.

As the levels of activism increased, the cast of characters tended to change. Some of the original demonstrators and picketers dropped out, apparently feeling uncomfortable with the more dramatic and hostile types of actions. At the same time, persons formerly in the background and some not previously involved were apparently attracted by the more dramatic actions and began rising to the forefront.[63]

There was a concurrent increase in the use of dramatic symbols. The original picketers carried simple, hand-lettered signs. Later additions included photos of aborted fetuses, tubs of red-paint-spotted infant dolls, and hanged effigies of Dr. Bagenholm and clinic manager Linda Taggart borne by dark-brown-shrouded and skeleton-masked demonstrators.

At first, Dr. Permenter was in a partnership with the Woman's Clinic, which was owned by a local woman. When she married a Pensacola attorney, John Burt claims he and others brought pressure on her husband by convincing some of his clients to withdraw their business. As a result, she sold her interest to Permenter and opened a new clinic in Fort Walton Beach, fifty miles to the east. That new clinic advertises in the Pensacola newspaper, but apparently the owner's husband is no longer under an economic boycott.

When all these tactics failed to yield significant change, the anti-abortionists began picketing the doctors' and manager's homes. The failure of this tactic led some persons, still unknown, to call offices, clinics, and homes threatening bombing and the harming of the operators' children and families. These calls were followed by pseudopatients entering the offices and releasing stink-bombs into the ventilation systems. Then an attempt was made to enter Bagenholm's office and directly confront the patients inside. The final and most dramatic escalation in the symbolic warfare was the introduction of Baby Charlie, the late-term fetus, to the picketing.

The increasing use of more and more radical dramatizations and tactics was not without a cost, however. The number of those willing to be associated with David Shofner[64] and, in particular, with John Burt has declined through time. Burt casts this consideration aside as a necessary cost of getting the job done. But while decreasing the numbers of people involved in the more dramatic actions, the use of radical tactics has left a fairly solid core of determined activists who receive public and media attention beyond what their number warrants. This has also forced the other anti-abortionists, those committed to more "polite" forms of protest, to differentiate themselves from Burt's tactics. For example, Penny Lea took great care to publicize her march as a "silent" one, a peaceful one. Although Burt participated as a coleader of the local forces, he did not produce Baby Charlie that day. The following event at Shofner's church attracted a relatively small audience. The primary result of the radicalization has been, except for the Lea march, Burt's co-optation of the public anti-abortion movement and a subsequent loss of public support for the movement as a whole and for all the individual groups. One effect of Burt's "radicalism" is seen in the response he got when, taking about fifteen Pensacolans to join Louisiana pickets at the site of the NOW national convention in New Orleans in July 1985, he marched before the hotel with Baby Charlie in his hand. According to the New Orleans paper, after one-and-a-half hours the Louisiana contingent asked him to leave, which he did. But, as the most radical person there, John Burt was the one featured on national television.

The escalation of picketer methodologies also led to the radicalization of some of the opposition. For instance, Dr. Bagenholm responded to the pressure by gradually increasing the time within which he would conduct abortions (from twelve weeks to eighteen) and by ceasing to perform adoption services. And although he wanted to leave Pensacola, and may likely have left it under other circumstances, he is now determined to remain there. Moreover, someone did apparently retaliate for the bombings by trying to burn the First Assembly of God. The anti-abortionists also claim to have received bomb threats, and in

July 1985 John Burt's Our Father's House was subjected to counter-picketing by the local NOW chapter, which followed with an additional counteroffensive by staging a "silent vigil" before the area's three most active anti-abortion churches in October 1985.

As recounted in chapters 3 and 4, fundamentalists have seen "sin" increasingly coming out of the closet in Pensacola over the past fifteen years. Public adherence to their definition of sacred morality has eroded with the legalization of alcohol sales, the abolition of blue laws,[65] the public display of prostitution, the dropping of sanctions against other "victimless crimes" such as homosexuality, the legal institution of gambling at the local greyhound track, and the decrease in the punishment of drug users (as opposed to distributors). Fundamentalists see their values publicly discarded and socially jeered, and, even worse, they see sin flaunted.

During the same period, the television medium in particular became an avenue for the expression of anti-abortion values and the anti-abortion movement's hostilities and anger. Religious broadcasts are no longer just a Sunday morning and midnight sign-off event. Programs such as "700 Club" and broadcasts by a variety of TV evangelists can be found on television at practically every hour of the day and night, every day. Perhaps more encouraging to the entire religious Right was the attention given these conservatives and their actions by local and national news programs. Media attention in front-page photos and articles and in lead TV news stories may have given the impression to them and others that they had a wide, receptive audience. Apparently media agents thought so, given the attention they devoted to conservative Christian activities and their mistaken attribution of Ronald Reagan's electoral victories, in part, to conservative Christian mobilization.[66] It is quite likely that the anti-abortion movement in general and its violent wing in particular, as with the civil rights movement and the anti–Vietnam war movement, would not have been nearly so effective without the skillful use of the media, which successfully portrayed their goals as widespread popular goals, if not moral or patriotic goals per se. It is one thing to read a newspaper story about an event in some other city across the nation, but television brings it to the living room and gives it a unique immediacy. Just the fact that television gives attention to an incident may cast an aura of power and strength, if not outright create such power and strength, to a far greater extent than the essential reported facts warrant. If national television takes something seriously, the public tends to take it seriously.

That members of the anti-abortion movement are aware of this is obvious. John Burt, for example, is clearly playing to the media with Baby Charlie. The importance of the media was made clear at the April 1990 anti-abortion rally in Washington, D.C., when a minister prayed, "Father, I ask that indeed you would give a very favorable report to the media."[67]

Media reports of bombings and arsons may have also had the indirect effect of encouraging additional such incidents. As anti-abortion organizations and congregations across the nation became aware of these local episodes, they would have instigated serious discussions about who might have committed them, and even praise for the perpetrators, judging from the various local reactions reported in the press about each incident. The adulation given the perpetrators in these anti-abortion networks would likely have cast them as models to emulate.[68]

Even more encouraging to the fundamentalists, giving the illusion of widespread popular support for their positions, was the organization of Jerry Falwell's Moral Majority. Persons and groups representing the religious Right have built huge edifices, perform before large audiences, and bring in large sums of money—all traditional American proofs of support, success, and popularity.[69]

An even greater and more dramatic sign of coming victory for the fundamentalists was the election of Ronald Reagan to the presidency with the vocal support of the Moral Majority and Reagan's concomitant vocal support of some of its key platforms, especially prayer in the schools and the abolition of abortion.[70] The fact that as governor of California Reagan had signed the most liberal abortion law in the nation at that time and that as president he did not attend church publicly more than a handful of times had no noticeable effect on this support for him. Again, the attention of the fundamentalists has been on outward form, the public rhetoric and presentation, rather than on the substance of conventional religiosity.

Numerous public polls and surveys have fairly well established that the Reagan electoral victories in 1980 and 1984 were the result of majority economic concerns and were achieved despite Reagan's religious positions, which, except for prayer in the schools, did not have popular support at all.[71] For example, a 1984 survey showed that 52 percent of those with an opinion believe "a badly deformed baby who could live only a few years" should be allowed to die. Furthermore, while 18 percent of the population believes abortion should be illegal under all circumstances, 53 percent feel it should be legal under "certain" circumstances, and 25 percent feel it should be legal under any circumstances. A 1980 poll showed that only 8 percent of the population approved of the Moral Majority.[72]

Other surveys have revealed that the Moral Majority and the overall fundamentalist program have the support of less than 15 percent of the voting population. At the same time, in the twenty years between 1963 and 1982, the number of Americans believing in biblical literalism has declined from nearly two-thirds of the total adult population to slightly more than one-third.[73] None of these facts have prevented the fundamentalist political activists from taking credit for the Reagan elections or from perceiving a public ground swell of support that does not exist. The "signs" have been seized upon to rejuvenate them and stimulate them to seek greater achievements.

When coupled with these seeming successes and the perceived support, the failure to achieve concrete goals has heightened the fundamentalists' frustrations. Several goals have appeared near at hand. A Prayer Amendment to the Constitution supported by President Reagan has been seriously debated in Congress. Federal support for abortions "of convenience" has ceased. The Supreme Court hears a new state abortion law case virtually every session. The fundamentalists keep feeling, "Maybe this time . . ." But most of these opportunities for true change have so far eluded them. As a result, the activism has heightened. The demands have broadened. The anger has increased.

Luker (1984, 145ff.) points out that the anti-abortion movement in California has changed character and personnel through time. She notes that the early activists were mostly professional males (doctors and lawyers) who were motivated by their awareness of the implications of the bending of the "health of the mother" clause in California abortions and the implications of proposed moderation of the state law.

They were followed after the 1973 Supreme Court decision by female activists who valued motherhood and pregnancy. This later group was largely self-recruited, searching for an avenue of protest. The first organizers, the professionals, dropped out of the movement due to cross-pressures from their community ties. The activist picketers, however, were not subject to those cross-pressures to the same extent.[74]

The bombers we studied are a third category of activists. They are also largely self-recruited and not subject to cross-pressures. A number of them were not involved in the previous protests, while some of them were but were disheartened by the apparent ineffectiveness of picketing. They differ most significantly in their age, being younger than Luker's California picketers, and their sex, being predominantly male. Like the female picketers in California, they value highly the traditional female role of mother and housewife. However, the males appear to act from a desire to keep females dependent, while females want to be able to hold the males responsible for the consequences of their sexual behavior (i.e., be responsible providers for the females and their offspring).

Thus, the increasingly radical groups involved in a social movement do not necessarily get recruited from the less radical elements, although some members may come through that route. For example, several bombers had previously been involved in picketing and other more peaceful activities. At the same time, however, at least half of them took up radical action as their first movement activity.

Both the sense of impending success and the experiences of frustration have been exacerbated by the fact that the fundamentalists tend to talk only among themselves. Many of them reinforce their common worldview by a lack of significant relationships with persons who contradict that interpretation.[75] Such limited interaction casts the aura of a closed corporate community around them. Such communities— found, for example, among many peasant societies or in the Appalachians in the United States—are accustomed to enforcing their own norms. They don't call the sheriff when someone violates community values; a private individual or group takes care of it on behalf of the community. Punishment is informal and personalized. Such worldviews at best offer amoral familism (a double standard for interpersonal dealings with insiders and outsiders) and at worst give community approval to the vigilantism of the Ku Klux Klan and similar organizations.

But social life is possible only with a modicum of trust that others will follow the rules, which enables us to predict others' behavior and their reactions to our own behavior. When others begin writing their own rules, when we cannot discern what rules they are operating under, it leads to the condition sociologists call "anomie" (normlessness). Because of the large number of subcultures that have different rules and different understandings of the rules, a degree of anomie is to be expected in modern society, especially in times of great social change when many rules are being redefined. A society can stand only so much anomie, however, before the situation deteriorates into such cases as Northern Ireland or Lebanon. Particularly during times of great change, it is important that the most elemental rules for solving differences of belief be adhered to. Otherwise the result is terrorism: a betrayal of our everyday, essential trust that people will follow the most basic rules of problem solving, that legal means of problem solving and resolution of grievances will be supported and obeyed.

The confessions of Jimmy Simmons and Matt Goldsby reveal that they were operating out of a perception of support for their violation of these most basic expectations. They both said they were talking about abortion when one of them said, in effect, "Somebody ought to do something about it." Implied in that statement is the belief that they had a community of support, that they would be enforcing community norms and values. Certainly they discovered such a community after their arrest when they received during their pretrial detainment a reported thirty to fifty letters a day supporting the bombings. Following the trial and prior to sentencing, letters supporting their deeds were also dropped in the First Assembly collection plate.[76] It is revealing that, insofar as we can determine, the clinic violence across the country has all been perpetrated by intensely religious, fundamentally religious, persons. It is apparently not enough that a person hold deep convictions against abortion. It is not sufficient that a person be a fundamentalist. An essential condition for the violence appears to be the presence of and interaction with a community that is perceived as a source of support, a community to act on behalf of, to give moral sanction to the act of violence.[77]

We hypothesize that this sense of support was heightened, perhaps even legitimized, by President Reagan's failure to condemn abortion clinic violence and bombings, despite frequent and strident public urgings. One significant piece of evidence is that while thirty-one clinics and offices were attacked between January 1, 1984, and January 1, 1985, only three attacks occurred in the eight months immediately after the president finally did speak against the violence in January 1985. Of course, the arrest and conviction of about a dozen persons for bombings and arsons of clinics and offices in 1984 and 1985 may well have added to the discouragement of others.

There was clear support of the Pensacola bombings and the bombers, not only in a few letters to the editor, but especially in the letters Simmons and Goldsby received while awaiting trial, in the attendance of sympathizers at the trial, and in the daily pickets outside the courthouse. In addition, the leaders of the Pensacola anti-abortion groups sent somewhat mixed signals, what William Brennan mistakenly called cognitive dissonance, to the bombers. While overtly disclaiming bombing and violence as a methodology, they unanimously said, in effect, "I'm glad it happened." The same response was expressed by fundamentalists in reaction to each of the other bombings across the nation. The Pensacola First Assembly of God pastor and congregation cooperated in this sub-rosa support through their reception of Simmons and Goldsby, in the name of condemning the sin while loving the sinner, and more specifically in their raising the defense fund for them. The most dramatic symbol of this support was probably the picketing and prayer demonstrations going on during the trial itself, as well as the large number of supporters present in the courtrooms. All these conveyed a clear, if sometimes silent, message to the defendants and to the public: "We approve of what you did. We commend you for it." The presence of a number of people from outside the local community added to their sense of defense by a national reference group.[78]

One example of an extreme form Christian fundamentalism is Christian reconstructionism, a radical, militant, political expression that constitutes virtually the ideal type of fundamentalism carried to its logical conclusion.[79] Its adherents, while a distinct minority, are gathered in congregations of various sizes—from quite small to as large as 12,000 members—and would install their brand of Christianity as the law of the land.[80] Reconstructionists are unabashed theocratists. Some (such as Gary North, a prominent reconstructionist and son-in-law of Rousas John Rushdoony, the "father" of reconstructionism) would deny religious liberty to "the enemies of God," whom the reconstructionists, of course, would identify.[81]

The reconstructionists feel that every area of life—law, politics, the arts, education, medicine, the media, business, and especially morality—must be ruled by them. They span a number of denominations: independent, Methodist, Presbyterian, Lutheran, Baptist, Catholics, former Jews, and others. Their goal is to establish a "God-centered government," a kingdom of God on earth, by instituting the Old Testament as the law of the land and executing criminals condemned to death by the Old Testament, including homosexuals, sodomists, rapists, adulterers, and "incorrigible" youths. They would censor extensively, so that media matters reflect their perspective. They would abolish public education and welfare (only those who work should eat) and limit taxes to the tithe (10 percent of everyone's income), most of it paid to the church. Other government taxes they define as theft. They would eliminate property, social security, and inheritance taxes. They desire to reestablish biblical, Jerusalemic society. They would have church elders acting as judges and courts that would oversee moral issues, while "civil" courts would handle other issues. The country would return to the gold standard. Debts, including the present thirty-year mortgages, would be limited to six years.

The reconstructionists want to reinstitute the medieval centrality of religion, the Puritan style of dominance in Massachusetts, and John Calvin's "Christian" government of Geneva, where heretics were burned at the stake. In their view democracy is opposed to Christianity, the rule of man placed above the rule of God.[82] Among the things they attack are property taxes and compulsory education. Jails would become primarily "holding ponds" for those awaiting execution or assignment as servants indentured to those whom they have wronged as one form of restitution. In addition, "true" Christianity is the road to economic prosperity; God blesses the faithful.

The fundamentalists' ultimate goal is the establishment of a theocracy, a government and laws in complete conformity with their definitions of the people of God. Law, economics, education, personal and public morality would all revolve around fundamentalist interpretations of the Bible.[83] Some, such as those who would disbar attorneys who defend accused pornographers, would not hesitate to abrogate some of our present basic civil liberties. All abortions would be illegal, prayers to Jesus would be uttered in every school, students would hear daily Bible readings, creationism would be taught in lieu of evolution, divorce would be outlawed except in cases of adultery, cohabiters would be jailed along with homosexuals and prostitutes, no stores would open on Sundays, prohibition would be reestablished, libraries would have unacceptable books removed, "non-Christian" (non-fundamentalist) teachers would be fired, public universities would become imitations of Falwell's Liberty College, and, in the visions of the most extreme, a grim Christ would scatter his gray breath over the land.[84]

It is questionable whether the majority of fundamentalists would themselves be content in such a society. While railing against the secular society they resent, many of them have enjoyed the fruits of the tolerance inherent in secularization. They have had the advantages of living in both worlds, their own and that of the society around them, and the ability to move back and forth between them. While some of them have delighted in blasting the "sinfulness" of society, they have also enjoyed slipping across the line on occasion to have a drink, to visit a prostitute, or to seek an abortion when an unwanted or threatening pregnancy occurred. This may help explain the differences in national polls between those who express support for the details of the Moral Majority agenda and the much smaller numbers who support the Moral Majority itself. For example, some people may not like the *idea* of abortion, but they may nevertheless want to preserve the option.[85]

### The National Scene and the Global Context

Is what happened in Pensacola typical of what has occurred across the nation, or is it a unique case? As discussed in chapter 13, the number of violent abortion-related incidents across the country in the 1984–87 period increased dramatically, to almost four times as many events as in the previous four-year period. And the greatest increase was in the most violent types of incidents: bombings, attempted bombings or arsons, and bomb threats.

Our survey of all facilities that were subjected to arson or bombing in 1984 and 1985 and were still operating in July 1985 reveals that all but one of them were subjected to intensive picketing, demonstrations, and techniques of harassment. While not all heavily picketed sites have suffered bombings or arsons, there is an obvious tendency for such actions to encourage more violent responses when milder behavior fails.

In this same time period, religious fundamentalism and its desire for theocracy have become a visible phenomenon worldwide. We see it voicing rejection of modernization, secularization, and toleration in Iran and Lebanon. It reveals itself in the Shiite movements throughout the Middle East, in the nativistic religions of Japan, in the fundamentalist stance of the Papacy against the liberation theologies of the Third World, in the mutually hostile and radical Protestant and Catholic positions in Northern Ireland, and in the extreme Orthodox position in Israel. The American fundamentalism with which we are concerned here, however, has its own international agenda, including political evangelism in the Caribbean and Latin America, and is totally opposed to most of the competing world fundamentalist movements.

American fundamentalism is haunted by a longing for an idealized bygone era when life was basically organized around kinship; when the family was self-sufficient on its farm and controlled its own everyday life; when roles were predefined and fixed; when behavior was regulated by gossip; when relations were warm, personal, and intimate; and people appeared to care deeply for one another. This longing leads to a correlative yearning for a new "Dark Age" in which religion will dominate politics, economics, education, and science.

The extent to which this is true is manifest in the resolve of the Reagan and Bush administrations to withhold support for international Planned Parenthood activities, justified mainly through arguments against abortion. The fact that in most countries no UN monies or U.S. government contributions are used to support abortions, or that where abortions are supported they are documented to be voluntary and represent only a very small fraction of all funds expended for population control, holds small sway with the religiously justified conservative U.S. administration.[86]

The abortion issue is not just a Pensacola issue, nor is it only an American issue. The bombings in Pensacola are not unique. Pensacola is a microcosm of global value conflict and only one stage enacting a worldwide issue: Can modernization continue with a vociferous minority that is willing to use violence to oppose it, that is unwilling to "live and let live," that refuses to compromise or to tolerate different life-styles, that finds any way other than its own absolutely unacceptable?

One possible beginning of an answer may lie in hearing the deeper cry behind the rhetoric. At least one thing the fundamentalists are saying to the nation and to the world is that they want control of their own lives, that they are not being listened to, that the "system" is no longer their system, is no longer responsive to them.[87] That cry is no longer a cry of only a few dispossessed religious conservatives but is the increasing lament of the middle class in America as well. More and more Americans perceive themselves as caught in a nonresponsive social structure, one that structures their lives without their consent and without their input.

The answer to that cry is not to accede to specific demands, but to empower people. It lies in providing avenues of communication from the individual to the collective structures, replacing the dominance of top-down communication typified by the characterization of the immediate past president as the "Great Communicator." It is clear that the American presidency is less responsive to the popular demands of a majority, or even to the viewpoints of consensus groups on particular issues, than it is ideologically motivated within a very narrow minority view. The presidency of Ronald Reagan, like the media-rich chairmanship of Mikhail Gorbachev and the current austere leadership of Iran, was a symptom of the underlying problem of delivering "democracy" in large-scale societies. It is easier to hold to an ideological principle that lacks popular support than it is to encompass the varieties of minority and majority positions that constitute the opinion fabric in mass culture.

All of the differences expressed in community and national debate cloud our vision of the shared problems of individual survival in our society and in world society. The economic and social boundaries separating us into subcultures are operative in our opinions and decisions about abortion. In a mass-communication culture even a minority opinion can hold political sway if it is given sufficient media exposure. The "majority" who hold weak opinions or who lack the critical capacity to form strong conclusions from manifest facts easily succumb to media manipulation. This difficulty of complex, mass society touches all classes, all socioeconomic groups, all religions—in short, all subcultures. Thus, even in the affluence that makes most of us middle class, we are all downtrodden, all struggling against ourselves, all cheapened by the values guiding our communities. The fundamentalists are not so much different from the rest of society as they are more aware, because of their founding premises, of the changes that confront us. Yet we must differentiate an "understanding" of the problem from the "solution" for a human future.

The conservative evangelical movement in the United States involves the wedding of an affluent core of ministers with the middle, lower-middle, and working classes.[88] Taking the nationalistic perspective legitimated by Ronald Reagan, such ministers as Jimmy Swaggart, Jerry Falwell, Oral Roberts, and Billy Graham pursue the notion that a successful future for the world is dependent on the economic success and well-being of the United States, that the bounty of capitalism in the United States will "trickle down" not only to the American middle classes and poor but also to the poor of the world who accept Jesus and American hegemony. Second, they argue that no other system has ever or can ever deliver the level of human comfort that the American system has, and on that basis it should be the standard against which all other societies should be judged. Often the message of the evangelists—interpreters of the gospel—rings clearly for male supremacy, white supremacy, and American supremacy, without regard for the cultures and aspirations of the rest of the world. It is not surprising that the "masses" within our nation respond, knowing how economically difficult recent years have been and how the international challenge to the United States seems irrational.

But "liberal" fundamentalist evangelist Anthony Campolo, in interpreting (but not espousing) Marx for Christian audiences, cuts through the heart of the conservative Christian complaint. Like other evangelicals, he stresses the necessity of Christian community as a means of achieving a full life. Like most fundamentalists, he argues for a full reading of a scripture he believes to be inerrant. His messages assert the gospel in the midst of a society that he argues is fundamentally secular, involving notions of individual autonomy and moral relativity. Yet he goes on to ask how people can hope to achieve a Christian life when they willingly participate in an economic system that dehumanizes people by devaluing their participation in production, by denying their creation as "creators in the image of God," by treating workers as objects in the system of production, and by magnifying the gap between the masses of the poor and the wealthy few.[89] In undermining the Marxist identification of liberation theology, Pope John Paul II has made the same points: human work should enhance the humanity of the worker, while profit, even in the capitalist mode of production, is always a secondary concern.

Such attitudes position Americans in the context of the world society as partners rather than as paternalistic physicians bleeding the poor to save them from their sins. This perspective is as valid for the abortion controversy as it is for economic issues. In the end we argue that the conservative fundamentalist critique of the world is as self-serving as the narcissistic secular ideology it despises. What all Americans need is the ability to struggle against blind self-interest, to fulfill the *promises* of capitalism everywhere, to support and expand programs for development such as the unimplemented and unpopular Caribbean Basin Initiative, to resist the kinds of ethnocentrism that made Union Carbide's response to Bhopal a travesty, to deny the principle of dictatorship wherever it occurs, to support Reagan's and Bush's resistance to protectionist laws, and to exercise restraint in processes of domestic collective bargaining. And all of this we need in the certain realization that by world standards our middle classes are fabulously wealthy and unimaginably free.

# ... 15
# Violence
# against Abortion
# and the
# Abortion of Violence

I came not to send peace, but a sword.
Matthew 10:34

## The Nature of Violence

The forms and motivations of violence are many. Violence may be the act of an individual or group. It may be premeditated or spontaneous. It may be directed against persons or property or both. It may be directed against persons as individuals or as representatives of the social system or some part of it. It may arise out of individual idiosyncrasies or out of group (social) processes and expectations. It may be a rational, an irrational, or a nonrational response. It may be a matter of ego defense, as in a subculture that demands violent defense of one's macho self-image. It may arise out of aberrational passion for control of others, or it may well up from cultural expectations, a learned response in defense of one's perceived status.

The violence most abhorred is that commonly defined as "criminal" violence—violence against "guiltless" others, as in a robbery or random murder—especially when it is premeditated. Less criminal, many people tend to believe, is violence against a cheating spouse or other "crimes of passion."

All violence has the effect of objectifying the victim; it "thingifies" him or her, dehumanizing the prey. This is a common self-perception of those taken hostage. They feel helpless, powerless, out of control.

Most of us go through our lives ordering our everyday experiences, making the details of our lives predictable so we can rely on the expectedness of events. Violence, especially random, "criminal" violence, shatters our illusion of control over the significant and mundane events of our lives. Violence reminds us very dramatically that we are vulnerable, contingent, dependent, and ultimately insecure in this universe. In short, it violates us. (It is no accident that the words *violence* and *violation* have the same Latin roots.) On the other hand, the violator, the initiator of violence, is declaring, "*I* am in control. The world shall be ordered *my* way! *I* shall decide the terms on which the others around me shall exist."

Thus, illegitimate violence is a threat to all of us. This is why most societies define such an act as an offense not only against the victim but, more importantly, against the entire society. And most societies regard the threat to society as more important than the threat to the individual who is violated.

And then there is the premeditated violence that is born of passion, the violence of a social movement, which is our concern here.

### Religion and Violence

History reveals a close connection between religion and violence. Such a connection goes back to long before the Crusades. However, picking up the threads of that relationship at the time of these "holy wars" is an excellent starting point for understanding religious violence.

The First Crusade arose in 1095 A.D. at the instigation of Pope Urban II. On their way to the Holy Land, many of the crusading groups became mobs who attacked the Jews of Europe, declaring that anyone who killed a Jew would experience complete remission of sin. Perhaps such violence against Jews was abetted by the Crusaders' frustration with the slow march to the infidel Muslims. In any event, the Jews experienced continued pogroms through successive Crusades. Later, with the onslaught of the bubonic plague, or Black Death, Jews again suffered as the scapegoat for it, even though they too perished in great numbers from the epidemic. Sometimes the violence against Jews was "legitimate," sanctioned by the political authorities. Other times, Jews were the victims of illegitimate violence, or mob action.

In sixteenth-century Europe, violence was expanded to internecine warfare—again, both legitimate and illegitimate—between Protestants and Catholics. As indicated by Davis (1975), such violence of Catholics against Protestants, Protestants against Catholics, and both against Jews was at times instigated by a desire to rid a community of "pollution" and at other times by class hostilities. In many cases the illegitimate violence occurred at the instigation and encouragement of zealous priests or ministers. Davis notes that "religious riot is likely to occur when it is believed that religious and/or political authorities are failing in their duties or need help in fulfilling them" (p. 169). Thus, one aspect of religious violence tends to be the conviction of the perpetrators that they are acting legitimately on behalf of community or divine values.

The United States has its own history of religious violence, such as that of the mob actions in Boston in the late 1800s against Irish Catholics in which communities and churches were burned and individuals were lynched. Also, Catholics in the South were the sporadic victims of violence.

In examining the more recent violence of Jim Jones's Jonestown, Ken Levi (1982, 175) concludes: "Sociologists (including myself) tend to view cult violence as a symptom of fervent commitment, similar in form to the kind of commitment that one might encounter in a business corporation or political party. The 'spiritually arrogant' cultist is self-willed (to the extent that anyone can be) because his actions are meaningful to him, in the same sense that the patriotic soldier fights for a cause that is meaningful to him." Levi maintains that "religious violence is most likely to occur in sects that enforce a single version of the truth by exercising total control and demanding total loyalty" and that "violent cultists come from cultures that already accept violence." He identifies the basic elements contributing to sect violence as centralized leadership under a charismatic leader, that leader's control of members through intense psychological manipulation, the thorough commitment of members to the group, isolation of the group from other social organizations, and "a set of beliefs that express hostility to outsiders" (pp. 177–79).[1]

## Abortion and Violence

There are parallels between the violence in the current abortion controversy and recent social movements and issues in America. In the 1950s and 1960s the civil rights movement spawned opposition on the part of the White Citizens Councils, who utilized primarily economic reprisals in their attempts to counteract the movement. However, their extreme oratory and rhetoric gave encouragement and comfort to the more violent wing, the Ku Klux Klan. On the other side, the non-violent civil rights movement provided an atmosphere in which the more extreme black power movement could arise.[2] The anti-war movement of the 1960s had its own protesters and demonstrators, such as Students for a Democratic Society, which produced the more impatient, more violent Weathermen.

As Joseph Fichter (1954) reports in his study of Catholic parishes, organizations have multileveled constituencies. At the outer edge of a parish, for example, are those non-Catholics for whom the parish bears some responsibility, such as spouses or children of Catholics. As one moves through concentric circles from the outer ring toward the center, the degree of involvement and commitment to the church increases. In the inner circle are the most committed, fully practicing members.

A social movement also has multilayered constituencies and participants.[3] At the outer edge are those who support its goals but are not actively involved in movement organizations. They may support the movement in voting or other political behavior, but they do not consider it a primary motivating factor. As one moves toward the core of the movement, behavior grows more activist and more radical. Organizations established to support the movement have different levels of commitment to its objectives, will use different tactics to achieve the goals, and will therefore be found spread out through the various inner-to-outer circles.

However, all other movement organizations and supporters will find themselves having to react to the behavior of more extremist movement supporters and organizations. And "moderate" organizations may find it necessary to become more radical to maintain their own constituencies.[4] The more moderate organizations may find themselves superseded in the public eye and even their own reputations characterized by more extremist groups. Individuals may move inward from one level of activism to more radical behavior. On the other hand, other persons may not involve themselves at all in the outer organizations but may leap into a superactivist position. Newcomers to a movement may feel a compulsion to jump beyond current levels of activism to prove their identification with the movement (what sociologists call the conversion syndrome).

At different stages of social movement development, different persons with different levels of commitment and activism, as well as different social profiles, will be attracted to organizations related to it. Willingness to become active in a movement will depend at least partially on one's social position and relations within the society and the relative costs of becoming active.[5] Earlier "activists" may withdraw as more persons willing to escalate the level of activism become involved and are willing to move toward greater degrees of radicalism. Also, as more extreme behavior develops in the movement, persons who might have united with less radical organizations may well pull back from being mobilized because of the entire movement's being identified with the radicals. Thus, the early, more civil activists may serve to recruit increasingly less civil members and move an organization beyond their own dreams and ambitions.

On the other hand, by attracting the primary attention of countervailing authorities, extremists may serve to free up more moderate members and organizations to a higher degree of activism. That is, extreme behavior may allow a redefinition of the situation in which slightly less extreme behavior now appears more or less moderate, when previously it would have been defined as most extreme (Killian 1972).

The anti-abortion movement has had several levels of membership involvement and degrees of activism (see figure 2).[6] The movement began activity beyond public opinion with (1) educational efforts, primarily by Catholic organizations, against contraceptives and abortion, and the formation of Right to Life committees. These efforts were followed by (2) organizing political action committees to support anti-abortion candidates and lobbying for laws, at first through (2a) state organizations in those states where there were efforts to liberalize state

**Figure 2. Levels of Involvement in the Anti-Abortion Movement**

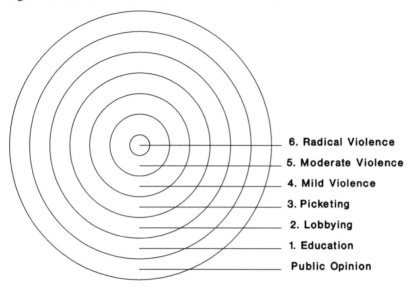

6. Radical Violence

5. Moderate Violence

4. Mild Violence

3. Picketing

2. Lobbying

1. Education

Public Opinion

laws and later, following the *Roe v. Wade* decision, through (2b) national organizations to develop and enact new legislation and elect candidates toward reversing the Supreme Court decision.[7] Using Lofland's (1985) categories, movement activity escalated into (3) "symbolic action," primarily picketing. When this failed to effect change, (4) intervention was utilized by a segment of the movement. Tactics included gluing clinic locks, setting off stink-bombs inside clinics, harassing clinic personnel, blockading entry to clinics, and occupying them. These activities may be characterized as forms of "mild" violence.[8] A stage of "moderate" violence followed, with (5) the destruction of clinic instruments and equipment. The final stage, (6) prevention, attempts to close clinics down through "radical" violence, including destruction of buildings through bombings and arsons, and kidnapping.[9] Each of these stages involves different kinds of persons based, at a minimum, on those persons' social positions and their social linkages, as well as on the organizations' degrees of inclusiveness and exclusiveness in recruitment of supporters, and their bases of recruitment.[10]

The bombings and arsons seemed to lead initially to a decrease among those willing to be publicly identified with the anti-abortion movement. This tendency was exacerbated by the identification of the slightly less radical activists, such as John Burt in Pensacola, with the bombers and arsonists. There has been an attempt since 1987 to recapture and revitalize the movement through Operation Rescue,[11] a group using civil disobedience by blocking entrance to clinics in targeted cities, an interventionist tactic. However, Operation Rescue depends on a coterie of national activists who target specific clinics in specific cities through serial sit-ins. The organizers of Operation Rescue have rarely been able to mobilize enough people in local communities to carry out their objectives in simultaneous demonstrations throughout the nation and have had to rely on a group of hard-core activists to move from city to city and recruit persons through their activism. However, they have garnered considerable support, with several hundred persons being willing to go to jail after taking part in demonstrations conducted in several cities at the same time.

On the other hand, the less radical activists may benefit from the greater "extremism" that tends to develop (Killian 1972). Such activists may be typed by the power structure as more reasonable and may therefore be able to negotiate movement in the society at large toward their objectives. Thus Operation Rescue tactics appeared to the public to be less radical than bombings and the National Right to Life Committee was viewed as less radical than Operation Rescue.

The escalation of radical behavior may well lie beyond the control of a movement's current leaders. But they still must respond to it, for they are linked in the public image with their radical wings. In the anti-abortion movement, the clear tendency of the "moderates" has been to deny the legitimacy of violence, such as arson and bombing, while at the same time welcoming it and using it to add to their own public exposure. The tactics of the moderates have consistently been to maintain the rightness of their cause while walking a nonviolent tightrope to try to maintain public credibility and approval.

John Burt is correct when he denies direct responsibility for the bombings. He is also correctly implying a partial responsibility when he says in effect, echoing both Protestant and Catholic pastors of sixteenth-century France, "I can't help it when what I do inspires someone to go off the deep end." Moreover, he is not discouraging bombing when he says, "I would go out and blow up a clinic and have no qualms about it except I am scared of being caught."[12] The violent wing of any movement can arise and continue to operate only with an approving audience. Private law, the use of force and violence by individuals to punish the "immoral," can be exercised consistently and over time only in the atmosphere of a supportive public. And across the nation the response of the anti-abortion demonstrators and figureheads has in every case paralleled that of the Pensacola leaders (John Burt and David Shofner, among others), who have as much as said, "I don't approve of violence, but I'm glad it happened."

A similar justification for the bombings and arsons came from none other than the Roman Catholic bishops of the United States when, in January 1985, they condemned the spate of bombings as a symptom of "the violence unleashed into society" by abortion itself and concluded that "violence begets violence." Statements like these by Burt, Shofner, the Catholic bishops, and similar others in communities across the nation add an air of legitimacy to the violence by blaming the victims.[13]

John Burt went further in a statement to a *New York Times* reporter shortly after the arrests of Goldsby and Simmons when he said, "Maybe like Harpers Ferry, where John Brown used violence to bring the evils of slavery into focus, these bombings may do the same thing on the abortion issue. . . . When the history of this period is written, it won't be the pickets or the letter-writers who will be the heroes. . . . It's going to be the bombers."[14]

Violence is inherent in the vituperative nature of much of the picketing and anti-abortion activities that have taken place across the country in the past few years. Many anti-abortion activists have displayed a murderous passion for the life of the fetus, a hate-filled love. Both psychologists and theologians have reminded us that love and hate are closely related emotions; one is never far from the other. Anti-abortion workers' love for the nameless, faceless fetus is reflected in dehumanizing and obscene behavior toward clinic patients and staff and their supporters. These displays have an uncanny ability to arouse similar emotions among the pro-choice supporters. Signs saying that God hates the sin but loves the sinner leave one unconvinced when the

facial expressions and vocal tones of the demonstrators are considered. The violence inherent in such picketing actions may serve as a catalyst to the less controlled among their followers.

Not unusual is an incident reported in the Buffalo, New York, *News* (June 2, 1986):

> During a morning service on June 1, 1986, the Rev. R. L. Hymers Jr., pastor of the fundamentalist Baptist Tabernacle, led an estimated 400 members of his congregation in prayer asking God to take Supreme Court Justice William J. Brennan Jr.'s life. Brennan was one of the seven justices who supported the 1973 decision legalizing abortions. His death, the group hoped, would enable President Reagan to replace him with a judge who opposes abortion. On the same day, the church chartered a plane to circle overhead while Brennan gave a commencement speech at Loyola Marymount Law School. The plane carried a banner reading, "Pray for Death: Baby Killer Brennan." According to Joseph Scheidler, executive

director of the Pro-Life Action League, Hymer's source for this appeal was Psalm 109, verses 8–9 and 16–17: "Let his days be few and let another take his office. Let his children be fatherless and his wife a widow . . . because he remembered not to show mercy, but persecuted the poor and needy, that he might even slay the broken in heart. As he loved cursing, so let it come unto him."[15]

Similarly, support for violence came at the 1981 National Right to Life Committee meeting at Disney World, where there was an "auditorium filled with people who bowed their heads at one point and prayed the Lord would 'send the enemy to the pit of destruction,' a congregation that enthusiastically applauded indirect references to vandalism and arson at abortion clinics."[16]

A more direct relationship between picketers and violence occurred in Birmingham, Alabama, when a clinic staff member discovered her beheaded cat on her doorstep. Arriving later at the clinic, she was faced with signs reading, "What happened to your cat?"

Violence is also encouraged by statements such as that by Teresa Lindley, who was arrested in Pensacola November 1986 for blocking a driveway at the Ladies Center:

We will not tolerate a place that is devoted to the destruction of children. God doesn't care how the walls come down. It can be economics, peaceful means like picketing, by people like Joan [Andrews] going in . . . but when judges and police of this community take away nonviolent means . . . then God is going to act.

Bombing is the only thing left if the other things don't work. This is a most dangerous place to be as long as that place is here. The person who makes the sacrificial effort to close that place down is saving the community from God's wrath. . . . Something will be done to close it because God has said to close it and I have no idea what God has in mind.[17]

In addition, Joan Bray, a member of the Pro-Life Nonviolent Action Committee, is reported to have said, "I am personally opposed to the destruction of property, but I respect the right of people who do it where babies are being slaughtered."[18] And statements by Randall Terry, head of Operation Rescue, indicate that "he does not see anything immoral in those who go further and bomb abortion clinics."[19] Even Pat Robertson has anticipated with pleasure the deaths of pro-choice Supreme Court justices.[20]

As we mentioned earlier, the kinds of participants in the anti-abortion movement have changed over the course of the movement's development. As the legal route faded in potential for success, a group of legal and medical professionals (in the California movement) were superseded by the more activist and primarily female picketers and demonstrators.[21] They in turn were overtaken by the predominantly male bombers and arsonists. Remarking on violence perpetrated by social movements, Anthony Oberschall (1973, 309–10) asserts: "Terrorism, bombings, and assassinations are resorted to by weak groups who already know their lack of mass support and their inability to generate more of it by other means and who therefore have nothing to lose by violence, especially if they have already been discredited in the eyes of the public."[22] Thus, the escalation of violence in the anti-abortion movement is an important indication of its failure to mobilize popular support.

### The Fundamentalist Ethic and the Spirit of Violence

We would go further and assert that violence is endemic to fundamentalism itself. The Christian Broadcasting Network (CBN), for example, includes on its regular weekend schedule of "family" programming reruns of "The Rifleman," "Wagon Train," "Laramie," "Cimarron Strip," "Branded," "Laredo," "I Spy," "The Cisco Kid," and "The Lone Ranger"—mostly westerns centered on violence between "pure" good and evil, white-hats versus black-hats. Indeed, the National Coalition on Television Violence (NCTV), which regularly monitors television broadcasting and grades programs, recently stated:

> NCTV has expressed its concern to CBN drama-action programming. Despite our best efforts, CBN has not been willing to meet with us to study this issue. NCTV has congratulated CBN on the low level of violence on its Monday through Friday daytime entertainment. However, Saturdays from 9 a.m. to 9 p.m. and Sunday 1 p.m. to 6 p.m. violent western programming takes over.

Also, "The Rifleman" and "Man From U.N.C.L.E." appear five days a week in early and late-evening programming.

It is about this programming that NCTV has the most concern. During these hours on Saturday and Sunday, CBN has the highest number of acts of violence per hour of any network in America. Although the violence is not as gruesome or vicious as in some pay-cable movies, it is an issue of concern.[23]

NCTV reports that CBN defends this programming as "helping fund the CBN ministry and thus bringing more people to Christ." This utilitarian ethic, soundly rejected by mainstream Christian denominations and, in theory, by most fundamentalists as well as most secular humanists, justifies the means used by the ends sought. It is the same justification given by those engaged in violence against abortion clinics and physicians' offices.

### Fundamentalist Theology and the Spirit of Violence

We maintain that violence is inherent in the central theological tenet of the fundamentalists—whether Protestant, Catholic, or Mormon. That doctrine is known as the substitutionary theory of the atonement, which is drawn primarily from the letters of Paul.[24] This theory holds that a righteous and just God is logically incapable of forgiving imperfection, even in creatures that he deliberately and consciously created and foreordained to be imperfect. Therefore, his righteousness can be assuaged only by a sacrificial offering, by *someone* suffering the penalty for human sin. Since in his mercy this God did not wish such deserved suffering for his creatures, he decided to punish himself for their inevitable disobedience. At the heart of the mood and intent of this theory is a violence consistent with a working-class approach to child-rearing techniques, which emphasizes obedience on the part of children and physical punishment for their disobedience. It is the theology that gave rise to the Crusades, the Inquisition, and the Salem witch trials.

The theology of the dualistic heaven and hell further contributes to the theme of religious violence. Fundamentalists and other dualists stress a literal, fiery hell of eternal punishment. While these images are drawn more from Dante's *Inferno* than from the scriptures,[25] they reinforce the notion of a God who is vindictive and unremittingly violent, a God of self-congratulating cruelty.[26]

These justifications for divine violence are reinforced by the violent eschatology of the dualists and fundamentalists, the millenarian expectation of Armageddon, the final all-out war between the forces of good and those of evil, between God and Satan. This bloody warfare is eagerly anticipated, one to be welcomed and hastened, for it will mark the vindication of God's chosen people.

This theology of violence carries over into the social and political perspectives of the fundamentalists. For example, Steve Zepp, an Assemblies of God minister and a picketer at the Ladies Center in Pensacola, frequently harassed women entering the clinic with his bullhorn-amplified question, "If you abort your baby, who's going to defend us against the Russians in twenty years?" The Moral Majority and religious Right have consistently advocated increases in the nation's military budget and nuclear capabilities. Violence is also implied, if not explicit, in the fundamentalists' opposition to social welfare programs such as Aid to Dependent Children, food stamps, and pre- and postnatal health care for the indigent. Ironically, they are thereby espousing social Darwinism, the survival of the fittest individuals. More explicitly, Randall Terry, national leader of Operation Rescue, stated, "I believe in the use of force. . . . I think to destroy abortion facilities at this time is counterproductive because the American public has an adverse reaction to what it sees as violence" (quoted in Kurtz 1989:A3).

This is not to say that all fundamentalists are violent, but that there is a coalescence of thought patterns, theology, values, and intracommunity interaction among fundamentalists that encourages and supports violence despite overt statements to the contrary. The theology and its adherents, by and large, do not recognize as a criminal act the bombing of abortion clinics and doctors' offices where abortions are performed. Even Pastor Lindell Ballenger, who clearly held that the bombings were wrong and supported jail terms for Simmons and Goldsby, struggled over whether they should actually serve prison sentences or not.

The more frequent reaction we found among the nonviolent anti-abortion leaders and acquaintances of Goldsby and Simmons was, "They're good, Christian people." Other responses were, "They shouldn't be placed with common criminals" and "They're not the criminals; the abortionists are." The head of the National Right to Life Committee, Dr. John C. Willke, asked, "Who are these folks? Not wild-eyed bombers. They come right out of the local Christian church. They do it as a present for Christ." Joseph Scheidler, Pro-Life Action League director, called the bombers "good Christians" and showed his support by attending the sentencing of the Pensacola Four.

Anti-abortion activists have overtly supported the violence against clinics by picketing the trials of the bombers and arsonists. They have, as mentioned above, also justified the violence. All these reactions are summarized in the one-word comment of activist Mary Yepez to the arson of the Everett, Washington, clinic: "Hallelujah!"

The anti-abortion activists have clearly been given to hyperbole, if not outright lies, which damages their credibility and questions their claim to the morality of their cause. They use pictures of very late-term abortions in their posters, but less than 1 percent of all abortions take place after the twenty-first week. They claim only 100,000 abortions per year took place prior to 1974, but the most conservative estimate by responsible sources is 200,000, while others maintain it could have been as many as 1.2 million per year. Anti-abortion spokespersons claim they speak for the majority of Americans, even though every opinion poll has shown for more than ten years that a minimum of 56 percent of the population support the *Roe v. Wade* decision. The anti-abortion leaders claim doctors are making huge profits from abortions, while illegal abortions cost ten times that of legal ones.[27]

Joseph Scheidler, while explicitly counseling against the use of violence, devotes a chapter of his *Closed: 99 Ways to Stop Abortion* (1985) to ways some anti-abortionists have destroyed and mutilated the signs of Planned Parenthood and other such groups. "While perpetrators of vandalism must be willing to accept the consequences of their act," he says, "in a real sense their actions may be more than an option. For many these actions constitute a moral obligation" (p. 296).

Not only the rhetoric but also the behavior of some of the activist anti-abortionists has bordered on the violent. They, or their sympathizers, have damaged property by placing glue in door locks, splashing paint on the buildings, harassing and intimidating patients and staff, seeking out patients in their homes, and approaching patients' families. Blowing up three buildings can be interpreted as a difference in degree of violence, not a difference in kind.

Matthew Goldsby, James Simmons, Kathy Simmons, and Kaye Wiggins were simply carrying the behavior of some highly visible persons in their community of faith to a logical conclusion. Of course, the next step beyond bombing and arson is direct, life-threatening violence against the abortionists themselves. That step was taken by Don Anderson, Wayne Moore, and Matthew Moore in their kidnapping of Dr. and Mrs. Zevallos.

Thus, there is a cooperative and mutually reinforcing relationship between the nonviolent public activists and the violent incognito actors. Each group uses the other for evidence of support and occasion for symbolic actions performed for the general public, as well as for one another. And the more extreme the behavior of the "nonviolent" activists and the closer their actions come to actual violence against persons, the higher the likelihood of "real" violence. (While we have not gathered sufficient data from all clinics across the country to establish the absolute truth of that statement, we have collected sufficient information to make the assertion with confidence.) Of course, with modern communications it is not necessary that the escalation take place within a single community, for someone in a relatively quiescent community may be inspired by media accounts of activists anywhere in the nation or world.

Jerome Himmelstein (1986) concludes that anti-abortion activism is primarily a function of those activists' being tied into religious networks. Kristin Luker (1984) notes that religious networks are a basic factor in mobilizing the anti-abortion activists in California. Cuneo (1989) finds this true also of his Family Heritage and Catholic Revivalist protesters in Canada. Harrison (1974, 49) concludes that "people are more likely to be attracted to a movement who are exposed to it in person, share its problem-solving perspective, have few social obligations that might conflict with membership, and have or develop social relationships with members."

Research shows that people join both mainline and sect religions primarily through personal contacts and relationships. The same is true of social movements. Religious networks, which tend to revolve around shared values, ideology, and worldview, are therefore fertile ground for induction into a social movement. We would add that the evidence indicates that the more exclusive those networks are and the less people are tied significantly to persons with countervailing or opposing opinions, the more likely network members are to engage in major acts of violence. This is especially true of those who are immune from loss of occupation or other forms of "normal" negative sanctions.[28]

In addition, our study of abortion-related violence indicates that Levi's (1982) contention that religious violence is more likely to occur among religious groups that are isolated should be modified in that small groups who are isolated within larger groups that are not necessarily isolated themselves, as groups, are also prone to violence. That is, small groups of fanatics may exist within less fanatic groups and may act on that fanaticism.

### The Politics of Violence

Thus, social movement violence does not occur in a vacuum. Aberrational as well as normal behavior may be culturally and socially formed. For example, one does not ordinarily dream of witches unless the cultural context provides some basis for belief in witches. As Émile Durkheim (1893) brilliantly pointed out, even suicide and its various forms are culturally shaped. And, as noted by the National Commission on the Causes and Prevention of Violence in its report *Violence in America*,[29] violence has always been part of the American fabric. As with suicide, a form of self-directed violence, violence against others or the property of others is much more frequent in societies that expect or allow for such behavior. Common among those who engage in forms of "morally" induced violence is the opinion that the person is acting for, on behalf of, and with the basic approval of his or her most intimate community or reference group. Most such violence tends to be what Tilly (1978) calls "reactionary . . . reacting to some change . . . backward looking."

Such "righteous" violence is more likely to occur in a small, corporate community, one in which the members share deeply held sentiments, values, and mores. It is less likely to occur when the majority are members of diverse groups with conflicting value systems and patterns of expected behavior, for in such groups one is faced with a number of cross-pressures and these mixed signals tend to moderate behavior, to keep one from overidentifying with any one particular group.

Thus Vicky Conroy, an anti-abortion activist from Pensacola, said there were limits to her activism against the abortion issue. She would not do something for which she could be put in jail, because she had several small children to care for. Implied in her statement is that, without this responsibility, she might indeed be willing to go to jail. On the other hand, the more actively involved people we talked with tended to be persons who were without day-to-day family responsibilities (their children were grown or they were men not required at home) and they had occupations that would not be endangered by a jail sentence of short duration (for example, pastor of a church, church staff member, and head of a shelter for pregnant and abused women). While the more daring activists were immune to normal sanctions for deviant behavior, this isolation also reinforced their values and beliefs—they were not in significant day-to-day interaction with persons who might disagree with them or voice countervailing opinions. Thus, the normal social constraints of a complex, urban society are relatively foreign to them. Their communities of interest are monolithic and mutually reinforcing.

As indicated above, Jerome Himmelstein (1986) has pointed out the importance of religious networks in the activation of those involved in the anti-abortion movement. This is clearly an important characteristic of those involved in violence against abortion clinics and doctors' offices. As asserted above, we would further hypothesize that the greater the exclusivity of those relationships and networks—that is, the less fundamentalists interact significantly with persons who might contradict or disagree with their positions—the more likely they will commit violence.

Goldsby and Simmons formed a tightly knit pair; as Kaye Wiggins testified, "They were a couple." Goldsby, in particular, found all his significant relationships in his religious group: Jimmy Simmons; Kaye Wiggins, who changed churches to be with him; his mother; his boss and father figure, David Del Gallo; and his co-workers at Del Gallo.

This is a pattern we found consistently among those committing abortion-related violence across the country.

## The Rhetoric of Violence

In his confession, Matthew Goldsby gave one justification for the bombings when he said, "I'd hate to see it come to the case when real estate meant more than human life." That is, he had weighed values, life versus property, and life had taken precedence. As if violence against property were not also a form of violence against persons, he raised an additional argument in support of the violence against buildings when he pointed to the ineffectiveness of political action and demonstrations. In effect, he was saying the bombings were "necessary" acts; there were no other avenues for redress. These arguments are essentially consistent with the approach of situational ethics, that anathema of the fundamentalists; that is, in the complex of competing claims, the most responsible thing for Goldsby to do was what he did.

However, Goldsby's rationale is an ill-informed example of situational ethics in that it is highly limited in its consideration of the competing "rights" and "goods" of the issue. There was no attempt to examine insofar as possible all the ramifications and alternative actions. Nor did Goldsby demonstrate, even when initially arrested, willingness to accept the guilt attached to every human ethical decision made in an ambiguous world. This acceptance of inevitable guilt is a hallmark of situational ethics. Indeed, through his arrest, trial, and conviction, Goldsby never publicly expressed remorse, never openly acknowledged any sense of guilt. Only two days prior to his sentencing, he told a reporter for the *Village Voice* who had asked if he still felt he had done right, "I know for a fact we saved one life. . . . How can I be sorry for savin' a life when I took no life? . . . Sometimes God has to create a spokesman—an oracle, so to speak—and maybe, you know, he chose me." The one emotion that comes through clearly was reflected in his confession when he expressed pride in doing the bombings well. The one vow heard was in his statement to the judge prior to sentencing: "I will not do it again." And when asked, on the morning of his sentencing, if he would recommend bombing to anyone else, Jimmy Simmons responded, "No, unless God tells them to."

Kaye Wiggins gave a new rationale when she said in her Cable News Network interview that God was using the four of them to publicize the abortion issue, a form of political action. Many of the leaders of the anti-abortion movement also used this rationale—especially David Shofner, John Burt, and Sharon Glass. This is basically an argument from the ancient school of ethical pragmatism: what is good is what "works." It is an ethical approach never accepted as valid in the mainstream of Christian thought—fundamentalist, liberal, neoorthodox, or whatever. However, we have seen no evidence that the bombings or other abortion-related violence has moved any segment of the public to relinquish a pro-choice stand and join the anti-abortion movement. The bombings and arrests did appear to solidify the radical anti-abortion fringe through their public demonstrations and press conferences. But the radicals' activities have also isolated them and eroded much of the support they may have once held. Furthermore, abortion-related violence appears to have no effect on the rate of abortions in the country.[30] In short, if the anti-abortionists are seeking increased public support, violence is nonpragmatic and counterproductive to that goal.

At the same time, however, the radical fringe has increased and heightened its dramatic actions. The accosting of patients and the invasion of clinics have increased dramatically since 1983. The anti-abortionists have opened counseling centers, misleadingly advertising them under "abortion services" in the Yellow Pages to attract women seeking abortions. Once women arrive at these "clinics," they are given a hard-sell effort to get them not to abort. The anti-abortionists claimed they would have about 2,900 of these centers in operation by the end of 1985.[31] In addition, since 1973 one in every fifteen family-planning centers has been the victim of bombing or arson.

Each of the users of violence—hammerers, bombers, and arsonists—gave almost identical justifications for their acts: God's law supersedes man's; a higher good—the saving of life—takes precedence over the preservation of property. The Pensacola experience is not unique in this respect, but it is a microcosm, a summation of what had been occurring all across the nation.

## Can Violence Succeed?

There is some evidence that violence may further a social movement's objectives. Gurr (1989, 498), for example, concludes that private violence can succeed when both the tactics and the objectives of violence are widely regarded as legitimate. This is not true of either the tactics or the objectives of the extreme anti-abortion violence. Thus, the continued use of such tactics as arson, bombing, and other violence, as well as some of the more "peaceful" harassment tactics, will probably guarantee a massive public reaction against the entire anti-abortion movement, especially as more and more local American communities are hit.[32]

What are we to do in the face of violence? The role of the state in human life is not to show mercy, nor is it to reflect Christian love. The role of the state is to maintain order and to institute justice, both of which may conflict with Christian principles of love and mercy. By its own nature the state cannot condone illegitimate violence of any kind, since by definition the state has a monopoly on violence, and the state's only option is to punish those who commit it. Thus, Christians or persons of any other religious or nonreligious persuasion who commit acts of violence against persons or property, as defined by the laws of the state, have no right to expect mercy. They can expect only justice, and, to maintain its own viability, the state must uphold a standard of justice firmly, or it will find its own authority on this and other issues undermined and usurped by vigilantes.

Under current law, cultural issues such as religious motivation are inadmissible as evidence or justification for violence. Furthermore, few avenues exist for responsible discussion of truly opposed cultural viewpoints. Matt Goldsby and Jimmy Simmons are victims of these inadequacies of our community praxis. The alternative choices of punishment and mercy offer a difficult dilemma in the case of the Pensacola Four and many other defendants and convicted bombers nationally. What is needed are community means of conflict resolution, as well as coordinated efforts to defuse the impetus to violence.

The public stance of the state in the person of its highest officers is important in the containment of violence. While the Bureau of Alcohol, Tobacco and Firearms was apparently diligent in pursuing perpetrators of clinic violence, they avoided media attention, purposely and rightly. President Reagan maintained a two-year silence on the violence despite well-publicized requests that he speak out firmly against it. Moreover, he took public stands against abortion in numerous speeches and in his essay published in the spring of 1983.[33] The wide circulation of this essay in the anti-abortion community was followed by a drastic increase in the rate of abortion-related violence, and the president's speeches before anti-abortion groups were interpreted by the violent radicals as tacit approval, support by silence. Even though bombers and arsonists may have misinterpreted Reagan's intentions and statements, his failure to speak strongly against violence meant nothing was done to counter the message of approval. The end effect of the bombings, moreover, was to legitimize the public anti-abortion movement as representing "moderates" with essentially democratic goals rather than inflexible minority positions.[34] This effect prevailed despite numerous polls indicating that the majority of the public feels that the abortion decision should lie solely with the woman and her physician.[35]

While we cannot "prove" a direct cause-and-effect relationship between Reagan's silence and abortion-related violence, the correlation is evident in the decline in violence following his eventual public condemnation of it on January 3, 1985—a movement toward delegitimation. The arrests of the Pensacola Four and three persons in Maryland early in January probably added significantly to the dampening effect. Support for our interpretation comes from none other than Don Anderson, who stated from his cell that he "agreed with pro-choice groups that bombers were encouraged by the absence of direct condemnations of their activities by Reagan. . . . [They feel] they have a green light from the president—that's the impression I got."[36] Moreover, testimony in the Pensacola trial and the assertions of the defense attorneys showed that Goldsby and Simmons believed they were acting on behalf of the president.

In addition, there was a dramatic increase in serious abortion-related violence following Reagan's election in 1980, compared with the number of such incidents during the Carter administration. Violent incidents in the first Reagan term were almost 450% of those in the Carter term (see table 3). One partial explanation for this increase

**Table 3. Acts of Violence against Abortion Facilities, 1977–80 and 1981–84**

| Type of Violence | 1977–80 | 1981–84 |
|---|---|---|
| Invasion | 35 | 65 |
| Vandalism | 6 | 62 |
| Death threat | 1 | 25 |
| Assault/battery | 5 | 13 |
| Burglary | 0 | 5 |
| Kidnapping/hostage taking | 0 | 2 |
| Attempted arson/bombing | 2 | 9 |
| Arson | 8 | 11 |
| Bombing | 4 | 25 |
| Total | 61 | 217 |

Source: National Abortion Federation.

probably lies in the defeat of the ERA, which likely led the radical religious Right to seek a new cause. But Reagan's stance on the abortion issue could only have encouraged the increase in violence.

In July 1985 the new attorney general, Edwin Meese, filed "friend of the court" briefs with the Supreme Court supporting the reversal of *Roe v. Wade*.[37] The Supreme Court rejected the government's position, fueling the national increase in efforts to close abortion clinics in 1988 through Operation Rescue.

The Reagan administration furthered its attack on abortion in October 1985 by proposing that Congress deny federal funding to family-planning clinics that provide abortion information to women. A Planned Parenthood officer responded that "it is impossible to operate a medically ethical program without telling pregnant women about their full range of options, including abortions." Supporters of the restriction also tend to oppose all counseling on contraception, since in their perspective such counseling is an encouragement to promiscuity. This effort to restrict funding was parallel to the administration's attempt to give government grants to anti-abortion church groups to advise pregnant women.[38]

Whatever the chief executive's actual intentions, the administration's stance on the issue was perceived by some extremists as endorsement and legitimization of private law enforcement or vigilantism. It is also clear that among some Christian congregations President Reagan was being interpreted as an "evangelical." His statements support a view of abortion argued on religious grounds and associated with central claims of the fundamentalist Christian message. Seen in this light, Reagan's stance on abortion and his silence regarding abortion-related violence confounded the functions of church and state.

# ... 16
# Will
# the Circle
# Be
# Unbroken?

,

It is a fearful thing to fall into the hands of
the living God.
Hebrews 10:31

Our task to this point has been as much descriptive as analytic, and to
some extent we have spread the many small generalizations of our
work through the text. Now we must review some of our key conclusions in an effort to reach the limited closure any book on such an
open and controversial social question can achieve. These conclusions
can be summarized in a few paragraphs, but they lead the way to a
central theme worthy of discussion at length: What is the place of and
limit of violence as a strategy of social change?

We have found that the broad anti-abortion movement is highly
complex in its development and has widely varied kinds of organizations and degrees of activism attached to it. We have found commonalities among Protestant, Catholic, and Mormon fundamentalists that
make them apt allies in the anti-abortion movement. We have also
seen that differing stages of the movement attract different constituencies, the most active and violent having less vulnerability to negative
sanctions and greater insulation from the prominent cultural beliefs of
the society at large, and even of their own denominations. We have
gone so far as to compare the profiles and motivations of those who
have resorted to abortion-related violence with those of violent males

**Figure 3. The Path to Anti-Abortion Violence**

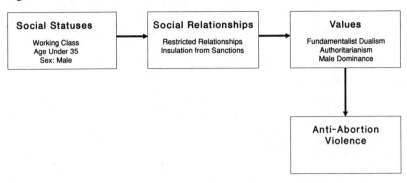

in general as well as rapists, torturers, and terrorists, and we have found a number of significant parallels between and among them. We conclude that acts of abortion-related violence are most likely to be carried out by persons who are less than forty years of age, working class, and male; have few, if any, close ties outside their religious community but enjoy what they perceive to be a community of support, usually a religious group and sometimes including the president himself; and reside on the edge, geographically or psychologically, of an urban community. Finally, such persons are likely to be thoroughly committed to a fundamentalistic orientation to their religion and culture (see figure 3).

In our examination of fundamentalism itself, we observed how its cultural premises might be a precipitating influence toward violence for certain individuals. The backgrounds of the bombers and arsonists indicate that they are uniformly fundamentalists, predominantly male, and operating out of a desire to control and even punish women, in contrast to female picketers, who appear to be acting out of a concern for their rights (Ginsburg 1990).[1] Among the social and sociopsychological variables that could well interact to foment violent actions from these particular fundamentalists, we have stressed the juxtaposition of a rigid moral worldview and a pattern of insecurity expressed in the overall life histories of the bombers and arsonists.

In sum, while the vast majority of violent acts in American society appear to be committed by persons who share the same kinds of social statuses and social relationships outlined in figure 3, abortion-related violence depends on a third factor: those statuses and relationships being filtered through the value system of fundamentalist dualism.[2]

Speaking metaphorically, abortion is only a skirmish in the battle over the nature of the family in a war to establish a theocracy. The fundamentalist Protestant-Catholic coalition maintaining the battle would fall apart over other issues in the overall war. Catholics and Protestants differ too basically, between and among themselves, on the whole range of contemporary social issues. That is, the different currents in contemporary Christian fundamentalism possess different visions of the nature of a proper theocracy.[3]

In one of his few lucid and valuable insights into religion, Sigmund Freud pointed to the essential ambivalence of the religious experience.[4] Although he did not use the term, he indicated that at the heart of religion lies *awe*, the experience of being at once attracted and repelled in the presence of the Sacred, the sensation of both fear and fascination before the Ultimate. This modern insight is reflected today in, for example, the philosophy of Paul Ricoeur, who stresses the core notion of *kerygma*—the announcement or proclamation of the gospel. For such modern theologians, this essential foundation of the Christian religion stands as "awareness" of the presence of the Spiritual Other, the source of human enigma and an equivocal intellect. This presence cannot be validated scientifically or perfectly codified through cultural expressions. Thus, people cannot escape ambivalence, for no human decision is "pure." All ethical and moral decisions bring human beings to a confrontation with their own temporality, their finitude, their contingency.

However, people at either extreme in the abortion debate seem unwilling to admit to their own ambivalence, their moral uncertainty. For example, the fundamentalists admit only to their delight in the presence of the Almighty and deny the terrible nature of God—except for others, in this case those they disagree with. On the other hand, pro-choice extremists adhere to a convenient definition of life, one based on the presence of brain functioning consistent with the equation of life and "intellect." This position not only denies the most basic understandings of cellular biology, but it also rejects the potential of medical technological advances in sustaining fetal life. Extremists on both sides are sure of the purity of their stance and are thereby closed to the ambiguities of their choices.

Abortion has become a focal issue of social conflict in the United States partially because it touches every community and, potentially, every family and every woman. Pornography, capital punishment, alcohol, topless bars, and similar issues vary widely in their immediacy to individual lives and communities. Abortion does not.[5]

Abortion has attracted extremists to both sides because the burden of decisions about abortion and the definition of life has rested with the courts, specifically the federal courts. Paradoxically, while the courts have maintained a rule of "community standards" on pornography, they have dictated one standard in the area of abortion, a standard based shakily on 1973 medical technology.[6] This immerses the abortion issue into such other controversies as states' rights, regional and cultural animosities, and radically different urban and rural life-styles. The majority of Americans, caught up in the tension of these controversies, have stood to the side as observers.

But as the extremists on both sides maintain, abortion is a basic and important issue. Its resolution, if there is one, will likely help shape the position the United States will take on many issues: the availability of birth-control information and devices, equal pay for equal work, the divisions of labor and responsibilities within families, the size of families and the ability to limit them as desired, the amount of education parents can give their children, and children's life chances. On an international level, the position taken on abortion by the United States may hold a key to potentials for development in the Third World, if not for the chances of survival without war in the next century.

Because the issues go far beyond abortion itself, the potential for violence is not limited to abortion alone. Indeed, in Pensacola abortion-related violence was preceded by several firebombings and arsons of gay bars. How the abortion issue is dealt with will likely affect the extent of violence in many other areas of disagreement in American society.

Concerted action continues against abortion clinics in the United States and has expanded toward organizations associated with birth control. The "moral necessity of protecting life" as a strategic argument has been a hallmark of public political opposition to abortion, even more so in the Bush years than during the Reagan administration. The public, however, has not been politically predictable where abortion rights are concerned. For example, former Governor Bob Martinez of Florida called a special session of the legislature to enact a new abortion law after the *Webster* decision, but he was unable to move a bill into consideration. His eventual unseating was at least in part attributable to his vocal anti-abortion stance. Yet the 1990 national elections saw little real transformation of the political landscape as a consequence of the abortion issue. One of our key conclusions is that violence follows inaction, or is linked to the perception that nothing is really being accomplished. We may well be entering a new period of abortion-related violence if the politicians, judges, and public at large allow the issue to remain pending.

If renewed social violence from a frustrated religious Right is a possibility, we should at least consider its meaning and consequences. Violence separates Christians from one another and infuses suspicion and fear into everyday affairs. Violence lurks behind the strident confrontation by anti-abortion demonstrators and their insensitivity to the women they accost and abuse at clinics across the nation. An involved and informed public could counter these effects, but probably not without some form of political or social accommodation of the moderate anti-abortion circles. But this means *real* changes in the frequency and availability of abortions, in the counseling associated with abortion procedures, and probably in the area of teen abortion and parental consent.

It would be possible, however, to go too far in accommodating a narrow moral worldview in our culture and law. Violence is inherent in the opposition to sex education in many small communities because such opposition condemns children to have babies.[7] In an ironic view of the protection of life, "having the baby" and dealing with the child after birth are even cited as *punishments* for sin in the narrow worldview of the most extreme fundamentalists. Thus violence is renewed by forcing teenage mothers to live with the consequences of actions most often contrived by cultural pressures and made bitter by parental condemnation and sexist pardon of boys' impulses. That this violence follows prohibitions on the use of contraceptives by fundamentalists and Catholics seems to us unpardonable. It forces women, sometimes children, into the servitude of procreation as though they had no other purpose in life.

Yet violence also persists in the cold, technical, and businesslike language the abortionists use to describe the interruption of fetal life and in the irresponsible way some people approach the act of abortion, again and again.[8] Violence lurks in the potentials created by the intent of the Pro-Life Amendment. The *form* of violence on one side or another in no way makes it more palatable, correct, or justifiable. One form of violence seems always to call forth another.[9]

Can the circle of violence surrounding abortion as a practice, as an issue, or as a reality ever be broken? Is breaking the circle of violence the purpose of the Pensacola abortion clinic trial and similar proceedings across the nation? Certainly, opinion is mixed on this issue in Pensacola. The prosecution contended throughout that violence, not abortion, was on trial. Yet in the minds of most people in the community, no matter what side of the issue they support, abortion was sustained by the refusal of the court to acquit any of the defendants.

The trial accomplished a necessary resolution for a particular case of violent action. Can we now say that it does not matter if one form of violence was sustained by the court and another rejected? Did the trial reduce the frustration of the anti-abortion activists? Did it reduce the fear of women going to the Ladies Center? Did it take away the apprehension of physicians, landlords, or insurance companies?

At this point, we may do well to recall the words of Thomas Jefferson, a founder of the country, a radical, a Christian (albeit one who considered himself above the myths of the faith), a scientist, and one of the framers of our law. Jefferson's approach to cultural change was to afford each generation its own definition of the social contract. Although he recognized that not all opinions in society would be held in "common law," he was extremely tolerant of cultural diversity. Consider Jefferson's words to Madison on the subject of rebellion: "I hold it that a little rebellion now and then is a good thing, and as necessary in the political world as storms in the physical. Unsuccessful rebellions indeed generally establish the encroachments on the rights of the people which have produced them. An observation of this truth should render honest republican governors so mild in their punishment of rebellions, as not to discourage them too much. It is a medicine necessary for the sound health of government."[10]

Jefferson was a champion of "responsible violence," such as that defined in the Declaration of Independence. Even "liberal" politicians today have difficulty understanding just how a system under the threat of "responsible violence" can be maintained. Perhaps Jefferson's vision is inappropriate to our time. Perhaps it is inappropriate to call abortion clinic violence (taken from either perspective) responsible, yet this is precisely the question before us today. Does not the "necessity defense," a successful legal plea in several abortion clinic cases involving civil disobedience, derive from the radical Jeffersonian posture?

Do we condone the taking of life, or individual choice in the taking of life, especially when the life involved is still intimately tied to the life of the mother?[11] It does no good to cite that other cultures all condone some form of life-taking or that Western civilization virtually condoned infanticide and child abandonment, given the frequency of those practices in previous centuries. We must decide if *we* condone any forms of institutional or individual life-taking, for *we* are not all other cultures. No matter what we decide, by whatever consensus we find possible, the result will be equivocal, and it will produce ambivalence and perhaps frustration and anger. At this point, it is most important that our leaders understand the consensus realistically and as representatives of the public will, for it often becomes necessary to enforce the public will by force.

The actions and statements of our nation's leaders, especially the president, may well determine whether we will move toward greater actualization of our claim to be a nation of laws or, alternatively, maintain the historical pattern of dealing with the most difficult issues through private or lynch law.[12] Passage of the Pro-Life Amendment could mark a drastic turning point toward the merger of religion and state, a movement toward a religiously dominated society such as we have not known since the original colonial period of our history. More alarming, responsible public figures seem disposed today toward the use of state power to enforce religious precepts.

On the other hand, secular thinkers self-righteously proclaim their values in school classrooms, while insensitively rejecting "religious" content in the schools as contrary to First Amendment protections.

While proselytization in schools is an important issue, the overreaction and domination of agnostic viewpoints puts us at risk of losing an important ethical heritage. State neutrality on religion is not the same thing as ignoring religion or forbidding its expressions. The contending vocal factions of our society seem universally motivated by fear of opposing opinions.

At the root of the abortion controversy lies the question of its need. That is, our society must examine and deal with those issues that give rise to some women's perceiving abortion as a necessity in the first place: unwanted pregnancies from incest, rape (both in and outside marriage), failed contraceptives, and inadequate socialization in sexuality and how to deal with it. As long as one in four minor females is a victim of incest and sexual abuse, as long as one in four females can expect to suffer from rape during her lifetime, and as long as teenage pregnancy is almost rampant, abortion will—and should—remain an issue. That is, American society must deal with the attitudes and behaviors of men that make abortion the only sensible option for some women. In addition, it must deal fundamentally with the status of women, for abortion is also an expression of the relative powerlessness of women, their both real and perceived lack of control over their own lives and reproduction.[13] Furthermore, we must deal with our culture's materialism and individualism, which are both protested and enjoyed by the fundamentalists, especially their figureheads.[14]

Like it or not, abortion involves us all, men as well as women, Christian and non-Christian, young and old, liberal and conservative, and especially those extremists and radicals on both sides of this issue who are experiencing acute alienation. We all have responsibility to face squarely the moral, biological, technological, and social ambiguities of abortion and to participate in the cultural resolution of the controversy. The alternative is to abandon the arena to the extremists of both sides and to learn to live with violence and the aroma of gunpowder and gasoline in the night air—not only at doctors' offices and clinics but also at churches, cathedrals, and probably homes.

# . . . Afterword

Contrary to Judge Roger Vinson's recommendation, Matt Goldsby and Jimmy Simmons were sent to the Federal Correctional Institution at Tallahassee, a level-two facility. Before leaving for prison, Matt suggested to Kaye Wiggins that maybe they should cancel their engagement, and she agreed. She shortly afterward began dating Arthur Shimek, the son of her attorney, Paul Shimek.

In December 1987, John Burt published a 1988 calendar with crude line drawings of "Pro-Life heroes" and began selling it on the street in front of the federal courthouse. In January 1988, Paul Shimek wrote Burt a letter demanding that Wiggins's picture be removed from the calendar since it was used without her permission. The letter also asserted that Wiggins had been trying to distance herself from the abortion issue and that the calendar was bringing her unwanted publicity and attention.

On the day Matt and Jimmy reported to prison, someone telephoned a bomb threat to a Tallahassee abortion clinic. Prison officials apparently felt that the reporting felons were responsible and refused to let Kathy visit her husband for sixty days. Matt was assigned to work in the kitchen, and he began taking computer-related college courses in the prison. He was also able to lift weights regularly, still in pursuit of the Mr. Olympia title. Jimmy was assigned to the bakery, where he could enjoy his hobby of cooking by making yeast breads and using leftover dough to make specialties for the baking crew. Both were allowed to have visitors for more than seven hours a day, five days a week.

On October 9, 1985, the federal parole board heard Goldsby's and Simmons's plea for reduction in their sentences. On October 13, 1985, the U.S. Parole Commission issued new guidelines abolishing the youthful-offender leniency agenda, which was established, ironically, in 1973. Hereafter, the comission said, youths would be treated the same as older offenders. With the "youthful-offender" argument no longer available, Matt's sentence was set at sixty-two months, with release scheduled for May 21, 1990, about twice as long as Judge Vinson had recommended. Jimmy's minimum sentence was set at about fifty-eight months, with release recommended for November 28, 1989. Both appealed to Judge Vinson to reduce their original ten-year sentences, thereby modifying parole options. However, on December 6, 1985, the judge held that the sentences were "just and fair" and refused to alter them, while reaffirming his prior recommendations for leniency. Simmons was placed at a work-release facility in Pensacola in 1989 and was paroled in October. Goldsby was paroled in November 1989.

Kaye Wiggins appealed her conviction. That appeal was denied.

Dr. Permenter quit his practice entirely to devote time to his other financial interests. Dr. Bagenholm secured another site for his practice but was unable to get insurance for it. A court order instigated by other residents of the medical condominium forced him to quit performing abortions. However, while still searching for insurance that will allow him to resume abortions in the office, he began performing outpatient tubal ligations, using local anesthetic, at a cost one-third that of those done in hospitals. He says he gets satisfaction from doing a procedure that reduces the demand for abortions. He hopes to expand his practice to include in vitro fertilizations.

Bagenholm maintains that the bombings had positive effects and that the changes in his practice and the loss of his building were easily worth the price. His practice continues to grow, perhaps at least partially because of all the publicity. He also perceives that the violence moved some "fence sitters" on the abortion issue to vocal support for women's choice. "Women's rights," he said, "are more important than my building."

The Ladies Center continues in operation under regular picketing. Those working there also continue to have their homes picketed. Shortly after the trial, the *Pensacola News Journal* quit publicizing any of the picketings or demonstrations. However, in March 1985 John Burt, Joan Andrews of the Defenders of the Defenders of Life, and two others burst into the Ladies Center and injured two persons inside, Linda Taggart, the manager, and Georgia Wilde, president of the local NOW chapter. Two of the invading women locked themselves into procedure rooms and destroyed some of the equipment. Released on bond, Burt and Andrews returned to the Ladies Center later that week to observe the regular picketing. That resulted in their bonds being revoked and their being sent to jail until their trials.

The election of Eleanor Smeal to the presidency of NOW resulted in renewed activism by the local NOW chapter, which picketed John Burt's Our Father's House and the area's major anti-abortion churches—Sacred Heart Cathedral, West Pensacola Baptist Church, and Pace Assembly of God—while continuing to provide escort services for the patients at the Ladies Center.

A split in the First Assembly of God resulted in the resignation of Pastor Lindell Ballenger and his organizing a new church, the Jubilee Christian Fellowship. The anti-abortion activists largely remained with First Assembly, while about one-half to two-thirds of the congregation reportedly left with Ballenger.

In March 1986, Joseph Scheidler, John Ryan, and Joan Andrews came to Pensacola to conduct a workshop. At that workshop, which was also attended by at least one deputy sheriff, a leaflet was passed out stating that a demonstration would be held the next day at the Ladies Center and that arrests were expected. The workshop attendees were outnumbered by the NOW pickets outside the Escambia County Health Center site of the meeting.

At the Ladies Center the next day, one deputy was present but, according to clinic personnel and others, he was unsure of how to respond when the demonstrators, including Scheidler with a bullhorn, came up on the porch of the clinic, which constituted trespassing. The demonstrators also entered the clinic parking lot to harass patients, with no law enforcement reaction.

According to several accounts, John Burt, Joan Andrews, Sarah Burt, and Karisa Epperley suddenly rushed the door of the clinic. According to testimony by Linda Taggart and Georgia Wilde, John Burt burst through the door and hurled the two against a banister and the wall, injuring both of them, while Sarah Burt and Karisa Epperly rushed upstairs to a procedure room, locked themselves inside, and began destroying some of the equipment. The four were charged with burglary with assault, criminal mischief, and resisting arrest. Following the arrests, Joseph Scheidler said, "We wanted to get more people in, but the front door was locked . . . the fact that we got in at all was quite a coup."

All the accused persons posted bond and were released. However, the following week John Burt, Epperley, and Andrews returned to the Ladies Center to talk with the demonstrators. On learning this, the prosecutor filed for revocation of their bail. The Escambia County judge, Lacey Collier, revoked their bail and had them incarcerated, saying that he could not guarantee the safety of the clinic personnel with Burt, Epperley, and Andrews out of jail, since the three of them had violated their bail.

Property damage was assessed at $1,800. Andrews was sentenced to five years in prison. In December 1987, Republican Governor Bob Martinez, referring to "humanitarian concerns during this holiday season,"[1] transferred her to a prison close to her home in Delaware.

The Escambia County Sheriff's Department filed charges of conspiracy against Joseph Scheidler, who was arrested on the warrant in Denver, Colorado, when he was attempting to register at the hotel site of the National Right to Life Committee meeting in June 1986.

In addition, the National Organization for Women, the Ladies Center of Pensacola, and the Delaware Women's Health Organization filed a federal suit in the state of Delaware through the Southern Poverty Law Center of Montgomery, Alabama, against Joseph Scheidler, John Ryan, Joan Andrews, the Pro-Life Action League (Scheidler's organization), and the Pro-Life Direct Action League (Ryan's organization). The class-action suit charged all the defendants with violations of the

Sherman Antitrust Act, with trying to drive "women's health centers that perform abortions out of business through a pattern of concerted, unlawful activity." The suit charged that the business of both of the leagues was "disrupting and closing women's health centers that perform abortions through the use of illegal activity." It also charged that all three individuals traveled throughout the United States "engaging in, or encouraging others to engage in, unlawful, concerted action, including repeated acts of trespass and vandalism."

Andrews was later dropped from the suit after her sentencing on the Ladies Center charges. At the sentencing the judge offered her probation if she would pledge to stay away from abortion clinics while on probation. However, she refused to give such a pledge and was sentenced to five years in prison.

In 1987 Susan Novotny was appointed U.S. magistrate, replacing Robert Crongeyer.

In December 1987, the *Pensacola News Journal* ran a follow-up article on the abortion controversy in the community. David Shofner said, "I got tired, myself. . . . I'd been in the fight so long I neglected my church. . . . I suppose when John Burt was prohibited from going to the Ladies Center, that took the wind out of everybody's sails."

Burt stated, "My probation officer won't let me go near the clinic." He noted that no more than fifteen or twenty Pensacola-area people were involved in most of the protests. He suggested that sentences imposed on some protesters scared other people and there was also a high burnout rate among the protesters.[2] At the end of his probationary sentence, he began picketing again.

On January 28, 1988, the Canadian Supreme Court erased the existing federal abortion law, enacted in 1968, because it denied women the right to "life, liberty and security of person," which are guaranteed by Canada's Charter of Rights and Freedoms. The rejected law required the approval of hospital committees of three persons before a woman could have an abortion.

We would predict that the confusion resulting from this could catalyze extremist acts in Canada similar to those in the United States since 1973, especially considering that 58 percent of the Canadian adult population believe in constraints on abortion. In 1992 a clinic in Toronto was destroyed.

On July 3, 1989, the Florida Supreme Court ordered Paul Shimek to cease taking new clients, to cease all practice of law with his current clients within thirty days, to refrain from withdrawing funds from any trust account, and to deposit any attorney fees in a trust account. Shimek was temporarily suspended from the Florida Bar under charges that he had a $50,000 shortage in his trust account of funds due clients. In June Shimek had requested permission to resign from the Florida Bar, while the bar was considering disciplinary action against him. His request was later granted by the state supreme court. Under state law, this means that he will never again be allowed to practice law in Florida.

In 1990 Shimek was convicted of grand theft and racketeering in the misappropriation of escrow funds of clients and funds of investors that Shimek transferred to others. The funds involved amounted to $297,000. He was sentenced to a three-year prison term.

# . . . Notes

**Foreword**

1. For an account of the Pensacola bombings from an anti-abortion perspective, see *Protectors of the Code* by Myra Sims-Shofner (1989), wife of David Shofner, one of the leaders of the Pensacola anti-abortion movement.

**Acknowledgments**

1. During the period this work covers, the *Pensacola News Journal* removed the hyphen in its name. We conform to the usage current at the time of each cited article.

**1. Introduction: The Abortion Stalemate**

1. For a general discussion of lawlike versus pattern theories in social science, see the excellent work by David Kaplan and Robert A. Manners (1972, 15–17). More comprehensive discussion by Abraham Kaplan (1964) provides independent epistemological bases for these theoretical styles. The work of several anthropologists of the "configurationalist" circle, most notably Clyde Kluckhohn, Ruth Benedict and Morris Opler, represents pattern theory in anthropology. On another intellectual front, the broad linguistic concepts of Ferdinand de Saussure (1966) not only gave rise to diverse "grammatically based" ethnographic styles in anthropology but also lie at the base of structuralism and much of poststructuralist contemporary theory. The most recent developments within these critical circles include rather open

interpretive frameworks similar, in particular, to Opler's theory of "themes." Our work, like the orientations only mentioned here, relies on the premise that understanding should be derived from some relatively global consideration of human situations, figured interpretively through large-scale models that, like grammars, inform us of principles through which human action signifies.

2. MacCannell and MacCannell (1982, 68–96) provide a modern critique of the ethnographic dilemma, how the student of culture can establish an account as authentic. The MacCannells stress the paradox that emerges wherein long-term contact produces cultural "familiarity" while it progressively blinds the ethnographic eye to "novelty." They also resist the intellectual movements that drive a wedge between humanistic and social scientific concerns with culture. In the end, no matter what one's perspective, what is necessary is that the student of culture observe and think. No amount of formality or intuition will save the ethnographer overwhelmed by cultural differences. We believe that our work represents a proper balance between the kinds of insights produced by familiarity or cultural immersion and the fresh view of the relative outsider.

3. Levi (1982).

4. See Gould and Kolb (1964, 312).

5. Granberg (1982, 562–64) maintains that "pro-life" would mean promotion of gun control; opposition to militarism and media violence; advocacy of high fertility, medical research, and preventive medicine; opposition to euthanasia, infanticide, suicide, and abortion; promotion of exercise, blood donation, vegetarianism, highway safety (as opposed to drunk driving and speeding), conservation, and redistributive domestic and foreign aid policies; and opposition to capital punishment. He asserts that "Labeling oneself as 'pro-life' is a form of self-aggrandizement, in part because it casts aspersions on one's adversaries, implying that these opponents are 'anti-life'" (p. 564).

6. There is evidence (Maxwell 1991) that individuals who join the movement are motivated not so much by the rhetoric employed but by their own life histories, circumstances, and values. That is, ethical principles are secondary. Life circumstances have a way of revealing and altering one's true ethical stance as a particular life circumstance arises. For example, *every* clinic that had been subjected to extreme violence reported that a former picketer had come seeking an abortion either for herself or for her daughter. Thus, as our life circumstances change, so do our ethical and moral principles alter to deal with them. Furthermore, our life concerns are shaped by our social, economic, and familial positions. One might conclude that necessity is the mother of morality. For example, those males and females most likely to cohabit without benefit of marriage, after young adults aged twenty to thirty, are those over sixty-five, in order to maintain both pension incomes.

A similar pattern develops in organizations. Traina (1975), for example, found that Roman Catholic dioceses in New York State responded more vigorously to enactment of a much more liberal abortion law when their maternity homes faced a drop in enrollments or when their hospitals were threatened by the law.

7. Medical technology has changed and blurred our definitions of both life and death. Biological life can be sustained through machinery far beyond the point of what would have been death fifty years ago. Technologists also are engaged in developing machines that can reason and think; a cutting edge in computers, for example, is the development of programs that reprogram themselves, that learn, and programs that practice "fuzzy thinking," comparable to that of humans. The distinction between animal and human has also been blurred, for chimpanzees have been taught to communicate with abstract symbols and relate their feelings. (See Hartouni 1987.)

8. The *New York Times*, in 1989, and the *Los Angeles Times*, in 1982, editorially adopted these conventions as being most accurate. James Kelly, a Catholic sociologist at Fordham University, distinguishes among the terms "anti-abortion," "right-to-life," and "pro-life" and equates the last with a broader, consistent ethic (Kelly 1991b) that would include social and economic justice for women, attacking what he perceives as underlying reasons for women to seek abortions in the first place. Even some spokespersons for the movement refer to it as "anti-abortion" (e.g., Hentoff 1989).

9. The only conviction for pro-choice-related violence we have been able to document is that of Dr. Arnold Ross, Gaithersburg, Maryland, who was convicted of assaulting a protester outside his clinic with a hypodermic needle. There were, however, questions of the legitimacy of that conviction. The only other incident, for which no one was arrested, was the arson attempted at First Assembly of God in Pensacola, which occurred shortly after the Christmas bombings.

10. For support for our view that the abortion issue and the resultant confrontations over it constitute a cultural conflict see Leahy, Snow, and Worden (1983).

11. On the same day that the Supreme Court issued the *Roe v. Wade* decision, it also issued the *Doe v. Bolton* ruling, which probably had broader implications for freedom of choice than *Roe*, but the first decision of the day on abortion has become synonymous with both.

12. To a degree this is already true, since there are reports that only one physician in the state of South Dakota is still performing abortions and the Allen Guttmacher Institute recently expressed dismay at the lack of abortion services generally in rural areas of the country.

13. Illegal abortionists traditionally have charged about five to ten times the rate for legal ones.

### 4. Onward, Christian Soldiers

1. While many people in the community refer to themselves as "Pensacolians" and "Floridians," we conform to the more historic and linguistically accurate terms *Pensacolan* and *Floridan*.

2. This constitutional provision later formed the basis of a state supreme court ruling overturning a law requiring parental consent for underage females seeking abortions.

3. Gracida was later transferred to the Corpus Christi, Texas, diocese, where he excommunicated a Catholic woman who worked at an abortion clinic there.

4. Zald and Ash (1966) point out the importance of rising expectations in the development of the civil rights movement and the consequent recruitment of previously marginal groups and persons.

5. On May 6, 1985, the U.S. Eleventh Circuit Court of Appeals declared the law a violation of First Amendment rights. The city council decided not to appeal the decision.

6. Arsons began in 1979, but this was the first bombing.

7. *Washington Post*, 10 January 1985.

8. Fundamentalism may be described as the right wing of evangelicalism. As Smidt (1989) has pointed out: ". . . biblical passages may be interpreted as either infallible, inerrant, or literal in nature. The infalliblist position is the least stringent, implying the Bible is without falsehood in matters of religious faith, while 'qualifying' the Bible's authority as a historical or scientific document. The 'inerrantist' position resists a distinction between authoritative and non-authoritative portions of the Bible, but might allow that some biblical 'truths' are either poetic or metaphorical. 'Literalism' is a particularly stringent position on biblical interpretation, suggesting that the text is to be taken without any qualification whatever." (Jelen, Wilcox, and Smidt 1990, 307–8).

Fundamentalists usually hold to the literalist position, while most other evangelicals hold the inerrant position, and some the infallible one.

### 5. Marching as to War

1. Florida law requires clinics and laboratories to dispose of suctioned uterine contents directly, through burial or cremation. All physicians and clinics in Pensacola submit the tissue to laboratories for analysis to check the potential presence of uterine cancer and to make sure there was an actual pregnancy. Thus, the disposal of the tissues is the responsibility of the laboratories and not the clinics. Proper disposal has never been seriously questioned by the authorities.

2. In the case of a security alarm at Permenter's, they figured they would still have time to escape and for the bomb to explode before an investigator would arrive.

### 6. The Visit of the Magi

1. This is a strong indication that the bombings were not a secret held only among the four principals.

2. There was testimony in one of the ensuing civil cases that indicated that a person experienced in munitions from First Assembly of God may have told Goldsby and Simmons how to build their bombs. However, no indictment followed this.

3. The phrase "it began to deal with us" is indicative of an important aspect of

the fundamentalist worldview. Internal feelings and thoughts are attributed to external forces; thus the individual is not responsible for his or her thoughts and feelings.

## 7. Between the Times

1. Burt makes explicit here one of our major contentions: that those most likely to commit violence are those who are less threatened by negative sanctions.

2. Lea later moved her organization's headquarters to a site just outside Pensacola, in Milton, Florida.

3. Diamond was pastor of a church in Baton Rouge to which some later Baton Rouge bombers belonged.

4. Students of religious sects will be familiar with the normal process of a religious group becoming more tolerant as its membership becomes more middle class and the group moves toward becoming a "church." Assemblies of God began among the working class and its membership continues to be primarily working-class. But in the last twenty years more of its members have become middle class and its working-class members have become more affluent. As a result, traditional strictures against the "popular" sins have relaxed. One indication of this is the substitution of a new ritual for infant baptism. Other indicants lie in the relaxation of women's dress code (many of them now wear slacks and blouses that open below the neck), their modern hair styles, and their use of makeup and jewelry. Also, it is clear that the male television ministers of the denomination use makeup and have their hair done. Most of the visible and obvious changes in traditional morality involve relaxation of rules for women, probably a result of the changing status and power of women—especially their economic power resulting from their working outside the home—and the consequent need to cater to them.

## 8. The Prosecution

1. Dallas Blanchard was the only one of the authors able to attend on the first day of the trial, and this chapter is presented primarily from his perspective. Blanchard attended each day of the trial but one, and Prewitt attended four days, including the one Blanchard missed. The trial notes of William Barnes, who was present during most of the trial, provided a cross-check. Thus the courtroom dialogue consists of direct quotations and paraphrasing from the notes of three observers.

2. Only one of the jurors, Glenda Stifflemire, claimed to have heard or read nothing about the case. In 1976 a Glenda Stifflemire wrote a pro-choice letter to the editor of the *Pensacola News-Journal*. We have not been able to determine whether this was the same person.

3. Although William Brennan, who was to testify in this trial on cognitive dissonance, had previously testified in another case, to our knowledge this is the first major abortion-related case in which this issue was raised. As discussed in the next

chapter, Monaghan's definition of cognitive dissonance is an inaccurate interpretation of this psychological term.

4. The vast majority of crimes committed in the United States are crimes against the state rather than crimes against the nation (federal). In most cases, for a crime to be a federal offense, it must in some way involve more than one state. Therefore, for these bombings to be valid federal crimes, as opposed to simply crimes against the state of Florida, the prosecution had to prove that more than one state was involved. Therefore Susan Novotny set about proving that the bombings interfered with interstate commerce.

5. With advances in medical technology, fetuses are more and more often treated by physicians while still in the womb. By 1990 some have even benefited from surgery. That is, the fetus has become a patient, which gives it a social role. This is also consistent with the medical movement away from the use of medications during pregnancy and anesthetics during birth because of potential harm to the fetus. Thus, Kasun's and Monaghan's line of questioning was certainly consistent with prominent medical viewpoints and underscores an important distinction between obstetric and abortion practices in their views of the fetus. The conflict inherent in these two views is heightened by the fact that most abortions are performed by obstetricians.

6. These questions by Shimek imply that abortion is a heartless, profit-seeking business.

7. This line of questioning reflects the view widely circulated in the anti-abortion community that fetal remains are sold to cosmetic companies for use in protein conditioners. There is no documentation that such sales are presently occurring. By state law, fetal remains are routinely sent to laboratories for analysis to determine whether there are cancerous conditions or uterine abnormalities. The laboratories are responsible for disposal. The Reagan and Bush administrations even banned the use of fetal tissues in medical research and treatment of illnesses such as Parkinson's disease, in which fetal tissue has appeared to be quite effective.

8. The first question reflects upon prior cases where fetal remains were found in trash cans and dumpsters of abortion clinics elsewhere in the nation. It also reflects the anti-abortionists' anger over disrespectful treatment of "human" (fetal) remains. The second question points to the alcohol-education function of the BATF and ties it to the assumed humanity of the fetus.

Theologians, scientists, and physicians disagree among themselves on the question of when life begins. Of course, biological "life" even precedes conception, for the sperm and egg are alive. The dispute arises over when that life becomes human. For some, humanness requires social incorporation into a human community. For others, it requires the psychological component of self-consciousness or self-awareness, which follows social incorporation.

9. The defense attorneys, especially Monaghan, continually referred to the defendants as "kids" to emphasize their youth.

10. There were originally twelve "Protectors of the Code" T-shirts that were

divided between Goldsby and Simmons. Because special-order T-shirts are usually sold in bulk, the numbers involved here do not necessarily indicate a wider conspiracy or some unusual fantasy on the defendants' part. We have not been able to establish that there was a connection between the T-shirts and the Gideon Project. Nor was such a connection made clear in the trial.

11. The social movement literature (see Zald and McCarthy 1987, 172) holds that highly publicized public events, such as this trial, serve to bring together movement activists and unite them by expanding networks. Joseph Scheidler has performed this function by attending a portion of the trials of a number of clinic bombers and arsonists, visiting them in prison, keeping in touch with them by writing them while they are in prison, and publicizing them in his newsletter. In fact, Scheidler's office furnished us with the addresses of all those imprisoned for abortion-related violence, including those who had completed their terms. Also, several arsonists or bombers attended Scheidler-sponsored events of various kinds prior to carrying out their criminal acts.

12. These manuals were handbooks of terrorist tactics produced under CIA sponsorship for use in Central America.

### 9. The Defense

1. The Dr. Seuss material concerned a statement from *Horton Hears a Who*: "A person is a person, no matter how small." The movie *Dune* is based on a series of science fiction novels in which good and evil are contrasted starkly and purely. The hero is a messianic figure whose mother conceived him against the orders of her superiors. When he becomes an adult, he conducts a Holy War or Jihad (terms used in the film) against those in power, the sinners. *Beast Master* features a cult that sacrifices "unborn infants." The hero was intended for such a sacrifice, snatched from his mother's womb, and branded preparatory to being sacrificed. At the last moment he is rescued from the would-be murderer and later becomes the savior of his people.

2. Kasun's general line of questioning about Simmons's relationship with her husband and the place of women in the Pentecostal community was designed to establish Jimmy's primary responsibility for Kathren's actions. Certainly the social pressure within that community is consistent with this cultural argument. There is, however, a wide latitude of opinion within fundamentalist circles regarding the interpretation of the obligation of obedience, which is not binding for immoral and, by extension, illegal behavior.

3. The use of denominational organizations, such as the Royal Rangers, to replace more ecumenical ones in the larger society serves to limit members' interactions with "outsiders."

4. This was the second mention of Raney, associate pastor of First Assembly. Although rumors suggested that others besides those on trial were linked to the bombings, actual involvement of George Raney or others in planning or executing the bombings has never been established as fact.

5. Actually, Wiggins's pronunciation is closer to the Hebrew rendering than is the usual "Bale."

6. This statement opens the controversy over interpretation of Goldsby's and Simmons's understanding of the Holy Spirit, a debate carried on through the testimony of Mullan and Manuel Cepeda, the prosecution psychiatrist who testified later. Mullan's view treats experience of the Holy Spirit as an illusion and thus relegates most manifestations of God in Pentecostal and charismatic religion to neurotic or psychotic origins, an interpretation consistent with Freudian psychology generally. Cepeda accepted the cultural milieu of charismatic fundamentalism and thus found no psychological abnormality in the search for the Holy Spirit by Simmons and Goldsby. Moreover, not all persons of Pentecostal faith would accept that the men's urges to do something about abortion were inspired by the Holy Spirit. In the context of diverse opinions about the validity of spiritual gifts and the authenticity of particular manifestations asserted in the case, neither psychiatrist was required to testify regarding the absolute authenticity of "inspired" behavior. This underscores the sense in which the court maintained a culturally indifferent or hostile attitude toward the religious claims of the defendants. At several points in the trial, testimony came very close to asserting that anyone who believes God talks to them is crazy.

7. Goldsby is not the only person convicted of abortion-related violence for whom Ronald Reagan has been cited as an inspiration. Nor does such inspiration necessarily suggest mental incompetence. Thus, from the prosecution's point of view, Goldsby indefensibly used Reagan, like Pentecostal religion, as a justification for a cold, calculated act of violence.

8. *Cognitive dissonance* is a term coined by Leon Festinger that essentially is defined as Dr. Daniel Dansak stated it later in the trial. Rather than referring to receiving "mixed signals" about what is right and wrong, the term denotes a disjuncture or incongruity between a person's beliefs or moral code and that person's behavior. See, for example, *When Prophecy Fails* (Festinger, Riecken, and Schachter 1956) and *A Theory of Cognitive Dissonance* (Festinger 1957).

9. Blanchard.

10. Michael Bray, who was convicted of several clinic bombings (see chapter 13), later told us that this organization was little more than a name on a letterhead and the membership actually consisted of his brother.

11. Compare this definition of splitting with Lifton's (1986) definition of the phenomenon in his study of Nazi doctors.

12. Simmons had to move back to her parents' home.

13. Mullan walked into Dillard's trap in her responses to these questions on cognitive dissonance. Dillard appeared to accept the defense's definition of it as getting "mixed signals," and Mullan's responses indicate that she did not really know what cognitive dissonance is and had accepted that erroneous definition as well.

14. Cepeda's resistance to Monaghan's questioning of his own beliefs under-

scores again the difference between his view of the supernatural and that of Nancy Mullan. While Cepeda's cultural empathy with the defendants was by no means perfect, he more clearly defended their cultural perspective than did the defense psychiatrist. Lack of cultural empathy was perhaps the central flaw in the strategy of the defense presentation, exposing the insanity plea as an effort to redirect the trial to the topic of abortion.

15. Most Baptists reject "full-gospel" interpretations of scriptural references to the "Gifts of the Spirit," especially speaking in tongues. Although perspectives in individual congregations may vary, Baptists who pursue a strict interpretation of biblical passages such as 1 Corinthians 12 usually become associated with non-denominational charismatic congregations.

16. The term *charismatic* has been introduced in recent years to indicate the extension to some "mainline" Protestant and Catholic congregations of "full-gospel" scriptural interpretations formerly associated almost exclusively with Pentecostal congregations. "Taking the Bible literally" is only one tenet of fundamentalist thought and is itself insufficient as a definition of the term *charismatic*. Some charismatics are fundamentalists, while others are not; and some fundamentalists are charismatics, while others are not.

### 10. Closing Arguments and Verdict

1. When questioned by officers on the day of Matt's arrest, Kaye Wiggins had three times asserted that she did not know Matt Goldsby.

2. We will later point out that this is a typical defense in abortion-related crime, called "blaming the victim."

3. Kasun ran through almost every defense ever used in an abortion-related violent crime: (1) necessity to save life; (2) persecution of the perpetrator; (3) absence of the real offenders, the abortionists; (4) insanity; (5) comparisons of abortion with the Holocaust; (6) the "illegality" of the Supreme Court decision; (7) lying investigators; (8) loyalty to family and family values; (9) youthful innocence; and (10) biblical imperatives.

4. The "necessity" defense, which holds that there was no legal alternative in the interest of saving a human life, has been frequently used in cases involving abortion-related violence. It has rarely succeeded and usually only in cases involving illegal demonstrations tried before a local, lower-court judge.

5. Another defense strategy: equating abortion to slavery of black Americans.

6. Blanchard.

### 11. Gifts of the Spirit

1. The offering of an interpretation is a typical validation of the authenticity of an instance of speech in tongues, that it is "of the Holy Spirit." Interpretation is itself one of the gifts of the Spirit; hence, in this instance several people were moved in what can be regarded as a unified act of Spirit-filled expression. Both interpreta-

tions on this morning were long, too long for us to render adequately in paraphrase, and very general in substance.

2. The strongest evidence indicates that the growth of conservative churches and denominations in recent years lies primarily not in their converting persons from liberal churches and denominations but in their higher birth rates and their better ability to hold on to their youth into adulthood. See Kelly (1977).

3. As Lofland (1966) and Lofland and Stark (1965) have pointed out, people have a predisposition to seek answers to problems in one of several avenues—e.g., politics, psychiatry, or religion. Prior socialization, especially as children or youth, weighs heavily in the choice of which type of solution to seek.

4. Indeed, Southern Baptist churches found to be practicing speaking in tongues are subject to dismissal from the state and national conventions.

5. There are indications from some informants that perhaps as many as a dozen members or attendees of First Assembly knew Jimmy and Matt had committed the June 25 bombing. Sims-Shofner (1989) supports this. There was also an indication that some knew of the Christmas Day bombings before they occurred, but this has never been proved legally.

6. In effect, Glass's conversion entailed no basic change in her worldview but simply a change in the side on which she stood in the cosmic battle.

## 12. Sentencing

1. Blanchard.

2. Federal prisons are graded by level of security, with level one reserved primarily for white-collar and minimum-risk prisoners.

## 13. The National Roll Call

1. Goffman (1981).

2. Thad Beyle, professor of political science at the University of North Carolina, maintains that a similar connection exists between the Reagan-Bush administrations and the charge of racism in the voting of David Duke, a former American Nazi and Ku Klux Klan leader, into a runoff election for governor of Louisiana ("Expert: GOP Policies Paved Way for Ex-Klansman Duke" [*Pensacola News Journal*, 21 October 1991, 2A]).

3. The table also includes attempted arsons and bombings.

4. Paul Weyrich, a right-wing strategist, said, "Some of the pro-life movement definitely feels that the Administration has given them rhetoric but not action" (*New York Times*, 26 January 1987, 22A). Spitzer (1987, 67) asserts, "Many in the right-to-life movement continue to voice dissatisfaction with candidates like Lehrman and Ronald Reagan. Even enthusiastic Reagan supporters in the RTLP view Reagan with suspicion and cynicism, calculating that his sympathies are founded in political expediency more than ideological fervor."

5. Merton (1957, 234–35).

6. Val Burris (1983, 305–17).

7. Nice (1988) analyzes the occurrences of bombings and concludes that they occur primarily in states having weaker social control, higher abortion rates, and greater tolerance of violence toward women.

8. Another significant factor is that the majority of abortion-providing physicians and clinics are located in coastal states. As of 1978, abortions were provided in only 23 percent of U.S. counties and were generally difficult to secure in central and midwestern states (Jaffe, Lindheim, and Lee, 1981, 15). Thus, abortion clinic violence is limited by the availability of potential victims.

9. Himmelstein (1986, 1–15).

10. Of course, the bombings and arsons have been concentrated in urban communities, for that is where the vast majority of abortion clinics and practicing obstetricians-gynecologists are located. However, Hunter (1984) maintains that it is in urban areas that fundamentalists will be less committed to religious belief and activism, since there they will be in closer contact with the functional rationality, cultural pluralism, and structural pluralism of modernity. We maintain, however, that just as individuals may more easily isolate themselves in urban centers than in rural areas, relatively isolated religious enclaves easily exist in urban areas and that the inevitable, even if limited and circumscribed, contact with modernity is one motivating factor in anti-abortion violence.

11. Randall Terry, head of Project Life in Binghamton, New York, is the organizer of Operation Rescue (OR). Some maintain that he is figureheading the organization for Scheidler, who has had several lawsuits filed against him by NOW and others. OR targets specific clinics and doctors' offices, and members attempt to close them down by chaining themselves to the doors and otherwise obstructing patient access. At this writing OR is in a severely reduced mode of activity due to judgments against the group amounting to about $500,000 in Atlanta and New York. OR activists differ in tactics from the bombers and arsonists in that they remain in place and seek arrest and imprisonment. Thus, they are a long step closer to traditional civil disobedience.

12. Scheidler, Terry, and Operation Rescue, among others, have suffered severe court defeats as a result of suits filed against them by clinics and NOW under RICO laws, which are antiracketeering statutes aimed primarily at traditional organized crime. Those decisions are still under appeal at this writing.

13. We were unable to obtain information on three convicted bombers or arsonists: David Holman, who committed five offenses in Rockford, Illinois, in 1986 and 1987; Lanning (first name not available), who pled guilty to a 1985 attempt on a clinic in Granite City, Illinois; and Frederick Gordon Tipps, who pled guilty to a charge related to an arson in Riverside, California, in 1986.

While virtually every individual and organization involved in the anti-abortion movement claims purely altruistic motives—i.e., unselfishly saving fetuses—we assume that no person acts without at least some ulterior motives. The issue of social movement altruism lies beyond our concerns here, but we recognize that it is an important issue in the field and that it is possible for persons to be more or less "purely" altruistic and minimally self-serving.

14. In an odd twist, in September 1985 Denis E. Dillon, the district attorney who prosecuted Burkin, joined and helped lead some one thousand protesters outside the Hempstead clinic.

15. Wood later sued Markley in civil court and was awarded $17,500 in compensatory damages and $100,000 in punitive damages. However, as a Benedictine, Markley has taken a vow of poverty. In January 1992 Wood, charging that Markley had paid nothing on the judgment, sued to have Markley's church in Foley, Alabama, garnish his wages.

16. *Action News*, March 1988, 1.

17. Beseda was convicted a second time, along with Dottie Roberts and Sharon Codispoti, by a federal court jury in August 1989 of conspiracy under federal racketeering charges of arson and extortion of an abortion clinic. He received a twenty-year sentence.

18. Michael Bray said in our interview in 1990 that the Defenders was never more than a paper organization; it consisted of "little more than a couple of letters."

19. Bray's conviction was later overturned. In 1987 he was rearraigned, and he entered an Alford plea, which is technically a guilty plea in which the defendant does not admit guilt. He was then sentenced to six years and served a little more than forty-six months in federal prison.

According to Bray, his attorney, Robert Muse of Washington, D.C., later defended some persons in the John Walker spying case and the Iran-Contra affair.

20. See chapter 14 for a discussion of reconstructionism.

21. In August 1987, a county circuit judge issued an order prohibiting Ross from doing abortions because demonstrators outside the office "were disturbing other businesses in the office complex" (Trafford 1987).

22. Diamond is the person who said at the Pensacola "I Believe in Life" rally in March 1984, "I wouldn't mind seeing those heathen doctors' hands cut off and hung up on a string for the world to see."

23. *Baton Rouge Morning Advocate*, 28 July 1987, 1A.

24. Ibid.

25. *Baton Rouge State Times*, 27 July 1987, 1A.

26. Ibid.

27. *Baton Rouge Morning Advocate*, 27 July 1987, 1B.

28. According to the *San Diego Union* (20 January 1988, 3B), several members of the church denied knowing Saie and claimed she was not a member of the church. Members describe the church as a "typical fundamentalist church," which includes assemblies on such topics as "God and Country" and support for President Reagan.

29. The son of a carpenter from Munday, Texas, the fifty-four-year-old Owens worked as a truck driver and plumber's assistant while a student at San Diego Bible College. Sixteen years before this bombing attempt, he founded his Bible Mission-

ary Fellowship. At one time he was reported to be a member of the John Birch Society.

30. Cheryl Sullenger and four others won a false-arrest suit against the Alvarado clinic for almost $59,000 when clinic personnel used a citizen's arrest to charge them with violating a court order against Owens and his followers in relation to their picketing. The court held that the five were not related to Owens and therefore were not subject to the injunction.

31. Owens was convicted in the same incident. The injunction was issued based on some of the activities carried out by Owens and his members, such as a sign in Spanish informing Mexican women that Mexican officials would be apprised of "persons who abort their babies in this clinic."

32. Christopher Harmon had been convicted of using a stun gun to shoot a man as he and his female friend were entering the Alvarado clinic. Harmon was sentenced to a year in jail and served a month before being released with orders not to picket or approach an abortion clinic.

33. *San Diego Union*, 2 December 1987, 1B.

34. See the discussion of Christian reconstructionism in chapter 14.

35. For his part in showing Brockhoeft the Ladies Center location, Burt had his probation revoked in August 1987 and was placed under house arrest, except to go to work or to leave with permission of his probation officer, for two years. While Judge William Anderson said he was convinced Burt was tricked into the trip, "I don't want you to accidentally lead another bomber to the Ladies Center or anywhere else." He also limited Burt to Santa Rosa County and ordered him to stay five hundred yards away from the Ladies Center under all circumstances.

36. This loose connection between various bombers and arsonists both before and after the offenses indicates that these persons constitute an approximation of what Oberschall (1980, 45) calls "loosely structured social action," which "refers to social action that is undertaken by a loose coalition of activists, part-timers, and sympathizers whose boundaries are ill-defined and shifting, who lack a common, central leadership, organization, and clear-cut procedures for deciding upon a common course of action."

37. This is a clear example of what is called "blaming the victim."

38. O'Hara (1991).

39. Ibid.

40. Bryant (1991) and Schlosser (1991).

41. This is in contrast to the far more public leaders of anti-abortion organizations, who tend to be "middle-aged or older, of both sexes, relatively well-educated, and have a history in public affairs" (Kriesberg 1985).

42. Physical violence has been predominantly a male activity in American society. However, with increased equality, females are now being arrested and charged more frequently than in the past for all forms of traditionally male crimes.

43. In line with this, one of the major defenses of Kaye Wiggins and Kathren

Simmons was that they were simply following the demands and needs of the dominant males in their lives—i.e., conforming to normal expectations in their religious community.

44. While we were not able to determine Marjorie Reed's mothering status, at the age of forty-six she was likely past the point where it was thought crucial to be at home with her children, if she had any.

45. As Muller and Godwin (1984) indicate, one important element in what they call "political aggression" is having the time to pursue such activities (p. 141). Members of the working class spend less time in work than do professionals: thirty-five to forty hours per week versus sixty to eighty hours. Those who are self-employed have even greater flexibility in their time allocation, as well as the greater ability to hide illegal activities under occupational guises.

46. McAdam (1986) calls this "biographical availability," which is "the absence of personal constraints that may increase the costs and risks of movement participation, such as full-time employment, marriage, and family responsibilities" (p. 70). On the other hand, Wood and Hughes (1984) maintain "that various structural conditions, such as being geographically mobile from rural areas, being self-employed, or being status discrepant, have no effect on anti-pornography social movement adherence when variables representing different socialization experiences and cultural environments are taken into account (religion, education, residence, age and sex)" (p. 86). Perhaps the major difference between our population and the sample used by Wood and Hughes lies in the *degree* of radical action, which might indicate differential factors in recruitment to differential levels of activism or radicalism.

47. Our use of the terms *social isolate* and *loner* is broader than the normal usage in the social sciences. Ordinarily these terms refer to a person totally shut out of close ties within any group. We maintain here that one can also be isolated through a lack of relationships with persons having differing worldviews, what is more typically called "encapsulated." Greil and Rudy (1980) posit three forms of encapsulation: physical, social, and ideological. Although our subjects are not isolated physically, they are isolated socially and ideologically. While Greil and Rudy use these concepts to explain identity transformation, we suggest that they may well be self-imposed methods of *maintaining* an identity. The higher incidence of mental illness in urban areas is partially explained by the ability of aberrant persons to withdraw and become anonymous in that environment. It is also possible for groups to effectively encapsulate or isolate themselves in cities. Furthermore, ritualizing and thereby limiting and strictly structuring contacts with "outsiders" may also serve to substitute for actual physical isolation. Hunter (1987, 178), for example, suggests that in environments that are more liberal "recognition of the minority status of their convictions . . . appears to foster a 'fortress mentality' among the strongly committed. . . . The evangelical in this context becomes even 'more' evangelical." Schmalzbauer's research (1991) supports this conclusion.

Luker (1984) documents that the earliest California anti-abortion organizations were composed primarily of professionals, physicians, attorneys, and social workers, who simply assumed that everyone would agree with their anti-abortion positions, that it was a general public value. Many of the physicians probably practiced in Catholic hospitals, where the anti-abortion stance was taken for granted. They tended to be shocked and shaken when their state enacted repeal or reform of abortion restrictions. Thus, even upper-middle class, educated professionals can be relatively encapsulated in modern society.

48. Scully and Marollo (1984, 530–44) interviewed a sample of Virginia prisoners convicted of rape. They found that 88 percent of them were eighteen to thirty-five years of age, 42 percent were married or cohabiting with a woman, only 20 percent of them had at least a high school education, and 85 percent were from a working-class background. Only 26 percent of them had a history of emotional problems.

The research on rape generally concludes that rape is less "sexual" than it is an effort to express contempt for and control of women. The research on opposition to abortion reflects the same position. Opposition to sex education in the schools, to use of contraceptives (a stand taken by many groups in the anti-abortion movement), and to the availability of private abortions appears also to arise primarily from a fear of females being able to control their own lives and no longer being subject to male dominance. As we cite elsewhere in this work, many anti-abortion spokespersons do not hesitate to assert that fear of pregnancy is important toward keeping women "in line," or moral. Our interviews with anti-abortion activists and bombers confirm this.

49. While fundamentalist males may appear more vocal about this, women in the movement also accept this ideology. Furthermore, they take abortion availability as a personal affront or an attack upon themselves. Spitzer (1987, 58) quotes one of the founders of the Right to Life Party and its two-time presidential candidate, Ellen McCormack, who, while not a fundamentalist herself, expresses an attitude common to the fundamentalist anti-abortionists we interviewed: "Decisions were being made by the politicians that had a tremendous control over our lives . . . we realized that the leaders in this country were giving a direction to society that we didn't benefit by. We felt that it [liberalized abortion legislation] was an intrusion in our lives and the lives of young children, and they were getting control over our lives that frightened us." Thus, the availability of abortion *to other women* is seen as a personal threat to them.

50. See, for example, Brinkerhoff and Pupri (1988) and Pollock and Steele (1968). In Florida the Department of Health and Rehabilitative Services (HRS) maintains a "hot-line" list of those reported to be possibly guilty of child abuse. No name may be removed for thirty days, and some not for five years, even if an investigation fails to support the report. In 1990 someone anonymously called the Florida hot-line and charged a couple with lifting a child, Princess, by the neck and locking her in the bathroom. Investigators discovered that Princess was a raccoon, but they still required the couple to undergo a state-mandated child-abuse counsel-

ing session. A number of fundamentalist groups have joined in a campaign against this hot-line law. For example, we recently spotted a car with two bumper stickers: "Be a Hero and Save a Whale/Save a Baby and Go to Jail" and "Stop HRS/Support Family Rights." HRS regulations define as abuse any physical contact that leaves a bruise for more than twenty-four hours. For many fundamentalists, physical punishment is a normal part of child rearing and should not be within the purview or under the control of the state.

Studies of slavery, in the United States as well as elsewhere, and studies of "on-the-job" status inequalities establish quite clearly that *wherever* women are in a subordinate status they are subjected to sexual exploitation, as well as other forms of exploitation. The authoritarian family is clearly structured for such exploitations as incest and wife rape.

51. DeBerg (1991) argues, based on early documents of the fundamentalist movement (1880–1930), that early twentieth-century fundamentalism was *primarily* a reaction to the changing roles of women, as opposed to the usual assumption that it was a reaction to the "larger" issues of modernism and theology. We argue, on the other hand, that the primary issue was a conflict of worldviews: that fundamentalists, then and now, wish to return to the Edenic era of the mechanical view of the universe, when religion was at the heart of all social institutions and organizations (i.e., the medieval worldview). In essence, DeBerg's argument supports this, for she maintains that fundamentalism arose from a desire to return to the Victorian family and its morality.

By the 1880s, when fundamentalism was gaining strength, the white Protestant hegemony was beginning its decline with the influx of European Catholics and Jews. At the same time industrialization was making inroads on traditional gender roles. For example, we had in our possession a letter from a young female to her attorney father in Maine (circa 1880) that declared that she would rather stay in Providence, working in a factory and being self-supporting, than return home to the life of a seamstress and dependency on kin. This supports DeBerg's thesis, but underlying the decline of Victorian family patterns lies the industrialization of the United States.

The fundamentalist movement clearly parallels other social movements. That is, while some have maintained that originally it was primarily a theological debate, others have contended that it was basically a protest against modernism, and De Berg argues persuasively that the basic issue was changes in gender roles. However, we argue that since its beginning fundamentalism has had multiple constituencies of varying social status, as have other social movements. Thus, theologians may have emphasized the theological issues, while the rank and file picked up on their own immediate concerns, which may have differed widely. For example, the rise of fundamentalism coincides with the rise of the Ku Klux Klan and the Know-Nothing Party. All are likely similar reactions to similar cultural and social changes.

52. We should note that the profiles of the bombers/arsonists, rapists, other violent criminals, and terrorists are virtually the same. Also, these profiles are rather

broad and demand further specification, which requires further research. In other words, the data are too general to draw any but the most tentative conclusions from them.

53. It is worth noting, however, that in 1988 the FBI did have an office assigned the task of developing profiles of abortion clinic bombers and arsonists. Indeed, the BATF had at least one of its personnel assigned to work at and with the FBI on this.

54. Of course, as the distinguished psychiatrist Thomas Szasz has pointed out, the definition of any act, person, or group as "terrorist" is a political act; that is, one person's terrorist is another person's liberator.

55. Gibbs (1989, 330) offers a sociological definition of terrorism: "Terrorism is illegal violence or threatened violence directed against human or nonhuman objects, provided that it: (1) was undertaken or ordered with a view to altering or maintaining at least one putative norm in at least one particular territorial unit or population; (2) had secretive, furtive, and/or clandestine features that were expected by the participants to conceal their personal identity and/or their future location; (3) was not undertaken or ordered to further the permanent defense of some area; (4) was not conventional warfare and because of their concealed personal identity, concealment of their future location, their threats, and/or their spatial mobility, the participants perceived themselves as less vulnerable to conventional military action; *and* (5) was perceived by the participants as contributing to the normative goal previously described (*supra*) by inculcating fear of violence in persons (perhaps an indefinite category of them) other than the immediate target of the actual or threatened violence and/or publicizing some cause."

Clearly, the acts against abortion facilities fit these criteria. They also fit the simpler definition of Gurr (1989): "the use of unexpected violence to intimidate or coerce people in the pursuit of political or social objectives." Furthermore, Wilson and Lynxwiler (1988) conclude that abortion-related violence fits the classification of "limited political" or "sub-revolutionary" terrorism.

56. Gurr (1989, 209). He adds, "Such tactics are a continuing reminder of the enduring potential for violence among conservative groups opposed to social change." Davis and Stasz (1990, 295) also include abortion clinic bombings among acts of terrorism.

57. Davis and Stasz, 302.

58. Ibid., 303.

59. *New York Times*, 15 November 1987, 3E.

60. Ibid.

61. Goleman, *New York Times*, 14 May 1985, 5C. Muller and Godwin (1984) conclude that "persons who are alienated from the political system, who perceive themselves to have insufficient political power, and whose ideology accepts political violence, should be predisposed to participate in aggressive political behavior. This would be especially true where they perceive such behaviors as effective methods for achieving political goals and *when they have available time to pursue these activities*" (140–41; italics added).

The reports on bombers and arsonists, especially from Ryan's Pro-Life Direct Action League and Scheidler's organization, read like hagiographies. The tone of their publications communicates astonishment that those who commit violence could be tried, much less convicted, for their acts.

62. Lifton (1986); Muller and Godwin (1984).

63. Ibid.

64. However, when the abortion issue gets personal, there are strong indications that persons in other segments of the anti-abortion movement are quite able to reevaluate their positions. For example, at *every* abortion facility that had suffered violence or attempted violence, the respondent said a demonstrator or picketer—that is, a strong activist—had later come to the clinic for an abortion for herself or a teenage daughter, a dramatic example of cognitive dissonance. When a woman is forty-five years old, thinks she has completed her family, and suddenly finds she is pregnant, or when she has a teenage daughter who is pregnant, then a reexamination of values and priorities is virtually inevitable. In every instance, the former demonstrator's opening statement had been, essentially, "I didn't realize . . ." McDonnell (1984, 50) cites corroborative evidence of this ability to reexamine one's moral stance with a changed life situation.

### 14. Sacred Universes in a Secular Society

1. As our colleague Ramon Oldenburg has pointed out, this issue goes back at least as far as the Middle Ages and Luther's execration of Copernicus and, we would add, the Vatican's condemnation of Galileo's discoveries. As we will argue later, the issue is basically centered on the conflicting claims for a religious hegemony consistent with an idealized memory of the Middle Ages and modern scientific views.

2. Please do not anticipate us and assume that we will characterize fundamentalism as a desire to establish a sacred society.

3. Cox is not alone in pushing the origins of secularization back to the Old Testament. See, for example, Berger (1969, 111ff.).

4. *De la division du travail social* (1893).

5. The following discussion is taken largely from "Cybernetics: Meta-Image of the Twentieth Century" by William H. Cozart. We realize full well that the following characterizations are simplifications of each of the various historical epochs. However, such oversimplification has analytical utility. In effect, we are drawing forth patterns similar to Max Weber's ideal types in order to highlight and contrast the dominant worldviews that developed in Western civilization.

6. Daniel J. Boorstin (1985, 64–72) emphasizes the role of the clock in forming the medieval mind-set. He refers to it as the "master metaphor of the universe" (p. 72). He is joined by Bronowski (1973) on the importance of the clock.

7. Cozart, p. 2.

8. As Robbins (1978) points out, the problem with the "normal" middle-class style of Christian religiosity lies in explaining its tolerance, since Christianity has historically been extremist and exclusive. As one of our reviewers, Judith Ochshorn, has pointed out, traditional Christian tendencies toward violence are well documented in the accounts of the Crusades, support for "just" wars, and witch-hunts. We would add to her list Savonarola's "cleansings," Luther's support for actions against the peasants, Calvin's burning of "heretics" in Geneva, and American Protestant riots against Irish Catholics, to name but a few such cases. To our knowledge, the introduction of tolerance into American Christianity of the last century is yet to be fully explained. For an analysis of contemporary mainline churches, see Roof and McKinney (1987).

9. James D. Hunter (1984, 11–14) maintains that modernity (secularization) is characterized primarily by "functional rationality, cultural pluralism, and structural pluralism." Functional rationality is comparable to what Munby (1963) calls "rational problem solving." The structural pluralism of Hunter is related to our use of the term *differentiation*, although Hunter stresses that its major aspect is the privatization of religion.

10. For descriptions of a variety of fundamentalist religious groups, see Ammerman (1987), Bradfield (1979), Dayton (1976), Fowler (1982), Hunter (1984), Liebman and Wuthnow (1983), Paloma (1982), and Quebedeaux (1978).

11. Smidt (1989a). However, Bruce (1988) maintains that even the middle-class members of the New Christian Right, which is largely an expression of fundamentalist values, have working-class values.

12. J. Milton Yinger and Stephen J. Cutler (1982, 83–84). See also Hunter (1984). Hunter defines evangelicalism essentially the same as we define fundamentalism. However, there are many self-identified evangelicals who do not subscribe to biblical literalism. They generally share with fundamentalists a conservative theology and an emphasis on soul-saving or individual conversion, as opposed to social activism, as the cure for the world's problems. Thus, as we use the terms, fundamentalism is a subset of the more inclusive group, evangelicals.

Most people in the United States, especially among the mainline religions, seemed to feel that fundamentalism disappeared after its becoming a national laughingstock in the Scopes trial. However, it continued as a force in American life, as in the prohibition movement, among other issues. See Marty (1991) for further influences and efforts of fundamentalism.

13. Ammerman (1991, 219) finds that the strong fundamentalists among Southern Baptist laity have at least a high school education but less than a college degree. "They had enough education to be full participants in the modern world, but not enough to have gained the credentials and status that might have made them more enamored of that world," she states. That in-between status corresponds with our contention that fundamentalists tend to have a rural orientation while living in an urban environment.

14. Many authors describe the basic elements of "documentary theory." See, for example, documentary treatment of Genesis, the first book of the Torah, in Gunkel (1910), von Rad (1972), and Coats (1983).

15. One of the most prominent founding documents of the Social Gospel movement is Rauschenbusch (1918).

16. The series was published over a period of years between 1910 and 1915 (Dixon, Meyer, and Torrey). In 1895 a conference was held at Niagara, New York, which essentially outlined the basic tenets of fundamentalism and formed the basis of the series. See Cole (1963) and Gaspar (1963).

17. Ammerman (1991, 217) maintains that theology alone is not a sufficient definition of fundamentalism, but that it is significantly marked by organizing to oppose social change. We differ with this. We contend here and below that fundamentalism is essentially a theological and ideological stance, that mobilization and organization for activism among fundamentalists, as in other ideological orientations, depends upon sociocultural and sociopsychological variables among the adherents.

18. Many also are opposed to the use of birth control. Recent studies of church growth among the conservative denominations have concluded that their increasing membership (as opposed to the declining membership of mainline denominations) has come primarily from higher birthrates and the ability to hold on to their children past adolescence (Kelly 1977).

19. Studies have shown that both Protestant and Catholic abortion protesters share in valuation of "traditional sexual morality"—i.e., opposition to premarital sex, birth control for those in their teens, sex education in the schools, and divorce (Granberg 1978; Fiedler and Pomerleau 1978).

Stets (1991) finds that the anti-abortionists have a unitary, absolutist attitude structure and "are more likely: 1) to engage in black-white, categorical thinking, 2) to minimize attitude conflict (dissonant stimuli either fit a class or are excluded, thus there is relatively little ambiguity), 3) to anchor behavior in external conditions (thus restricting internal integrative processes and the self as causative agent in interpreting stimuli) and 4) to consider change as sometimes necessary. . . . Such individuals are interpreting the different issues in the same way; they see them as representing the same underlying dimension. This underlying dimension might symbolize 'adhering to authority,' 'following one's conscience,' or 'abiding by one's religious beliefs.' . . . Pro-lifers may see that there is only one issue: doing the right thing as defined by those in authority."

20. Cuneo (1989, 42) maintains that there are significant numbers of Catholics who share with fundamentalist Protestants a belief in and emphasis on biblical inerrancy, the physical resurrection of Jesus, and the requirement of a personal relationship with Jesus for salvation.

21. There is debate at present about the applicability of the term *fundamentalism* to non-Christian and Christian religions other than Protestantism. Cuneo (1989) limits the term to Protestants. Others would disagree with that position. For exam-

ple, Martin E. Marty of the University of Chicago is currently working under a five-year grant from the American Academy of Arts and Sciences on commonalities among various "fundamentalisms" across the spectrum of world religions (see Marty and Appleby 1990; Lawrence 1989).

22. One of the reviewers of this work questioned our inclusion of "a justification for violence" as a defining characteristic of fundamentalism. As we will argue later, this is a common thread in all fundamentalisms. Most fundamentalists readily support the use of *state* violence in the death penalty and war. Furthermore, recent research indicates a higher incidence of child and wife abuse among them. Only a minority carry this justification to the use of personal violence against abortion clinics, homosexuals, or other violators of their private morality. Violence is clearly a part of the theology. The only questions revolve around against whom and by whom it should be used. For additional support for our position, see Frenkel-Brunswick (1954) and Lifton and Strozier (1990).

These characteristics of fundamentalism, especially dualism and absolutism, are reflections of Piaget's (1967) pre-formal thinking pattern and the elaborations of it in the work of Perry (1970), Wilcox (1979), Kohlberg (1983), and Fowler (1981) on cognitive, social, and moral development. For a good summary of these perspectives, see Roberts (1986). It should be noted, however, that Kohlberg's work has been questioned because his research was based only on study of male subjects (see Albert, Hanley, and Rothbart 1986; Beal, Garrod, and Shin 1990; Donenberg and Hoffman 1988; Gallotti 1989; Toronto 1987).

23. As we have seen, essential elements of modernism include acceptance of ambiguity, contingency, probability (vs. certitude), and a unitary understanding of the universe.

24. See Peter Steinfels, "Dissecting Fundamentalism" (*New York Times*, 20 November 1988, 24E).

25. Social Darwinism, whose origins predate Charles Darwin, opposes assistance to the poor and other "less fortunates" on various grounds, including the classic religious proposition that people are in poverty because they have sinned and are being punished by God, and the more overtly racist and secular proposition that the weak should die out to keep from degrading the human species by having progeny, a misuse of Darwin's proposition of natural selection. Some have characterized those following this position by opposing abortion, Aid to Dependent Children, prenatal health care, and other social welfare programs for mothers, infants, and children as believing that life begins at conception and ends at birth.

26. Redekop (1968) points to three basic ties between fundamentalism and the radical Right: a simplistic dualism that views virtually everything in a stark black-white dichotomy, a conspiratorial view of the world, and individualism. However, we would qualify "individualism." For while both groups emphasize the rights of individuals to operate in the economic sphere without governmental regulation and the importance of the individual's spiritual experience, the extremists of both groups would impose their definitions of morality in a collective fashion.

27. See, for example, Hunsberger and Altemeyer (1991). Robert Jay Lifton (1986) points out in his discussion of totalitarianism what we see as an interesting potential corollary with authoritarianism. Those who seek total control over others may well be frightened by their own dark, potentially uncontrollable urges. Therefore, in fear of their own internal selves, they seek total control over their external world and especially other people. The fear of oneself may lead to a desire to institute one's omnipotence.

Indeed, there is an intimate relationship between authoritarianism and totalitarianism. The original studies of the authoritarian personality by Theodor W. Adorno et al. (1950) arose from interest in German actions under the Nazis. Fundamentalism stresses obedience and submission to authority, usually in the form of a charismatic leader, not at all unlike "normal" German submission to Hitler.

Another tie between fundamentalism and totalitarianism is indicated by Lifton (1986, 494) when he asserts that Nazism was a form of "reactionary modernism." That is, the Nazis used modern technology to its fullest in killing millions of people in an attempt to return to a "primitive" German myth. At heart they were, Lifton asserts, antitechnological and antimodern, while at the same time using technology to its ultimate.

Research into the relationships between fundamentalism and authoritarianism has shown that fundamentalism is quite authoritarian (Shils 1954). Photiadis and Johnson (1963) also found that "orthodoxy," measured in terms of fundamentalist theology, is correlated with authoritarianism. They concluded that authoritarianism links orthodoxy with prejudice. For a survey of findings on authoritarianism see Kirscht and Dillehay (1967).

There is also a close connection between authoritarianism and what sociologists call "cultural fundamentalism." Wood and Hughes (1984, 89) describe the latter as "adherence to traditional norms, respect for family and religious authority, asceticism and control of impulse. Above all, it is an unflinching and thoroughgoing moralistic outlook on the world; moralism provides a common orientation and common discourse for concerns with the use of alcohol and pornography, the rights of homosexuals, 'pro-family' and 'decency' issues." Clarke (1987) maintains that the abortion protest in England is primarily an expression of cultural fundamentalism.

As Stets (1991, 16) asserts from her analysis of pro-life thought patterns, "Pro-lifers may see that there is only one issue: doing the right thing as defined by those in authority." She concludes that while it may be important to examine social movements from the resource-mobilization perspective, "it is equally important to examine the individual actors in a movement and the extent to which their attitude structure influences a movement's activities." Several authors—e.g., Wilson (1983, 55)—have pointed out that the basic mistake of resource-mobilization theorists lies in their making the organization the unit of analysis. However, Wilson concentrates on the lack of consideration of the role of government and misses the roles of the supporters' social positions, of culture, and of ideology.

28. When one Operation Rescue member was asked if he would approve of an abortion of a "12-year-old rape victim whose health would be harmed by a full-term pregnancy," he responded: "I hope you don't think we're being insensitive. . . . We're aware of what the flip side is. It comes back to the matter of absolutes. It's just easier to have a blanket absolute, which Scripture provides, than to grapple with these tough questions" (Morris 1989, A10). Falik (1975) found that anti-abortionists were characterized by "conventionalism, authoritarian submission, exaggerated identification with masculine and feminine stereotypes, extreme emphasis on discipline, and a moralistic rejection of the impulse life; degree of religious identification; an inability to tolerate ambiguity." Johnson and Tamney (1984; 1988, 44) found that those with "inconsistent life views," such as opposing abortion while favoring the death penalty, "tend to be authoritarian, and dogmatic authoritarians tend to ignore or compartmentalize inconsistent beliefs."

29. Some studies of authoritarianism have shown a correlation between authoritarianism and family ideology that parallels the fundamentalist ideal family. For example, Levinson and Huffman (1955) found that authoritarianism correlates with an ideology of the autocratic family, which emphasizes conventionalism, authoritarian submission of women and children, exaggerated masculinity and femininity, strong stress on discipline, and rejection of impulse life. Furthermore, Frenkel-Brunswick (1954, 237) found that authoritarian children, who usually come from authoritarian families, "tend to display authoritarian aggression, rigidity, cruelty, superstition, externalization and projectivity, denial of weakness, power orientation and more often hold dichotomous conceptions of sex roles, of kinds of people, and of values." Lifton and Strozier (1990, 25) conclude from their work at the Center on Violence and Human Survival that fundamentalism comes "close to sadism" and that fundamentalism has "the need for total control of children."

30. Cuneo (1991) reports hearing a Scheidler call-in tape in which he stated that 70 percent of American women had had sexual relations either before marriage or with someone other than their husbands during marriage. According to Cuneo, Scheidler went on to conclude that "seventy percent of American women are sluts."

31. A similar philosophy is espoused by John Burt's Our Father's House. One of his brochures asserts, "They [the Burts] set down and enforce house rules that help the individual develop self-discipline" (Burt, "Welcome to Our Father's House," n.d.). Residents are not allowed to send or receive mail or telephone calls without Burt's censoring; may not leave the house unaccompanied or without permission; may not have another person, even of the same sex, in their rooms with the door closed; and may not touch the house television channel setting (set on a Christian network). In addition, they must turn over all income, such as welfare payments, to the house. In short, it is assumed that total dependence is the pathway for the development of responsible independence.

32. The sociologist Everett Hughes once said, "Every child has an inalienable right to authoritarian parents against whom to rebel."

33. See DeBerg (1991) for the importance of this in the origins of fundamentalism. DeBerg argues, based on early documents of the fundamentalist movement, that early twentieth-century fundamentalism was *primarily* a reaction to the changing roles of women, as opposed to the usual assumption that it was a reaction to the larger issue of modernism. Of course, it can be easily argued that the changes in the roles of women were just one of the multiple results of the complex of changes wrought by modernism. While many of the early fundamentalists may have centered on female roles as *the* central problem (possibly because it was the most obvious and personally threatening change for them), others quickly saw that the issue was larger and deeper.

34. There are disagreements in the research on this issue. It may well be that those disagreements arise over the subjects of the different investigations. It is likely, for example, that upper-middle-class Catholics, who are more apt to be involved in the educational and political efforts of the movement, function out of a broad "pro-life" ideology and motivation, while the more activist, working-class Catholics, who are more likely to picket or participate in more violent activities, operate out of an ethic centering on sexual behavior and the status of women. Ellen Willis put it this way in the *Village Voice*: "the nitty-gritty issue in the abortion debate is not life but sex" (quoted in Petchesky 1984, 263). Her observation may apply primarily to the more activist wing of the anti-abortion movement. Johnson and Tamney (1988, 44–45) hypothesize that those with "inconsistent" life views "are not really as concerned with the life-taking aspect of abortion as with their opinion that abortion promotes sexual promiscuity. These people are not so much 'right-to-lifers' as sexual moralizers." For an analysis of recruitment and membership of different types of persons in different levels of the anti-abortion movement, see Blanchard (forthcoming).

35. Johnson and Tamney (1988, 44–45) identify four traits of those with inconsistent life views (e.g., opposing abortion while affirming the death penalty): membership in fundamentalist Protestant churches, concern about the sexual behavior of young adults, belief in physical force to solve problems, and social traditionalism.

36. Hall and Ferree (1986, 201) hold that "attitude toward premarital sexual relations becomes the best predictor of abortion attitudes for both blacks and whites."

Turner and Killian (1987, 256) point to the importance of several factors in the success of a social movement, one of which is "benefits for members." This implies that no movement is entirely altruistic, that it is able to recruit supporters at least partially on the basis of what it can offer those supporters. Thus, we began our analysis by asking ourselves, What do these people have to gain?

Clarke (1987, 235) concluded that abortion protest in England arose from cultural values as opposed to status discontent, a desire to enhance participants' social status. We claim that there is another "style" of status discontent, one that desires to *maintain* a social position vis-à-vis significant others, such as in the family, and that coincides with cultural values. The definition of a status group by Page and Clelland

(1978, 275) as "defined by its way of life" approaches what is termed "cultural fundamentalism." In examining the school textbook controversy, they find "four basic thematic complaints: (1) disrespect for traditional orthodox conceptions of God and the Bible; (2) use of profanity and vulgar language; (3) disrespect for authority; and (4) advocacy of moral relativism. In general these four themes can be viewed as objections to secular humanism as a substitute for a preferred authoritarian theocentrism. As such, they are statements of concern about the destruction of a way of life" (p. 274). However, their definition of secular humanism is a quite distorted one.

37. Lawrence (1989, 100) maintains that one of five basic traits common to all fundamentalists (Protestant, Jewish, and Islamic) is "secondary-level male elites. They derive authority from a direct, unmediated appeal to scripture, yet because interpretive principles are often vague, they must be clarified by charismatic leaders who are invariably male." We maintain that the ideology of male dominance extends well beyond the masculine elite, that an exaggerated masculinity infuses the entire ideology itself.

The official pronouncements of both the Catholic and Mormon churches support male dominance in the family. And the literature of the various religious segments of the anti-abortion movement, as well as the public utterances of innumerable leaders of it, overwhelmingly support our contentions here.

Cuneo (1989) maintains that his "Family Heritage" Catholics involved in the Toronto anti-abortion activism are those primarily interested in maintaining "traditional" family statuses of males and females. The females, in particular, desire to hold both males and females responsible for their sexual behavior in defense of their prized mothering role.

Komarovsky (1964) describes vividly the blue-collar women who place priority on their mothering role. They view their husbands in a utilitarian fashion, prizing and evaluating the men primarily on the ability of the husbands to provide the means for the women to perform their mothering role.

38. See, for example, LaHaye (1980). Phyllis Schlafly words it vividly: "It's very healthy for a young girl to be deterred from promiscuity by fear of contracting a painful, incurable disease, or cervical cancer, or sterility, or the likelihood of giving birth to a dead, blind, or brain-damaged baby (even ten years later when she may be happily married)" (cited in Planned Parenthood pamphlet, no title, [1990]).

Judie Brown, president of the American Life League, is virtually as harsh in her judgment: "The woman who is raped has a right to resist her attacker. But the preborn child is an innocent non-aggressor who should not be killed because of the crime of the father. More to the point, since a woman has a right to resist the rapist, she also has the right to resist his sperm . . . However, once the innocent third party to a rape, the preborn child, is conceived, he should not be killed . . . Incest is a voluntary act on the woman's part. If it were not, it would be rape. And to kill a child because of the identity of his father is no more proper in the case of incest than it is in the case of rape" ("The Human Life Amendment," n.d., 18).

Mary Ellen Fulda, who was arrested for blockading a clinic, said, "Today it's popular to have your pleasure and not to be responsible. The bulk of women getting abortions are not responsible" (Smith 1989). Hall and Ferree (1986, 201) found that "attitude toward premarital sexual relations was the best predictor of abortion attitudes."

39. Fear is an important component of the entire fundamentalist syndrome—fear of Satan's wiles, fear of pregnancy outside marriage, fear of the wrath of God, fear of the consequences of any form of disobedience. Barbara Ehrenreich (1983) says that the easy availability of abortion "has upset a system in which the only 'honorable' outcome of an unwanted pregnancy is marriage" (quoted in Joffe 1985).

40. Some refer to this as the "sow image" of females: their task is to bear male children who will change history and female children who will bear female children, who will bear male children . . . .

41. See Komarovsky (1964).

42. Recall that Nancy Mullan's testimony in the Pensacola trial indicated that both Kathy and Kaye were, in a sense, outsiders inserting themselves into the relationship between Matt and Jimmy. "Matt and Jimmy were a couple," she said. In her own testimony about the "Defenders of the Code," Kaye Wiggins emphasized the strength of Matt and Jimmy's relationship. And Kathy's teacher, Grace Madison, asserted that Kathy "showed obedience" to her husband, a point that was formerly stressed by Kathren Simmons's defense attorney. Although these limited facts do not point to an "abnormal" relationship for either couple, the characterizations of Matt and Jimmy as "carrying on like little boys," which even contributed to Monaghan's characterization of the men as Huck Finn and Tom Sawyer and Goldsby's depiction of himself and Simmons as Spanky and Alfalfa, suggest at the least that the typical behavior of the "boys" was idealistically juvenile.

43. However, Cuneo denies that "Catholic fundamentalist" is an appropriate term for this group, because it would invite easy comparisons of these people with Protestant and Islamic fundamentalists. We maintain that the term is appropriate because, as Cuneo himself states, they share significant and key beliefs with Protestant fundamentalists—namely, "an inerrant Bible, the literal existence of a heaven and hell, and a demonic force active in the world personified as 'the devil'" (Cuneo 1989, 100). He also says that these Catholics have a "missionary zeal and ideology of crisis" (p. 186) and fit Troeltsch's sectarian type of religion (p. 201). He adds that "the Revivalist imagination interprets everything in terms of a dualistic drama of light versus darkness. And in spiritual warfare, where everyone is aligned on the side of either angels or demons, there is no point in sparing feelings or reputations, in passing over scandal, or in deferring to qualms of civility. The enemy must be exposed and brought to judgment" (p. 191). The parallels are too striking to ignore and they do most certainly invite comparisons with Protestant and Islamic fundamentalists.

44. Kriesberg (1978, 150) points out that "the anti-abortionists are apparently less concerned about abortion per se than with its legalization which signifies, to them, a decline in traditional American religious and moral values, as well as governmental intrusion into private affairs—especially the family" (Leahy 1978).

45. There is a rising interest in family violence as it relates to fundamentalist religion. See, for example, Horton and Williamson (1988).

See also Prescott (1989), who maintains that "the 'anti-choice' personality or culture has a consistent profile of tolerance of and even support for human violence and pain with authoritarian control over personal liberties" (p. 115). He summarizes the anti-choice profile: "(a) an intolerance for the dignity, integrity, and life of the human body; (b) a high tolerance for and/or indifference toward human pain and suffering; (c) a lower value on nurturance of children and families; and (d) an anti-sexual pleasure ethic" (pp. 115–16). Prescott's contentions may need some qualification. For example, there are in anti-choice circles overwhelming rhetorics about "family" values. However, the emphasis ultimately is on control by men of women and children, as exemplified in the writings of LaHaye. And while much is said of the value of children, behavior toward them stresses physical discipline in achieving control. Frequently, the emphasis on control extends to physical violence toward women.

Johnson and Tamney (1988, 45) find that one characteristic of the Christian Right, besides fundamentalism, is "the belief that physical force, and in some cases weaponry, is needed to solve problems."

46. Francis Schaeffer, who lived from 1912 to 1984 and is still frequently quoted by contemporary fundamentalists, proclaimed that "The Renaissance, with its emphasis on man-centeredness, autonomy, and individuality, is bad; the God-centered Reformation, with its emphasis on moral absolutes of right and wrong, is good" (Faux, 1990, 134–35). The Reformation was still centered in the medieval worldview and values. Martin Luther, for example, assumed the existence of Satan—even "saw" him once and threw an inkwell at him—and demons, and he supported a strong centralized government's repression of religious dissent. Schaeffer's evaluation of the Renaissance is shared by LaHaye.

47. When we were attending the trial and interacting almost exclusively with fundamentalists, and when we were interviewing them, only John Brockhoeft among them asked us about our beliefs or our perspectives on the abortion issue. However, Brockhoeft interrupted Blanchard's opening sentence of explanation and embarked on a ten- to fifteen-minute dissertation of his own stance. On the other hand, when we contacted clinic managers and physicians who had been targets of abortion-related violence, not a single one of them would talk with us until we had clarified our position on abortion and detailed the purposes of the interview.

48. Postmillenarians believe that Christ's return will follow a thousand-year reign of peace and righteousness that has been instituted by his elect. Premillenarians believe Christ's return will precede such a period; therefore they tend

to be socially passive since they cannot hasten his return. Postmillenarians are more likely to be activists in trying to bring the world closer to the millennium (Roberts 1990, 244–46).

49. Marty (1987, 300) describes fundamentalism as "an almost Manichean world of black/white, God/Satan, Christ/Antichrist, Christian/'secular humanist.' . . . People who seek authoritarian solutions are likely to follow charismatic fundamentalist leaders in such a time." Nonetheless, we are surprised at how infrequently works on fundamentalism (e.g., Sandeen 1970; Jorstad 1970; and Caplan 1987) mention its Manichaean dualism. Manichaean or Zoroastrian dualism is commonly found in Jewish, Islamic, Sikh, and Hindu fundamentalisms, as well as in the Christian expressions. Dualism in Christianity probably originates with the imposition of Greek (particularly Platonic and Gnostic) thought on the New Testament, as well as the influence of Zoroastrian thought on Judaism in the intratestamentary period. The Old Testament is clearly this-worldly and unitary in its view of human existence.

50. Sugawara (1985). The Pro-Life Action Network (PLAN), one of Scheidler's projects, began sponsoring training sessions in 1984 based on the tactics of Scheidler's book (National Organization for Women, "Project Stand Up for Women Now: Operation Rescue Fact Sheet, n.d.).

51. Thus when the revelations of Jimmy Swaggart's sexual misconduct became public, a Pensacola fundamentalist said on WEAR-TV on February 23, 1988, that if a person is doing the work of the Holy Spirit, then Satan will strive ever harder to discredit that ministry. Therefore, the logic goes, Swaggart's aberrations prove the validity of his being a chosen agent of God.

Furthermore, virtually any event can be taken in personal and egocentric terms. For example, with the revelation of Swaggart's sexual misbehavior just two weeks before the March 1988 "Super Tuesday" presidential primaries in a number of Southern states, Pat Robertson interpreted the whole thing as a plot by George Bush to discredit Robertson. He did not delineate how Bush had engineered the Swaggart situation. As Robertson stated it, "Nothing happens unplanned."

This mind-set, which sees virtually all events as the work of either God or Satan, is particularly attractive to working and lower social classes. For example, it is important in those groups that no individual be better than his or her fellows, that their community of fate maintain its solidarity. Therefore, even the type of gambling popular in those groups, such as bingo and lotteries, involves no skills but only pure chance; thus winners cannot claim any kind of superiority to their fellows (Morris and Mogey 1965, 70–73). In this theology all events, good and bad, are the result of external forces and are only to be discerned as the work of God or Satan and responded to by the individual. Angela Means of Atlanta expressed it well: "God speaks to me through signs and different events that I know can only be through his hand. For example, I had this designer's dress on and, not knowing, right next to me was the designer's sales rep. I immediately got booked for the job. I'm guided and led to places that have the answers to my prayers like that all the time" (*Creative Loafing*, 18 November 1989). In short, significant events are externalized to a source other than the individual.

52. See note 44. There is something to be said for this approach to morality since it allows both sides of a dispute to develop a modus vivendi. For example, those on the inside of religious organizations—both lay and clerical—have been aware that there are homosexual ministers. But it was no issue as long as they kept their homosexual activities outside the parish and outside the public purview—i.e., were "discreet." Now that homosexuals (even some homosexual ministers) are "coming out" and demanding public, as opposed to private, rights and statutory recognition, a great deal of strife has arisen within religious and public groups. It is at least in part a dispute revolving around disagreements over de facto and de jure rights. Essentially, the same change is occurring regarding the abortion issue. Indeed, one mark of deep social transformation in current American society may be the sheer number of issues for which organized groups are seeking as never before de jure rights: abortion, homosexuality, prostitution, pornography, and atheism, to name a few.

53. Although much of Cash's representation may be dated and an oversimplification of the South generally (even at the time he wrote), among the most culturally conservative populations in the South today (rural or urban) there certainly exist enclaves where the themal dichotomies of public and private life satisfy the letter of Cash's model. One might even suggest that the contemporary case is not so much one of Southern conservative culture having changed, but rather that this culture has had a significant impact on ethical and moral standards outside the region or that this is more a mark of American culture than merely the South's. One might even maintain that this dichotomy is a mark of human nature that happens to be more evident in some social groups, such as extremely conservative religions.

For contemporary substantiation of Cash's characterization as it applies to fundamentalists see, for example, Roebuck and Hinson (1982, 71 and 122–24). While Roebuck and Hinson label these working-class Southerners as "rednecks," which is a pejorative term to Southerners, Reed (1983) calls this value orientation "Local" or "Peasant," which harks back to feudal or medieval social structures. It is found primarily among those who have experienced "immersion in the traditional rural culture of the South and isolation from the influences of education, city life, travel, and the mass media" (p. 48). Reed adds that these elements are common to all preindustrial peasants, who, we add again, exist largely in feudal, mechanical-worldview societies. Furthermore, "peasants" also exist in cities, may have had some higher education, and may be exposed to the media without losing their local orientation. As one United Methodist minister in Alabama said, "I went to Vanderbilt [for a master's degree in theology], but I didn't let it affect me." And, if a person watches primarily religious evangelists on television or other specialized programming, we would argue that person has not really been exposed to the media.

Furthermore, a person may watch television and merely react negatively against its influences toward toleration of different values and thus have her or his prejudices reinforced by it.

54. The sexual scandals attached to evangelists Jimmy Swaggart, Jim Bakker, and Marvin Gorman are, we submit, prime evidence of this "split" in the Southern and fundamentalist psyche between publicly espoused belief and private behavior (a form of cognitive dissonance). The illustrative force of their cases is heightened by the fact that Jimmy Swaggart reportedly instigated the charges leading to the dismissal of Gorman; severely chastised Bakker for his behavior; and had been guilty, according to first news reports, of his own form of sexual misbehavior for several years. Furthermore, all three were members of a single denomination, the Assemblies of God. The cumulative evidence is that there is a problem with repressed or hidden sexuality among fundamentalists, which, of course, is not limited solely to them.

Despite his tearful repentance, Swaggart was again arrested in Indio, California, in October 1991 for picking up a prostitute while there with his wife on an evangelistic mission.

55. For a good analysis of the relationship between work roles among the male working class and their effect on involvement in other social institutions, especially religion, see Knight (1978). Neitz (1981) points out that there are two "conceptual frameworks" within the Right to Life movement. The elite (primarily the Catholic church hierarchy) operate out of a "pro-life" perspective and are therefore opposed to the death penalty, euthanasia, and nuclear arms. On the other hand, for the rank and file of the movement, Protestant and Catholic, the issue is the family: ". . . freedom to abort breaks the connection between sex and procreation, denies the sanctity of motherhood and the authority of the father, and implies that it is the individual and not the family which is the basic social unit" (p. 271). See also Luker (1984) and Cuneo (1989).

56. During one of the local school controversies over evolution/creationism, Blanchard wrote a letter to the editor of the *Pensacola News Journal*, and suggested, tongue in cheek, that if we are seriously going to consider teaching creationism, then we should also add to the curriculum the flat-earth theory of geography, the foreign-object-in-the-body theory of physical illness, and the demon-possession theory of mental illness, among other similar viewpoints. He received a number of telephone calls from fundamentalists, including one biology teacher, thanking him for the letter as if it were serious. This idiosyncratic incident not only supports our contention that fundamentalism operates out of the mechanical worldview but also suggests that fundamentalists may have difficulty in dealing with figurative speech, such as metaphors, irony, and satire. To our knowledge there has been no research on this issue of the relationship of religious ideology and use and interpretation of language.

57. A letter to the editor sums up the stance: "The Bible still stands firm . . . 'In the beginning God created the heaven and the earth.' That is real science" (*Pensacola*

*News Journal*, 19 November 1990, 6A). As the creation-science/evolution debate has progressed from intellectual to political action on both sides, the creation-science position has become increasingly rigid. Since it has become clear that creation science will not be mandated in the public schools, creationists have shifted toward a position calling for the removal of evolution from the curriculum. If successful, of course, such a campaign would violate the academic freedom of authentic scientists (who should, after all, define what science is) and destroy science teaching in the public curriculum entirely. Although Peter Berger (1969) has argued eloquently that religion is essentially a social construction (apart from any arguments about the objective existence of divine beings), the social constructions of this form of fundamentalism build only the elaboration of very old cultural themes. Indeed, the building process is entirely devoted to the protection of those themes to the extent that these fundamentalists want to co-opt science to demonstrate what they claim to believe on the basis of faith.

A large number of scientists accept the proposition that science itself, particularly social science, cannot be value-free or totally objective. The mere choice of a topic to research and the choice of a theoretical perspective from which to proceed are themselves value judgments that tend to be self-fulfilling prophecies. However, such biases can be somewhat controlled by the researcher's making clear what her or his biases are (much as we did in our first chapter) in order to allow the reader to make informed judgments.

The difference between that approach and that of the fundamentalists lies in the scientist's relative openness to conflicting and disconfirming evidence. While fundamentalists deny or totally discount conflicting data, the scientist has an obligation to deal with them, take them into account, and modify theory to fit them.

58. Marty (1987, 300) points out that fundamentalists "have 'borrowed' the technology of modernization with all its bewilderments and used it substantially to promote nostalgic and simplistic visions of the past as models for the future." They are New Luddites with an ironic twist: using technology in an attempt to destroy the effects of that technology.

59. One of our arsonist interviewees has for several years sent Blanchard ten-to-twenty-page, single-spaced expositions on the changing dates for the coming Armageddon and has even called him, collect, to tell him that "tomorrow is the day." For an excellent discussion of fundamentalism across cultures and the thought patterns of modernism and fundamentalism, see Lawrence (1989).

60. See Marty (1987, 287–302) and Lawrence (1989) for a similar perspective.

61. See Zald (1980) for an analysis of the interaction between social movements and countermovements and their dependencies on one another.

62. For the processes in developing commitment to religious organizations, see Kanter (1972) and Festinger, Riecken, and Schachter (1956).

63. Muller and Godwin (1984, 140–41) support this analysis: ". . . persons who are alienated from the political system, who perceive themselves to have insufficient political power, and whose ideology accepts political violence, should

be predisposed to participate in aggressive political behavior. This would be especially true where they perceive such behavior as effective methods for achieving political goals and then they have available time to pursue these activities. Conversely, persons who believe that their participation in governmental decision making is important, who believe that they have influence on these decisions, and who are not only interested in politics but supportive of the political system, belong to relevant organizations, and have attained the education necessary for acceptance by other participants, are likely to exhibit above average levels of democratic participation."

This is essentially a distinction between lower- and working-class individuals versus upper-middle-class professionals. Thus, a person's position in the social structure may have a decisive effect on that person's degree and type of involvement, if any, in a social movement. Therefore, specific organizations within social movements may succeed or fail based at least partially on the audience from which they seek recruits and support.

64. Shofner and his wife left Pensacola in 1990 to become missionaries in Latin America.

65. So named because the first ones enacted in the United States (in Connecticut) were printed on blue paper.

66. See the discussion of this following.

67. Goodman (1990).

68. Bruce (1988, 47) points out the "morale-boosting effect [to the New Christian Right (NCR)] of the high profile which fundamentalist preachers acquired in the late 1960s and 1970s." There is considerable evidence that it had the same effect on the anti-abortion wing of the NCR. By extension, we hypothesize that the publicity given to early and continuing clinic violence and the positive responses of the less violent wing of the anti-abortion network became a catalyst for greater violence, a kind of self-fulfilling prophecy where one act increases the likelihood of future similar acts.

69. Of course, the collapse of the PTL Club with the revelations of Jim Bakker's sexual behavior with Jessica Hahn, Jerry Falwell's attempt to resurrect the Bakker enterprises, Jimmy Swaggart's problems, and the attendant negative publicity have given television evangelism a setback. A number of those media evangelists and others have said these events hurt their revenues. On the other hand, organized religion, both conservative and liberal, has gone through periods of growth and decline throughout American history, and it is likely that this setback is a temporary one and one that may have occurred before long anyway.

70. Bruce (1988, 45) maintains that a crucial element in the rise of the New Christian Right was finding "in various elements of the political structure . . . some hope of success to the aspiring activists." We maintain that this is also true of the more extreme anti-abortion activists, the bombers and arsonists. For an analysis of the connections between the anti-abortion movement and the NCR, see Conway and Siegelman (1982).

71. See, for example, Donovan (1988) and Bruce (1988).

72. *emerging trends* (June 1983; February 1981; January 1981).

73. *emerging trends* (December 1982).

74. Ginsburg (1990) found that activist females on both sides of the issue were operating out of a concern for the role of female reproduction in the society. Both anti-abortion and pro-choice groups arise from the problematic position of women in American society "in which wage labor and individual achievement are placed in conflict with reproduction, motherhood, and nurturance" (p. 220).

75. Hunter (1984, 67) indicates that fundamentalists are far more involved in church activities and less involved in other community organizations than are other religiously oriented persons. One effect of high religious participation is that less time is left for other organizations and activities. It also means that such people run less risk of having serious relationships with those who differ with them, which might encourage or force them to question their belief system.

Zald and McCarthy (1987, 67–95) also point out that religious groups, especially those that are strongly ideological (e.g., fundamentalist), are ready-made infrastructures for mobilization.

76. This post-offense support has risen from a spectrum of people in the anti-abortion movement. Joseph Scheidler has been a key networker in inspiring such support. Scheidler maintains correspondence with and visits offenders in prison. After their release, some of them are invited guests of honor at his gatherings, where he presents awards to them. Randall Terry of Operation Rescue provided financial and moral support to Michael Bray and his family while he was in prison. Bray's wife has also been an active participant in Operation Rescue efforts in the New York, Atlanta, and Washington, D.C., areas, and probably others. John Ryan of the Pro-Life Direct Action League features and praises the bombers and arsonists in his publications. Some maintain that Operation Rescue is a "front" for Scheidler.

77. Largely through the efforts of Joseph Scheidler, who maintains files on them and has publicized their addresses, the bombers and arsonists themselves have formed a small community of mutual support in addition to receiving letters of support from other sympathizers. For example, Michael Bray's wife has visited Curtis Beseda in prison at least twice, and the Brays named their child born in 1990 Beseda Bray. There have also been at least limited communications between various perpetrators, frequently through intermediaries, since prison and parole regulations prohibit communication with other felons.

78. Segaller (1987, 291–92) points out that terrorists and terrorist groups rely on support from persons on the fringe who do not cross the line into violence themselves. For example, there are "suppliers" of material and funds and attorneys who may "float" from defendant to defendant. There are some parallels to the defenses in the anti-abortion movement. At least two attorneys in the Pensacola case had defended others in cases of abortion-related violence, and William Brennan had testified in at least one other case, as had Nancy Mullan.

79. See Bill Moyers's *On Earth as It Is in Heaven* segment of his "God and Politics"

series on PBS (Moyers and Pratt 1988). In this program he interviews a number of Christian reconstructionists, including R. J. Rushdoony, and illuminates some of the disagreements among them. The prominent theologian of the movement is Cornelius van Til (1967a, b, and c).

80. The influence of their major authors, especially Rushdoony, extends widely within the larger fundamentalist community.

81. Rushdoony disagrees with North on this point and would not impose reconstructionism antidemocratically. Rushdoony has written more than thirty books. Other prominent authors and figures in the movement are David Chilton, Gary North, and Robert Thoburn.

82. Rushdoony unabashedly asserts that democracy is "the great love of the failures and cowards of life" and that Christianity is basically and radically antidemocratic, "committed to a spiritual aristocracy" (Moyers and Pratt 1988). See also our earlier discussion of fundamentalism and authoritarianism. Fields (1991) supports our contention that fundamentalists seek to reinstitute the dominance of religion over all other social institutions.

83. As Scheidler expressed it, "For those who say I can't impose my morality on others, I say just watch me" (Planned Parenthood flyer, n.d).

84. With apologies to Algernon Charles Swinburne. Marty (1987, 301) gives a similar prognostication: "If there has to be a new social contract some day, it is likely that there must be a state religion, compulsory in character, authoritarian in tone, 'traditional' in outlook. America would be 'socialized' not in the name of Marx but of Jesus, not in the name of communism but of Christian republicanism."

85. Attorneys are reported to have an adage about private morality laws: "They are on the books to help preserve our morality; at the same time they are not enforced in order to preserve our conduct" (Schmidt 1990, 9).

86. For specific data on international political action on population, see the newsletter of the Population Institute, *Popline*, which has been in print since the late 1970s.

87. See, for example, Bruce (1988, vii), who concludes that "American fundamentalists are (a) sufficiently numerous that when organized they can bring their issues into the public arena for discussion but (b) too weak to significantly change the socio-moral climate of America." A similar but not so well-stated conclusion is offered by Kelly (1991a and 1991b) in regard to the current anti-abortion movement in the United States.

88. "Born-again Christians" tend to have a high school education or less, earn incomes of less than $30,000, and are older than the larger population (*emerging trends*, September 1990). However, they do span all social class, income, and education groups. As of 1990, 38 percent of the population can be identified as "born-again" (ibid.). Bruce (1988) maintains that even those who are middle class have come from a working-class background and have working-class values, which is consistent with the findings of Kelly (1977).

89. There are anti-abortion groups that also uphold the breadth of Campolo's

critique and that fit Kelly's (1991a, 316) definition of "pro-life" in that each "contributes to the just and compassionate society." Among these are Sojourners, JustLife, Prolifers for Survival, Pax Christi, and Evangelicals for Social Action, currently relatively weak organizations but groups that Kelly maintains are the movement of the future. As Kelly (1991a, 316) puts it: "As with all authentic social movements, the *primary* aspiration of the pro-life movement should not be that of changing the laws but of creating a world that welcomes and finds a place for all of us simply because we—and the unborn—share a common humanity."

Arguing for a truly "seamless garment" that would be as active against poverty and war as against abortion, and chiding the Roman Catholic Church for demeaning women, Gudorf (1984–85, 490–91) has stated a similar position: "We will never convince those involved in the taking of one and a half million aborted lives a year to consider the life of the unborn reverently if we do not evince reverence for the mothers of those unborn, for the starving millions of our world, the hundreds of thousands of innocent civilians threatened by death in war. We will be accused of romanticizing the unborn out of disdain for the already born, of ignoring the personhood of women, and of passing the burdens of protecting life onto the shoulders of pregnant women rather than accepting the very real burden belonging to all of us to protect all human life."

### 15. Violence against Abortion and the Abortion of Violence

1. Snow, Zurcher, and Ekland-Olson (1980, 479) maintain that "the fewer and the weaker the ties to alternative networks, the greater the structural availability for movement participation."

2. We point out, however, that the black power movement espoused violence only in self-defense.

3. McCarthy and Zald (1977).

4. Zald and Ash (1966).

5. In the anti-abortion movement, and probably also in the pro-choice movement, crucial social positions appear to be gender, social class, occupation, education, and age, and all of these tend to be interrelated. Ginsburg (1990), for example, finds differential experiences of American society by different age cohorts to be a crucial factor in activists joining one movement or the other. Among males involved in the anti-abortion movement, social class appears to be a crucial factor. Professionals are more likely to be involved in the educational and political-action arms of the movement, while working-class males appear to predominate among the more strident activists and those prone to violence. The type of occupation also appears to be crucial. That is, the more discretion a person has over his or her own time, the more likely one can be recruited into activism. See also Seaton (1990) for a socio-psychological perspective on those who blockaded abortion clinics in Vancouver, Canada.

Maxwell (1991) finds that the specific personal meanings and needs of individuals are also a crucial factor in movement involvement. For example, some persons may have a "need" to stand out or in some way become a public figure.

Leahy (1975) finds that social networks are an important element in recruitment into the movement, especially for leaders in it. He also finds that those who hold occupations that allow them considerable time to devote to movement and organizational activities are more likely to get involved.

6. McCarthy and Zald (1977) have maintained that there are several levels of participants in a particular social movement *organization*. But as Staggenborg (1985, 585) has indicated, "there are different types of movement participants and different types of SMOs [social movement organizations], which require different levels and types of participation."

In fact, it might be more appropriate to speak of anti-abortion *movements*. Those opposing abortion are not at all unified. Some organizations are single-issue, opposing abortion alone, while others are multiple-issue, opposing abortion and other "life" issues, such as euthanasia, capital punishment, and nuclear and chemical arms. The importance of abortion varies among the latter groups. There are also paper organizations, which are usually front groups for other groups on temporary issues, such as Defenders of the Defenders of Life. Furthermore, some organizations arise and die or wax and wane through time, especially amidst the shifts of national and local issues and events.

In addition, various organizations within the movement differ on the goals, tactics, and strategies to be used. Therefore, various organizations distance themselves from others within the overall "movement." One of the hypotheses generated by this research is that social movement organizations are most likely to support other organizations that are in penultimate and ultimate proximity to their own positions and to distance themselves from organizations beyond those points.

Just as the organizations differ, individuals vary in their motivations for joining particular segments of the movement. Some anti-abortionists clearly operate out of an antifeminist orientation, while others may act from a communitarian, familistic concern, and still others may act out of personal crises or life-history events (e.g., those handicapped from birth defects). Thus the type of organization that an individual joins and its degree of radical action may well arise from a combination of factors in the individual's life history and social location.

7. Spitzer (1987, 56–57) enumerates these and adds a fourth group, those performing extralegal activities. We contend that this last category is more complex and includes a wider range of types. These first two levels of the movement appear to be dominated by male professionals in positions of leadership. Leahy (1975) found that anti-abortion leaders tended "to be well-educated with occupational and professional interests that allow for devoting significant time to the controversy; they have a history of participation in voluntary civic and political organizations, a number of which are compatible with the anti-abortion position." Given the time of his survey and the development of anti-abortion organizations at that

322 . . . Notes

period, this profile fits the leaders of the educational and lobbying types of organizations more than those of the more violent wing.

8. Women comprise the majority of those who take part in marching and picketing. They are also heavily involved in the "soft" interventionist tactics such as stink-bombs and glue in locks, but the leadership shifts toward working-class males (e.g., Randall Terry and John Burt).

We would include in this "mild" violence category the establishment of fake abortion clinics (estimated in 1991 at between 2,000 and 3,000) because this involves intentional deception and, usually, exaggerations to a woman in distress.

9. This stage involves almost exclusively working-class males.

10. Cable, Walsh, and Warland (1988, 951) point to at least two sources of recruitment: "utilitarian alliances grounded on shared grievances," and "existing friendship networks." These, we contend, may vary in importance with level of involvement in the movement.

Those groups that engage in educational and political reform efforts might be compared with Merton's (1957) "conformist" response to society's goals and the means for achieving those goals; according to McCarthy and Zald's (1977) economic concept of social movement industries, those engaged in moderate activism might be categorized as entrepreneurs within the industry trying to cut into the "conformist" or corporate market; and those engaged in extreme violence would be comparable to Merton's "innovators," developing new, illegitimate means for achieving industry goals.

11. According to Suh (1989, 92), Operation Rescue was organized in 1986 with the help of Joseph Scheidler. Some maintain that it became a "front" for Scheidler following the several suits against him. Tumulty and Smith (1989) say basically the same thing.

12. *Pensacola News Journal*, 2 December 1986, 1A.

13. The sociological concept of "legitimacy" refers to a consensus among the public that an act is "right." For example, a significant percentage of the public perceives speed-limit laws as too low. Thus many people regularly exceed those limits by five to ten miles per hour. Police forces respond to this perception by normally not ticketing speeders until they exceed ten miles per hour above the speed limit; that is, the police accept the public definition of what is legitimate.

14. Nordheimer (1985).

15. *Conscience* (July/August 1986, p. 20). Similar sentiments have been expressed by others. Pat Robertson, 1988 presidential candidate, told one anti-abortion gathering to look to "the wonderful process of the mortality tables" to change *Roe v. Wade* (Diamond 1989, 94). Diamond also cites: "Joseph Morecraft, 'reconstructionist' pastor of Chalcedon Presbyterian Church in Georgia, said in 1986 that God should remove Supreme Court Justices 'in any way he sees fit' to get constitutional interpretations that are anti-abortion. 'I've prayed God would remove the Supreme Court Justices . . . who have consistently voted for the legaliza-

tion of abortion . . . and I'll leave it to God to determine how he wants to do it'" (pp. 94–95).

16. English (1981, 16). As previously stated, we contend that those groups most likely to support other groups are those that are closest to one another in their anti-abortion positions. These responses from Right to Life delegates indicate that they are closer to the violent wing than their official positions and their leadership are willing to admit.

17. *Pensacola News Journal*, 2 December 1986, 8A.

18. Thomas (1984, 5).

19. Tumulty and Smith (1989, 12–14).

20. Diamond (1989).

21. Luker (1984).

22. We argue that such violence might also be committed by those who sense a broad support base in a local community against some outside force, such as in the case of bombings of schools and buses in some Southern communities during the early period of school integration.

23. *Pensacola News Journal*, 25 October 1986, 7C.

24. The typical fundamentalist relies most heavily on Pauline theology, especially the radical justification of the individual by faith alone (Romans 1:17), one of the foundations of Protestant individualism. Charismatics and Pentecostalists stress the portion of Paul's first letter to the Corinthians dealing with the gifts of the Spirit (1 Cor. 12:4ff.). They ignore or discount the differing understanding of speaking in tongues in the earlier Acts account of Pentecost, when everyone is reported to have heard what was said in his or her own language (Acts 2:1ff.). Also, Paul is anti-intellectual when he asserts that the gospel is foolishness to the Greeks (philosophers) and that God turns normal logic on its head (1 Cor. 1:18–23; 2:14; 3:19). These passages ground and justify the fundamentalist hostility to the (secular) "world" and its interpretations of reality. For more detail on the Pauline bases of fundamentalism, see Machen (1921), one of the "fathers" of fundamentalism, and McKown (1984, 1985, 1987, 1990).

On the other hand, theological "liberals" and supporters of the Social Gospel tend to cite the Jesus of the Gospels, especially the Sermon on the Mount (Matthew 5–7), and the works of the Prophets—i.e., the doing, ethical, aspect of religion, such as expressed in Hosea 6:6 and Micah 6:8.

This is consistent with the findings of Glock and Stark (1965) that "orthodox" (fundamentalist) parishioners stress beliefs and religious experience as the basis of salvation and denigrate social ethics, while "liberals" emphasize ethical behavior as opposed to orthodoxy or any other particular belief system.

25. Many modern, non-fundamentalist scholars question the existence of an eternal hell in biblical theology of both the Old and New Testaments.

26. Hunter (1984, 125) maintains that current fundamentalists have down-played the judgmental nature of God. However, he bases this conclusion primarily on books written for popular fundamentalist consumption and on advice given by

leaders to laypersons on how to evangelize. Based especially on our observations and interviews, we contend that this shift is a marketing strategy, not a basic change in theology. Hell and damnation are alive and well among anti-abortion activists, especially the arsonists and bombers. Perhaps the evangelist Billy Sunday voiced it most succinctly, "I have no interest in a God who does not smite" (McLoughlin 1955, 158).

27. As David Carlin, the Democrat majority leader of the Rhode Island senate and a supporter of restrictions on abortion, said, "When you're trying to address the mushy middle, the more extreme you can make your opponent look, the better off you are" (Dionne 1989, 14).

28. Snow, Zutcher, and Ekland-Olson (1980, 792–93) indicate movement participation "is largely contingent on the extent to which extra-movement networks function as countervailing influences." See also Harrison (1974).

29. Graham and Gurr (1979).

30. Grimes et al. (1991).

31. We have not been able to verify how many they have actually opened, but a 1991 congressional hearing estimated the number of such centers at more than 2,000. Other responsible estimates run as high as 3,000.

32. Gamson (1968) points out that the use of violence "can undermine the persuasion resources which a group possesses. Such resources as reputation and personal attractions may be diminished or destroyed since they depend on the attitudes of the target of influence toward the group" (p. 166). He also indicates that the resort to force is used primarily by alienated groups who perceive no other options (pp. 169–70).

33. "Abortion and the Conscience of the Nation," *Human Life Review* (Spring 1983).

34. Reagan's contribution to an aura of legitimacy for those ideologically supporting violence was exacerbated by his entertainment of Joseph Scheidler, among other anti-abortion figures, at the White House following one of his addresses to a Washington anti-abortion rally. Scheidler followed this up with publicity of it in his newsletter. Scheidler is active in networking the convicted bombers and arsonists. He has attended many of their trials and maintains contact with them in prison. His office furnished us with the current addresses, in and out of prison, of those convicted. He also presented Edward Markley with his Defender of Life Award in 1988. A number of bombers and arsonists have also attended Scheidler-led functions prior to their acts. Other prominent national anti-abortion figures have targeted previously damaged clinics with civil disobedience, as well as continuing pressure at the homes of physicians and judges previously involved in abortion clinic issues. Thus the national anti-abortion movement has successfully exploited violence to make itself appear more moderate.

While the public has not generally accepted the violence as legitimate, the anti-abortion movement has widely used its perception of presidential access to increase support among its sympathizers. As Zald and McCarthy (1987, 280) point out, "A social movement must not only justify its goals, but also justify its *modus operandi* as a social movement. Legitimacy of means helps a movement recruit new members and gain access to the media, and makes government repression less likely and less effective." To draw a rude political analogy, however, Reagan's hosting Scheidler is inconsistent with George Schultz's refusal to allow Yasir Arafat to address the United Nations in New York.

McCarthy (1987, 65) points to the fact that anti-abortion sympathizers have held the presidential office since 1975 as an important element in the anti-abortion movement mobilization. We contend that this also enhances the perception of legitimacy by the violent wing of the movement. Among the few issues separating George Bush and Michael Dukakis was abortion, but concern was raised that Bush would be less active on the anti-abortion agenda. This concern was enhanced by his controversial choice of Louis Sullivan as secretary of health and human services. Further evidence of Bush's distancing himself from the anti-abortion movement lies in his statement on August 17, 1991, that, regarding the Wichita Operation Rescue protests, the protesters should obey the law and the federal judge's injunction against their blocking entrance to a clinic there. Also, Bush refused to see Randall Terry when Terry and a priest flew to Kennebunkport, Maine, to protest the arrest of protesters by U.S. marshals. Bush also characterized Operation Rescue's tactics as "excessive."

In regard to Reagan, Spitzer (1987, 67) asserted that "many in the right-to-life movement continue to express dissatisfaction with . . . Ronald Reagan. Even enthusiastic Reagan supporters in the RTLP [Right to Life Party] view Ronald Reagan with suspicion and cynicism, calculating that his sympathies are founded in political expediency more than ideological fervor."

35. Numerous polls reveal that the public is ambivalent toward abortion. Those wishing to outlaw all abortions and those wishing to allow total choice to women about whether or not to have an abortion are both minorities. The majority appear to believe that there should be some restrictions on the availability of abortions, but the ultimate choice should be left to the woman (significantly, without the veto power of the physician, which goes beyond the *Roe* and *Doe* decisions).

36. *Washington Post*, 4 January 1985, 27A.

37. In a welcome speech at a conference of evangelicals in Washington, D.C., in September 1988, Ed Meese asserted that the source of all authority in government was the "Word of God."

38. Despite these varied efforts, the Reagan administration became a source of frustration to many anti-abortionists. For example, Paul Weyrich, a strategist for the movement and one of the masterminds behind the formation of the Moral Majority (Bruce 1988), said, "Some of the pro-life movement definitely feels that the Administration has given them rhetoric but not action" (*New York Times*, 26 January 1987, 22A).

In May 1991, the Supreme Court upheld the right of Congress and the president to withhold funds from organizations such as Planned Parenthood that provide abortion information to clients. Planned Parenthood said it would give up federal funding rather than change its policies.

### 16. Will the Circle Be Unbroken?

1. Jelen, Wilcox, and Smidt (1988) finds that while in 1977 Catholics tended to oppose abortion primarily from a respect for life and fundamentalist Protestants opposed it out of a conservative sexual ethic, by 1985 all groups had shifted to a conservative sexual morality base.

2. In the language of causality, these are all *sufficient*, but not *necessary*, conditions for the precipitation of violence. That is, violence does not seem to occur without the majority of these factors being present, but their presence does not necessarily result in violence. However, the more these factors are present, the more likely it is that violence will occur.

3. Kelly (1991b) argues that the anti-abortion movement will die, while the broader pro-life movement will remain viable, if marginal, in American society.

4. *Totem and Taboo* (Freud 1950, 145ff.).

5. It is estimated that one in every four women in the United States will have an abortion at some time in her life, given current abortion rates. This is approximately the same rate of abortion Kinsey (1948) estimated twenty years before *Roe v. Wade*. Various estimates indicate essentially similar or larger frequencies for the 1860s (Mohr 1978, 76–82). It appears that neither the medical safety nor the legality of abortion has a real impact on its frequency, except in terms of which social classes tend to have the greatest access to it.

6. One recent Supreme Court case, *Webster v. Reproductive Health Services*, hints that a "community standard" for abortion may be forthcoming. To the extent that the Reagan and Bush appointments to the Supreme Court ultimately speak with a unified voice, a possibility by no means certain at this writing, limitations on the availability of abortion could be permitted in the laws of the states. Under such a legal climate, some religiously conservative states have moved to change their existing laws to make them much more restrictive. While *Webster* gives states the right to place some restrictions on abortions and the acceptable limits of those restrictions are yet to be determined, theoretically states would have the right to empower cities and counties to enact their own restrictions.

7. A number of studies have shown that teenage females who have a course in sex education also have both a lower rate of pregnancy and a lower frequency of sexual intercourse. However, fundamentalists are threatened by formal sex education, almost as much as they are threatened by abortion, and hold that both are attacks on traditional morality. For example, an Operation Rescue recruitment tract charges, "Euthanasia and infanticide are commonly practiced, school sex clinics are being established, and a political solution is as far away as ever." A number of anti-abortion organizations equate any form of contraception with infanticide.

8. However, research universally indicates that a very small number of women seek repetitious abortions.

9. S. M. Miller (1990, 5) argues that Americans are now experiencing a series of crises of

a) *social structure* (poverty, homelessness, loss of hegemony, role of media, inequalities, schools, household changes), b) *culture* (fragmentation, me-ism, fear of the economic future, sense of decay, violence, materialism, commercialization, isolation), c) *the state* (poor functioning bureaucracies, inadequate funding, anti-tax feelings, elitism), and d) *progressive-liberal ideology* (uncertainty about expanded state vs. non-governmental institutions, the roles of civil society, effects and attractiveness of left-liberal policies, especially for overcoming inequalities).

It may well be that the general social crisis pervading all our social institutions plays a major role in the social unrest and increasing violence in American society, one more indication of a social structure and culture in potential collapse or fundamental transformation.

10. Quoted in Matthews (1984, 85).

11. Traditionally, our society has made distinctions in the "value" of a life depending on the point of time at which it "dies." For example, prior to twenty weeks in a pregnancy, both spontaneous and induced termination are medically and legally labeled as abortion. At or beyond the twentieth week of pregnancy, it is called a fetal death and a fetal death certificate is filed. If the baby is born alive but dies at any time within the first year of life, an infant death certificate is issued. After the first year of life, a normal death certificate is prepared. Furthermore, those deceased before birth and shortly thereafter usually receive much more simple funerals than infants who die after being incorporated into the family system—that is, have been given a social role. Thus changes in medical technology—such as the ability to treat the fetus in the womb, which gives the fetus the social status of "patient"—cloud our previous, simpler understandings of the meaning of both life and death.

12. The revelations surrounding the Iran-Contra affair and the Reagan administration's admission (despite Ronald Reagan's frequent protestations to the contrary) of attempting to trade arms for hostages tempt us to suggest that the Reagan administration supported terrorism both at home and abroad. While that administration and Bush's sought to limit accessibility to abortion information and appointed a number of conservatives to the Supreme Court, and a number of states ceased public funding for abortion and passed more restrictive laws, anti-abortionists were still frustrated. They were increasingly disillusioned by the fact that although Reagan spoke to pro-life rallies against abortion (always by telephone rather than in person), he and his staff did little to actually push the Pro-Life Amendment or the Prayer Amendment. That is, they increasingly reported feeling that he talked a good game but pushed very little for action.

13. Ginsburg (1990, 222–26) tells of an interesting dialogue between pro-life and pro-choice activists in Fargo, North Dakota, and its potential ameliorating

effects. The groups discovered, to their surprise, that they had some common concerns.

14. As Ginsburg (1990) points out, women activists on both sides of the issue are acting out of a nurturance motivation, anti-abortionists for nurturing roles in the family and pro-choicers for a wider realm for nurturance in the larger society (e.g., for more humane social relations in the workplace). Perhaps this common concern is a beginning place for ameliorative dialogue and common action among women to address the root causes of abortion. That still leaves hanging, however, the problems of male attitudes and behaviors.

### Afterword

1. *Pensacola News Journal*, 25 December 1987, 1B. She was later transferred back to Florida, where Martinez pardoned her. She then resumed her national activism.

2. *Pensacola News Journal*, 27 December 1987, 1B, 3B.

# . . . Bibliography

"Abortion Foes Ponder Setbacks." 1987. *New York Times*, 26 January, 22A.

Adorno, Theodor W., et al. 1950. *The Authoritarian Personality*. New York: Harper.

Albert, M., D. Hanley, and M. Rothbart. 1986. "Gender Differences in Moral Reasoning." *Sex Roles* 15:645–53.

Ammerman, Nancy Tatom. 1987. *Bible Believers: Fundamentalists in the Modern World*. New Brunswick, N.J.: Rutgers University Press.

———. 1991. "Southern Baptists and the New Christian Right." *Review of Religious Research* 32, no. 3 (March): 213–36.

Barr, J. 1977. *Fundamentalism*. London: SCM Press.

Beal, C., A. Garrod, and Patrick Shin. 1990. "Development of Moral Orientation in Elementary School Children." *Sex Roles* 18:13–27.

Berger, Peter. 1969. *The Sacred Canopy: Elements of a Sociological Theory of Religion*. New York: Anchor Books.

Blanchard, Dallas A. n.d. *The Anti-Abortion Movement*. New York: Twayne Publishers. Forthcoming.

Bonhoeffer, Dietrich. 1966. *Ethik*. Munich: Chr. Kaiser Verlag.

Boorstin, Daniel J. 1985. *The Discoverers*. New York: Vintage Books.

Bradfield, Cecil D. 1979. *Neo-ism: A Sociological Study*. Washington, D.C.: University Press of America.

Brinkerhoff, Merlin B., and Eugen Pupri. 1988. "Religious Involvement and Spousal Abuse: The Canadian Case." Paper presented to the Society for the Scientific Study of Religion.

Bronowski, Jacob. 1973. *The Ascent of Man.* Boston: Little, Brown.

Brown, Judie. n.d. "The Human Life Amendment." Stafford, Va.: American Life League.

Bruce, Steve. 1988. *The Rise and Fall of the New Christian Right: Conservative Protestant Politics in America, 1978–1988.* New York: Oxford University Press.

Bryant, Cedric. 1991. "Arson Suspected in Abortion Clinic Fires." *Greensboro News and Record,* 18 March, 1.

Burkitt, F. C. 1923. *The Religion of the Manichees.* Cambridge: Cambridge University Press.

Burris, Val. 1983. "Who Opposed the ERA? An Analysis of the Social Basis of Antifeminism." *Social Science Quarterly* 64 (2): 305–17.

Burt, John. n.d. "Welcome to Our Father's House: A Place for New Beginnings." Pensacola, Fla.

Cable, Sherry, Edward J. Walsh, and Rex H. Warland. 1988. "Differential Paths to Political Activism: Comparison of Four Mobilization Processes after the Three Mile Accident." *Social Forces* 66, no. 4 (June): 951–69.

Caplan, Lionel, ed. 1987. *Studies in Religious Fundamentalism.* Albany: State University of New York Press.

Cash, W. J. 1941. *The Mind of the South.* New York: Alfred A. Knopf.

Catholics for a Free Choice. 1986. *Conscience* 7(4) (July-August).

Chalfant, H. Paul, Robert E. Baeckley, and C. Eddie Palmer. 1981. *Religion in Contemporary Society.* Sherman Oaks, Calif.: Alfred Publishing Co.

Clarke, Alan. 1987a. "Collective Action against Abortion Represents a Display of, and Concern for, Cultural Values, Rather Than an Expression of Status Discontent." *British Journal of Sociology* 38 (2): 235–53.

———. 1987b. "Moral Reform and the Anti-Abortion Movement." *Sociological Review* 35 (1): 123–49.

Coats, G. 1983. *Genesis with an Introduction to Narrative Literature.* Grand Rapids, Mich.: W. B. Eerdmans.

Cole, Stewart G. 1963. *The History of Fundamentalism.* Hamden, Conn.: Archon Books.

Conway, Flo, and Jim Siegelman. 1982. *Holy Terror: The Fundamentalist War on America's Freedoms in Religion, Politics, and Our Private Lives.* New York: Delta Books.

Cox, Harvey. 1965. *The Secular City.* New York: Macmillan.

Cozart, William. "Cybernetics: Meta-Image of the Twentieth Century." *ie* 3(2). Chicago: Ecumenical Institute.

*Creative Loafing* (Atlanta). 1989. 18 November, 6.

Cuneo, Michael W. 1989. *Catholics against the Church: Anti-Abortion Protest in Toronto, 1969–1985.* Toronto: University of Toronto Press.

———. 1991. Statements made at the annual meeting of the Society for the Scientific Study of Religion, Pittsburgh, 10 November.

Davis, Nanette J., and Clarice Stasz. 1990. *Social Control of Deviance: A Critical Perspective*. New York: McGraw-Hill.

Davis, Natalie Zemon. 1975. *Society and Culture in Early Modern France*. Stanford, Calif.: Stanford University Press.

Dayton, Donald. 1976. *Discovering an Evangelical Heritage*. New York: Harper and Row.

DeBerg, Betty A. 1991. *Ungodly Women: Gender and the First Wave of American Fundamentalism*. Minneapolis: Augsburg Fortress.

Diamond, Sara. 1989. *Spiritual Warfare: The Politics of the Christian Right*. Boston: South End Press.

Dionne, E. J., Jr. 1989. "Two Sides in Abortion Debate Crowd the Center." *New York Times*, 13 August, 14.

Dixon, Amzi C., Louis Meyer, and Reuben A. Torrey, eds. 1910–15. *The Fundamentals: A Testimony to the Truth*. 12 vols. Chicago: Testimony Publishing.

Donenberg, Geri R., and L. W. Hoffman. 1988. "Gender Differences in Moral Development." *Sex Roles* 18: 701–17.

Donovan, Patricia. 1988. *When the Conventional Wisdom Is Wrong: A Reexamination of the Role of Abortion as an Issue in Federal Elections*. Washington, D.C.: Alan Guttmacher Institute.

Durkheim, Émile. 1893. *De la division du travail social*. Paris: Alcan.

Ehrenreich, Barbara. 1983. *The Hearts of Men: American Dreams and the Flight from Commitment*. Garden City, N.Y.: Anchor Press/Doubleday.

Eliade, Mircea. 1991. *The Eliade Guide to World Religions*. San Francisco: Harper.

English, Deirdre. 1981. "The War against Choice." *Mother Jones*, Feb., 16–32.

"Expert: GOP Policies Paved Way for Ex-Klansman Duke." 1991. *Pensacola News Journal*, 21 October, 2A.

Falik, Marilyn M. 1975. "Ideology and Abortion Policy Politics." Ph.D. diss., New York University.

Faux, Marian. 1990. *Crusaders: Voices from the Abortion Front*. Secaucus, N.J.: Carol Publishing Group.

Festinger, Leon. 1957. *A Theory of Cognitive Dissonance*. Stanford, Calif.: Stanford University Press.

Festinger, Leon, Henry W. Riecken, and Stanley Schachter. 1956. *When Prophecy Fails*. Minneapolis: University of Minnesota Press.

Fichter, Joseph H. 1954. *Social Relations in the Urban Parish*. Chicago: University of Chicago Press.

———. 1951. *Southern Parish*, vol. 1. Chicago: University of Chicago Press.

Fields, Echo E. 1991. "Understanding Activist Fundamentalism: Capitalist Crisis and the 'Colonization of the Lifeworld.'" *Sociological Analysis* 52, no. 2 (Summer): 175–90.

Fowler, James W. 1981. *Stage of Faith: The Psychology of Human Development and the Quest for Meaning*. New York: Harper and Row.

Fowler, Robert Booth. 1982. *A New Engagement: Evangelical Political Thought*. Grand Rapids, Mich.: W. B. Eerdmans.

Frenkel-Brunswick, Else. 1954. "Further Explorations by a Contributor to 'The Authoritarian Personality.'" In *Studies in the Scope and Method of "The Authoritarian Personality*," ed. R. Christie and M. Jahoda. Glencoe, Ill.: Free Press.

Freud, Sigmund. 1950. *Totem and Taboo*. New York: W. W. Norton.

Fuchs, Dieter. 1983 "Politischer Protest und Stabilitat des politischen Systems." In *Wahlen und politisches System*, ed. Max Kaase and Hans-Dieter Klingemann, 121–43. Opladen, Germany: Westdeutscher Verlag.

Galotti, Kathleen M. 1975. *The Strategy of Social Protest*. Homewood, Ill.: Dorsey Press.

———. 1989. "Gender Differences in Self-Reported Moral Reasoning: A Review and New Evidence." *Journal of Youth and Adolescence* 18:475–87.

Gamson, William A. 1968. *Power and Discontent*. Homewood, Ill.: Dorsey Press.

———. 1975. *The Strategy of Social Protest*. Homewood, Ill.: Dorsey Press.

Gaspar, Louis. 1963. *The Fundamentalist Movement*. The Hague: Mouton.

Gibbs, Jack P. 1989. "The Conceptualization of Terrorism." *American Sociological Review* 54, no. 2 (June): 329–40.

Ginsburg, Faye. 1990. *Contested Lives: The Abortion Debate in an American Community*. Berkeley: University of California Press.

Glock, Charles Y., and Rodney Stark. 1965. *Religion and Society in Tension*. Chicago: Rand McNally.

Goffman, Erving. 1981. *Forms of Talk*. Philadelphia: University of Pennsylvania Press.

Goleman, Daniel. 1985. "The Torturer's Mind: Complex View Emerges." *New York Times*, 14 May, sec. C.

Goodman, Walter. 1990. "Jennings on Abortion: Looking at Both Sides." *New York Times*, 1 November, 3B.

Gould, Julius, and William L. Kolb, eds. 1964. *A Dictionary of the Social Sciences*. New York: Free Press of Glencoe.

Graham, Hugh Davis, and Ted Robert Gurr, eds. 1979. *Violence in America*. Beverly Hills: Sage Publications.

Granberg, Donald. 1978. "Pro-Life or Reflection of Conservative Ideology? An Analysis of Opposition to Legalized Abortion." *Sociology and Social Research* 62 (April): 421–23.

———. 1982. "What Does It Mean to Be 'Pro-Life'?" *Christian Century*, 12 May, 99: 562–66.

Greil, Arthur L., and David R. Rudy. 1980. "Sociological Cocoons: Organizations for the Transformation of Identity." Paper presented at the annual meeting of the Society for the Scientific Study of Religion, Cincinnati, 1980.

Grimes, David A., Jacqueline Forrest, Alice L. Kirkman, and Barbara Radford. 1991. "An Epidemic of Antiabortion Violence in the United States." *American Journal of Obstetrics and Gynecology* 165, no. 5 (November): 1263–68.

Gudorf, Christine E. 1984–85. "To Make a Seamless Garment, Use a Single Piece of Cloth." *Cross Currents* (Winter): 34 (4): 473–91.

Gunkel, Hermann. 1910. *Genesis*. 3d ed. Goettingen, Germany: Vandenhoeck and Ruprecht.

Gurr, Ted Robert. 1989. "Political Terrorism: Historical Antecedents and Contemporary Trends." In *Violence in America*, vol. 2, ed. Ted Robert Gurr. Newbury Park, Calif.: Sage Publications.

Hall, Elaine J., and Myra Marx Ferree. 1986. "Race Differences in Abortion Attitudes." *Public Opinion Quarterly* 50 (2): 193–207.

Harrell, David Edwin, Jr. 1975. *All Things Are Possible: The Healing and Charismatic Revivals in Modern America*. Bloomington: Indiana University Press.

Harrison, Michael I. 1974. "Sources of Recruitment to Catholicism." *Journal for the Scientific Study of Religion* 13: 49–64.

Hartouni, Valerie Anne. 1987. "Abortion Politics and the Negotiation of Public Meanings." Ph.D. diss., University of California, Santa Clara.

Hentoff, Nat. 1989. "Civil Rights and Anti-Abortion Protests." *Washington Post*, 6 February, 11A.

Himmelstein, Jerome L. 1986. "The Social Basis of Antifeminism: Religious Networks and Culture." *Journal for the Scientific Study of Religion* 25 (1): 1–15.

Horton, Anne L., and Judith A. Williamson. 1988. *Abuse and Religion: When Praying Isn't Enough*. Lexington, Mass.: D. C. Heath.

Hunsberger, Bruce, and Bob Altemeyer. 1991. "Authoritarianism, Religious Fundamentalism, Quest and Prejudice." Paper presented at the annual meeting of the Society for the Scientific Study of Religion, Pittsburgh, November 1991.

Hunter, James Davison. 1984. *American Evangelicalism: Conservative Religion and the Quandary of Modernity*. New Brunswick, N.J.: Rutgers University Press.

———. 1987. *Evangelicalism: The Coming Generation*. Chicago: University of Chicago Press.

Jaffe, Frederick S., Barbara L. Lindheim, and Philip R. Lee. 1981. *Abortion Politics: Private Morality and Public Policy*. New York: McGraw-Hill.

Jelen, Ted G., Clyde Wilcox, and Corwin E. Smidt. 1988. "Changes in the Attitudinal Correlations of Opposition to Abortion, 1977–1985," *Journal for the Scientific Study of Religion* 27 (2): 211–28.

———. 1990. "Biblical Literalism and Inerrancy: A Methodological Investigation." *Sociological Analysis* 51, no. 3 (Fall): 307–13.

Joffe, Carole. 1985. "The Meaning of the Abortion Conflict." *Contemporary Sociology* 1 (1): 15–29.

Johnson, Stephen D., and Joseph B. Tamney. 1984. "Support for the Moral Majority: A Test of a Model." *Journal for the Scientific Study of Religion* 23: 183–96.

———. 1988. "Factors Related to Inconsistent Life-Views." *Review of Religious Research* 30 (1): 40–46.

Jorstad, Erling. 1970. *The Politics of Doomsday: Fundamentalism of the Far Right*. Nashville: Abingdon Press.

Kanter, Rosabeth. 1972. *Commitment and Community: Communes and Utopias in Sociological Perspective.* Cambridge, Mass.: Harvard University Press.

Kaplan, Abraham. 1964. *Conduct of Inquiry: Methodology for Behavioral Science.* San Francisco: Chandler Publishing.

Kaplan, David, and Robert A. Manners. 1972. *Culture Theory.* Prospect Heights, Ill.: Waveland Press.

Kelly, Dean M. 1977. *Why Conservative Churches Are Growing.* New York: Harper and Row.

Kelly, James R. 1991a. "Abortion: What Americans *Really* Think and the Catholic Challenge." *America* 165 (13): 310–16.

———. 1991b. "Seeking a Sociologically Correct Name for Abortion Opponents." Paper presented at the annual meeting of the Society for the Scientific Study of Religion, Pittsburgh, November.

Killian, Lewis M. 1972. "The Significance of Extremism in the Black Revolution." *Social Problems* 20 (Summer): 41–48.

Kinsey, Alfred C., Wardell B. Pomeroy, and Clyde E. Martin. 1948. *Sexual Behavior in the Human Male.* Philadelphia: W. B. Saunders.

Kirscht, John P., and Ronald C. Dillehay. 1967. *Dimensions of Authoritarianism: A Review of Research and Theory.* Lexington: University of Kentucky Press.

Knight, Edward L. 1978. "Working-Class Whites in the New South: A Community Study." Ph.D. diss., New School for Social Research, New York.

Kohlberg, Lawrence. 1983. *The Psychology of Moral Development.* New York: Harper and Row.

Komarovsky, Mirra. 1964. *Blue-Collar Marriage.* New York: Random House.

Kriesberg, Louis, ed. Vol. 1, 1978; vol. 8, 1985. *Research in Social Movements, Conflicts and Change.* Greenwich, Conn.: JAI Press.

Kurtz, Howard. 1989. "Operation Rescue: Aggressively Antiabortion." *Washington Post,* 6 March, 3A.

LaHaye, Tim. 1980. *The Battle for the Mind.* Old Tappan, N.J.: Fleming H. Revell.

Lawrence, Bruce B. 1989. *Defenders of God: The Fundamentalist Revolt against the Modern Age.* New York: Harper and Row.

Leahy, Peter J. 1975. "The Anti-Abortion Movement: Testing a Theory of the Rise and Fall of Social Movements." Ph.D. diss., Syracuse University.

Leahy, Peter J., and Allan Mazur. 1978. "A Comparison of Movements Opposed to Nuclear Power, Fluoridation, and Abortion." In *Research in Social Movements, Conflicts and Change,* vol. 1, ed. Louis Kriesberg. Greenwich, Conn.: JAI Press.

Leahy, Peter J., David A. Snow, and Steven K. Worden. 1983. "The Anti-Abortion Movement and Symbolic Crusades: Reappraisal of a Popular Theory." *Alternative Lifestyles* 6 (1): 27–47.

Levi, Ken. 1982. *Violence and Religious Commitment: Implications of Jim Jones's People's Temple Movement.* University Park: University of Pennsylvania Press.

Levinson, D. J., and P. E. Huffman. 1955. "Traditional Family Ideology and Its Relation to Personality." *Journal of Personality* 23:251–73.

Liebman, Robert C., and Robert Wuthnow. 1983. *The New Christian Right*. New York: Aldine.

Lifton, Robert J. 1986. *The Nazi Doctors: Medical Killing and the Psychology of Genocide*. New York: Basic Books.

Lifton, Robert Jay, and Charles B. Strozier. 1990. "Waiting for Armageddon." *New York Times Book Review*, 12 August, 1, 24–25.

Lofland, John. 1966. *Doomsday Cult*. Englewood Cliffs, N.J.: Prentice-Hall.

———. 1985. *Protest: Studies of Collective Behavior and Social Movements*. New Brunswick, N.J.: Transaction Books.

Lofland, John, and Rodney Stark. 1965. "Becoming a World-Saver: A Theory of Conversion to a Deviant Perspective." *American Sociological Review* 30:862–74.

Luker, Kristin. 1984. *Abortion and the Politics of Motherhood*. Berkeley: University of California Press.

Lupfer, Michael B., Patricia L. Hopkinson, and Patricia Kelley. 1988. "An Exploration of Attributional Styles of Christian Fundamentalists and Authoritarians." *Journal for the Scientific Study of Religion* 27 (3): 389–98.

McAdam, Doug. 1982. *Political Process and the Development of Black Insurgency, 1930–1970*. Chicago: University of Chicago Press.

———. 1986. "Recruitment to High-Risk Activism: The Case of Freedom Summer." *American Journal of Sociology* 92:64–90.

MacCannell, Dean, and Juliet Flower MacCannell. 1982. *The Time of the Sign: A Semiotic Interpretation of Modern Culture*. Bloomington: Indiana University Press.

McCarthy, John D. 1987. "Pro-Life and Pro-Choice Mobilization: Infrastructure Deficits and New Technologies." In *Social Movements in an Organizational Society*, ed. Mayer N. Zald and John D. McCarthy. New Brunswick, N.J.: Transaction Books.

McCarthy, John D., and Mayer N. Zald. 1977. "Resource Mobilization and Social Movements: A Partial Theory." *American Journal of Sociology* 82:1212–41.

McDonnell, Kathleen. 1984. *Not an Easy Choice: A Feminist Re-examines Abortion*. Boston: South End Press.

Machen, J. Gresham. 1921. *The Origin of Paul's Religion*. New York: Macmillan.

McKown, Delos B. 1984–85. "Are American Educational Reforms Doomed?" *Free Inquiry* 5, no. 1 (Winter): 11–15.

———. 1987. "The 'Escape Goat' of Christianity." *Free Inquiry* 7, no. 2 (Spring): 32–34.

———. 1990. "Humanism, Disbelief, and Bibliolatry." *Humanist* 50, no. 3 (May/June): 7–9.

McLoughlin, William G. 1955. *Billy Sunday Was His Real Name*. Chicago: University of Chicago Press.

Marty, Martin E. 1987. *Religion and Republic: The American Circumstance*. Boston: Beacon Press.

———. 1991. *The Noise of Conflict*. Chicago: University of Chicago Press.

Marty, Martin E., and R. S. Appleby, eds. 1990. *Fundamentalisms Observed*. Chicago: University of Chicago Press.

Matthews, Richard K. 1984. *The Radical Politics of Thomas Jefferson: A Revisionist View*. Lawrence: University of Kansas Press.

Maxwell, Carol J. C. 1991. "Where's the Land of Happy? Individual Meanings in Pro-Life Direct Action." Paper presented to the annual meeting of the Society for the Scientific Study of Religion, Pittsburgh, November.

Merton, Robert K. 1957. *Social Theory and Social Structure*. Glencoe, Ill.: Free Press.

Miller, S. M. 1990. "Breaking Taboos and Changing Assumptions." *Social Report* (Department of Sociology, Boston College) 9, no. 1 (Fall): 5, 7.

Mohr, James. 1978. *Abortion in America: The Origins and Evolution of National Policy*. New York: Oxford University Press.

Morris, Holly. 1989. "Reluctant Couple Converts to Activism." *Washington Post*, 2 February, 10A.

Morris, R. N., and John Mogey. 1965. *The Sociology of Housing: Studies at Berensfield*. London: Routledge and Kegan Paul.

Moyers, Bill, and Greg Pratt, exec. eds. 1988. *On Earth as It Is in Heaven*. In the "God and Politics" television series. Greg Pratt and Jan Falstad, producers. Public Broadcasting System.

Muller, Edward N., and R. Kenneth Godwin. 1984. "Democratic and Aggressive Political Participation: Estimation of a Nonrecursive Model." *Political Behavior* 6:129–46.

Munby, D. L. *The Idea of a Secular Society and Its Significance for Christians*. New York: Oxford University Press.

*National Catholic Reporter*. 1978. Review of *Are Catholics Ready?*, by Maureen Fiedler and Dolly Pomerleau. 14 November.

National Organization for Women. n.d. "Project Stand Up for Women Now: Operation Rescue Fact Sheet."

Neitz, Mary Jo. 1981. "Family, State and God: Ideologies of the Right-to-Life Movement." *Sociological Analysis* 42:265–76.

Nice, David C. 1988. "Abortion Clinic Bombings as Political Violence." *American Journal of Political Science* 32 (1): 178–95.

Nordheimer, Jon. 1985. "Bombing Case Offers a Stark Look at Abortion Conflicts." *New York Times*, 18 January, 12A.

Oberschall, Anthony. 1973. *Social Conflict and Social Movements*. Englewood Cliffs, N.J.: Prentice-Hall.

———. 1978. "Loosely Structured Collective Conflict: A Theory and an Application." *Research in Social Movements, Conflict and Change*. Vol. 1, ed. Louis Kriesberg. Greenwich, Conn.: JAI Press.

O'Hara, Jim. 1991. "Arsonist Given Five Years Probation: She Tried to Burn Planned Parenthood." *Syracuse Herald-Journal* (Syracuse, N.Y.), 19 April, 1B.

Opp, Karl-Dieter. 1988. "Grievances and Participation in Social Movements." *American Sociological Review* 53:853–64.

Page, Ann L., and Donald A. Clelland. 1978. "The Kanawha County Textbook Controversy: A Study of the Politics of Life Style Concern." *Social Forces* 57 (1): 265–81.

Paloma, Margaret. 1982. *The Charismatic Movement: Is There a New Pentecost?* Boston: Twayne.

People for the American Way. 1986. *Forum* (Fall), 12.

Perry, William G., Jr. 1970. *Forms of Intellectual and Ethical Development in the College Years: A Scheme.* New York: Holt, Rinehart and Winston.

Petchesky, Rosalind Pollack. 1984. *Abortion and Woman's Choice: The State, Sexuality, and Reproductive Freedom.* New York: Longman.

Photiadis, J., and A. Johnson. 1963. "Orthodoxy, Church Participation, and Authoritarianism." *American Journal of Sociology*, 69:244–48.

Piaget, Jean. 1967. *Six Psychological Studies.* New York: Random House.

Pollock, C. B., and B. F. Steele. 1968. "A Psychiatric Study of Parents Who Abuse Infants and Small Children." In *The Battered Child*, ed. R. E. Helfer and C. H. Kemp. Chicago: University of Chicago Press.

Prescott, James W. 1989. "The Abortion of *The Silent Scream*." In *Abortion Rights and Fetal 'Personhood,'* ed. Edd Doerr and James W. Prescott. Long Beach, Calif.: Centerline Press.

Princeton Religion Research Center. *emerging trends*, 3(1), 3(2), 5(6), and 12(7).

Quebedeaux, Richard. 1978. *The Worldly Evangelicals.* New York: Harper and Row.

Rauschenbusch, Walter. 1918. *A Theology for the Social Gospel.* New York: Macmillan.

Reagan, Ronald. 1983. "Abortion and the Conscience of the Nation." *Human Life Review* (Spring).

Redekop, John H. 1968. *The American Far Right.* Grand Rapids, Mich.: W. B. Eerdmans.

Reed, John Sheldon. 1983. *Southerners: The Social Psychology of Sectionalism.* Chapel Hill: University of North Carolina Press.

Robbins, Thomas. 1978. "Milton Yinger and the Study of Social Movements." *Journal for the Scientific Study of Religion* 17: 302–5.

Roberts, Keith A. 1986. "Sociology in the General Education Curriculum: A Cognitive Structuralist Perspective." *Teaching Sociology* 14 (October): 207–16.

———. 1990. *Religion in Sociological Perspective.* Belmont, Calif.: Wadsworth.

Roebuck, Julian B., and Mark Hinson III. 1982. *The Southern Redneck: A Phenomenological Class Study.* New York: Praeger.

Roof, Wade Clark, and William McKinney. 1987. *American Mainline Religion: Its Changing Shape and Future.* New Brunswick, N.J.: Rutgers University Press.

Runciman, Steven. 1947. *The Medieval Manichee: A Study of the Christian Dualist Heresy.* Cambridge: Cambridge University Press.

Sandeen, Ernest R. 1970. *The Roots of Fundamentalism: British and American Millenarianism 1800–1930.* Chicago: University of Chicago Press.

Saussure, Ferdinand de. 1966. *Course in General Linguistics*. Ed. Charles Bally, Albert Sechehaye, and Albert Reidlinger; trans. Wade Baskin. New York: McGraw-Hill.

Scheidler, Joseph M. 1985. *Closed: 99 Ways to Stop Abortion*. Westchester, Ill.: Crossway Books.

Schlosser, Jim. 1991. "Insanity Plea Planned." *Greensboro News and Record*, 16 August 16.

Schmalzbauer, John A. 1991. "Evangelicals in the New Class." Paper presented at the annual meeting of the Society for the Scientific Study of Religion, Pittsburgh, November 1991.

Schmidt, William E. 1990. "Treating Adultery as Crime: Wisconsin Dusts Off Old Law." *New York Times*, 30 April, 1, 9.

Scully, Diana, and Joseph Marollo. 1984. "Rapists' Vocabulary of Motives." *Social Problems* 31 (5) :530–44.

Seaton, Craig E. 1990. *Altruism and Activism: Character Disposition and Ideology as Factors in Blockade of an Abortion Clinic*. New York: Cummings and Hathaway.

Segaller, Stephen. 1987. *Invisible Armies: Terrorism into the 1990s*. New York: Harcourt Brace Jovanovich.

Shils, E. A. 1954. "Authoritarianism Right and Left." In *Studies in the Scope and Method of "The Authoritarian Personality,"* ed. R. Christie and M. Jahoda. Glencoe, Ill.: Free Press.

Sims-Shofner, Myra. 1989. *Protectors of the Code*. Pensacola, Fla.: Privately published.

Smidt, Corwin E. 1989a. "Identifying Evangelical Respondents: An Analysis of 'Born Again' and Bible Questions Used Across Different Surveys." In *Religion and Political Behavior in the United States*, ed. Ted Jelen. New York: Praeger.

———. 1989b. "'Praise the Lord' Politics: A Comparative Analysis of the Social Characteristics and Political Views of American Evangelical and Charismatic Christians." *Sociological Analysis* 50 (1): 53–72.

Smith, Lynn. 1989. "Four Voice Their Operation Rescue Stories." *Los Angeles Times-Mirror*, 23 March, 3, 29.

Snow, David A., Louis A. Zurcher, Jr., and Sheldon Ekland-Olson. 1980. "Social Networks and Social Movements: A Microstructural Approach to Differential Recruitment." *American Sociological Review* 51: 787–801.

Spitzer, Robert J. 1987. *The Right to Life Movement and Third Party Politics*. Westport, Conn.: Greenwood Press.

Staggenborg, Suzanne. 1985. "Patterns of Collective Action in the Abortion Conflict: An Organizational Analysis of the Pro-Choice Movement." Ph.D. diss., Northwestern University.

Steinfels, Peter. 1988. "Dissecting Fundamentalism, the Principles and the Name." *New York Times*, 20 November, 24E.

Stets, Jan E. 1991. "Attitudes about Abortion and Varying Attitude Structures." Paper presented at the annual meeting of the American Sociological Association, Cincinnati, August 1991.

Sugawara, Sandra. 1985. "Abortion Opponents Pledge 'New Era of Activism,'" *Washington Post*, 7 March 7, 3B.

Suh, Mary, and Lydia Denworth. 1989. "The Gathering Storm: Operation Rescue." *Ms.*, April, 92–93.

Thomas, Cal. 1984. "Bombing Abortion Clinics: It's Violent, But Why Not?" *Los Angeles Times*, 27 November, 5.

Tilly, Charles. 1978. *From Mobilization to Revolution*. Reading, Mass.: Addison-Wesley.

Toronto, Joan C. 1987. "Moral Orientations: Both Justice and Care." *Signs* 12:644–663.

Trafford, Abigail. 1987. "The Rise of Medical Vigilantes." *Washington Post*, 8 September, WH 15.

Traina, Frank J. 1975. "Diocesan Mobilization against Abortion Law Reform." Ph.D. diss., Cornell University.

Tumulty, Karen, and Lynn Smith. 1989. "Operation Rescue: Soldier in a 'Holy War' on Abortion." *Los Angeles Times*, 17 March, 12–14.

Turner, Ralph H. and Lewis M. Killian. 1987. *Collective Behavior*. Englewood Cliffs, N.J.: Prentice-Hall.

van Til, Cornelius. 1967a. *A Christian Theory of Knowledge*. Philadelphia: Presbyterian and Reformed Publishing Co.

———. 1967b. *The Defense of the Faith*. Philadelphia: Presbyterian and Reformed Publishing Co.

———. 1967. *The New Hermeneutic*. Nutley, N.J.: Presbyterian and Reformed Publishing Co.

von Rad, G. 1972. *Genesis: A Commentary*. Philadelphia: Westminster Press.

Wilcox, Mary. 1979. *Developmental Journey: A Guide to the Development of Logical and Moral Reasoning and Social Perspective*. Nashville: Abingdon Press.

Wilson, Michele, and John Lynxwiler. 1988. "Abortion Clinic Violence as Terrorism." *Terrorism* 11 (4): 263–73.

Wood, M., and M. Hughes. 1984. "The Moral Basis of Moral Reform: Status Discontent vs. Culture and Socialization as Explanations of Anti-Pornography Social Movement Adherence." *American Sociological Review* 49:86–99.

Yinger, Milton, and Stephen J. Cutler. 1982. "The Moral Majority Viewed Sociologically." *Sociological Focus* (October): 289–306.

Zald, Mayer N. 1980. "Issues in the Theory of Social Movements." *Perspectives in Social Theory* 1 (1): 61–72.

Zald, Mayer N., and Roberta Ash. 1966. "Social Movement Organizations: Growth, Decay and Change." *Social Forces* 44 (2): 327–40.

Zald, Mayer N., and John D. McCarthy, eds. 1987. *Social Movements in an Organizational Context*. New Brunswick, N.J.: Transaction Books.

# . . . Index